SOCIO-ECONOMIC DYNAMICS IN RURAL BANGLADESH

Socio-economic Dynamics in Rural Bangladesh

The individual and societal effects of opportunities and obstacles

DIETMAR HERBON

Avebury

Aldershot · Brookfield USA · Hong Kong · Singapore · Sydney

Published by
Avebury
Ashgate Publishing Limited
Gower House
Croft Road
Aldershot
Hants GU11 3HR
England

Ashgate Publishing Company
Old Post Road
Brookfield
Vermont 05036
USA

British Library Cataloguing in Publication Data

Herbon, Dietmar
 Socio-economic Dynamics in Rural
 Bangladesh: Individual and Societal
 Effects of Opportunities and Obstacles
 I. Title
 338.95492

ISBN 1 85628 681 9

Printed and Bound in Great Britain by
Athenaeum Press Ltd, Newcastle upon Tyne.

Table of Contents

2

4

List of Tables

7

9

List of Figures

14

15

Preface

This study is the result of several years of theoretical and empirical research on Bangladesh carried out in cooperation with the Rural Development Academy, Bogra, and the Institute of Rural Development at the University of Göttingen.

The Institute of Rural Development was the perfect surrounding in which to take up the task of writing this study. I especially appreciate the support which I received from Prof. Dr.Dr.Dr.hc. Frithjof Kuhnen, who provided me with the opportunity to write this study, who let me use the technical resources of the Institute and who was available for advice at all times. Prof. Dr. J.O. Müller and Prof. Dr. W. Manig also supported me in many different ways over the years. The same applies to the members of the Bangladesh research team: Dr. F. Kahrs, Dr. H.-P. Müller, Dr. C. Räder and R. Piesch. The many discussions with the other researchers at the Institute most certainly provided me with many insights, constructive criticism and ideas. I want to thank all of them.

Without the technical support of the excellent library at the Institute of Rural Development and the German university libraries system and without the support and guideance of the Göttingen University Computer Center, this study would not have been technically feasible.

This study is based on experience and material gathered during two longer periods of stay in Bangladesh (1979-81, 1985-86) when I carried out empirical research in various villages in Bogra District. The then Directors of the Rural Development Academy in Bogra, M.N. Nurul Haq und Abdul Muyeed Chowdhury, gave me substantial support. In particular my collegue Shahadot Zzaman Sarkar (Tuku), the other Bangladeshi staff members who worked with me and the many friendly and patient neighbors from those villages in which I lived were central to the success of my work. It is not possible here to mention each and every collegue and companion individually.

Kenneth Muller is the person to whom my special gratitude for this book goes. The original manuscript was written in German, and he took up the challenge of translating it into English.

Many people have contributed to this book. My family had to cope with long periods of strain and little spare time. They all have their share in the result presented here.

Of course the entire responsibility for what is expressed here lies with me. Nevertheless, I would welcome any constructive criticism from the readers.

D. H., July, 1993

1 Introduction to the Study

1.1 "The Case" of Bangladesh

Bangladesh is, according to international public opinion, an exceptional country about which one generally only knows that masses of people live there in abject poverty and that they are "regularly" afflicted by catastrophes. As a rule, the country appears in the headlines with its 110 million inhabitants only when it is hit once again by a catastrophe in the form of a flood or cyclone. [1] The resulting picture is not false, but it is also not complete. The same is true regarding the image of the masses sinking into abject poverty. With a population density of more than 750 people to each square kilometer of land [2] – excluding the areas covered by water – Bangladesh is the most densely populated country in the world. Thus the country is comparable with, e.g., the extremely densely populated regions of the Nile delta and Java. [3] At least 80 % of the population lives in rural regions and is generally engaged in agriculture, either as farmers or farmhands. Only a small percentage of the population earns its living outside the agricultural sector.

Between the population growth, which amounts to ca. 2.5 % per annum, and the economic growth, a "race" is taking place of hardly comprehendible and, in some cases, tragic dimensions. In international public opinion – as well as among Bengali observers – the country is permanently just this side of bankruptcy, and the impoverished population is just short of starving in masses.

These impressions of the situation in the country and among its people are only slightly distorted, and the earnestness of the situation hardly allows any illusions to arise. The final catastrophe has already been prophesized for a long time now, and the anticipation of its arrival hangs over many journalistic, scholarly and visionary studies like the sword of Damocles over the description of the situation and the future. But the horrendous catastrophe has still not taken place. That, indeed, cannot draw our attention away from the many daily and annual small, individual catastrophes, but it confronts us with the question of whether we (1) *perceive* and *interpret* that which we *"see"* correctly and (2) whether we *draw the correct conclusions from it*, both political and scholarly.

---

1   Cf., e.g., [231] Kunert, 1985; [334] Venzky, 1985; [335] Venzky, 1987; and [336] Venzky, 1987.

2   Cf., [126] Government, 1988: p. 42. (The abbreviation *Government* stands for *Government of the People's Republic of Bangladesh* and refers to government publications.)

3   A general and exhaustive description of the country and its people can be found, for example, in [9] Ahmed, 1968; [10] Ahmed, 1976; and [138] Haroun er Rashid, 1977. Detailed descriptions can also be found in [18] Ahmed, 1988; [203] Johnson, 1975; [205] Johnson, 1979; [205] Johnson, 1981; and [359] Zingel, 1978.

18

confronts us with the question of whether we (1) *perceive* and *interpret* that which we *"see"* correctly and (2) whether we *draw the correct conclusions from it*, both political and scholarly.

What is the cause behind this picture and the resulting negative expectations? Why are (implicit) prognoses about Bangladesh's development so difficult? Are our impressions exhaustive and correct? What is the situation like from the viewpoint of Bangladesh's society, especially from the angle of the people concerned? These questions will be discussed in the following chapters.

1.2 Objectives and Concept behind this Study of Bangladesh's Agrarian Society

The purpose of this study is to throw a little light on the *"phenomenon Bangladesh."* It can, however, not provide a generally valid *social theory*, and cannot even be *comprehensive*. Instead, the purpose is to throw a spotlight from the angle of an (as yet unusual) *perspective* on the living conditions of the agrarian population.

There is a large number of questions that imply both theoretical measures and conclusions to which various authors have tried to give consistent answers.

- Is the problem *agricultural stagnation under population pressure* ? [4]

- Is the country in an *agrarian cul-de-sac* ? [5]

- Is the population caught in a *below poverty level equilibrium trap* ? [6]

- And is the country, thus, a *test case for "development approaches"* ? [7]

- Will the result be *differentiation, polarization and confrontation* ? [8]

- Can the situation be explained on the basis of the *behaviour* and poverty of the people ? [9]

The attempt will be made to present the individual and systemic dynamics of the people and the agrarian society in Bangladesh against the background of the description of a few theoretical interpretations of Bangladesh's

---

4   [7] Ahmad, 1984, (Agricultural Stagnation under Population Pressure).
5   [63] Boyce, 1987, (Agrarian Impasse).
6   [23] Alamgir, 1980, (Below Poverty Level Equilibrium Trap).
7   [104] Faaland, Parkinson, 1976, (Test Case of Development).
8   [190] Jahangir, 1979, (Differentiation, Polarization, and Confrontation).
9   [245] Maloney, 1988, (Behaviour and Poverty).

drawn to other studies for these aspects. [10] The *first goal* instead is to present and explain

- the *structure and dynamics of the society* from an *individualistic, structural perspective*. This perspective is based on an *individually-structurally integrated net-utility optimization model* that was developed on the basis of *methodological individualism*. [11]

The objective of the model is to be able to study the

- *economic and social activities* of individual people,

- the *decisions and "concepts of life"* behind them,

- the *situation* and the *logic* in which the activities are embedded and

- the *individual behavioural strategies* that the individual follows with respect to his *individualistic, teleological goals*.

One of the *primary goals* is to utilize this approach in order to reach a comprehensive understanding of the conditions in rural Bangladesh and, thus, partially explain them.

A *second goal* of this study is to sketch

- the *economic and social effects resulting from the goal-oriented activities of many individual people* in Bangladesh that in their "sum" lead to superordinate, social phenomena and structures, as well as to specific dynamics, or "development processes" in the course of time.

The *overall goal* of the present study is, then, to deliver

- an *empirical model based on behavioural-theory* in order to enable a *comprehensive explanation of the dynamics of individual and social self-production and reproduction* against the background of the generally acknowledged situation in Bangladesh, which at times is dramatic and shaken by crises.

The resulting improved understanding of the individualistic, structural conditions in rural Bangladesh and the change trends that have taken place

---

10 Cf., e,g,: [23] Alamgir, 1980; [27] Alamgir, 1980; [101] Etienne, 1985; [102] Etienne, 1985; [103] Faaland, Parkinson, 1976; [104] Faaland, Parkinson, 1976; [190] Jahangir, 1979; [286] Rahman, Islam, 1985; [316] Siddiqui, 1982; [323] Stepanek, 1978; [337] Vylder, 1982; [338] Vylder, Asplund, 1977; [342] Wennergren, Antholt, Whitaker, 1984; [345] Westergaard, 1985; [353] World Bank, 1974; and [354] World Bank, 1984.
11 [155] Herbon, 1992: p. 23 ff.

to date could deliver indications as to where a *"development"* policy [12] could be introduced, or seen normatively, would have to begin.

The *statement of the problem* to be dealt with in this study is, thus:

- what are the living conditions under the existing structural framework conditions in Bangladesh – which still have to be sketched – that are faced by the individual people;

- which are the strategies they use to secure their lasting subsistence in connection with other people, and, thus, ensure a minimum livelihood; and

- which intended and which not intended (macro)effects result from this that, once again, reciprocally determining one another, dictate the chances the individuals have in life by determining the existing structure, its dynamics and potentials.

The *result* of these deliberations cannot be transformed into behavioural stipulations and specific prognoses. The perspective of this study is a *behavioural and systems theoretical approach*, not a *systems technical one*. It will perhaps be possible for the development-policy oriented reader, however, to gain a few *insights into the interrelating factors*; perhaps it will be possible for the development planner to be able to judge the *necessity and consequences of his measures* more thoroughly; and the reader interested in Bangladesh may perhaps be able to *better understand* the *world* in which the people in Bangladesh live; however, he will not find any solutions here. Perhaps, however, it will be possible for the reader to develop them more easily.

1.3 The Structure of the Presentation

In the first chapter following this introduction (Chapter 2) – "General Dynamics of Development in Bangladesh" – a few significant approaches for presenting and interpreting the development dynamics in Bangladesh will

---

12 *"Development"* is placed in quotation marks here in order to illustrate the fact that this term has cultural and ideological implications. In the first place, it is based on *teleological concepts* with *controlling pretensions*: an embroiled situation develops which leads to a better and more progressive situation. Secondly, no one in the first or second world speaks of development policy if he means economic, financial, internal, or cultural policy. And thirdly, the (for many people) morally positively biased term embellishes the hard power and interest policy reality (sometimes military policy). The term "development" shrouds the ideological and political implications for which there are usually more precise terms. If the term is used here anyway, then with the awareness of this background.

be presented and critically discussed. In the next step (Chapter 2.3), a few key national-statistical indicators will be presented in order to demonstrate the fact that the present conditions are determined by dynamics that, until now, have theoretically neither been recorded nor explained. Against the background of the problems resulting from the inconsistency between indicators and interpretations in Chapter 3, the spectrum of *conceivable*, strategic, socially differentiated individual behaviour will be described. The resulting presentation of the contingencies in the individual behaviour system is a technical and theoretical prerequisite and consequence of the concepts on the dynamic "processes" in the agrarian system included in the following chapter, Chapter 4. The contingencies are conceived as the consequences of and preconditions for individual behaviour. In the final chapter, Chapter 5, the circle leading back to the theoretical and empirical statements made at the beginning will be closed by a few fundamental conclusions. This provides a few basic inferences and insights for principle, theoretical and empirical reconstructions of the conditions in Bangladesh in the future.

The succession of chapters and ideas sketched here and in the text does not imply *any* formal and sequential succession. Instead, the attempt will be made here to present interdependent and *non*-linear theoretical and empirical chains of thought that in "reality" are integrated, e.g., take place simultaneously and necessitate a recurrent presentation and analysis in order to be linearly and stringently presented. The structure of the presentation should be understood as "interlaced" and "circular."

"... for its size of population Bangladesh is the most densely populated country in the world and its position will almost certainly get worse, terribly worse, unless something is done or happens to check the natural increase in population."

Just Faaland und J.R. Parkinson [13]

" ... the interaction between population and agricultural growth is considerably more complex than acknowledged ... The historical record indicates that population growth can have *positive* effects on the level of agricultural output ... by inducing land-saving technological change."

James Boyce [14]

2 General Dynamics of Development in Bangladesh

2.1 General Data

Bangladesh's situation can be described on the basis of a few key data. The societal complexity is, indeed, not done justice to by this method; however, it is possible to make the key problem areas of the country and its people recognizable and help categorize them.

In 1990, the population of Bangladesh amounted to approximately 110 million people. [15] The actual surface area (not counting the area covered by water) amounts to ca. 119.624 km^2; [16] i.e., an average population per km^2 of 920 people. There are, however, regions in which the population density amounts to more than 1500 people per km^2. Each year, the population grows by approximately 2.4 %, and doubles over a period of 25 to 30 years. The country has to annually offer subsistence to ca. 2.75 million additional people per year. That means that presently per year, about 1.3 million additional

---

13   [104] Faaland, Parkinson, 1976: p. 1.
14   [63] Boyce, 1987: p. 252.
15   For a general introduction to the country and the people and a description of the geographical, economic and political conditions in Bangladesh cf., e.g., [9] Ahmed, 1968; [10] Ahmed, 1976; [18] Ahmed, 1988; [138] Haroun er Rashid, 1977; [203] Johnson, 1975; [204] Johnson, 1979; [205] Johnson, 1981; [302] Sadeque, 1986: p. 71 ff.; and [359] Zingel, 1978.
16   It amounts, thus, to approximately the same surface area covered by Bavaria and Baden-Württemberg together.

people have to find a means of earning a living, to find jobs that offer enough to live on. The present population growth, in other words, makes expansion in the economic activities and services necessary. This signifies exploiting and mobilizing additional resources that open up acceptable opportunities for the population to earn a living.

The *drastic* increase in the population growth did not begin until the 60's of this century as a consequence of the decrease in the mortality rate. The rough birth rate remained relatively constant during the first half of the 20th century and amounted to 5 %. In the 60's, it even fell to 4.5 % and has remained at approximately that level since then. [17] The rough mortality rate sank during the 50's in the 20th century to about 4 %. Around 1960, it amounted to approximately 2.3 %, and since the mid 80's, it has amounted to 1.5 - 1.7 %: i.e., the general life expectancy has grown to about 55 - 60 years of age. If the population in Bangladesh continues to grow at the present rate, the population will double every 28 years. At the moment there are no indications that the present growth trend will change in the "foreseeable" future. [18]

The present living conditions are characterized by the fact that approximately four-fifths of the population live in the rural regions and just under two-thirds of this rural population is directly involved in agriculture. This percentage decreased from 84.6 % in 1961, to 58.8 % in 1983/84, while the trading and private and public service sectors expanded tremendously. In absolute figures, the number of employees increased in all sectors. [19]

---

17 This is, thus, the factor that shifts to the distant future any adjustment in the population growth that would allow the population to reach a constant level and, therefore, will continue to lead to much greater population density. Bangladesh is very different from other countries in this sense, including India and Sri Lanka, in which the birth rates and fertility are receding.

18 [342] Wennergren, Antholt, Whitaker, 1984: p. 57 ff.

19 The statistical data bases are often deceptive and appear to supply exact data that is not realistic. Ignoring the inaccuracy that occurs when the data is collected (frequently the data is based on mere guessing), the basis for the surveys and criteria have changed so much that the data from various years are not always comparable. Thus, e.g., the definition of what a city is and, as a result, which groups belong to urban and rural populations has changed. Hence the percentage of the population designated as the urban population has increased drastically without a dramatic exodus from the rural regions having taken place. In the case of statistical data, the definitional basis and, thus, the delimiting criteria are not always clear and – at least in the case of the official statistics – not published so that, e.g., what an *agricultural occupation* is, is not defined.

In the case of all of the data presented here – as in the case of the following statistical data – they consequently present the *trends* and the *rough conditions*, but are hardly exact enough to give fluctuations of a few percent an interpretable significance.

In reference to the presented data, cf. [120] Government, 1986: p. 31 ff.; [122] Gov-

Bangladesh's two key characteristics are, thus, (1) a fixed and rather densly settled mass of land and (2) a continually and rapidly growing population. Despite an economic growth of approximately 4 % per annum, [20] the dynamics do not suffice to banish the widespread poverty that can be recognized on the basis of indicators [21] such as:

- an average life expectancy of 55 years;

- an average birth rate [22] of 34.4 per 1000 inhabitants;

- a total fertility rate [23] of 4.7 children per woman, which signifies that

- women in the age group of 45 - 49 years of age gave birth to an average of 6.5 children;

- a literacy rate of ca. 24 %;

- poor nutritional and health conditions; and

- an overall discrimination of women, among other things.

On the contrary, "unemployment" and "underemployment" are increasing while the number of landless grows rapidly at the same time. A specific power structure in the villages, unequal elite and urban-centric power structures within the national framework, an inadequate general and technical educational level, inadequate administrative and budget structures and various other factors are made responsible for inadequate dynamics in the system, i.e. for insufficient "development." [24]

In this study, a detailed analysis and evaluation of the general *causal factors* of *underdevelopment* and their reciprocity will not be carried out. On the contrary, the existing conditions will be used here as the point of departure. In the following sections, however, a few attempts will be made to scientifically explain the present *change trends*.

2.2 Interpretations of the Dynamics of Development

The picture of Bangladesh, as it has been roughly sketched with the help of a few important socio-economic factors, was the occasion for several concepts

---

ernment, 1988: p. 28 ff.; and cf., e.g., [18] Ahmed, 1988: p. 30 ff.

20 [357] World Bank, 1986: I.
21 Cf. [124] Government, 1988: p. 55, Tab. 2.40, and p. 519, Tab. 12.1; and [126] Government, 1988: p. 42, Tab. 3.01.
22 CFR, crude fertility rate.
23 TFR, total fertility rate.
24 Cf., e.g., [357] World Bank, 1986.

that describe the societal dynamics of the country on the basis of structural analyses and projections. It is possible to differentiate between a few typical approaches that, however, do not completely exclude one another. They will be briefly sketched in the following. (1) On the basis of an analysis of the *dynamic processes*, as can be derived from the national statistics, a résumé will be drawn up of the concepts that have been utilized and developed to date. (2) Based on this, the question of the individual life strategies will be substantiated in the following.

From among the multitude of concepts that make statements on the *direction* and *potentials* of development, [25] two main theoretical perspectives and analytical approaches can be recognized.

1. In the first approach, the question of *social inequality* is dealt with. As a rule, this question is studied within the framework of a Marxist approach with respect to the control of resources and chances to gain power, as well as opportunities in life. The basic concept of this approach can be briefly sketched as follows.

The agrarian, post-colonial society in Bangladesh is characterized by the contrast between the capital and land-accumulating landlords and large farmers and the small farmers who are being reduced to poverty and the proletariat consisting of a growing number of landless farmworkers. The owners of the major means of production – land – the landlords, exploit the farmhands and petty tradesmen. This group is caught up in the net of the dynamics of a capitalistic system that is forcing its way into a partly feudal, partly small farmer, communally based society and driven into polarizing, impoverishing and antagonistic class conflicts. The dominant interests, i.e. the large landowners, the comprador bourgeoisie, the military and the foreign capital and power interests manage in the course of the conflict to

---

25 Two fundamental perspectives can be differentiated here with respect to the *"problem"*: (1) application-oriented and (2) social-theory oriented studies. Indeed, the application-oriented studies are also based on substantiated analyses; however, at the same time they have, as a rule, *"policy-oriented"* and *"programme"* or *"project specific"* (systems technical and optimistic) goals. Social theoretical studies also follow more or less explicitly the goal of presenting the reader with consequences from their analyses, i.e. of influencing him by presenting him with knowledge, interpreting the system and giving meaning (unspecified) so as to create a change (consciousness altering and more pessimistic).

These fundamental perspectives will not, and cannot, be gone into here. It should, however, be kept in mind that various projections and prognoses and, as could be demonstrated in principle but will be ignored here as it would go beyond the scope of this study, a priori methodological and theoretical perspective limitations can result from varying perspectives and goals. Thus "systems technicians" derive their justification from *success*, even if it is merely optimism with respect to the goal, and "systems analysts" derive their justification from *criticism* and pessimism.

stabilize the power and production structures at first by means of (1) formal political structures and institutions, (2) anchoring the values and ideologies that legitimize the existing order and (3) military interventions. When the exploited class becomes aware of its situation and gains a class consciousness, a situation arises in which the class develops solidarity and begins purposeful, directed actions supported by the grass-roots level which bring about (1) a revolutionary change in the conditions, (2) the abolishment of antagonisms and (3) the end of poverty because the producers are no longer separated from their means of production.

2. The question as to *societal efficiency* is raised in the second approach. Thereby, the questions of the availability of resources and their allocation, as well as the inefficiency that results from the unequal control over resources and income, and the problem of the cause of the population growth are placed in the foreground of interest. The basic concept (the accents with respect to the importance given to inefficiency vary greatly in the diverse approaches) can be sketched as follows.

The agrarian society in Bangladesh is – firstly – characterized and changed by uncontrolled population growth that forces socio-structural adaption. The control over the means of production and the organization of the production have to be changed by developing adequate technology and know-how based innovations in order to cope with the pressure arising from the needs of the growing population. The organization and the yields from production are often inadequate. This can also be partly traced back to (1) insufficient access to the unequally distributed resources and (2) "development inhibitions" that are caused by inefficient organizational and institutional structures. In addition, the (1) extreme pressure on the resources that is caused by the drastic increase in the population and (2) the existing poverty with its socio-economic and mental-cultural consequences are regarded as the reason for the stagnating economic development. Structural and institutional change is, thus, the prerequisite for a production that is adequate enough to (1) eliminate the prevalent poverty, (2) compensate for the population growth, (3) perhaps initiate growing affluence and (4) finance socio-institutional change.

These two fundamental approaches can be complemented by still one further approach. **3.** This approach can include the first two perspectives from the viewpoint of socio-cultural complexity.

These three basic perspectives, which more or less complement each other in specific studies and are more or less usage oriented, as well as the resulting perspectives for the development in Bangladesh, will be presented in the following section using the example of a few specific approaches.

- The studies on societal inequality: [26]

  - the "revolutionary" class conflicts perspective;
  - the "revolutionary" agrarian reform perspective;
  - the "involutionary," mobilization strategy perspective.

- The studies on societal inefficiency: [27]

  - the "innovative," population dynamics perspective;
  - the "transformative" agrarian development perspective;
  - the "technocratic," development planning perspective.

- The studies on socio-cultural complexity: [28]

  - the "evolutionary," cultural dynamics perspective;
  - the "microscopic-structural," village perspective.

These first two approaches, which have specific theoretical and methodological implications, make statements on the *development of an entire society*, i.e. they contain macro-theories. This is also true in the case of most of the village or case studies that try to make statements on the general or specific aspects of socio-economic development. These approaches do not exclude each other mutually. On the basis of theoretical analyses of their own empirical data and experience, most of the authors as a rule deviate only in the significance they place on the importance of the causal factors and the consequences, and they differ only in a more or less stressed transposability of the approach. The implications for the usage of the approaches will be briefly presented here; however, the development policy implications and plausibility will not be discussed. The approaches have only been given labels in order to furnish them with a name: the intention was not to qualify them polemically.

In this brief sketch of the theoretical models behind the studies, it is not possible to (1) judge the empirical substantiation and the theoretical conclusions contained in the published material; (2) to deepen and individually understand the conceptual and theoretical position of the specific approaches; and (3) to carry out a detailed, substantiated and fair analysis, i.e. to examine each study on the basis of findings from other studies or offical statistics that may contradict them. On the contrary, in section

---

26   Cf. page 29.
27   Cf. page 39.
28   Cf. page 48.

2.3, my own and partially deviating picture will be presented and current macroscopic and statistical material introduced on the basis of several indicators and, thus, unspecific criticism will be implied. In addition, when (2) presenting the micro-theoretical and empirical findings of other authors, it will be necessary to take their individual hypotheses and findings into consideration. In connection with my description of the societal dynamics, (3) in the last chapter, Chapter 5, I will refer back to the explanations contained in the approaches.

2.2.1 Studies on Social Inequality

2.2.1.1 The Revolutionary Class Conflict Perspective

The control over the means of production, the resulting power structures and the ensuing socio-political dynamics are the focal points in Jahangir's study. [29] On the basis of a Marxist approach, he describes the structural dynamics of the production conditions in the agrarian society in Bangladesh. His study is based on suppositions that he attempts to support by argumention. They can be summarized as follows.

1. The class of "wealthy farmers" has succeeded since the independence of the country in 1971, in contrast to the poorer and average farmers, in stabilizing their economic basis and maintaining their political power. This class strengthens its position by increasing investments in agricultural and nonagricultural enterprises that they attempt to secure by means of political influence at the national and urban levels. Hence, a confrontation between the underprivileged rural population and a class alliance of the ruling classes supported by horizontal urban-rural relations is presently taking place. Vertical clientelistic interdependencies are dissolved by the processes of differentiation and polarization and the structural contradictions in the class relations. [30]

2. The "land reform ideology," i.e. agrarian reform, the state promotion of the small farmers by means of subsidies and the formal political structures serve the dominant interests and are oriented towards them. Despite this fact, there are internal struggles to gain the control over the means of production. The use of and access to power is important because the control over the means of production and the possibility of steering the political, social and economic change in the desired direction is dependent upon it. Presently, however, this has resulted in an inability to resolve the fundamental contradictions in the society.

---

29   [190] Jahangir, 1979.
30   Cf. [190] Jahangir, 1979: p. 21 ff. and p. 199.

Thus, at the moment, the hierarchic, family-relationship/alliance oriented, basically static village system is disintegrating and classes are evolv-
ing instead. The land concentration is increasing because the possibilities of
increasing the agricultural productivity are improving and investment opportunities outside agriculture are opening up. The subsistence farmers'
situation has become aggravated because of their integration in the market
economy and the reduction in the size of the farms that resulted from fragmentation through inheritance and forced sales. This leads to increasing
polarization. [31]

3. A growing coalition of interests between the rich agriculturists and
urban investors, firstly, and, secondly, the natural catastrophes that additionally lead to predicaments and distress for the poor and uproot them, result in polarization, i.e. an increasingly marked division between the classes
with the corresponding tensions and conflicts. This polarization results from
the fact that the wealthy classes are successful in stabilizing their wealth by
taking advantage of the possibility to generate income outside agricultural,
despite the creeping fragmentation and dissolving of their landed properties
as an outcome of inheritance. [32]

Colonial policies and the implementation of development strategies led
to a deformed capitalistic economy that superimposed an economic system
based on value added on top of a survival-oriented economic system. Impacts of natural catastrophes aggravated the situation of the small farmers
even more without their having developed a class consciousness and having
taking up political activities as a reaction to exploitation and appropriation
by force. However, Jahangir stated that there were at times situations in
which conflicts regarding access to resources resulted in confrontation and,
on the basis of the solidarity resulting from the conflict, in a social class
consciousness. At the time (the mid 70's), this was accelerated by left-wing
political groups, but the question of the development of a class consciousness
cannot be clearly answered because, firstly, the left was divided and quar-
reled and, secondly, the class consciousness in the villages was too weak. [33]

---

31 [190] Jahangir, 1979: p. 157 ff., p. 198.
32 Cf. [190] Jahangir, 1979: p. 199.
33 "It appears that the poor peasants of Bangladesh are beginning to operate as a
    class-for-itself in the Marxist sense. They have found forms of organization and
    ideology adequate to express their demands. They are also organized in relation
    to an underground revolutionary movement but exhibit levels of class consciousness
    which are more closely connected with their immediate situation than that of national
    politics." ([190] Jahangir, 1979: p. 238.)
    "... we find that the stabilization of a rich peasant class and the political mobilization
    of the underprivileged peasants into peasant unions has resulted in radical change in
    the rural areas. The expression of class solidarity at the village level is weak. ... In

30

Summarizing, Jahangir cites the following factors: [34]

- Capital accumulation is taking place in the hands of the ruling rural groups.

- This leads to a vertical socio-economic differentiation process in the small farmer economy.

- Market pressures, consequences resulting from political decisions and the structure of the state have contributed to the present rural land tenure and labour organization systems.

- Manpower and land have become sellable commodities.

- The differentiation process led to polarization in a rich class and a class of small farmers living in abject poverty.

- Small farmers are not only forced to become farmhands and impelled to sell their manpower, but they also have to purchase the food they consume on the market with the wages they earn.

- This market is controlled by the rural rich and urban investors and steered by state intervention.

On the basis of a political evaluation of the situation, [35] he concludes with respect to the development of the political situation that "... certain new forms of consciousness are revealed by peasant action ... expressing new structural alignments and contradictions and antagonisms. They are most marked in the relations between peasants and the local agents of the state bureaucracy. Whereas the rural rich are structurally aligned with the bureaucracy and the dominant political parties, the poor peasants, organized by the left-wing, operate mainly in the local arena. The latter attempts to challenge the existing national power structure from a class position,

---

the case of underprivileged peasants, class solidarity arises at the village level and undermines pre-existing loyalties and dominant ideologies." ([190] Jahangir, 1979: p. 278.)

34 [190] Jahangir, 1979: p. 279 ff.

35 This evaluation results from the author's extremely committed political viewpoint. He quite positively judges the role and the significance of left-wing Bengali local organizations and policies at the grass-roots level. As to the question of the extent to which this corresponds to the present situation in Bangladesh, an answer cannot be given here. In my opinion, the real situation in the villages and bazaars is not as positive. The author's position, however, is based on his experience at the beginning of the 70's when in Bangladesh many things were still not clearly defined and flowing, and the revolutionary potential still seemed to be strong.

31

which, because of increasing economic differentiation and polarization, is more clearly defined, and they form a local political base. In this way, the process of differentiation expands the potential area of tension and dissatisfaction, and gives shape to the forms and intensity of political confrontation at both village and national level." [36]

2.2.1.2 The Revolutionary Agrarian Reform Perspective

Rahman's class analytical and agrarian policy approach is similar to that of Jahangir. [37] He developed his approach for an empirically founded theoretical study on the basis of an analysis of the Russian/Soviet debate on the "agrarian question" and a dialectic-antithetic comparison of Lenin's and his successors' position with that of the "Chayanov school" (production organization school). [38]

In Lenin's case, according to Rahman, a number of contradictions that cause and influence each other lead to "differentiation" among the farmers dividing them into a rural bourgeoisie and a rural proletariat (class differentiation). According to Chayanov, a demographic phenomenon – the creation and disintegration of household and farm units – is the significant driving force behind socio-economic "differentiation" (demographic differentiation). [39] On the basis of this theoretical comparison of the conditions leading to socio-economic differentiation – class formation –, he developed "verifiable hypotheses" for both approaches [40] which he investigated within

---

36 [190] Jahangir, 1979: p. 290 f.
37 [281] Rahman, 1986.
  Interestingly, Rahman pays no attention to Jahangir's writings.
38 He characterizes Lenin's position as follows:
  "The sum total of all these contradictions among the peasantry, according to Lenin, is the *differentiation*. 'Depeasantization' is almost synonymous with this term. Lenin further emphasized that the process of disintegration of the peasantry and the emergence of property inequality was not sufficient to be termed differentiation. Differentiation signified much more. More importantly, it ousted the old peasantry and brought in new types of inhabitants – the rural bourgeoisie – chiefly petty bourgeoisie and rural proletariat ..." ([281] Rahman, 1986: p. 15.)
  He sketched Chayanov's concept as:
  "... the Organization-Production School led by Chayanov viewed the differentiation of the peasantry primarily as a demographic phenomenon. To them, it was more a measure of relative family size and decomposition than of differential economic success. Farm size being the most important indicator of a peasant's wealth, it was argued that farm size tended to follow a cycle coincident with the family life cycle, increasing as family members matured into workers and declining as the family aged and disintegrated with the formation of new families." ([281] Rahman, 1986: p. 24.)
39 [281] Rahman, 1986: p. 12 ff.
40 The hypotheses based on Chayanov's statements are:

32

the framework of his own empirical studies of two villages in Bangladesh and tested against the background of a Marxist approach to explain the evolution of a class society. His findings and conclusions will be briefly presented in the following.

1. Despite the implementation of rural development programmes, in-

---

- "Peasant households do not employ wage labour. ...
- ...the motive behind production organization by an individual family unit is not profit-maximization but establishing and maintenance of the labour-consumer (or subsistence) balance. ...
- Land is flexible in supply to all households ...
- For each household family size influences the size of cultivated area ... the correlation between the operated area and consumer-worker (c/w) ratio shall be positive.
- For each household the c/w ratio influences the hours worked per adult. In other words with increase in c/w ratio, hours worked per adult also increases. ...
- Similarly, with the increase in c/w ratio, output/worker shall also increase. ...agricultural income per capita shall also increase.
- The family life cycle influences the relative wealth of a family. ..."

And as hypotheses derived from the Chayanov approach by Shanin:

- "Rich families are becoming poor over time by partitioning and other demographic processes and poor families are becoming rich as their family size increases. ..."

([281] Rahman, 1986: p. 67 f.)
The hypotheses based on Lenin's statements are:

- "... the control over the means of production at a point in time is distributed very unequally.
- ... the concentration in the ownership of means of production ... [is] getting worse over time.
- ... one shall observe differences in techniques of production, income and expenditure pattern, food intake and standard of living, extent of market participation and any other aspects connected with such differences.
- Differences in the distribution of material elements of production shall have roots in social relations of production and exchanges ...
- ... the extent of labour exploitation and impoverishment shall increase ...
- The state shall get increasingly involved in displacing the poorer peasantry and helping the process of concentration in the hands of a few. ...
- ...capitalistic relations ... will increasingly subordinate all other relations in agriculture."

([281] Rahman, 1986: p. 68 f.)
These abridged hypotheses that were drawn up by Rahman have been given here in order to (1) illustrate his quite precise theoretical position, (2) to clarify the validity of his conclusions on Bangladesh that will be presented in the following without being able to discuss the empirical analysis in detail and (3) in order to be able to refer back to these hypotheses once again later in this study.

equality and poverty are increasing. Inequality with respect to land ownership and usufruct is pronounced: the concentration in the hands of the richest is increasing, while the majority is being slowly dispossessed. [41] This is also valid with respect to other agricultural means of production.

2. The rich have greater control over the means of production and can, hence, appropriate the surplus and surplus value generated in the agrarian economy by means of rent, lending money, market mechanisms and exploiting the labour of others.

3. The increasing exploitation leads to a "dispossessing" of the poor and, finally, to proletarization which can be see by the *increase in*

- wealthy farmers farming land themselves that had formerly been leased to tenants,

- large farms renting additional land,

- wage labour,

- manpower layoffs and

- the monetarization of wages.

---

41 Cf. the analysis of part of Rahman's data in Chapter 4.1.2 on page 227 ff.
In anticipation, however, the following methodological comment is appropriate. The empirical proof that he delivers for these statements is presented in such a way that it seems to support this theoretical finding. A detailed presentation of the empirical data in an earlier article suggests, in my opinion, other, contradictory, or at least deviating interpretations (Cf. [279] Rahman, 1982).
In this source, (see pages 56, Tab. 2a; 57, Tab. 2b) namely, it can be seen that

- the absolute number and the percentage of landless households and households with little land *increased* rapidly from 1951 to 1981, while those of the rich *decreased*; and

- the area of land belonging to the individual land-ownership groups among the poor *increased*, even if not to the same extent as their number, while that of the rich *decreased*.

Thus in the course of time, there is general *fragmentation of the property*, a *decrease in the size of the farm units* and, by implication, evidently *general impoverishment* and *no "concentration"*!
This discrepancy can be explained by the change in the descriptive, statistical analysis methods: in 1982, fixed land-ownership size classes were described with respect to their quantitative development. 1986, relative, percentile land-ownership categories were surveyed. Thus the fact can be established that even if the rich are *absolutely decreasing* in significance both in number and regarding the area they own, they are *relatively* becoming *richer* (!) in comparison to the overproportionally increasing landless. This permits completely different political arguments.

Class consciousness and the disintegration of family and communal relations are further indicators of class differentiation.

4. The state promotes these processes actively by helping the wealthy farmers to secure their economic position and, thus, allows the distribution of income and power to become even more unequal. Hence, it promotes the disintegration of the small farmer stratum and the unequal and, thus, deforming capitalistic penetration. This leads to a still unclarified situation and even unclearer relative significance of capitalistic and feudal methods of production. [42]

Based on this development, he comes to the conclusion that there are, in principle, two alternatives for the future societal development:

- the path of socialism and a step by step transition to collective property in order to reverse the trend of increasing poverty and create a basis for progress; and

- the path of capitalism which benefits the rich farmers and aggravates class differentiation and poverty. [43]

In summary, to quote Rahman himself: "The way the sheer volume of the pauperized and to some extent proletarized rural poor is increasing, neither the agrarian sector nor the industrial sector under present structure will be in a position to support the swelling millions. The prospect of dependent capitalism, the model the donor countries and agencies prescribe for Bangladesh, has, therefore, no bright future either. The solution

---

42 "As trends indicate the gains of rapid expansion of productive forces have been expropriated by the rich peasantry, leaving the other half into utter ruin. In other words, differentiation is proceeding fast, along with simultaneous polarization and *immiserization*: the poor peasantry are denied the technical advancement and the number of wage labourers is rising without much scope for employment either in agriculture or in industry. It is apprehended that many more peasants will become landless and the competition for obtaining sharecropping rights and employment will harden in the coming years. The way the great majority of the rural poor cope with the lack of resources will shape the destiny of Bangladesh society in the coming years. It is most likely that they will get further alienated from the more well-to-do peasants. Of course, many factors external to the village society will have profound influence on this outcome." ([281] Rahman, 1986: p. 256 f.)

43 "... if the society at large decides to solve its agrarian question in a socialist way there is no alternative but to aim at collective ownership through successive stages. This alone can reverse the present trend of exploitation and pauperization and build a basis for future progress. On the contrary, however, if the society opts for a capitalist road notwithstanding the Populist rhetorics – the rich peasantry will be the ultimate beneficiaries, giving a further twist to the pace of differentiation and impoverishment. And that is what seems to be in the agenda, at least for the moment, of Bangladesh state." ([281] Rahman, 1986: p. 258.)

undoubtedly lies in the socialist transformation of Bangladesh society." [44]

Siddiqui [45] likewise based his analysis on a Marxist approach. His starting point is, despite the ambitious title, a description of poverty in Bangladesh within the framework of a village study. It seemed to him that the problem had been poorly described and explained until then. It is not possible to present his empirical findings here. The starting point and conclusion of his presentation are:

1. Poverty is increasing in the course of time in rural Bangladesh, both according to relative as well as absolute standards.

2. The economy is stagnating, a fact that is reflected in the gross domestic product, the per capita availability of food and the per capita industrial production.

3. The exchange of resources with foreign countries as well as foreign aid aggravate the poverty creating structures and, thus, poverty itself.

The statements on the international involvement and its negative consequences cannot be discussed here: the statements on the growing poverty and the stagnating economy will be examined in section 2.3 of this chapter.

2.2.1.3 The Involutionary and Mobilization Strategy Perspective

Another model for interpreting social development in Bangladesh was developed by Alamgir. [46] He derives his theory from historical materialism and based his studies on a model that he calls the *below poverty level equilibrium trap*. Alamgir supplied evidence to substantiate the fact that during the period from 1949/50 until 1969/70, the rural income situation, particularly with respect to the poor, worsened to a level below the subsistence or poverty level. While the number of people living below the threshold to poverty has been steadily increasing, hardly anyone who has passed this threshold manages to ascend beyond this level once again. On the other hand, a certain number of people who have periodically or permanently passed the famine threshold die a silent death. [47]

---

44 [281] Rahman, 1986: p. 259.
45 [316] Siddiqui, 1982: "The political economy of rural poverty in Bangladesh."
46 [23] Alamgir (1980).
47 "Trends of real income per capita, real wages, income inequality and poverty ... indicate that the base of Group A [*] is becoming narrower but its members are gaining control over a greater proportion of total income and wealth while the rank of Group B [**] is swelling. Available evidence suggests that the level of welfare of Group B is fluctuating between the poverty line and the famine line. This has been the situation throughout the period under consideration with no indication of any change. However, ... in this period the oscillations have grown much smaller and they have stayed very close to the famine line. Some people are continuously falling below the famine line and perishing either due directly to lack of basic food or indirectly to

36

According to Alamgir, Bangladesh is subject to the following regular development processes or laws of motion. [48]

1. There is a steadily increasing concentration in the ownership of the means of production. The unequal distribution of land from the beginning is significant here (concentration of land holding).

2. The population growth and the rules governing inheritance cause splitting and fragmentation of the land. This leads (1) to uneconomical farm units and hits the small farmers in particular, (2) to an emigration to the cities and (3) to larger families and greater fertility as a strategy for securing their subsistence [49] (law of population). The increasing pauperization of the people and the necessity to secure their survival force them, under the pressure of increasing debts and decreasing per capita real income, to surrender assets (distress sales and transfer of assets, alienation).

3. Both the percentage of households without land as well as the percentage of agricultural labourers among the total number of those employed in agriculture are increasing. This cannot be traced back to the increase in the population and the negative effects of market forces alone, but rather to antagonistic class relations. [50]

---

the diseases related to a famine situation. ... Therefore, what one observed has been called the 'Below Poverty Level Equilibrium Trap' depicted by the situation reached today ... The state of equilibrium referred to is defined with respect to the famine line in the sense that if some forces act to raise the income/welfare level above the famine level there are opposing forces that quickly retort by pushing it down to the famine level. ... more and more people are getting trapped into this situation thus making the society bottom heavy implying that any reversal in the trend will require fundamental structural change." ([23] Alamgir, (1980): p. 87 f.)

---

* "Group A includes the semi-colonial forces, the bourgeoisie (national and comprador) including commercial, agricultural, industrial, and financial elements and the upper crust of professionals and civil bureaucracy." ([23] Alamgir, (1980): p. 86)
** "Group B includes poor peasants, agricultural labourers, the proletariat, the lumpenproletariat, petty professionals and low paid fixed income groups." ([23] Alamgir, (1980): p. 86 f.)

48 [23] Alamgir, (1980): p. 90 ff.
49 "The semi-feudal/semi-colonial social formation leads to an exploitative social relationship which produces increasing poverty, among the masses and the 'Below Poverty Level Equilibrium Trap' which on the one hand combines some exogenous forces to make fertility raising forces stronger than fertility depressing forces, on the other hand, give rise to unique factors that tend to encourage a relatively large family size and consequently a high rate of population growth." ([23] Alamgir, (1980): p. 100 f.)
Alamgir takes up – without indicating it in any way – one of the hypotheses developed by Geertz ([111] 1963).
50 "It should be noted here that landlessness, giving rise to a loss of staying power, makes rural households susceptible to pressure from exploitative forces in society.

4. Sharecropping is losing significance, a fact which is reflected in the decrease in the number of tenants who own land themselves; i.e., the land is increasingly farmed by the owners themselves, whereas the number of real tenants and the land they farm has remained the same. [51]

5. The relation between the "weaker" and the "dominant" sections of the population is characterized by a decrease in solidarity, by the collapse of "exchange entitlements," the "moral economy." [52] This is explained by (1) sinking real wages that are caused (a) by monetarization and fixation without the seasonal fluctuations in the price of grain being taken into account and, thus, unreliable purchasing power which is (b) characterized by a general deterioration in the working conditions without "wage adjustments." The worsening of the situation is explained (2) by a drastic reduction in incomes and employment at the time of the flood catastrophe in 1974, (3) by a negative development in the sharecropping conditions and (4) by a deterioration in the market position of the consumers. Furthermore, the "traditional" system of social security based on solidarity within the "extended family" and the "kin group" is also disappearing. The same is true in the case of the patronage relations that have been undermined by better education, political patronage, migration and alternative employment and income opportunities. This results in the loss of a few advantages found in larger socio-economic units that exhibit solidarity: (1) the scale advantages and (2) the absorption effects for insecurity and risks during the necessary and frictionless implementation of technological innovations.

6. The market orientation in production decisions is becoming more important because more and more is being sold and must be sold than the traditional "surplus after subsistence." The supply of consumer goods is being provided increasingly via the market (1) in order to compensate for seasonal fluctuations (2) because the needs can frequently no longer be met by means of self-production. [53] Furthermore, the general increase in the significance of markets, especially rural markets, the market for means of

---

Under the semi-feudal mode of production ... there are many instruments through which the dominant groups extract surplus from peasants and landless labourers." ([23] Alamgir, (1980): p. 102.)

51 "... there has probably been some amount of substitution of landless tenants for landed ones. Therefore, the traditional equalizing effect of sharecropping on the distribution of land holding has been weakened." ([23] Alamgir, (1980): p. 133.)

52 Alamgir refers to Sen here (cf. [312] Sen, 1982) who uses the term *"exchange entitlements."* He does not mention Scott's (cf. [311] Scott, 1977) parallel concept of the *"moral economy."*

53 Alamgir does not indicate the importance and value he places in this phenomenon that he does not quite seem to find substantiated. He explains this by a lack of empirical material supporting the hypotheses.

production and the market for industrial goods, plays a role.

Alamgir develops political-programme-based behavioural stipulations from his knowledge of the societal "development laws": [54] in order to dispose of the forces that are responsible for the situation in Bangladesh, political perspectives and the identification of the forces and classes that are responsible for the exploitation of the majority of the masses are necessary, in addition to economic and technical measures. Therefore, it will be necessary to mobilize the masses and dispose of the exploiting forces. Traditional economic theories do not offer any concepts for solving the real problems. Pragmatic approaches for raising the level of prosperity cannot function since they cannot do away with the real causes of underdevelopment, or what is called the "below poverty level equilibrium trap." Hence, the conditions in Bangladesh can only then be improved if the dominance of the comprador bourgeoisie or other classes which represent semi-feudal and semi-colonial interests has been ended.

2.2.2   Studies on Societal Inefficiency

2.2.2.1   The Innovation and Population Dynamics Perspective

Ahmad [55] presented her approach for analysing Bangladesh on the basis of Boserup's hypothesis [56] that an agrarian society which is confronted by independent population growth will increase the yields in agricultural production by means of technological innovations. Her position, thus, contradicts the Malthusian concept [57] that population growth is limited by the shortage of resources and is, hence, *dependent* upon the available resources. Under the existing natural conditions, the present situation in the agricultural sector is characterized by the following features:

- divers farm sizes and structures (fragmentation),

- a traditional sharecropping system,

- a large number of landless,

---

54   Cf. [23] Alamgir, (1980): p. 163.
     At this point and in this context the problem of the development policy programme, which is contained in another facile list of good advice covering all possible areas, should and cannot be further examined here. The significance of the political or pragmatic orientation of the literature has already been pointed out in footnote 25 on page 26.
55   [7] Ahmad, 1984: p. 18 ff.
56   [60] Boserup, 1981. Cf. also [61] Boserup, 1985.
57   Cf., e.g., [71] Bähr, 1983; [142] Hauser, 1982; and [268] Pulte, 1972.

- marked population density,

- limited capital endowment in the agricultural sector,

- primitive technology and

- subsistence production is very significant.

The potential for compensating for the population pressure is, accordingly, very limited. Her arguments can be summarized as follows.

1. The drastic increase in the population did not begin until the 30's in this century. Since then, according to Ahmad, the production of food has no longer been able to keep up with the increasing number of people so that it became necessary to increase the importation of food. The growing quota of food imports became necessary, although at the same time the main concentration in agricultural production shifted from the production of raw materials and fruit for marketing purposes to the production of food for consumption purposes. As the agricultural production could no longer keep up with the population growth, the average income per capita sank - i.e., the result was mass poverty and income disparity.

Ahmad sees proof in this development of the notion that population growth is not dependent upon a successful and adequate supply of food for the population. On the contrary, the autonomously growing population attempts to adjust the production of food to its needs. [58] She sees another proof of this in the fact that while the death rate sank, the birth rate in Bangladesh has remained constant and there has been no reduction in fertility despite the fact that migration did not provide an adequate outlet for the population. This development took place on the basis of individual perceptions of utility and led at the collective level to sinking wage rates and increasing unemployment. [59]

2. From this one can see that in the case of Bangladesh, a change for the worse in the economic situation has no, or only an insufficient, decelerating influence on the population development. And vice versa, the assumption that population pressure will bring about production increases is not valid in the case of Bangladesh, at least not to a sufficient extent. [60] On the one

---

58 [7] Ahmad, 1984: p. 42 ff.

59 [7] Ahmad, 1984: p. 54 ff.

60 "The application of labour input per crop season on operations like irrigation, water control, intensive cultivation practices and the cultivation of labour intensive high yielding crops have not proceeded at a fast rate. Capital formation through investment of unpaid family labour has also been insignificant." ([7] Ahmad, 1984: p. 108.)

hand, this can be traced back to insufficient or belated state interventions [61] and, on the other hand, to structural and institutional inefficiency.

3. The deviating and inadequate endowment with land, either owned by the peasants themselves or rented, led thus to differences in the extent to which family and hired manpower were employed and, as a consequence, to differences in productivity that were dependent upon the size of the farms. In addition, inefficient institutional arrangements also played a role such as sharecropping and informal credit, which are – in addition to other factors – indicators of the imperfection of the factor markets. [62]

4. The inadequate, inefficient and belated government policies have led, instead of doing away with structural and institutional bottlenecks, to an aggravation of the problems. The introduction of innovative technology and organizational forms by means of government measures has furthermore – under the existing conditions of overpopulation, poverty and a concentration of economic and social power – proven to be very difficult. [63]

Thus it is possible to see – according to Ahmad – that the presumption is incorrect in the case of Bangladesh which assumes that population growth will internally induce adequate production of food by means of technological innovations as a result of a worsening of the situation faced by the population. On the contrary, by means of externally induced change it is necessary to prevent the negative productivity development and the increasing poverty from continuing to progress. Thus, the goal is to prevent, before it is too late, a negative, self-reinforcing spiral that could otherwise no longer be slowed down. [64] She is not very optimistic about the future. "In view of the existing situation it is difficult to be optimistic about the fate of the rural population in Bangladesh. It is a fact that the present government (or government in recent years) lack the strong political will to transform the political economy. But the balance between population and resources has become so unfavourable that it is difficult for any government to achieve a miracle. With some marginal progress in the new technology the majority of the rural population will probably manage to survive but not enjoy a rising per capita income." [65]

---

61 [7] Ahmad, 1984: p. 110, and p. 176 ff.
62 [7] Ahmad, 1984: p. 113 ff.
63 [7] Ahmad, 1984: p. 226.
64 [7] Ahmad, 1984: p. 10 ff., and p. 227.
65 [7] Ahmad, 1984: p. 16.

2.2.2.2 The Transformative Agrarian Development Perspective

Boyce's key hypothesis concerning the agrarian development in West Bengal and Bangladesh [66] contains the presumption that the introduction and adoption of production increasing innovations, despite the establishable potentials, did not take place to a sufficient extent and in the awaited form because the resulting collective benefits did not correspond to the benefits for those that held the power, influence and wealth in their hands. The present agrarian structures are based on the attempt to attain and enforce individual interests, whereby the powerful and rich have the advantages, and changes that are not beneficial to them, or even endanger their position, are blocked. This has the systemic consequence of slowing down the dynamics of change [67] that are mainly based on an efficiently coordinated and collective utilization and control of the key factor water.

Boyce bases his study on the analysis of statistical documents and published studies [68] and arrives at the following conclusions.

1. Population growth induces agricultural growth. Population growth has, presuming that a delay of approximately 30 years played a role, induced increasing agricultural production and led to a corresponding growth rate in the yields. This can be traced back to: (1) the increasing availability and

---

66 Boyce ([63] Boyce, 1987) explores the historical development and the reasons for the increasing poverty in the region in a comparison between the Indian state of West Bengal and Bangladesh: both belong to the same "cultural circle" and "eco-geographical region."
    Only his remarks on Bangladesh will be referred to in the following.

67 He establishes a "... need for an 'impure' theory of induced innovation, one that recognizes that the self-interest of powerful individuals or groups may retard the pace and bias the direction of technological and institutional change. In so far as features of the agrarian structure constrain the level and growth of agricultural output, the invisible hand fails to work its magic. ... it does undercut the 'rationality implies efficiency' paradigm, which holds that, 'where potential gains exist to overcoming economic inefficiencies, one should presume that the gains will be exploited ...' ... The present study will argue that, in the agriculture of Bangladesh and West Bengal such blockages [by powerful interest groups or the expectation of activities of powerful groups] are not the exception but the rule." ([63] Boyce, 1987: p. 49 f.)
    "The key question is why, despite intense demographic pressure, this agricultural potential remains unfulfilled ... [It] underlines the need for an 'impure' theory of induced innovation, which seeks to explain technological and institutional changes, or their absence, not only in terms of relative factor endowments and product demands, but also in terms of conflict among individuals, groups, and classes. The outcome of these conflicts may have profound implications not only for distribution, but also for production. In purely technical terms, there can be little doubt that Bangladesh ... ha[s] the capacity to feed the[ ] present population[ ] and more... " ([63] Boyce, 1987: p. 255.)

68 Cf. among others, [63] Boyce, 1987: p. 49f., and p. 251 ff.

input of manpower that is independent of technological innovations; however, (2) some labour intensifying and land-saving innovations took place; and (3), in addition, the improvement in the water control was important.

Rapid population growth does, thus, not have a slowing down effect on the increases in the agricultural outputs. But in the long run, it could turn out that the increases in the population will neutralize the yield-increasing effects of the innovations. If, thereby, the two growth rates should neutralize each other, there would be no improvement in the population's situation. The standard of living and the agrarian structures would basically remain the same on a higher level with respect to numbers. [69]

2. The most important production factor and the innovative key technology is water and its societal and technological control, i.e. irrigation and drainage and flood control. Until now (1980), the use and spreading of irrigation were relatively insignificant. At the end of the 70's, only approximately one-eighth of the gross cropping area in Bangladesh was irrigated. This lack partly explains why the increase in agricultural production did not keep up with the population growth, but rather lagged behind it. [70]

3. The inadequate utilization of the factor labour is based on the unbalanced and, thus, inefficient landownership structures (land tenure). The existing differences in the size of the farms have, among other things, the following effects. [71] (1) Small holdings farm their land more efficiently because, on the one hand, they employ both more family as well as hired, wage-earning manpower and, on the other hand, they farm the better and less flood endangered land. (2) Shorter tenancy contract durations are accompanied by greater employment of inputs, mainly fertilizers. Short tenancy periods meet, in other words, the interests of the landowners if they want to achieve higher yields. It can be seen that (a) tenancy positively correlates with agricultural productivity – a correlation that has not been quite elucidated empirically – and (b) the hypothesis that tenancy is inefficient is

---

69 "If increased output leads to higher fertility and lower mortality, this would testify to the inadequacy of past agricultural growth, which has failed to lift living standards above the abysmal levels at which these deadly mechanisms [nutritionally based infertility and a generally higher mortality rate] operate.
The reverse linkages from agricultural growth to population growth would tend in the long run, to offset the positive effects of induced innovation upon per capita agricultural output. ... Few would argue that rapid population growth in Bangladesh ... is an unmixed blessing, but the above analysis suggests that it is not an unmitigated evil, either. The fashionable view that population growth is the fundamental economic problem in countries such as Bangladesh fail to take into account the positive impact of population growth via the process of induced innovation." ([63] Boyce, 1987: p. 159.)

70 [63] Boyce, 1987: p. 199.

71 [63] Boyce. 1987: p. 245.

incorrect.

4. A lack of cooperation and inadequate creation of institutions above the farm level hinder collective control of the water, i.e. the utilization of water for irrigation and prevention of floods. Projects for improving water control are hindered by the social conditions. The landowners are not unreservedly interested in, or in the position to (1) cooperate with one another and (2) to allow a large number of workers to be tied to one job or project for a longer period of time. Inappropriate utilization of inputs and technological and financial mismanagement hamper the construction of canals to take advantage of the relatively inexpensive surface water. [72]

The lack of control and common-cooperative utilization of the various existing irrigation facilities, which resulted from socio-institutional difficulties, has led to limited utilization of the existing potential. The social and economic inequality within the group of landowners posed large obstacles to the organization of the technological improvements. [73]

According to Boyce, the fundamental problem that, on the one hand, the "powerful" have no interest in technological innovations and that, on the other hand, collective or administratively organized measures for creating a "water infrastructure" are necessary, can be solved in three different ways.

1. Government measures for expanding the canal system or the irrigation pump facilities. If enough external resources are available, this might be successful. [74]

---

72 "Possibilities for labour-intensive water control development projects, which could make use of surplus labour in the slack season, are undermined by landowner disinterest, attributable not only to the formidable difficulties of cooperation among themselves, but also, it is hypothesized, to their reluctance to employ large numbers of agricultural labourers at a single work site for a sustained period for fear of potential repercussions. Attempts to substitute government initiatives for local resource mobilization, via rural works programmes are undermined by misappropriation of resources by large landowner-controlled project committees, biases in project selection, shoddy execution, and a lack of institutional mechanism for maintenance." ([63] Boyce, 1987: p. 246 f.)

73 "... deep tubewells are ... chronically underutilized, an outcome to which disarticulation and inequality in the agrarian structure again contribute. The siting of tubewells to maximize individual interests rather than total irrigation capacity, favouritism and monopoly pricing of water allocation, the deliberate withholding of water to facilitate land acquisition, and the sabotage of tubewells by resentful neighbours all contribute to rates of capacity underutilization that often make a mockery of the cost-benefit calculations on which their installation was based. Similar problems afflict low-lift pumps and smaller-capacity shallow tubewells. In many places, manually operated hand tubewells for irrigation appear a more appropriate technology ..." ([63] Boyce, 1987: p. 247.)

74 "This strategy can be criticized, however, for its high cost, its dependence upon external finance and consequent political viability, and its implications for equity

2. Redistribution of land rights in order do away with the limitations that are caused by the interests of the rural elite.

3. The creation of institutions for the purpose of collective water control, for carrying out collective activities such as construction measures and for further capital intensive measures, later on, which are adapted to the local conditions. [75]

Summarizing, Boyce's findings can be quoted as follows, [76] "Increased agricultural output ... would not automatically translate into less hunger, for the production and consumption of food are separated by the intervening dynamics of distribution... But to say that agricultural growth is not *sufficient* to eliminate hunger does not mean that it is not *necessary*. On the contrary ...

The historical record indicates that population growth can have *positive* effects on the level of agricultural output – even in the densely populated environment of the Bengal delta – by inducing land-saving technological change. Moreover, there remains substantial scope for major production increases in the region notably via water control development." [77]

2.2.2.3   The Technocratic and Development Planning Perspective

Wennergren, Antholt and Whitaker are representatives of an approach that can be labeled a *"modernistic"* and *"development planning"* approach. [78] After diagnosing the situation, their goal is to make suggestions for overcoming the limitations of the agrarian structure in Bangladesh. [79]

The food and nutrient supply available to the growing population is inadequate. This is evidenced by the fact that (1) children under 15 years of age receive too few calories on the average, (2) every seventh child is underfed, (3) only every fourth child under 11 years of age is of normal weight and normal size and (4) many people suffer from anemia and night blindness due to a lack of vitamin A, etc. Thus, many people suffer from disorders

---

and income distribution." ([63] Boyce, 1987: p. 255.)

75   "Whether such changes can or will be brought about ... is a matter about which one can only speculate. At the moment the prospects do not seem bright." ([63] Boyce, 1987: p. 255.)

76   [63] Boyce, 1987: p. 251 ff.

77   [63] Boyce, 1987: p. 255.

78   Cf., e.g., among others, [104] Faaland, Parkinson, 1976.

79   Wennergren, Antholt, Whitaker ([342] Wennergren, Antholt, Whitaker, 1984.) explicitly claim to argue pragmatically, i.e. not to supply fundamental knowledge on the long-term societal trends, etc. "This book analyzes the agricultural sector in Bangladesh since 1972, identifies the positive factors that are the bases for progress in the sector, and pinpoints the constraints that must be corrected if more equitable growth is to occur." ([342] Wennergren, Antholt, Whitaker, 1984: xiii.)

due to malnutrition that affect their intellectual and bodily abilities. [80]

According to the authors, (1) the majority of the employment opportunities will continue to be in agriculture, (2) even under the most favourable assumptions concerning the growth of the agrarian sector the new employment opportunities will not suffice to supply everyone with work and (3) the nonagricultural job opportunities will not grow and expand to the necessary extent. This will lead to depressed labour-market conditions and minimal wages. [81] The consequences for the purchasing power and nutrition, among others, are obvious.

Agriculture, which has to supply the growing population with food, is faced by an enormous task that can in principle only by solved by (1) an intensive promotion of education, training and organizational abilities; (2) the creation of institutions; and (3) broad social support of this kind of policy. [82] The authors' source of optimism and belief that this will take place is drawn from (1) the fact that they see large unused potentials in Bangladesh and from (2) the historical experience that other nations with likewise limited natural resources have been successful. [83]

Positive characteristics and potentials that give grounds for hope in the future are, according to the authors: [84]

1. The government has announced a strong interest in promoting agriculture and set the corresponding priorities.

2. An impressive basis of natural resources is present that can serve as a foundation for an improvement in the agrarian production capacities: namely, (1) good and uniform soil quality, (2) large quantities of surface and ground water and (3) relatively constant temperatures that make year-round cultivation possible.

3. The farmers react increasingly positively to the new production possibilities that result from the improvements in biological technology.

4. A promising technological basis exists, as well as a research system that serves the agricultural production. The fact that Bangladesh has a

---

80   [342] Wennergren, Antholt, Whitaker, 1984: p. 22.
81   "When one links the low-skill levels of rural Bangladeshis with their large numbers and limited job opportunities, depressed rural markets and wages are inevitable." ([342] Wennergren, Antholt, Whitaker, 1984: p. 33.)
82   "The challenge to agriculture in Bangladesh is only symbolized by the thousands of tons of rice, vegetables, and fruit that must be produced. The real challenge is to create the mix of technical talent, technical innovation, institutions, and enlightened public policies which are supported by a popular will and sustained to at least the turn of the century. It is a formidable challenge, but not impossible." ([342] Wennergren, Antholt, Whitaker, 1984: p. 121.)
83   [342] Wennergren, Antholt, Whitaker, 1984: p. 315.
84   [342] Wennergren, Antholt, Whitaker, 1984: p. 315 ff.

rather large cadre of agricultural scientists and technicians should be regarded in this context.

5. The denationalization of a growing industrial sector that is oriented
towards the agrarian sector and a reduction in the state market intervention
raise the allocation efficiency.

6. Foreign donors support the national development efforts relatively
generously and extensively. Furthermore, the foreign debt is quite small.

On the way to turning the potentials into reality and, hence, developing
the agrarian sector, however, there are a large number of obstacles that have
to be overcome. [85] These are:

- an inadequate research basis and performance;

- an inefficient agricultural extension system;

- insufficient investments in human capital (people);

- little diversification in the production;

- excessive market intervention on the part of the administration;

- inadequate services and poor performance on the part of the marketing
  system;

- an inadequate physical infrastructure;

- a rapidly growing population that has to compete for the resources;

- limited internal resource mobilization and, thus, a growing dependency
  on external support;

- not enough export capacity and, as a result, not enough opportunities
  to earn foreign currency which, therefore, is scarce;

- an inadequate energy supply;

- and inadequate and inefficient administration;

- a limited basis of information and knowledge with respect to political
  decisions;

- discrimination of women; and

- a problematical land tenure system.

---

85   [342] Wennergren, Antholt, Whitaker, 1984: p. 322 ff.

On the basis of this list of problems, which comprises nearly all of the development problems that one could imagine, according to the authors the task is to free agriculture from its "chains" and find a lasting and efficient path to implement technological change. [86]

This insight leads to a reversal of the catalogue of problems into a catalogue of goals, all the way from reducing the population growth to improving the production for export. [87] The theoretical conclusion the authors draw is consequently that: "Characterizations of Bangladesh as a developmental 'basket case' are inaccurate and misleading, but more importantly, they distort the realities of the present and the potentials for the future ... It is true that Bangladesh still faces substantial obstacles ... But, conventional wisdom which characterizes Bangladesh's situation as irremediable, belies the strength and potentials existing within the agricultural sector that provide a basis for cautious optimism about the future." [88] "Investing in people and institutions represents the only realistic long-run solution to the dilemma facing Bangladesh." [89]

2.2.3 Studies on Socio-cultural Complexity

2.2.3.1 The Evolutionary and Behaviour-theoretical Perspective

From the *evolutionary* perspective, the present societal situation in Bangladesh is regarded as the result of and an "intermediary step" in a 3000 year history of development. From this perspective, the period covered by the last centuries – at the most – and usually the last decades is too short a span of time to judge a culture's ability to perform and its dynamics. From the *cultural-evolutionary* viewpoint, as represented by, e.g., Maloney, [90] the problems faced by Bangladesh take on another colour than in the perspectives that have been described until now. The cultural and behaviour-theoretical concepts behind this perspective were not conceived by Maloney as alternatives to the usual economic and political-economic approaches, but rather as a kind of supplement that placed the approaches in the correct perspective. The approach can be sketched on the basis of the following hypotheses.

---

86 It is the task "... to devise and follow, on a sustained basis, a path of technological change in agriculture that is economically efficient. In short, technological changes must free agriculture from constraints imposed by inelastic (relatively scarce) supplies of land and labor." ([342] Wennergren, Antholt, Whitaker, 1984: p. 346.)
87 [342] Wennergren, Antholt, Whitaker, 1984: p. 348.
88 [342] Wennergren, Antholt, Whitaker, 1984: p. 315.
89 [342] Wennergren, Antholt, Whitaker, 1984: p. 360.
90 [245] Maloney, 1988.

1. The ability to adapt itself to an ecological niche and fill out the niche reproductively makes Bangladesh a successful society to which there are no parallels. Its adaption to the existing conditions found in the alluvial delta put the population in a position to *secure a subsistence for very many people* (1) on the basis of rice growing and (2) by means of a sustained and resource conserving economic system while (3) being faced simultaneously by a very great population density. This led to specific adaptive forms of social and economic organization, to particular personality characteristics and to its own biological reproductive conditions. [91]

2. From the *"humanitarian"* perspective, Bangladesh is likewise singularly successful. Crass violations of the *"internationally accepted humanitarian standards"* do indeed take place, but this should not obstruct the eye from taking in the finer aspects of their personal qualities, social relations and "verbal" culture. [92]

3. The Bengali [93] society will in the future for various reasons question some of the basic values of Western societies and thus show that the Western way of looking at things and the Western humanistic expectations for the future and desires regarding progress are *by no means* inevitably valid. [94]

Maloney prognosticated that:

1. Dealing with the population growth will lead to massive violations of the presently accepted human rights. In the same way, the contingent reciprocity between high fertility and a high mortality rate that is accepted both by the society and individually contradicts Western concepts.

2. The stability of the way of life in Bangladesh that is based on growing rice proved to be a remarkable achievement since this combination of a high population density with a sustained adaption to the eco-systemic and mineral resource base may prove in the long run to be more stable than Western industrial civilization. [95]

---

91 "There is probably no other society in the world in which such a heavy population can subsist on the land without destroying the resource base. It is long adaptation to the deltaic land by a rice-growing peasant-urban culture that makes this possible. Adaptive interaction between the geographical base and the culture has produced the Bangladeshi social organization, kinship system, settlement pattern, economic transaction pattern, beliefs, modal personality and even reproductive biology – all these evolved in close symbiosis with the land." ([245] Maloney, 1988: p. 1 f.)

92 "... the more subtle qualities of personality and behavior are as important in judging the overall quality of life. ...the rural people stress the human relational aspect and the expressive and verbal culture." ([245] Maloney, 1988: p. 2 f., p. 69.)

93 Indian East Bengal and Bangladesh.

94 [245] Maloney, 1988: p. 3, p. 84 f.

95 "Because of the enduring potential of this life style, it might be conceded to be more successful in the long run than societies which over-exploit the world's limited mineral and energy resources for industrialization. Bengali peasant life can support

3. The definition of the standard of living based on consumed goods and services could become questionable. In fact, instead, the standard of living could be measured by aspects such as (1) the quality of the "network" of personal relations (social network), (2) personalized (personal) organization forms and (3) the wealth of the verbal culture.

4. The atomistic and dynamic network of personal relations could prove to be a saving feature in the face of comprehensive collective and collectivistic demands made on the individual. [96]

These premises are simultaneously the basis and results of Maloney's concept. From the perspective of long-term cultural evolution and the concomitant social and individual adaption, he puts forward behaviour-theoretical reasons – i.e., among other things, cultural and physical – for specific behaviour and institutions. He does indeed agree with the general political, socio-demographic and economic framework data and extrapolations and also sees thereby – a fact which will be demonstrated in the following – the fatality of further systemic development along the lines of the presently valid parameters; however, he goes beyond the presently foreseeable catastrophe to draw *"transcendent" conclusions.* In a first step, he relativizes the "end of the world perspective": "... who would have believed, when Bangladesh became independent in 1971, that by 1988 it would have 30 million additional people? And that they would be living at more or less the same level of subsistence? The peasant society is extremely absorptive and resilient, not because it is organized for production, but because of the infinite variety of subtle adjustments and personal relations that allows this demographic growth.

But if there is one lesson the long anthropological perspective can give, it is that growth is not forever. There are always cycles of adaptation and overadaptation." [97]

Maloney's perspective oscillates, in other words between (1) illuminating the enormous adaptive achievements of the social system, (2) the certainty that the present dynamics cannot continue unbroken and (3) the elucidation of individual behaviour and behavioural strategies as simultaneously the prerequisites for and consequences of past and future developments. The conclusion he draws from his general description of the dynamics of the

---

the greatest population density on the land, without destroying the resource base." ([245] Maloney, 1988: p. 85.)

96 " ... behavioral tendencies in which the individual remains atomistic but in an ever-dynamic web of personal relations, and not selling himself to any abstraction or ideology, may prove to be a saving feature of the society." ([245] Maloney, 1988: p. 85; cf. p. 52 f.)

97 [245] Maloney, 1988: p. 79 f.

Bengali population, social tensions, involutionary developments and new ecological problems such as, e.g., the global "hothouse effect" and the resulting increase in the level of the oceans with its catastrophic consequences for Bangladesh, which lies just above the present sea level, is: "Our vision is short and we cannot foresee how, but through the suffering of change, the genius of the culture and the innate intelligence of the Bengali people will create a new synthesis." [98]

2.2.3.2   The Microscopic, Structuralist Perspective

The majority of the social, economic, agricultural economic and demographic studies on Bangladesh and the human and scientific problems there are based on one-time studies of single holdings or households and villages or – very seldom – re-studies. As the official, national data material suffers from the well-known limitations in their quality and there are absolutely no census data for many phenomena and the accuracy of the categorical structures does not always suffice for scientific purposes, it proves necessary for many researchers to collect their own data. As this can only take place on the basis of limited means with respect to time, personnel and finances, the predominant level of the studies is the individual, or microsocial, or microeconomic unit of the village. [99] At this level, as a rule, the attempt is made to record empirically as far as possible all of the relevant structure data and variable interactions in order to dare extrapolations into the future and develop macroscopic interpretations on this basis and – occasionally – suggest more or less daring and progressive policies.

It is not possible here to go into the individual, implicit or explicit models and the theoretical progress in connection with the individual studies, or certain types of approaches. On the contrary, empirical material that has been generated in this manner and the conceptual suggestions will be collected and treated as far as possible in the following presentation within the framework of the summarizing approach that will be presented here. Before this can happen, however, in the following I will present my own social theoretical interpretation of (1) the new statistical material that has become available in the meantime in order to (2) to confront the above-sketched macro models with it. This macroscopic interpretation will make the comprehensive individualistic, structuralist and systems dynamic approach understandable that has been developed here and will be used in this study.

---

98   [245] Maloney, 1988: p. 84.
99   Cf., e.g., the bibliographies in: [5] Adnan, 1988; [6] Adnan, 1990; [178] Hye (ed.), 1986; and [304] Saqui, Akhter, 1987.

The development of (1) the population, (2) the production of food, (3) consumption of food, (4) wages, (5) income and (6) the right to utilization of land were used as general indicators of the development dynamics. These indicators will be briefly presented in the following in order to dare, on this basis, to make a *preliminary* evaluation of the situation as presented by the national data. Following that, one of the main hypothesis will be presented upon which the further study is based.

2.3 Indicators of the Dynamics of Development

2.3.1 Population Growth

Two key variables in the social system that have been observed until now – and all of the macro approaches agree on this point – are the available land in Bangladesh, in particular land used for agricultural purposes, and the population living on and off the land. The reciprocal effects ensuing from a fixed area of land and a rapidly growing population – mediated by the potentially and currently available technology that is employed to cultivate the land in order to maintain the subsistence of the people and the dynamics resulting from this – are the major points of interest on which all of the macro concepts concentrate.

Bangladesh's population is growing presently by about 2.5 %, or doubles approximately every 28 years, and at the moment amounts to around 110 million people. In comparison to a longer period of history, at the moment a *population explosion* is taking place. Figure 1 shows the population development in this century. Included in the presentation are three projections showing the growth until the year 2000 on the basis of more or less "favourable" assumptions. The population of Bangladesh will, accordingly, in the year 2000 have grown to approximately 140 million people and have *quintupled* in this century. With this, a never before and nowhere previously found dimension has arisen, a *new quality in the population density and dynamics* beyond all past historical and evolutionary achievements and experience. On the basis of mathematical extrapolations and demographic analogies alone, one can say that this process will not continue this way for a long time. What will follow will definitely be quantitatively and qualitatively new.

In the following presentation, the attempt will be made to show on the basis of a few statistical indicators which consequences for the living conditions of a population growing that rapidly will probably take place. In the case of these *indicators*, they are descriptive, statistical *relations* that, however, do not show any reciprocity, any structural complexities, or any

52

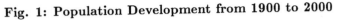

Fig. 1: Population Development from 1900 to 2000

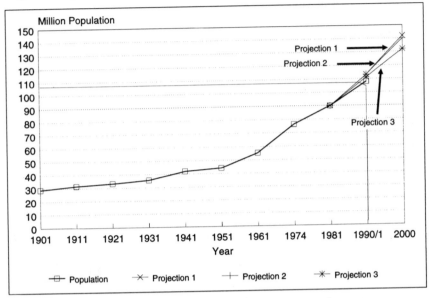

Source: [114] Government, 1984: p. 31, Tab. 1 and p. 144, Tab. 10; [126] Government, 1988: p. 62, Tab. 3.25 and Tab. 3.26; and [130] Government, 1991: p. 4.
Note: For the numerical values, see Table 23 in the appendix.

individual fates. The attempt to do this will be made later on. At the moment, the objective is to substantiate macro dynamics that (1) – and this will be significant later on – describe dynamic framework conditions for the activities and chances in life for individual people and which (2) relativize the models presented in Chapter 2.2.

2.3.2 The Development in the Production of Food

For a population in which the majority of the people live on the edge of the existence minimum, the general production of food is significant. Thereby, it is necessary to examine whether the total yields:

- suffice to feed the population;

- increase, and to what extent; or

- increase sufficiently to keep step with the population growth.

Fig. 2: Developments in the Areas Cropped with Rice, 1960/61 - 1988/89

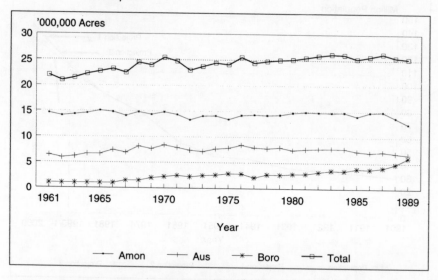

Source: [80] Chen, 1975: p. 205, Tab. 3; [124] Government, 1988: p. 180; and [128] Government, 1990: p. 169, Tab. 4.46.
Note: For the numerical values, see Table 24 in the appendix.

The arable land in Bangladesh, with the exception of a few hilly marginal regions, is intensively used and could only be insignificantly increased to the *detriment* of the non-Bengali ethic peoples in the marginal areas. Since rice is the staple food, the production of rice can be regarded as an indicator of the population's supply – with the limitation that these are only average values that give no information as to the distribution of the rice.

Figure 2 shows that for the years 1961 - 1989, there was a general production increase in rice (total) that, however, did not take place on the basis of of an increase in the cropped area, but was due rather to an increase in the cropping of winter rice (Borro). In the main rice cropping season during the monsoon period (Amon), the entire available area that is not flooded is cultivated. The size of the cropped area does not increase. The same is true in the case of the pre-monsoon summer season (Aus) in which the cropped area does indeed shrink slightly due to the overlapping of the season with the winter season in which irrigated rice is cropped (Boro); however, the size of the cropped area remains basically constant. The increase in the cropped area per year is due to irrigation of what would otherwise be fallow land.

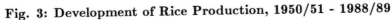

Fig. 3: Development of Rice Production, 1950/51 - 1988/89

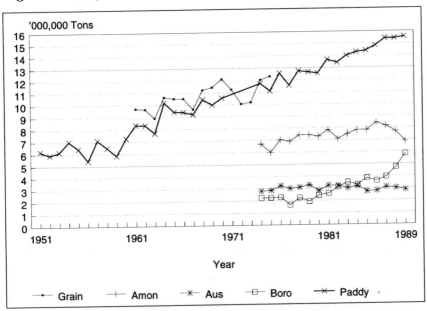

Source: [80] Chen, 1975: p. 204, Tab. 1; [124] Government, 1988: p. 180; and [128]
  Government, 1990: p. 169, Tab. 4.46.
Note: For the numerical values, see Table 25 in the appendix.

Figure 3 shows that the cereal yields – mainly rice (wheat is also gaining importance) – have increased since 1951 by just under 150 %. This growth is due to higher per acre yields of monsoon rice (Amon) and an extension of the irrigated winter rice area (Boro).

If one takes a look now at Figure 4 then it becomes obvious that during the period between 1961 and 1973, the cereal yields (including wheat) kept essentially up with the population growth. The per capita yields for rice at the beginning of the 70's sank because of the struggle for independence: in the meantime, however, they have become stable once again. The rice yields have increased since then and have, basically, been able to keep up with the population growth. [100]

---

100 The fluctuations and, perhaps, slightly sinking per capita yields that are particularly obvious in Table 26 in the appendix do not seem to be significant. The available figures and the harvest *estimates* upon which they are based are so imprecise that they can be ignored here. Naturally such fluctuations can have local and class specific catastrophic and fatal effects. This will be discussed later on. At the moment, the

Fig. 4: Developments in the Rice Yields Per Capita per Annum, 1961-1989

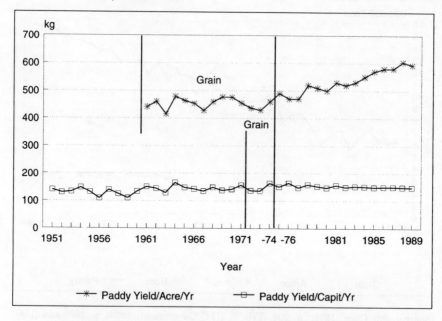

Source: [80] Chen, 1975: p. 204 Tab. 1 and p. 205, Tab. 3; [124] Government, 1988:
p. 180; [128] Government, 1990: p. 169, Tab. 4.46; and [190] Jahangir, 1979:
p. 169, Tab. 28.
Note: For the numerical values, see Table 26 in the appendix.
In the case of the data on the rice yields per area from 1961 - 1973 and 1971-1973,
the data refers to cereals, i.e. a minimal percentage of wheat has been included.

In the case of other foodstuffs though, such as, e.g. the protein rich
pulses, meat and milk, there have been decreases in the average per capita
availability. Merely the values for meat made an unexplainable jump of
nearly 100 % around 1980. [101] Pulses – which are the most important suppliers of protein – and milk, however, recorded slumps. In the case of pulses,
this could possibly be explained by the increasing cultivation of those areas that were otherwise used for growing pulses with irrigated rice during

objective is to concentrate on *highly aggregated* and (as precisely as possible) *estimated
basic trends.*

101 This is certainly caused by a change in the registration and calculation procedures.
Cf. in addition [124] Government, 1988: p. 620 ff., Tabs. 14.2, 14.6, 14.8, 14.11 and
14.12.

Fig. 5: Availability of Food Per Capita, 1960/61 - 1988/89

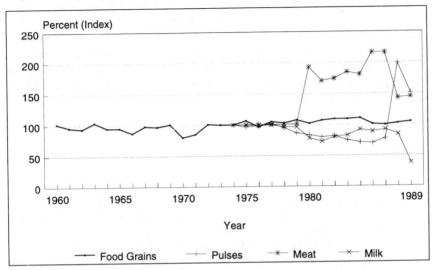

Source: [124] Government, 1988: p. 617, Tab. 14.1; [128] Government, 1990: p. 611,
Tab. 14.01; and [80] Chen, 1975: p. 208 Tab. 4.
Note: For the numerical values, see Table 27 in the appendix.

the dry season. Regarding milk, the explanation could lie in a smaller feed basis and increasing over-usage of the milk cows as draught animals. [102] In this respect, it is not possible to supply a reliable causal explanation. The decreases in the protein suppliers could, hence, (1) be traced back to the growing population pressure that forces an increased production of calorie suppliers, or (2) it could indicate comparative cost, yield and import advantages.

The overall and average availability of food cereals has, calculated on the basis of per capita of the growing population, thus remained relatively stable. In the case of the availability of protein suppliers this does not appear to be true. More reliable data would be necessary before far-reaching conclusions could be drawn because the production figures used in the national statistics refer to products that have a large self-sufficiency component and, therefore, do not always appear on the market. An indicator that could bring clarity here, however, could be the development of the real food consumption.

---

102 This is based on hypotheses that were formulated on the basis of village studies that have not been empirically substantiated until now. Cf. [144] Helmrich, 1986. Also see Chapter 4.2.2.1, page 256.

2.3.3 Development in Food Consumption

The development in the overall average food consumption is not clearly recognizable (Figure 6). [103] It seems to have become stable once again after a slump in the second half of the 70's. It increased in 1985/86 in comparison to 1973/74 by as much as approximately 20 %. The increase in consumption, however, is essentially based on the consumption of rice. The consumption of pulses, milk, meat and fish has not increased much. The nutritional level attained in the 60's does not seem to have been quite reached again.

---

103 From Figure 6 as well as Table 30. in the Appendix, which presents the controversial data from Hassan and Ahmed and the official statistics, and Table 28 in the Appendix, which is based on a Table in [342] Wennergren, Antholt, Whitaker, 1984: p. 21 and [18]Ahmed, 1988: p. 46, that tends to contradict the official data in Figure 6, it can be seen that the per capita consumption of cereals did not decrease by very much during the period from 1962 until 1975/76, but that it did decrease after that until 1982. This is a fact that cannot be explained by a general shortage. In the case of animal products, in contrast, during the course of the 60's there was a slump, while the supply seems to have remained stable during the 70's. This development is also contrary to the trend in the supply. The percentage of plant foodstuffs (with the exception of cereals) decreased slightly: data broken down according to components is not available.

The consumption of the nutritional elements protein, fats and carbohydrates, on the one hand, and the number of calories, on the other, create other indicators that are presented in Table 29. The per capita supply of protein seems, accordingly, to have remained approximately the same during the last ca. 25 years. This fact shows, in comparison to Table 28 that the published figures are not consistent because if this figure were correct then the decrease in the consumption of animal products and, thus, animal proteins would have been compensated for by an increase in the consumption of pulses in order to keep the percentage of proteins constant. That can, however, not be the case according to Table 28.

The same difficulty in interpreting the available material is true in the case of the other indicators. The methodological problem cannot be discussed here, and a methodological criticism of the statistics was not carried out. It should be kept in mind, however, that the figures are, at best, rough, unreliable, and inconsistent, but that they are simultaneously absolutely necessary indicators that allow many trends to be recognized. Before, however, they can be used to draw largely practical conclusions, either further empirical studies would be necessary, whereby the precise historical data *basis* is missing in order to evaluate the development trends, or it would be necessary to reprocess the unpublished source-data material. This comment on the quality and dependability of such difficult national key data and statistics is naturally true in the case of the other figures presented in this study and in those of other authors. In order to save space and time, this information will not be repeated in connection with other contexts.

Fig. 6: Food Consumption Per Capita/Per Day, 1973/74 - 1988/89

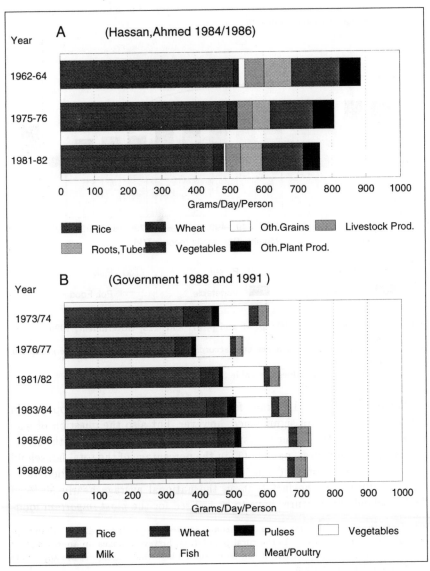

Source: [123] Government, 1988: p. 20; [129] Government, 1991: p. 21, Tab. 4.8; and
[139] Hassan, Ahmad, 1984: p. 164 ff., Tabs. 2, 3, 5, 6.
Note: For the numerical values, see Table 30 in the appendix.
Cf. footnote 104, p. 60.

Fig. 7: Expenditures for Food by Per Capita Household Income, 1988/89

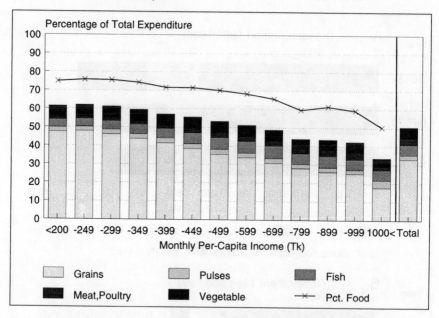

Source: [123] Government, 1988: p. 51 and p. 57; and [128] Government, 1990: p. 65,
Tab. 1.14.

Note: Monthly expenditures (in percent) according to per capita expenditure group (in Tk) in 1985/6.

For the numerical, values see Table 31 in the appendix.

Not only the general average food consumption and its development in the course of time is of significance, however, but also the question of who has access to and the power to dispose of food. This is reflected in the structure of the expenditures, namely (1) in the percentage of the total household expenditures spent on food and (2) in the allocation of certain foodstuffs. Figure 7 illustrates the fact that on the national average nearly 50 % of the household expenditures have to be utilized for the *most important* food-

---

104 Unfortunately, only time series data separated according to the rural and urban populations were available. As the rural population, however, makes up approximately 90 % of the total population, it can be presumed here that the figures are applicable to the entire population.

[139] Hassan, Ahmad, 1984; and [140] Hassan, Ahmad, 1986, presented less satisfying findings on the basis of smaller surveys.

stuffs. [105] Rice alone makes up more than 30 % of the monthly household expenditures. In the case of the groups in the poorest categories, according to per capita spending capacity, the expenditures for the basic foodstuffs amount to nearly 60 % of the household budget, and nearly 50 % of the household budget is spent for the calorie source rice. The expenditures for the protein sources fish, meat and pulses are correspondingly small. [106]

Thus, the possibilities many households have to eat anything else than rice are limited and, frequently, insufficient. It is, however, important that the food supply and food consumption seem to have become stabilized and even slightly improved.

Tab. 1: Development of the Number and the Percentage of Poor According to the Criterion of the Supply of Calories, 1973/74 - 1988/89

| Year | Poverty Line at 2122 Cal/Day./Pers. [a] | | | | Poverty Line at 1805 Cal/Day./Pers. [b] | | | |
| | Rural | | Urban | | Rural | | Urban | |
	Mio.	(%)	Mio.	(%)	Mio.	(%)	Mio.	(%)
1973/74	57.4	82.9	5.6	81.4	30.7	44.3	2.0	28.6
1981/82	60.9	73.8	6.4	66.0	43.1	52.2	3.0	30.7
1983/84	47.0	57.0	7.1	66.0	31.3	38.0	3.8	35.0
1985/86	44.2	51.0	7.0	56.0	19.1	22.0	2.4	19.0
1988/89	40.5	48.0	10.8	44.0	24.9	29.5	5.0	20.5

Source: [123] Government, 1988: p. 33, Tab. 2; and [129] Government, 1991: p. 33, Tab. 6.2.
Note: Percentages (%) refer to the specific total population.

a   Recommended Intake.
b   Abject Poverty – "hard core poverty."

Table 1 clearly shows that the thresholds to poverty and abject poverty have shifted in favour of many poor if seen on the basis of the supply of calories. *The number and percentage of those who cannot meet their recommended and minimum calorie requirements has decreased greatly. At the time, it would not be possible to speak of increasing impoverishment.*

In the following, the development of the purchasing power will be discussed. This can be regarded as an indicator of the potential food consumption and standard of living. The wages after adjustment for inflation and the per capita income will be used as indicators of the purchasing power.

105 Cf. [123] Government, 1988: p. 50, Tab. 1.12.
106 The general income development will be discussed once again on p. 63.

2.3.4 Wage Developments

The level of the wages and their development over the course of time is a further indicator for the chances that the working class has in life, i.e. wage-earners in the lower socio-economic strata. A sinking or rising wage rate can indicate how the purchasing power of those develops who cannot feed themselves off their own land, or who are not active as self-employed entrepreneurs. The wage ratio, however, can also be used as a rough indicator for those who earn their income as small traders and thus, with only a few exceptions, earn an income that is comparable with at least that of a worker's wages. The developments in the wage rate are presented in Figure 8.

Fig. 8: Wage Development, 1963/64 - 1988/89

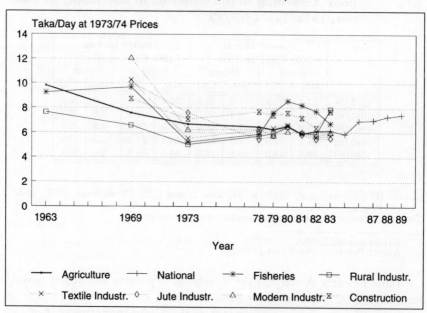

Source: [126] Government, 1988: p. 249, Tab. 11.08; [128] Government, 1990: p. 495, Tab. 10.35; and [355] World Bank, 1985: Annex I, Tab. 5 and Tab. 6.
Note: For the numerical values, see Table 32 in the appendix.

The general wage rate sank in the years before 1973/74, i.e. essentially before and during the struggle for independence, by approximately 30 %, a trend that caused many authors to speak of a general drop in the wage rate. This trend, however, did not continue: instead, the wages evidently *remained and became stable at a minimal level* after it had once been reached. There are no figures broken down according to sector for the years after 1983/84, but rather only the overall national figures. The situation has evidently become stabilized all in all here, if not having even improved. This seems to be the case despite the fact that the additional manpower that is continually pushing its way onto the labour market have essentially only the possiblility of taking up wage labour, [107] and should, thus, depress the wage rates.

The economic system as a whole has obviously developed enough job opportunities to stabilize the wages in the face of a growing demand. In the following, the attempt will be made to clarify whether this can eventually be traced back to the fact that the wages have already reached a level at which only the minimum physical reproduction is possible, i.e. a level under which even starving people would no longer accept the work because the wage would no longer cover the reproduction costs.

2.3.5 Income Development

Figure 9 shows the development of the average per capita income of the population in Bangladesh from the year 1973/74 until the year 1988/89. These figures have been adjusted to make up for inflation. [108]

It can be seen that (1) the average per capita income *increased* over the fifteen year period from 1973/74 to 1988/89 by almost 80 %; (2) the average national income, in which the urban working class's income is included, had not distanced itself significantly from the average urban income; and thus (3) there was no growing disparity between urban and rural income. The general trend in the development of the per capita income proves that it has been possible – *despite the population growth* – *to maintain the income level*, i.e. to stabilize the positive trend.

Mean values, naturally, do not say everything. On the contrary, the income distribution and, hence, buying power play a special role. An important aspect, thereby, is the development of the distribution. As can be seen in Figure 10, the income is distributed very unequally among Bangladesh's population.

The poorer 50 % of the population in 1973/74 had only a little more than approximately 26 % of the total income at its disposal. That corresponds approximately to the amount that the upper 10 % has for itself alone. With 24.5 % of the total income for the lower 50 % of the population, in 1988/89 this percentage, at an overall higher level, had hardly worsened. The rich

---

107 This will be discussed later in connection with the question of increasing landlessness and the impossibility of employing one's self on one's own land. See Chapter 4.3.1, p. 268.

108 Cf. [355] World Bank, 1985: Annex I, Tab. 9.

Fig. 9: Development of the Per Capita Income, 1973/74 - 1988/89

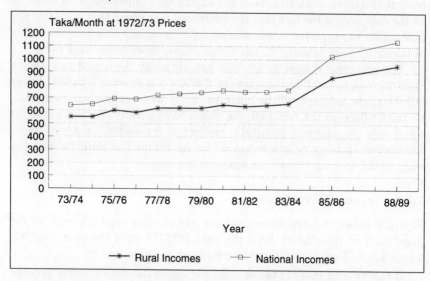

Source: [129] Government, 1991: p. 18, Tab. 4.5; and [355] World Bank, 1985: Annex I, Tab. 9.
Note: The data for 1973/74 up to 1983/84 were calculated on the basis of the gross domestic product according to the 1972/73 prices and the national population figures. The data of 1988/89 were taken from [129] Government, 1991. For the numerical values, see Table 33 in the appendix.

have, however, managed to improve their position to the detriment of the well-to-do. [109]

Apart from the (1) *tremendous inequality*, however, the fact is remarkable that the (2) *distribution structure*, although it has *not improved*, has *also not worsened*. It can indeed be seen that the percentages of the individual groups during the final phase of Pakistani rule around 1968/69 shifted slightly in favour of the poorer groups and at the beginning of Bangladesh's independence once again slightly in favour of those better-off; however, they essentially *remained the same* over the total period of 20 years. Thus, structurally there was no shift in favour of the poorer and poor; however, the fact that there was also *no polarization* and *there was no worsening of the impoverishment* is remarkable.

A look at a few national data and taking them as indicators for the long-

109 The eighth and ninth-tenth, the 70 % - 90 % group.

Fig. 10: Developments in the Income Distribution, 1963/64 - 1988/89

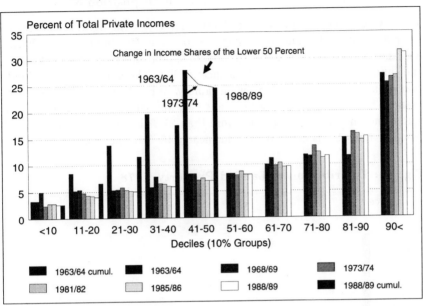

Source: [123] Government, 1988: p. 33, Tab. 1; [129] Government, 1991: p. 32, Tab. 6.1; and [288] Rahman, 1988: p. 1010.
Note: Percentage of the total income in percent per 10 percent of the population. For the numerical values, see Table 34 in the appendix.

term development of the overall societal conditions makes it seem reasonable to come to the conclusion that despite the drastic population growth, despite the catastrophic consequences arising from the war of independence in 1971, and despite the recurring natural catastrophes, [110] a drastic worsening of the situation did *not* take place. The general income development and distribution instead allows one to recognize a positive overall trend and make an optimistic evaluation. This is especially true in the case of the *current situation* of the poor. Their *long-term chances* are questionable, but

---

110 The country is hit nearly every year – in some years not at all, but in other years several times – by cyclones that cost many lives and cause enormous damage, particularly in the southern coastal and delta regions. The cyclones 1970 and 1985 cost 30,000 and 110,000 lives, respectively. It is nearly impossible to capture in figures the corresponding damage to property which repeatedly reoccurs in the interims. Cf. [124] Government, 1988: p. 18 ff.

that was true in the past as well.

2.3.6 The Distribution of the Power of Disposition of Land

The key resource, i.e. the key production factor, in the agrarian society of Bangladesh is land – land for a house, or to use for farming purposes. Farming land and, in particular, the *ownership* of land contribute to one's status and influence and improve one's chances in life. The number of households that do not own any land is growing rapidly. While in 1978 just a little less than 15 % of all of the houses did not own any land, the number of those who owned no land increased to more than 27 % by 1983/84. Agricultural labourer households account even for nearly 40 % of the households. [111]

Fig. 11: Distribution of Landed Property, 1978

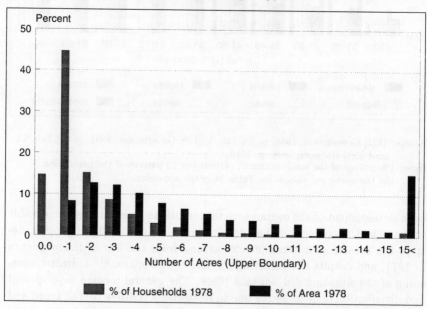

Source: [196] Jannuzi, Peach, 1980: p. 19
Note: For the numerical values, see Table 35 in the appendix.

Figure 11 clearly shows that in 1978 nearly 60 % of the (poorer) house-

---

111 Cf. [196] Jannuzi, Peach, 1980: p. 19; [126] Government, 1988: p. 99, Tab. 5.9 and p. 85, Tab. 5.2.
Unfortunately no *data on property* was available to me for various years.

Fig. 12:   The Development in the Number of Holdings per Holding-size Category, 1960 - 1988/89

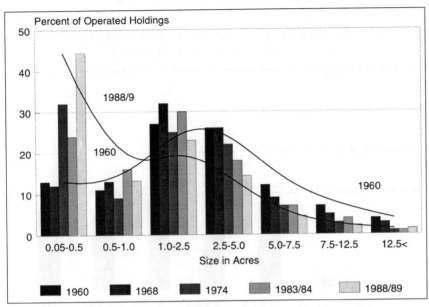

Source: [125] Government, 1988: p. 139; [129] Government, 1991: p. 141, Tab. 3.02; and
[7] Ahmad, 1984: p. 30 (from Alamgir, 1975).
Note: For the numerical values, see Table 36 in the appendix.
Cf. also [289] Rahman, Ali, 1984.

holds which owned less than one acre [112] of land owned, all in all, only about
8 % of the land, whereas approximately 4 % of the households with more
than 9 acres each owned a total of 30 % of the land.

In addition to the ownership of land, however, the possibility of *farming*
one's own or leased land is of importance since in order to earn one's living
it may also be favourable to cultivate land that is not one's own. Such
opportunities, however, are not equally distributed. Figure 12 shows (1)
the relative number of *holdings* in the corresponding holding size category
and (2) how the number of holdings changed from 1960 to 1988/89. In the

---

112 In the following, I will speak of acres and not hectares. In the figures, I use *decimal*
for the unit of land as a rule. One hundred decimal (dec.) corresponds to one acre.
As the unit acre is frequently too rough a measuring unit and the indigenous unit is
bigha (= 33 dec., = one-third acre and locally, sometimes. specifically 57 dec., etc.),
this seems appropriate.

following figure, Figure 13, the corresponding percentage of the total area is presented that was cultivated in the individual holding categories during the same period of time. [113]

Fig. 13:   Development of the Percentage of Cultivated Area per Holding-size Category, 1960 - 1988/89

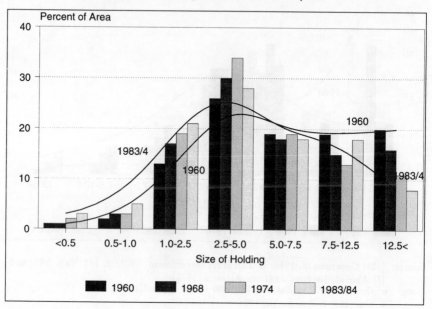

Source: [125] Government, 1988: p. 139; [129] Government, 1991: p. 141, Tab. 3.02; and
    [7] Ahmad, 1984: p. 30 (from Alamgir, 1975).
Note: For the numerical values, see Table 36 in the appendix.

Figures 12 and 13 clearly show that:

1. The size distribution is also in this case unequal since 40 % of the holdings with less than 1 acre of land cultivated in 1983/84 a total of only 12 %, whereas 5 % of the holdings with land amounting to more than 7.5 acres cultivate 24 % of the total farmland.

2. The small holdings (up to 2.5 acres) are increasing in number and the area they cultivate. In the case of the larger holdings, the process is the exact opposite. The transition to more small holdings, the stabilization

---

113 Unfortunately there are only a few ([289] Rahman, Ali, 1984) absolute figures for the years referred to because only on this basis can one judge absolute changes. This would be the only way to recognize the changes in the significance of large land ownership.

of the larger middle-sized holdings (5 to 12.5 acres) and the decrease in the very large holdings signalize a complex structural change in the case of *holdings* that cannot be covered by the term *polarization.* On the contrary, it seems necessary to speak of an *increase in small holdings*, a *stabilization of larger middle-sized holdings* and a *decline of the largest holdings.*

3. The degree of concentration – [114] which does not reflect the structural shifts and quantitative, absolute increases – exibits for the time before independence from Pakistan a slight trend towards more equal distribution, whereas afterwards, especially in the case of the smallest and small holdings, there was an increase in inequality. This trend has reversed in recent years in the case of small holdings. *There is a continually increasing number of small and smallest holdings that tend to unite an increasingly large share of the land among their numbers.*

4. As a result of the increasing number and importance of the small holdings, the structure is presently changing with respect to a *leveling off at the threshold to poverty.* Thus, despite the continued inequality, it is not possible to speak of *polarization.*

5. Presently there is a massive increase in the number of households that can *no longer earn their own living off their own land.*

6. The number of large holdings is decreasing and the amount of land they cultivate as well. That means that the rich, large holdings *do not accumulate land.*

7. If one only regards the distribution and volume of landed property, then presently there is a trend towards increasingly *spread and shared poverty.*

2.4 An Evaluation of the Dynamics of Development

The preceeding brief and indicative examination of the economic dynamics under the conditions of a rapidly growing population clearly shows the following aspects.

1. During recent years, a stabilization of the economic conditions and difficult living conditions has taken place. The overall *average situation* became stabilized during the course of the 70's, following a rapid deterioration towards the end of Pakistani rule that was at times accelerated by the process of independence.

2. Poverty and wretchedness are still pressing, but still, the availability of food, its consumption and the income situation have *improved slightly,* and the number of those who suffer from undernourishment seems to have decreased.

---

114 Also see the discussion in Chapter 4.1.3 on page 231.

3. This happened *although* two powerful trends – that have been strongly stressed in the relevant literature – consisting of enormous population growth and increasing landlessness and marginalization of farms worked in the opposite direction.

4. This also took place in spite of social, political and cultural "inefficiency" and "inequality"and lacking institutional efficiency and political will.

Within the scope of this study, it will not be possible to present, let alone discuss, the details of the multifaceted critical and constructive analyses on these aspects of the societal dynamics. The sketch of the economic dynamics rather aims at demonstrating that:

- on the basis of *past* experience, reversals in trends that might take place as a result of complex factor interdependency cannot be grasped and prognosticated correctly;

- Marxist-Leninist development prognoses *do not mirror reality*;

- prognoses, hence, have more of a *legitimating character* in order to propagate political measures which may serve general or particularistic interests and – possibly – also enforce them;

- societal development dynamics are non-linear and, therefore, it is not possible to make more than hesitant trend prognoses.

These statements do *not* mean that (1) the increasing fragmentaion of the holdings, (2) the growing number of people, (3) the limitation and shortage as well as unequal distribution of the resources, (4) the interests and class conflicts and (5) the globally increasing warming of the atmosphere will not sometime and somewhere end catastrophically. Whether and how, that is the question. *It must remain unanswered here.*

As the result of the above presentation and analysis, we find depressing and simultaneously fascinating dynamics in the economic and societal conditions in Bangladesh. The structures are not improving essentially, as far as recognizable. Despite this fact, they have prevented the individual living standard from rapidly falling in the face of the increasing population and, instead, stabilized it.

The following chapter, Chapter 3, will *not* deal with the question as to which factor constellations, historical laws, or political strategies may be behind this phenomenon of *"systems stabilization in the face of rapid population growth."* An attempt will instead be made to clarify *which microstructures in the agrarian society,* i.e. in the rural regions, *and their own dynamics led to the temporary stabilization of the conditions.*

70

Hypothesis:

Hence, the hypothesis that is presented here is that these agrarian societal structures that are generated, pushed, changed and accepted by the people working individually or collectively, hand in hand, or against each other, lead via intended and unintended actions in their sum and interdependence to a dynamic system. This system creates the framework for further activities. This leads to a concept of a multistable, self-propelling, systemically and autopoietically generated network of acting people who create their future through their activities in the present.

With reference to the agrarian society in Bangladesh, this means that in the following (1) the way individually *acting individuals* that live in the rural regions and directly or indirectly off the land *manipulate and use the natural and agrarian-structural factors in their struggle for securing their own livelihood and opportunities* – and those of the people close to them – will be elaborated, as well as (2) *which consequences this has* for them and the system they must live in. Stated briefly, the question is which individual behavioural strategies are used by the people in Bangladesh?

"The strategy any one individual adopts is in terms of an ideal. And the ideal exists in a particular form, which reflects the ideological and economic system ... Everybody aspires to a similar ideal but must act in terms of his or her own starting point, options, and circumstances. It is the difference in these not the difference in ideal which determines people's strategies."

Bangladesh Rural Advancement Committee [115]

"Whatever one's doubt about the numbers, they do roughly indicate reality."

Michael Lipton [116]

3 Individual Action Strategies

The social conditions were, and are, created by multifarious and multiple individual strategical actions and form the conditions at the same time for these actions. In the following chapter, individual actions will be presented on the basis of (1) individual perspectives: (a) goals, (b) rights, (c) access to resources, (d) results and (e) autopoietic aspects. In the next step, a few interdependent action strategy complexes will be depicted: (2) relationships, (3) production, (4) exchange, (5) acquisition and (6) crisis management. This will present a picture of the perspectives and strategies for individual actions, as well as their contingencies, within the context of Bangladesh.

3.1 The Approach: The Individual Perspective

The holistic, macro-theoretical and development-law perspective for Bangladesh, as it has been elaborated in the preceeding chapter, is *not* the perspective of the individual. His perception, the spectrum of possible actions he may choose and the goals he follows under the existing conditions in his attempts to determine and pursue his own life are not – from his point of view – primarily tied to and correlated with the overall societal developments. These – conceivably negative – developments do indeed influence him "objectively," but can as far as he is concerned, if he recognizes them

---

115 [68] BRAC, 1983: p. 177.
116 [239] Lipton, 1988: p. 4.

at all, not be influenced, nor are they relevant for his individual, existential actions.

The objective in the following is to show how

- the individual's perception, in particular his perspective for specific actions, and

- the possible strategies for actions within the existing societal and natural framework

present themselves to him.

The individual is, as has already been theoretically discussed, a part of and participant in a system that ensures his reproduction and livelihood and that binds him, limits him and determines his life in multifarious ways. At the same time, however, he is – in his limited scale – the manipulator and founder of the thus generated system. The individual initial conditions, chances and success vary greatly. They are, in part, "caused" by the system and changed, i.e. either consolidated or partly dissolved. The structure and the dynamics of these framework conditions that limit the individual's opportunities to carry out possible actions are the focal point of the next chapter.

In this chapter I will describe the individual and institutional opportunities allowing actions *available to the individual people in Bangladesh. In other words, I will elaborate the possibilities the individual in Bangladesh has* in principle *to pursue his goals; that is, which structurally determined options he has at all.* Whether he actually does that, or can do that, which he desires depends on specific, individual and empirical environments and personalities; in other words, the "objective world around him." [117]

The following discourse can be understood firstly as a system of equations, as an algorithm that formulates the fundamental *opportunities* that exist for the individual in Bangladesh. For this purpose I will use empirical, statistical and quantitative material. The initial conditions and situation the individual is confronted by will be conceived as being given. This presumption will then in the following chapter, Chapter 6, be revoked and the variability and dynamics of development in the initial conditions will be elaborated. [118] The extent to which the differences in the control of resources, opportunities in life and perceptions of individuals allow only specific limited

---

117 [233] Lewin, 1963.
118 The complexity of the system of actions that is described here demands a step by step presentation of the correlations and conditions. This may awaken the impression on the part of the reader that certain interdependencies have not been taken into consideration. I cannot guarantee that this impression will not prove to be correct in the end. I would like to ask the reader, however, to follow the formally structured

actions will be more extensively elaborated there. The question as to which concrete, specific values are filled into the "variables" of the individuals' "algorithms" is an empirical question.

3.1.1 Goals: Normative and Individual Concepts

The people in Bangladesh pursue benefits and utilities. As to what they consider to be their specific benefits can until now only be indirectly inferred on the basis of actions and their consequences, i.e. expectations they have stated. [119]

The Islamic-Bengali culture's normative system implies that, within certain limits, the individual is free to make his own decisions and is responsible for his actions. In the last instance, however, they are subject to God's will and must answer to him for what they do. Each person is, thus, an active, acting part of Allah's divine will and divine plan, and at the same time subject to them.

The Islamic laws (*"śāriā"*) [120] *regulate the individual's relationship to Allah and his fellow members of creation and the actions of conscious and rational human beings.* There are imperative, forbidden and permissible actions that are judged on the basis of their societal functions and considered either to be absolutely necessary, or as need fulfilling, or facilitating to life. The basic values are to respect the faith (the religion), life, property, family (household), lineage (the honour and names of the ancestors and their descendants) and rationality. The rules are established in detail in the Koran and Hadith and present clear, normative instructions governing most of the actions carried out in daily life. [121]

---

and drawn out chain of interwoven reasoning and pursue my thoughts before deciding in the end. The presentation of systemic interdependencies can only be sequential. The multifarious circular chains of thought should, however, at the conclusion be resolved.

119 Until now I have discovered no studies that attempt to specify on the basis of empirical, psychological studies what the individual needs and goals of the people of Bangladesh consist of. *I* in no way doubt that – after spending approximately 3 years in Bangladesh – they are "rational" and that their "logic" is comparable to European logic and can be grasped on the basis of European logic, and this is implied in the following elaborations. The chain of reasoning, emotions and actions seem to be intersubjectively comprehensible. Those members of the various disciplines in Bangladesh who study the diverse fields involving mankind and his society and culture have until now not seemed to find this worthwhile studying.

120 Cf. [228] Kreiser, Diem, Majer, 1974: p. 56 ff.

121 For the philosophy and rules of Islam see, e.g., [158] Hitti, 1970; and [262] Nomani, 1977. For the rules governing economic activities, see [299] Rodison, 1971; and [340] Weber, 1972: p. 375 f.

For Muslim Bengali that signifies more concretely stated: [122] each person obeys the *"śāriā."* That means that it is of great value to him to be a member of a family and household and own land one day – in other words, to become a landowner (*mālik*). This can, however, only take place on the basis of the true belief (*islām*), by means of good, benevolent and righteous deeds (*halāl*), while avoiding harmful and unrighteous acts (*harām*). Furthermore, the true believer should gain merits by being helpful (showing solidarity), using his influence for others (patronage) and supporting others in their belief (conforming to the norms, among other things). Sinful acts should be avoided.

Muslims believe that Allah has absolute control over four essential aspects of an individual's life: birth, death, subsistence and wealth. At birth, one's starting position in earthly life is established by being born in a more or less well-to-do or poor family. Allah, however, intervenes each year and adjusts a person's life according to which *efforts* and how much effort the individual has shown on his part. Hence in the course of time, one can improve one's fate by means of one's own efforts. The final balance is drawn up and the final judgement is made on Judgement Day when the decision falls as to whether one will be allowed to enter heaven (paradise) or be sent to hell. The final and highest earthly goal, however, is achieved by proper conduct in the pursuit of (1) land and property, (2) in the pursuit of the head of the household (*kartā*) to maintain the proper dignity and (3) in his pursuit of the well-being of those who are entrusted to him. Therefore a prerequisite is to be a landowner and the head of a household. Other possessions are useful, but they never reach the value of owning one's own land. One either gains possession of land as the son of a landowner (*mālik*), or by purchasing it, or by means of marriage or inheritance from a distant relative. "A person becomes a *mālik* through time, and he also remains a *mālik* by properly meeting the vicissitudes of time, all of which are determined as part of his destiny by Allah." [123]

A *mālik* has the following rights and duties. [124]

1. He is the absolute lord of his land. He alone has the right to make decisions regarding the utilization of and purpose for which the land is used. He must, however, utilize it optimally in order to be considered a successful *mālik* and, thus, become a respected man.

2. He must gain knowledge, abilities and skills in his role as the cultivator

---

122 [327] Thorp, 1978: p. 21.
123 [327] Thorp, 1978: 23 f.
124 [327] Thorp, 1978: pp. 23 ff.; and [246] Maloney, Aziz, Sarkar, 1980: p. 9 ff. For a criticism of the patriarchal-society orientation of these two studies see [57] Blanchet, 1984: p. 15 ff.

of his own land and make use of them. Furthermore, he must know the qualities of his land (soil quality, availability of water, etc.), be able to judge and take the weather conditions into consideration and cultivate the land correctly and enduringly.

3. He must farm his land by (1) deciding on the employment of and employment conditions for household members and hired hands; (2) seeing to it that the proper cultivation measures are carried out; (3) organizing the harvest on time and making certain that as little losses as possible take place during the harvest and storage; (4) making certain that the yields are marketed properly; and (5) deciding when and how to cooperate with others by arranging tenancy agreements, borrowing money, lending money, etc.

4. He must prove his abilities on the basis of successful and enduring decisions and activities with respect to cultivating the soil and use them to his advantage by consuming some of the energy from his soil in the form of food and, simultaneously, gaining the physical and mental strength to carry out just that task.

5. He must provide for the members of his family and, if need be, other members of the extended household and, as the head of the household (*mālik, kartā*), for the welfare of those people entrusted to him. "His decision making and disposition of tasks with the family *ultimately aim at making his family a happy family.*" [125]

6. He has to account for the position of his wife and his children. This position is characterized by the fact that (1) *all* humans are equal, (2) that the head of the family represents the family outside the family and (3) women are equal to men within the house. The woman is part of the man as she (Eve) was created out of his (Adam's) rib. At the same time she is his counterpart in the task of reproduction and his companion throughout life.

7. He must, as an equally entitled member of the community *(shamāj, jāmāt)*, observe both his religious as well as his social rights, obligations and duties.

8. Only by deciding and acting jointly with the others in accordance with, and while taking all of the individual demands, needs and performances into consideration, is it possible for the head of the household to be successful and fulfil the will of God.

---

125 [327] Thorp, 1978: p. 3. The italics are mine.

This framework of religious concepts [126] describes the emic, [127] normative system that demands specific actions and which, it is presumed here, also leads to actions, i.e. *justifies* them. Under the conditions found in Bangladesh with its unequal distribution of opportunities and resources, the pursuit of the goal of gaining enough land of one's own and cultivating it is, for at least a large section of the landless – which make up more than one-third of all of the households – illusory at best. For those households, therefore, a "second best" system of goals has to be presumed as a result: an independent, honourable and productive life on the basis of a regular and secure social and economic livelihood as a good Muslim. Similar modifications must also be presumed in the case of women as the ownership of land and farming are values that belong to the men's realm. In this case, the goal of being a good woman consists of respecting and loving her husband and playing a subordinate role, in providing for the house and children on her own responsibility and, in particular, in bearing him at least one son. As the man's success is also advantageous for the woman's welfare and status, it is important for her to support him. This relation is reflected in the official term with which a husband is addressed *"śāmi"* – master ([The] Lord). The real relation is, however, somewhat more prosaic and the woman's position is without a doubt complementary to that of the man. [128]

3.1.2 Rights: Decisions and Responsibilities

Depending upon the individual's starting chances in life, the attempts to achieve a more or less plentiful existence, a more or less sociable and pious life and an adequate number of male and, because it does happen, female offspring implies strategic behaviour. Both the intended actions – as well as those actions that are then carried out in reality – are based on the anticipation of necessary and desirable conditions and living situations for the future and concern the entire spectrum of human basic needs. Fields of

---

126 The normative statements that are presented here are based on empirical findings. There are certainly variations and different attitudes according to person, gender, religion, education, sect, etc. Only a general picture is presented here that definitely needs to be corrected empirically.

127 *Emic* = societal *immanent* (self-)definition.
In contrast:
etic = *objectified* conceptualization of the outside observer.

128 The attitudes concerning the formal and practical role of women range from: exploited and suppressed (negative) to complementary-equal and in accordance with God's will (positive). The theoretical implications, the *emic* and *etic* concepts as well as the subjective variations, will not be gone into further here. A sociological analysis of the marriage relationship and conjugal bliss and an intercultural comparison still have to be made.

decision and behavioural competence are normativelly regulated within the framework of the role concepts which are individually interpreted and to a greater or lesser extent complied to. Thus both the emic and etic concepts are dominated by the idea of a household and head of a household. [129] The head of the family is considered to be the guardian of the social sphere of the family that is entrusted to him (as a rule, his wife and children). He cannot be ignored by outsiders. In the economic sphere, he is the one who makes the decisions regarding the utilization of the resources available to the family according to the stipulations of the goals, necessities and individual needs. In accordance with the Islamic mentality, no outsider has the right to interfere in the internal affairs of the head of the household as every Muslim is free and equal, i.e. his own master.

These concepts are indeed dominated by patriarchal thinking, but in reality the women are their own masters. Thus they are in part (1) included to varying degrees in decision making, depending upon the specific field of the decision and individual partner; (2) women run their own businesses and enterprises and maintain their own contacts; and (3) as widows they are, in some cases, very independent heads of households. [130] Widowed women who have growing sons and wealth at their disposal are without a doubt active as independent heads of households. They make all of the decisions themselves, but frequently ask for the advice and support of male relatives. The extent to which the patrilineal influence bears weight in the concrete case depends upon the personality, the status and the wealth of the family.

In principle, each individual adult male – with or without family – is his own master and can make decisions at his own risk. According to the norms, women are entrusted to their husbands, but in reality within the sphere they are assigned to, they are quite independent and, in some cases, as a widow they assume a man's role. A widower, however, refuses to assume the role of a woman. He is dependent upon a woman and must remarry.

With respect to the internal affairs in the household, the woman is responsible for most of the upkeeping in the household and has a corresponding field in the decision making. "The social emphasis of the leading role of men and the patriarchal structure should not hide the fact that the wife of the *karta* (male head of the household) plays a decisive role within the family." [131] Hence, within the household and the family, role and personality-

---

129 [147] Herbon, 1984: p. 252, [243] Luchesi, 1983: p. 119 ff., [327] Thorp, 1978.
130 Cf. [243] Luchesi, 1983: p. 128 f.
131 [243] Luchesi, 1983: p. 125. "Seen from without, it often appears as if the woman of the house unquestioningly obeys the instructions of the *karta*, that her only function is to carry out his orders, and as if she has no access to the financial resources of the household and can neither calculate nor plan economically. This impression is

specific spheres of competence do exist. Age, gender, property rights and personal characteristics lead to very special individual interests that are pursued on an individual and/or household basis within the framework of more or less extensive social alliances consisting of followers and relatives and both men and women. [132] In the following, in order to simplify the description and train of thought, the gender and role specific power of decision and the existing fields of actions will be ignored. Following a few additional introductory thoughts, the (1) fields in which individuals strategically act in a socially oriented, pertinent manner with an implicit meaning behind it and (2) the resulting *cumulative and structural aspects and consequences* will be presented in the following on the basis of the projected action-theoretical concept. Synergetic and structural dynamic consequences will be reverted to once again in Chapter 4.

3.1.3 Resources: The Household Endowment

Economic activities are carried out by households or enterprises, according to common opinion. In reality, however, it is not the households that produce and act, but rather *temporarily interacting individuals* and the groups they form. As the organizational framework, they establish households and enterprises. The official statistics and most empirical studies, however, collect data on resources and the utilization of resources for pragmatic reasons at the level of the *survey units household or enterprise.* In this context, therefore, on the basis of the information and data situation it must be presumed that individuals act – i.e., produce, consume, etc. – within the framework of the comprehensive organizational unit household. [133]

Some producing activities are based on a resource *pool* that includes the material resources (land, labour and capital) and the immaterial resources

---

supported by the information that the women give upon being interviewed and in which they, in accordance with the social norms, present themselves as being ignorant and dependent. In reality, however, they are autonomous in their own sphere..."([243] Luchesi, 1983: p. 126.)

132 For more on the aspect of group-strategical orientation in decision making see, e.g., [146] Herbon, 1984, [147] Herbon, 1984: p. 252.

133 This supposition has been discussed in another place: [155] Herbon, 1992: p. 95 ff. The acquisition of data at the household level, however, also includes exchange and consumption; that is why it is not possible to avoid speaking of households and enterprises in the following sections insofar as empirical material is used. It must, however, not be forgotten that behind such activities are always the individuals with a specific set of personal characteristics. As a rule, this manner of studying the households implies the dominant, patriarchal role and position of the male head of the household. There is a latent danger that not enough attention will be paid to the role of the woman and her activities and chances in life.

Fig. 14: Developments in Manpower, Persons 10 Years or Older, 1961 - 1985/86

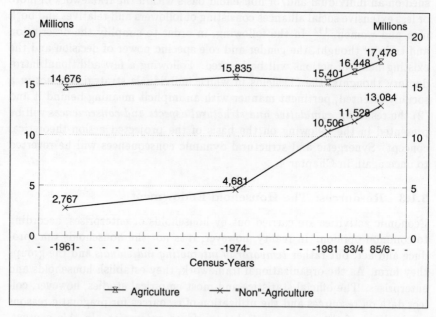

Source: [120] Government, 1986: p. 33, Tab. 1A; [128] Government, 1990: p. 97, Tab. 3.01 and p. 98, Tab. 3.02.
Note: For the numerical values, see Table 37 in the appendix.

(e.g., rights, claims, knowledge and power) that are usually contributed to by several household members. And they take place with a view to at least a partial replacement of the yields and income in this resource and consumption means *pool*.

The volume and the potential of the available resource pool and the potential degree to which the consumption needs of the participating household members can be fulfilled through their use determine the number of household members and are determined by them. Thus, before various individual activities can be introduced, a few "basic data" will be presented that characterize the endowment of the household units in which the social, economic and reproductive activities take place.

The agricultural sector seems in essence to be saturated with manpower due to the growing population. Figure 14 shows that the absolute number of labourers active in agriculture has hardly, or only underproportionally, in-

80

creased. In contrast, the number of nonagricultural labourers [134] has grown approximately four-fold in recent years. It seems, in other words, that the "employment growth" is not taking place in agriculture itself. Accordingly, the relative significance of the agricultural sector is sinking. [135]

Tab. 2: Development in the Number of Households, 1960 - 1991

Year	Number of Households	% in 1960
1960	9,603,000	100
1973/74	12,676,000	132
1981	14,785,000	154
1988/89	18,788,869	196
1991	19,617,506	204

Source: [124] Government, 1988: p. 77 ff. Tab. 2.66 to 2.70; [129] Government, 1991: p. 47, Tab. 1.01; and [130] Government, 1991: p. 8, Tab. 1.

In 1991, approximately 110 million people lived in the 19.6 million households in Bangladesh. In 1985, out of approximately 14.8 million households, ca. 10 million households that owned land of their own had a total number of members amounting to ca. 63 million people. Of these, about 40 million were over 10 years of age and were counted as belonging to the gainfully employed population according to the standards in Bangladesh. Of these, 21.5 million are males and 18.5 females. [136]

The "Labour Force Survey," however, found 16.2 million males and 0.2

---

134 In the statistics, it is unfortunately not recorded whether the people are active in rural regions or in the cities. It is also not said whether the people work as wage labourers (farmhands or industrial workers), or whether they are active in the tertiary sector.

135 "Bangladesh is a country with a very high population density and widespread poverty. ... The high rate of population growth (2.6 %), a very low literacy level (about 25 %), poor health and nutrition, and the weaknesses in public administration and the financial system act as major constraints on economic and social development. However, despite the country's structural constraints and repeated disruption caused by natural disasters, Bangladesh has made significant progress during the late 1970's and early 1980's. ... an overall rate of economic growth of about 4.0 % per annum was achieved during the past five years. ...despite expected growth in the economy, the *employment* and poverty situation will continue to cause concern. In addition to the existing unemployment/underemployment, a labour force growing by over 1.3 million every year will find it difficult to secure adequate productive employment. The solution of the problem is further complicated by increasing landlessness, the rural power structure and limited capital and skills relative to employment needs." ([357] World Bank, 1986: I, IX.)

136 [125] Government, 1988: p. 139 f., Tab. 1.

81

million females working actively in agriculture, a number that is difficult to reconcile with the data above. The number of people working in agriculture, however, make up only 59 % of the total number of gainfully employed, as is made clear by Figure 14.

Even if these figures are problematical from a statistical and theoretical standpoint, they reflect the fact that (1) *only about 60 % of the people live in households which own more than 0.05 acres of land*, but they do not necessarily also cultivate the land. It is also clear that (2) despite the deviating absolute figures published by the "Labour Force Survey," *60 % of the gainfully employed population work in agriculture.*

The index numbers in Figure 15 and Table 3, which have been complied on the basis of various holding-size categories, refer to this part of the population amounting to approximately 10 million households in the mid 1980's, while neglecting the "landless" households.

Fig. 15: **Ratio of the Agricultural Population to Farms and Land According to Holding-size Categories, 1983/84**

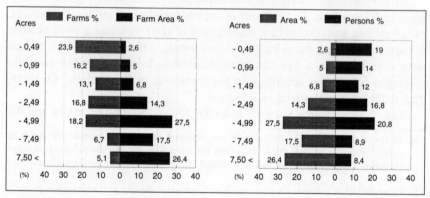

Source: [125] Government, 1988: p. 139 ff., Tab. 1.

Farms with less than one-half acre of land (marginal farms) and farms with up to one acre of land (small farms) represent ca. 40 %, cultivate ca. 7.6 % of the farmland and make up approximately 33 % of the population. Middle sized and large farms of 1 to 5 acres make up 48 %, which corresponds to a percentage of the farmland equaling ca. 48 %, as in the case of the percentage of the population they represent amounting to ca. 49 %. The just under 12 % made up by the large farms cultivate about 44 % of the total area, on and off which 17 % of the population live.

The (average) number of people that live off a farm is, hence, nearly

Tab. 3: Index Numbers for the Ratio of the Agricultural Population to the Farms According to Holding-size Categories, 1983/84

Holding-size Category (Acres)	Percent of Farms	Percent of the Total Farm-land	Percent of Agri-cultural Population	Number of People per Acre of Farm-land	Adults (10 < Years) Among the Farm Popula-tion
		(%)		(N)	(%)
0.05-0.49	23.9	2.6	19.0	20.3	62.6
- 0.99	16.2	5.0	14.0	7.8	62.6
- 1.49	13.1	6.8	12.0	4.9	62.7
- 2.49	16.8	14.3	16.8	3.3	63.2
- 4.99	18.2	27.5	20.8	2.1	64.2
- 7.49	6.7	17.5	8.9	1.4	65.4
7.50 <	5.1	26.2	8.4	0.9	66.0
Total	100.0	100.0	100.0		
Average of All Households				2.8	63.6

Source: [125] Government 1988: 139 ff. Tab. 1.

independent of the farm size and equally distributed over all of the holding-size categories. That leads to a population density of over 20 people for marginal farms and not even one person for the largest farms. On the average, each *agricultural* household cultivates 2.26 acres, while the average is ca. 0.25 acres per capita of the population. [137] Thereby, the relation of workers to consumers (w/c-ratio) on all of the farms is nearly equal, an indicator for the basic family farm structure. [138]

Figures 16 and 17 show that a low household per capita income correlates to a limited number of household members. The number of people in a household increases, however, nearly proportionally with the household income. Thereby, particularly in the case of the wage earner-consumer ratio (c/w ratio), it becomes clear that it remains nearly constant, independent of the size of the household income. Thus, for each wage earner there are approximately 3 to 3.5 dependent persons (women and children), independent of the total size of the household income. Furthermore, the larger the total household income, the more people there are who share it. Hence, the

---

137 [126] Government, 1988: p. 89, Tab. 5.02.
138 Cf. Figure 17.

Fig. 16: **Average Number of Wage Earners and the Individual Contributions to the Income of the Rural Households - 1988/89**

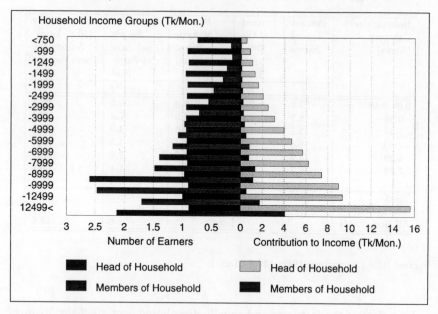

Source: [129] Government, 1991: p. 48, Tab. 1.02.
Note: For the numerical values, cf. Table 38 in the appendix.

differences in per capita income are indeed still impressive; however, they are no longer nearly as extreme as the absolute values would make it appear.

Vice versa, it can be said that – on the average – there is a (statistical) optimal household size that results in a wage earner-consumer ratio that is striven for, more or less consciously. There is a statistical indication that the household size is adapted to the available income by including or excluding members. Merely in the case of the very lowest income category of up to 750 Tk per month per household is the w/c ratio even more compressed. In this income category, which includes rest families that have been destroyed or uprooted or single persons (widows, orphans, beggars, etc.), nearly everyone has to take care of himself.

Figure 18 clearly shows that the relative significance of non-family members likewise increases with growing household income and increasing per capita income. These people are certainly integrated in the household in

Fig. 17: Average Number of Household Members and the Ration of Consumers to Wage Earners and the Average Total and Per Capita Income of the Rural Households, 1988/89

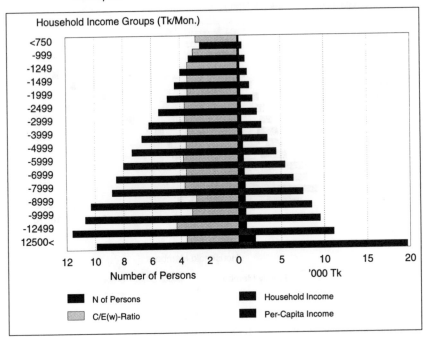

Source: [129] Government, 1991: p. 48, Tab. 1.02.

Note: For the numerical values, see Table 39 in the appendix.

some cases only because they are social cases. Otherwise they are integrated into the household as manpower. There is a – statistical – adaption in the size of the households that evidently "regulates" itself in the course of time. [139]

It is clear that the population "pressure" on the small farms in particular is enormous and that their endowment with land of their own does not suffice for adequate subsistence. They attempt to compensate for this handicap, as can be seen in Table 4, by means of *intensive cultivation*. The small farms are indeed hindered in this by the lack of disposition of water, but their

---

139 Short-term adjustments of this type are not described in the empirical literature on the subject.

Fig. 18: Absolute and Relative Percentages of Family Members
and Other Persons Among the Total Number of Members of Rural Households, 1988/89

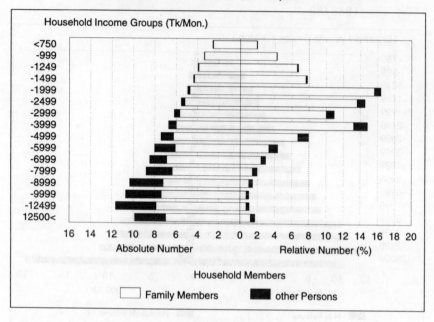

Source:[129] Government, 1991: p. 47 f., Tab. 1.03.
Note: For the numerical values, see Table 40 in the appendix.

average cropping intensity is higher.

The heads of the small farms have, with respect to the percentage of land belonging to the farms, less access to irrigation water than large farms. This is based, however, on probability distribution – as a result of the limited, decentralized, irrigation perimeters that do not cover the whole area and the chess-board-like and scattered distribution of the individual plots over the countryside. Twice as many individual plots per farm, for example, result in twice as high a probability of "falling" within the irrigation system with a field. If, however, any field belonging to a farm is located within an area that is accessible to irrigation, then this automatically results in a percentage of irrigation per farm that *increases* invertedly in correlation to the decrease in the size of the farm because this means that already a very large percentage of the land belonging to the farm can be irrigated; i.e., the smaller the farm, the larger the percentage of the land that is irrigated.

Tab. 4: Index Numbers on Land Utilization of Farms According to Holding-size Category, 1983/94

Holding-size Category (Acres)	Percent of Farms	Number of Plots of Land	Percent of Farms w. Irrigation of All Farms	Percent of Irrigated Area Among the Farm Area		Cropping Intensity	Percent of the Total Farm Area
				Irrigating Farms	All Farms		
	(%)	(N)			(%)		
0.05-0.49	23.9	2.4	21.1	77.6	20.7	196.8	2.6
- 0.99	16.2	5.0	37.9	61.7	24.5	195.0	4.6
- 1.49	13.1	5.5	43.0	53.4	23.3	192.0	6.8
- 2.49	16.8	7.2	47.5	44.8	21.5	188.3	14.3
- 4.99	18.2	10.0	50.4	37.8	19.2	181.6	27.5
- 7.49	6.7	13.6	52.2	34.7	18.4	175.8	17.5
7.50 <	5.1	26.2	56.2	26.0	17.3	167.1	20.4
Total %: Average of All Households:	100.0	6.9	40.3	38.2	19.5	179.3	100.0

Source: [125] Government, 1988: p. 139 ff. Tab. 1, Tab. 7 and Tab.8.

This effect is an indicator of the fact that the successive introduction of irrigation technology in the organizational framework of large farms by means of including limited areas can gradually be put into effect, integrated and adapted, whereas small farms must, or can, react relatively abruptly to these changes with their entire farm organization. This, then, is an indication of the fact that small farms have very different chances and productivity according to whether they are dependent upon rain or not. In the case of large farms, the change in the ratio of rain-fed and irrigated cropping takes place gradually with respect to the entire farm. As small holdings, seen absolutely, are less well endowed with *capital*, [140] it is clear that capital "extensive" and labour intensive irrigation technology would be advantageous at the time of the introduction of the technology. Also in view of the well-known limitations in the capital and factor markets, simple technology

---

140 Cf. the indicators such as endowment with means of transport and storage capacities in [125] Government, 1988: p. 455, Tab. 23, p. 479, Tab. 26.

would support the chances of access and application for the smallholder. The opposite is true in the case of large farms as they are more likely to have access to subsidized capital on the basis of their power position and connections. Greater labour intensity complicates the organization of large farms. [141]

The ratio of land and the people dependent upon the land is a basic condition with which the people must plan and operate. They have to take into account the type of available land (e.g. rainfed or irrigated) and the type of persons belonging to the farm household (workers or dependents). In the case of the generally accepted size of a self-subsistence holding of ca. 1 to 2 acres, the *chances of survival on the basis of farming activities on one's own holding are very unequally* distributed, depending on the productivity of the factors land and people. The smaller holdings, in particular, can only meet their needs by means of over-proportional intensity and nonagricultural activities and wage-earning jobs, as well as differential strategies that will be discussed in the following.

Within the scope of this study it is not possible to do justice to the empirical differentiation, complexity and contingency of the quantitative and qualitative disposition and utilization opportunities. Summarizing, it should be kept in mind that the control over resources is very unequally distributed if one takes the Gini coefficient of concentration as a basis; however, the overall level is so low that the extent of individual control of agrarian resources is seldom very opulent. Under these circumstances, hence, very many people are faced by the problem of having to provide for their existence and survival on the basis of too little, too poor quality land, or no land at all, not to speak of the inadequate access to inputs and the markets.

The objective of this differentiated picture of the resulting unequal and insufficient opportunities in life, which in the following will be for the moment tentatively "fixed" on the farm size, is to help to reflect in the following sections the perspectives and contingencies of the people who operate and act under these circumstances. One should, however, be aware of the fact that subsistence and survival are not *necessarily* based alone on control of the resource land. On the contrary, the "income per capita" is the relevant dimension, i.e. income independent of its source while taking the lowest level per capita into consideration, even for the poorest, and keeping the overall distribution within the society in mind. Thus, for example, the per capita income of a "landless trader" or of the members of his household can be much larger than of people who live in the household of a "half-feudal landlord." Due to the dominant position of agriculture in rural regions, however,

---

141 Cf. [154] Herbon, 1990.

one can tentatively operate with the indicator holding-size while remaining aware of the fact that the overall social and economic stability of the country, despite a sinking per capita access to land, as was established in Chapter 2.1, cannot be explained by this factor. [142]

3.1.4 Results: Food and Energy Supply

At the end of all social and economic activities carried out by many single individuals, i.e. their household among other things, is the control over a supply of the most important provisions, foodstuffs and fuel. The objective of the following presentation is to give a rough analysis of the status and the structure of the standard of living and the supply. The strategies that lead, and led, to the conditions briefly sketched in the following will be presented in detail in Chapters 3.2 to 3.6.

The *individual* supply and consumption of food is more difficult to establish than the supply of the *entire economy*. [143] Hassan and Ahmed [144] illustrate in a study: (1) a general change for the worse with respect to the nutritional situation; and (2) the fundamental, differential social conditionality of the consumption of foodstuffs. With respect to the worsening of the general situation, though, they contradict all official statistics.

Figure 19 illustrates [145] the per capita food supply available to four socio-economic categories in absolute figures and clearly demonstrates the social conditionality of the nutritional situation. With these foodstuffs, the

---

142 Farms comprise (cf. [125] Government, 1988) own land – leased-out land + additionally leased land. The percentage of leased land can, for the individual tenant "only," be very large and very important, but absolutely, the percentage of the leased land among the overall farmland is 12 %.
Cf. Chapter 3.4.1.1, p. 150.

143 It is difficult to ascertain the nutritional situation of the population, and especially that of the many individual people living in various situations in life. The general tendency in the *supply of food*, which will be dealt with once more in the final chapter, indicates that the per capita supply of grain remained relatively constant as a result of various controlling intervention methods on the part of the state (storage, market interventions, marketing and imports), as well as increasing production, whereas the supply of sugar, for example, seems to be faced by large fluctuations. The supply of plant proteins in the form of legumes appears to have continually worsened.
For an analysis of the factors hindering an expansion in the production of legumes cf. [99] Elias, 1988.
On the other hand, the supply of animal products per capita seems to have improved.

144 [139] Hassan, Ahmed 1984.

145 The socio-economic categorization of the population in four groups on the basis of the amount of taxes they pay is considerably problematic and unsatisfactory. As aiding indicators, however, they will be adopted here as there is no better material available.

Fig. 19: Food Consumption per Capita According to Household Category, 1982

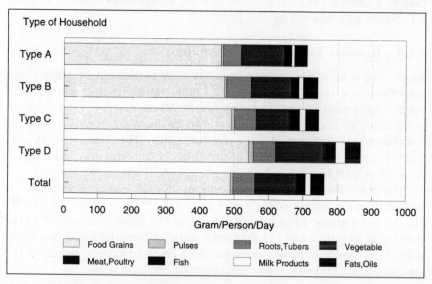

Source: [139] Hassan, Ahmad, 1984: p. 146, Tab. 1.

Note: For the numerical values, see Table 41 in the appendix.

"In rural Bangladesh populations are classified into four groups A, B, C, and D. (According to the authors' opinion.) The A group are the poorest, most certainly landless and are not required to pay any local tax. The B group are a little bit better off and pay a token tax. The C group may be regarded as a rural middle-class and pay an appreciable amount of tax. The D group are the richest and pay the highest proportion of tax." ([139] Hassan, Ahmad, 1984: p. 144.)

household type category A (poor) manages to meet approximately 80 % of its own energy requirements, and the households in category D (rich) nearly their entire energy requirements (98 %). [146] In the case of protein, on the other hand, all of the strata seem to be sufficiently supplied. In the case of trace elements and vitamins, more or less the same deficit is found in all of

---

146 This figure, only 98 % of the energy requirement supply for the rich, makes the entire data questionable. The problem of analysing the requirements and their supply is clearly illustrated here on the basis of the income situation of the rich and the fact that the rich can afford as much food as they want and are in some cases definitely overfed. It is necessary, however, to fall back on the available material as there is a lack of better figures to illustrate the social differences. In doing so, it is not the correctness of the absolute level that should be stressed, but rather the differential aspects.

Fig. 20: Food Situation of Children According to Household Income Category, 1981

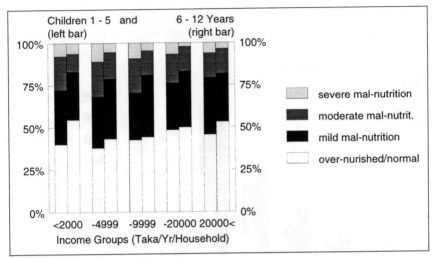

Source: [356] World Bank, 1985: p. 77, Tab. 2.06; p. 80 , Tab. 2.10.
Note: For the numerical values, see Table 42 in the appendix.

the strata. This deficit, as well as a certain oversupply, can be traced back not only to socio-economic factors, but is rather also the result of culturally based food preferences. [147]

Figure 20 clearly shows, on the basis of a very sensitive indicator – the food situation of the children – that the food situation is to a certain extent dependent upon the general income situation of the households. Hence, a higher income signifies a slight improvement in the food situation – measured on the degree of malnutrition. Important in order to judge the situation is, however, the fact that (1) even in the wealthiest families nearly half of the children suffer from malnutrition and that (2) the children can to a certain extent overcome the deficit and the after-effects during the course of their lives – if they survive. It is interesting that (1) it is in the poorest category that one finds the largest percentage of properly nourished older children; however, this category also includes those that suffer drastically from malnutrition. [148] In addition, it is once again clear that (2) a large

---

147 [139] Hassan, Ahmad, 1984: p. 153, Tab. 10.
148 To some extent this phenomena can be explained by the fact that the children in this economic situation begin to work earlier and earn a – no matter how miserable –

Fig. 21: Non-food Biomass Production and Utilization According to Socio-economic Household Category, 1976/77

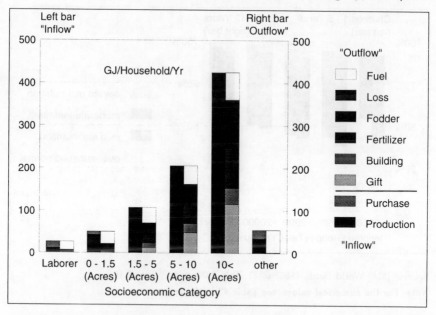

Source: [215] Kennes, Parikh, Stolwijk, 1984: p. 231. Tab. 7.
Note: For the numerical values, see Table 43 in the appendix.

income does not necessarily result in a better food supply, i.e. other factors play a role.

To sum it up, the fact can be established that – with reference to the relatively complex and ambiguous problem of nutritional conditions in their economic, social and cultural conditionality – the *poorer households are faced by a poorer supply and the members seem to be more poorly fed* than the relatively and absolutely prosperous. It is not possible within the scope of this study to completely clarify the question as to what extent the malnutrition is the result of improper nutrition with respect to calories or the quality of

income that contributes to their nutrition. Furthermore, the physiological mechanism by which growth stops as a result of malnutrition also plays a role. Since nutrition indicators are also based on the indices height correlated to weight and children suffering from malnutrition stop growing too early or their growth is slowed down ("stunting," cf. [356] World Bank, 1985: p. 79.), the energy balance can be more favourable in the cases of a more limited supply of food.

the nutrition. [149] It should be pointed out here that the relative percentage of expenditures used for food out of the overall expenditures of the households is larger in the poorer than in the rich households. These expenditures obviously do not suffice, however, in order to ensure an adequate supply of food. On the other hand, however, – if one takes the miserable starting position into consideration – the poor come surprisingly close to the same level of food consumption as the prosperous.

The poor nutritional situation – seen absolutely – corresponds to the situation of the supply of *fuel* for cooking. Fuel for cooking consists basically of a biomass that is produced and available on the spot. Fossil fuels (gas, coal and oil) do not play a role in the rural areas. The production and supply of fuels made of biomasses [150] is very dependent upon the volume of the general household plant production that itself is dependent on the available, or cultivated land.

The biomass/plant production is not carried out merely for the purpose of producing fuel, but also for the purpose of producing food and raw material. Thus, the utilization of plant material for the purpose of energy for cooking is only one goal among others. Figure 21 illustrates the absolute and relative importance of fuel for the overall balance in a few significant socio-economic household categories. The fact evolves that the landless and those households that have very little land do not produce sufficient plant material in order to produce fuel and building material, and fodder and fertilizer in sufficient volumes. They have to obtain biomass, i.e. collect manure, foliage, stubble, straw and waste [151] by hard work and even buy wood during the damp rainy season when other products hardly serve to heat or supply any thermal value.

Middle-sized to large holdings are net-energy producers and deliverers. A considerable percentage of the fuel energy is delivered to households that do not have enough fuel and building material at their disposal. Those households that find themselves in a more favourable position can afford to recycle a growing percentage of plant materials as fertilizer for plant production, or process it in animal production. Thus, these holdings are privileged both because they have enough fuel and energy for cooking at their

---

149 Cf., among others, with respect to the entire complex of the nutritional situation in Bangladesh: [53] Bhuiya, Zimicki, D'Souza, 1986; [52] Bhuiya, Wojtyniak, D'Souza, Zimicki, 1986; [77] Chaudhury, 1986; [78] Chaudhury, 1988; [86] Chowdhury, 1985; [139] Hassan, Ahmad, 1984; [140] Hassan, Ahmad, 1986; [141] Hassan, Khuda, Ahmad, 1985; [300] Roy, Haider, 1988; and [356] World Bank, 1985.

150 When in the following *fuel* is mentioned, the fuel is made of biomasses, i.e. plant residues, raw material and manure.

151 Cf. [215] Kennes, Parikh, Stolwijk, 1984: p. 224 f. Tab. 6.

Fig. 22: Percentage of Traditional Energy Derived from Biomass According to Farm-size Category, 1980/81

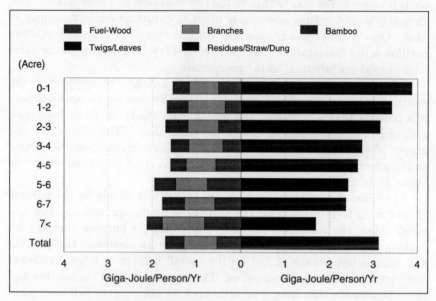

Source: [183] Islam, 1984: p. 68, Tab. 5.
Note: For the numerical values, see Table 44 in the appendix.

disposal, as well as because they can "invest" a large part of the biomass in the soil and plant production cycle and animal production. In addition, they have the advantage of the monetary and immaterial value of the fuel that is derived from selling or trading it.

Prosperous households consume more than three times as much fuel in comparison to the landless households. This fuel is derived (net) to 100 % from their own production. Per household member, however, they need – as can be seen in Figure 22 – more valuable energy than the poor households. This seems to be caused by scale effects. The significance of the five most important fuel sources is also illustrated in this figure with respect to the diverse farm-size categories. As various fuels have diverse fuel values and qualities, the prosperous households have, accordingly, large quantities of excellent fuel at their disposal, whereas deficits with respect to good fuel have to be – and evidently can be – compensated for by intensive utilization of inferior materials for fuel, foliage among others. These sources of energy can, however, only be collected and dried by means of relatively labour-

94

intensive methods (e.g., sweeping the leaves together in bamboo thickets); tasks that can, and are, for the most part carried out by children.

All in all, in other words, it is thus obvious that the poor households (1) have to use a larger percentage of their income for food and are, despite this fact, not as well nourished, and (2) have to use part of their *monetary income for fuel* and accept part of their *income in kind in straw or the right to use wastes.* [152]

3.1.5 Autopoiesis: Children – Preconditions, Consequences and Functions

The household, farm and other economic and social organizations serve the individual, with respect to ensuring reproduction, with varying degrees of success. The process of ensuring reproduction – i.e., (1) ensuring self-preservation, (2) raising children and (3) maintaining the socio-economic system in which the individual carries out actions in order to maintain his existence and attempts to secure his opportunities in life – takes place in real, concrete situations. Actions are carried out as an answer to momentary necessities as well as with a view to long-term consequences and opportunities.

Securing *long-term opportunities* does not only signify a lasting organization of the individual's production and social systems, but also that he will be provided for in old age, or in case of illness. One of the best guarantees for acceptable security in old age is raising children – particularly male offspring in Bangladesh – who provide for their parents when they become old. The children also maintain the "farm" and carry on their parents' achievements and, thus, make a transcendental contribution (1) towards securing their parents "existence" beyond the grave, (2) towards fulfilling Allah's will, towards the creation of the world. [153] Furthermore, children also make up part of the manpower available in the household or on the farm. This manpower helps earn income and other proceeds that can then be added to the common income and expenditure *pool* and then allotted and utilized.

The "production" of man, he himself and his children, is hence the most common goal and basic function of individual acts and collective control.

---

152 With respect to the fuel complex and the energy cycles in Bangladesh, see [8] Ahmad, Hossain, Mian, Hossain, 1986; [39] Asseldonk, Stolwijk, 1983; [42] Bala, Karim, Dutta, 1980; [65] Briscoe, 1979; [183] Islam, 1984; [184] Islam, 1987; [215] Kennes, Parikh, Stolwijk, 1984; [260] Nannen-Gethmann, 1983; and [266] Parikh, Krömer, 1985.
   For information on the conditions in India see, e.g.: [51] Bhagavan, Giriappa ,1987; and [62] Bowonder, Rao, Dasgupta, Prashad, 1985.
153 Cf. Chapter 3.1.1.

The philosophical/ideological and religious/moral (emic) arguments for the procreation and raising of children will be only be briefly sketched here.

- Raising children is a religious duty. [154]

- Raising children is a social and moral duty because they increase the capacity of the family they descend from, strengthen the kinship group in its competition for scarce resources and increase the social and political influence. [155]

- Children can and should be a pillar in old age. Parents should be able to count on and place their trust in their children with respect to their security in old age. [156]

The parents' desire to have children or not to have any more children is the manifest expression of the desire to satisfy certain needs of a socio-moral and economic type, or secure their satisfaction in the future. The desire to have children is, of course, not alone dependent on moral and economic *deliberations and considerations* on the part of the parents, nor is it purely emotionally based. On the contrary, it is dependent upon the *judgement* of how good the chances are of really being secure in old age. This judgement itself is, among other things, dependent upon: (1) the number of already born, living, adult and male children; (2) the parents' ages, specifically the mother's; (3) the economic endowment, i.e. the control of means of production and the (still) closely tied (4) degree of formal school education. The extent to which the goals are achieved – i.e., the number of children who can potentially contribute to security in old age and the, should the case arise, availability of alternative means – thus has reciprocal effects individually and statistically on the current desire to have children.

Figure 23 illustrates on the basis of empirical material from Maloney et al. [157] the fact that this desire is dependent upon the number of children

---

154 "Having children is a moral duty in Islam on several grounds ... It is believed that Allah wishes to keep up the continuity of the world through human actions ... from the religious point of view while procreation is a worldly duty, it is also a compulsory (*faraj*) duty. Child raising is also a religious duty, for if children are not raised well for undertaking worldly and religious responsibilities the parents will be answerable to Allah." ([246] Maloney, Aziz, Sarkar, 1980: p. 100).

155 "The sense that greater numbers of family members mean strength of the kinship group is known to be true especially by the males, who deal every day with the factionalism and alignments of village politics. ... A *guṣṭhī* or *bangśa* that loses many contests will decline in economic position as well as in prestige (*gaurab*)..." ([246] Maloney, Aziz, Sarkar, 1980: p. 101).

156 Cf. [246] Maloney, Aziz, Sarkar, 1980: p. 108.

157 [246] Maloney, Aziz, Sarkar, 1980: p. 311, Tab. 36.

Fig. 23: Desire to Have Children, Men and Women, Dependent Upon the Number of Already Existing Sons and Daughters *

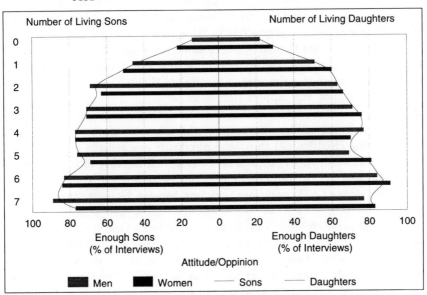

Source: [246] Maloney, Aziz, Sarkar, 1980: p. 311, Tab. 36.

Note: For the numerical values, see Table 45 in the appendix.

* The publication nowhere states in which year the data were gathered.

the parents already have and, even if the correlation is only faintly clear, upon their gender. This is illustrated on the basis of the percent of parents – men and women – who are of the opinion that they have *enough children* – sons or daughters. It is clear that the desire to have no more sons or daughters is rather low when a family has only one or two children, but after that it increases strongly. The desire to stop having further children increases less strongly up to the fourth child, and finally levels off at about 80 % to 90 %. After the fourth child, the parents generally accept their "fate." As the number of children, however, has nothing to do with the "quality," namely whether they are male or female, the desire to have more children is dependent upon the gender of the already existing children. This is, however, not easily recognizable on the basis of the material. [158] It is

---

158 This fact demonstrates the methodological problems involved in utilizing data that was collected and recorded for other purposes and the interpretation of the data in

possible to recognize the fact, however, that if there is *no living son* then more people want more children than if they have no living *daughter*. If the parents have a son and a daughter, the difference in the gender-specific desire for children disappears, although there is a greater preference for a second son than a second daughter. Above and beyond this fact, the gender of the children does not play a role in the group that was studied. [159]

It is also clear that women – understandably – sooner come to the conclusion that they have enough children, both sons and daughters. This seems to be true although it is the women themselves that with all probability will be dependent upon the support from sons.

It is normal that parents with increasing age (have to) reduce their desire to have additional children because (1) they have, to an increasing extent, enough living children, (2) they have physically reached the limits of their strength and fertility, (3) they accept the actual number of children with increasing age, [160] (4) the chance that one of the partners will die grows and takes place and (5) additional children become an increasing economic burden.

The number of children is subject to, in addition to the age of the mother, socio-economic influences. [161] Figure 24 illustrates the dependency of the number of children that are born per family on economic conditions for which the family's ownership of land is an indicator. The figure illustrates the fact that poorer women have, on the average, less children *at the end* of the fertile period of their lives than better-off women. This is an indicator of the differences in the economic strength of the families and could also be traced back to differences in fertility.

It is striking that although – as will be demonstrated [162] – girls in the poorer strata marry *earlier* than the others, their comparative reproduction performance (number of children) per age group is much lower, catches up slightly with increasing age, but never reaches the same level.

The number of children, even sons, does not say anything about the real success in ensuring security in old age. Cain [163] comes to the conclusion on the basis of an empirical study that an individual's opportunities in life and his poverty situation can result in varying degrees of success in ensuring

another context. In many cases it is not possible to derive the information necessary for a study with any degree of certainty from the tables and discourses presented by various authors. Sometimes it is even impossible to comprehend the author's own interpretation on the basis of their own data.

159 [246] Maloney, Aziz, Sarkar, 1980: p. 108 f. and p. 310, Tab. 3.3; p. 311, Tab. 36.
160 [246] Maloney, Aziz, Sarkar, 1980: p. 309, Tab. 32.
161 Cf., for example, [56] Bhuiyan, 1986; and [208] Kabir, Ahamed, Moslehuddin, 1986.
162 Chapter 3.6.1.3, p. 207 ff. and Tab. 16, p. 210.
163 [73] Cain, 1986.

Fig. 24: Number of Births per Woman According to Landownership-size Category and the Woman's Age *

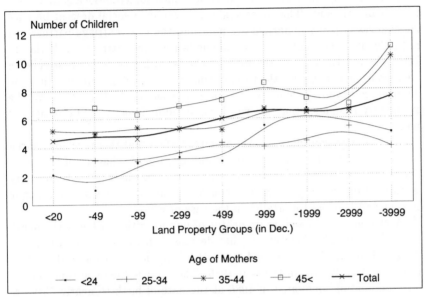

Source: [246] Maloney, Aziz, Sarkar, 1980: p. 316, Tab. 41.

Note: For the numerical values, see Table 46 in the appendix.

* The publication nowhere states in which year the data were gathered.

security: poverty increases the mortality rate for adult men and women. It increases the possibility and probability that their reproduction will be limited (reproductive failure). The poor are somewhat less fertile, and their children are more likely to die. Their chances of raising a son that stays alive are, hence, more limited from the very beginning. It should be mentioned, however, that the factor *"chance"* plays a much more important role for the success in reproduction and, thus, for security in old age than the factor "differences in the socio-economic situation."

Independent of their original material situation, all old people are threatened by social and economic decline if they do not have the *luck* to have at least *one* living adult son. Old people are more "vulnerable" in the case of economic crises because no one is directly obliged to support them. The possibility of increased poverty and the danger of being reduced to the state of pauperization in old age leads to greater mortality among poor people.

The danger of a lack of security in old age is greater in the case of women than men because (1) it is always more difficult for women to live without a male "provider" without suffering economic and social losses and decline. Furthermore, (2) infertility on the part of women sometimes leads to divorce or their banishment. This, once again, (3) results in social descent because the chances of being remarried are poor and the new marriage partner will certainly be – especially in an economic sense – less attractive. If the infertility is not the fault of the woman, she (4) will receive her first child in the second marriage later than other women in her age group and, thus, on the average have less chance of "reproductive success." That is to say, the probability is smaller that she will have an adult living son during her old age.

If a marriage continues to exist despite the fact that there are no children and if this results in pauperization in old age, the (5) chances of becoming a widow early grow for the woman on the basis of the increased morbidity resulting from poverty. The consequence is an increased socio-economic descent and increased mortality in the case of widows.

A clearer, even if sadder, indicator of opportunities in life is the death rate. The mortality (death rate) has decreased drastically in recent years: the rough death rate decreased from 41.3 $^0/_{00}$ in the years 1881-1891 to approximately 12 $^0/_{00}$ in the year 1986. The average life expectancy of the rural population amounted in 1986 at the date of birth to nearly 55 years and, if the first year was survived, more than 61 years. The opportunities are, however, indeed surely not equally distributed over the entire range of the various socio-economic classes. In this respect, however, no publicized figures are available. [164]

As there is no information on the class-specific mortality rate, the reproduction success that is correlated with the social and economic situation of the parents can only be derived on the basis of three "soft" indicators: (1) the socially differentiated mortality of children due to malnutrition and undernourishment, [165] (2) the slight differences in the birth rates if one uses the landownership-size categories as a basis and (3) the socially differentiated death rate among mothers that can presently only be surmised. [166]

---

164 I was unable to find data on the general mortality and, in particular, the death rate for children that could be correlated with the economic situation of the family or household from which they come. Merely Sohail ([321], 1979: p. 71, Tab. 5, p. 73, Tab. 6) registered survival rates according to household categories. The categories "Landless Farmer, Owner Cultivator, Non-Agricultural," which do not contain very much socio-economic information, do not register any significant differences. In the literature on the subject, however, such differences are presumed. National data are evidently (very wisely?) not broken down according to economic conditions.

165 [356] World Bank, 1985: p. 100 ff.

166 It is only possible to mention the fundamental risks of death among mothers here.

With these consequences in mind, people are aware that reproduction success is dependent upon "chance," i.e. the will of Allah, and tend to "plan" their lives and have and raise children just as it happens. Furthermore, they tend to create the social and economic conditions that allow them to raise their children and increase their children's chances in life as much as possible.

Increasing and maintaining one's own chances in life directly by means of economic and social actions or indirectly by means of reproductive acts is both theoretically and statistically as well as emic-normatively the goal and purpose of specific acts. While the subjective perceptions and anticipations that are determined by the situation are always relevant for human acts, normative expectations are less relevant, and theoretical expectations hardly relevant at all. On the other hand, not only the *subjectively intended* acts are decisive for human behaviour, but also *unintended* side-effects and consequences and the collective, "aggregate consequences" that become evident in statistical patterns. These consequences, in turn, form the basis for further human decisions and acts. The resulting contingencies – socio-economically differentiated spectrum of possibilities – and individual and solidary-common acts will be elaborated in the following sections. Thereby, the behavioural strategies resulting from the individual perspective will be presented in order to develop conclusions regarding the dynamics of the overall system in Chapters 6 and 7.

3.2 Relations: What Ties Who to Whom and Why?

3.2.1 Contingencies in the Relations System

Manifold social relations are a fundamental aspect of Bengali society. The people cannot imagine a life without manifold, extensive and deep relations. To a much greater extent than in the "modern Western world" – in which human interaction is dominated by considerations of functionality, by the media and the masses – the network of manifold personal relations plays in Bangladesh an important role regarding all human and existential purposes.

The people perceive themselves *not as parts* of groups and social entities, but rather as *active individual participants* in various social communities. The individual actor is embedded in a social-normative and role-ascribed framework of expectations and duties. The individual person, however, perceives himself as an individual personality with individual relations and interactions. This leads to contacts to others and strangers and dyadic inter-

---

The data that is presented here is also not socio-economically differentiated. Cf. [106] Fauveau, Koenig, Wojtyniak, Chakraborty, 1988; and [227] Koenig, Fauveau, Chowdhury, Chakraborty, Khan, 1988.

actions that can be regarded as the foundation for each individual network of social relations. This network of relations is constantly built up by each individual, maintained, utilized and possibly dropped.

With respect to completely marginalized, uprooted beggars or refugees, they have in extreme cases either no network of relations or only one in which merely a few people are included. Regarding the members of the village, regional, or national elite groups, the networks are extremely extensive and complex. This gives them – and we will come back to this point later [167] – an a priori advantage over others.

Status and role expectations and the roles ascribed to the individuals as well as their membership in a group predetermine the awaited interaction pattern, but if and how this is used is left to the individual. An essentially "atomistic" and "segmentary" social structure is the result from the viewpoint of society. A pronounced individualistic and autonomy-oriented basic attitude accompanied by a marked ability to fit in and to establish networks is the result from the viewpoint of the individual.

The individual is a member of a social group – seen from the standpoint of structuralists – and participant in and manipulator of an extensive and multiple network of relations – seen from an individualistic standpoint. In the following, the types of individual relations will be briefly sketched. The resulting group network structures should be regarded as the consequences which are perceived as separate entities. Thus, they may become "reference systems" for individuals and their individual acts. Figure 25 elucidates the way in which membership in a group is based on an individual network of relations, as seen from the standpoint of the individual. This network, thus, is structured by membership in groups.

The multiple relations that any single individual has and which do not exclude one another, but rather in many cases even overlap, superimpose and determine one another, can be broken down roughly into the ideal types (1) family, (2) household, (3) consaguineal and affinal, (4) client and (5) "functional" [168] relations. These relations are woven into an individual social network in the centre of which is the individual himself. The individual does, indeed, feel that he belongs to and is affiliated with certain groups; however, this feeling of belonging is always only the cause and normative background of specific, concrete interactions.

---

167 Cf. Chapter 3.5.1.2, p. 189.
168 The term "functional" is used here in the sense of "issue-related" and "impersonal" without any further connotations that would give them a specific value. I have put it in quotation marks in order to indicate that other relations are naturally also *functional*.

Fig. 25: Schematic Presentation of an Individual, Multileveled Network of Relations

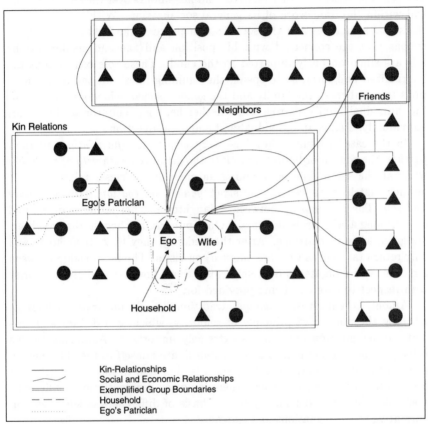

Source: the author.

Note: The figure illustrates in an exemplary and schematic way some of the principally possible regulations of the *ego* and/or his wife. Households, family, patri clan, family relationship and relations to friends, neighbours and a patron represent the possible memberships in groups. They are the results of individual relations (ascribed or gained) that have been tied. The network of relations is much more complex empirically.

3.2.1.1 Relations in the Nuclear Family

As a child, the individual has the "natural" relationships of a child to its parents and other people around it. [169]

---

169 With respect to the "interpersonal" relations in detail within the family, cf. for example: [40] Aziz, 1979: p. 46 ff.; [243] Luchesi, 1983: p. 145 ff.; [251] Mashreque,

A child is dependent upon the care of its *parents* and only begins to develop its own active relationships to members of the family such as its brothers and sisters or other relatives and neighbours over the course of time and within the framework of its general socialization. Within the scope of the social structures and the socialization process, the behavioural expectations that are connected with his position and age and gender-specific role are simultaneously imparted to the child. These role conceptions are internalized and form, so to speak, the "guiding lines" for the future relations to members of the family and the general social behaviour. As to how the individual fulfills his role and whether he, e.g., reinterprets the norms individually, etc., is an individual and empirical question.

In the case of adults, they have very *gender-specific relations* to their *parents*: the son subordinates himself to the distanced *authority of his father* while at the same time maintaining an emotionally closer relation to his mother that is distanced by the strict *gender segregation between mother and son*. The relationship between a daughter and her father is direct and open as long as the girl is still small. Once puberty has begun, the daughters are given away in marriage. After the wedding, they leave their home and only return (as long as they are married) on visits. The relationship between a mother and daughter is relatively close. Sons, however, are given priority with respect to care and being provided for. [170]

Among themselves, *siblings* traditionally demonstrate solidarity, whereby the normative principle of seniority, which also defines and regulates other position relations, is extremely important. According to this principle, the younger person has to subordinate himself to the older person and, on the other hand, the older person is obligated to show solidarity and provide for the younger. At first there is no sex differentiation. Differentiated roles come to exist merely on the basis of differences in socialization, normative role designations and exogamy.

The relationships to parents and siblings are consanguineous relationships. These relationships are de facto and normatively predetermined for the individual, but the specific form they take arises out of his personal

---

1986; and [15] Ahmed, 1985.

For the terminology on relationships within the family see: [40] Aziz, 1979: p. 197 ff.; and [243] Luchesi, 1983: p. 199 ff.

"The chief principles that govern the relationship between parents and children are loving care on the part of the parents and respectful obedience on the part of the children. The obligation to provide for the children reverses over the years: it shifts from the parents to the children, especially the sons, who have to provide for their aging parents. Nevertheless, the respectful subordination of the younger in dealing with the older remains unchanged."([243] Luchesi, 1983: p. 145).

170 Cf. [243] Luchesi, 1983: p. 153.

behaviour and living conditions.

The *married couple* forms, generally and normatively, the central family dyad. The individual sex role of men and women and, thus, also the individual specific behaviour are complementary. By isolating the women from strangers and the outer world within the framework of the "veiling commandment" (*purdā*), women are forbidden to carry out certain activities and spared from having to carry them out. Men, as a rule, are active outside the house and work in agricultural or as craftsmen. Within the house, with respect to caring for the children and preparing meals, they play a subordinate role. [171]

---

171 The complementarity, the non-interchangeability and the inequality in the sex-specific roles are regarded from an Islamic-normative (emic) point of view as being completely normal. Emancipatory (etic) principles, however, contradict this.

The non-public forms of life and working spheres have led to a greater awareness of and more attention being paid to the male sphere of existence in academic studies: the agrarian and political economies, as well as the social system of the men. The female sphere of existence was frequently neglected thereby until towards the end of the 70's: the household and reproduction economies and the women's social system. This has three consequences: (1) for those who did not know the society, the impression of the insignificance and the deprivation of the women was unreflectedly cemented; (2) the significance of the female activities was falsely judged and underestimated with the result that the socio-economic conditions and processes were inadequately presented; and (3) the perception of the inadequacies led to increased attention and concentration on "women's topics." In the meantime, there are a number of studies and bibliographies focused on women. A few are mentioned in the following:

With respect to the topic of general empirical "studies on women" see, e.g.: [2] Abdullah, 1976; [11] Ahmad, 1980; [37] Arens, Beurden, 1977; [75] Cain, Khanam, Nahar, 1979; [132] Halim, McCarthy, 1985; [133] Hannan, Islam, 1986; [170] Huq, Begum, Salahuddin, Quadir, 1983; [177] Hye, 1985; [180] Islam, 1980; [181] Islam, 1984; [182] Islam, 1985; [188] Islam (ed.), 1982; [192] Jahangir, 1986; [193] Jahangir, 1987; [202] Jiggins, 1986; [206] Kabeer, 1985; [209] Kabir, Moslehuddin, Howlader, 1988: [214] Katona-Apte, 1988; [222] Khan, 1985; [223] Khandker, 1987; [224] Khandker, 1988; [244] Mabud, 1985; [248] Martius - von Harder, 1978; [250] Marum, 1982; [263] Nur Begum, 1987; [275] Quddus, Solaiman, Karim, 1985; [291] Rahman, 1986; [292] Rahman, 1986; [293] Rahman, 1986; [306] Sattar, 1974; [310] Scott, Carr, 1985; [314] Sharma, 1985; [320] Sobhan, 1987; and [344] Westergaard, 1983.

With respect to the complex of more pragmatically oriented studies on socio-economic status and activities of the women see, among others, e.g.: [1] Abdullah, 1985; [3] Abdullah, Zeidenstein, 1976: [34] Ali, Rahman, 1978; [69] BRAC, 1983; [107] Feldman, Banu, McCarthy, 1986; [112] Gerard, 1977; [136] Haque, 1986; [137] Haque, 1988; [187] Islam, 1979; [207] Kabeer, 1985; [221] Khan, 1987; [270] Qadir, Quddus, 1979; [301] Sadeque, 1986; [308] Sattar, Showkat Ara Begum, 1988; [326] Tahziba Khatun, 1975; [328] Todd, 1987; [330] UNICEF, 1977; [331] UNICEF, 1977; [332] UNICEF, 1977; [333] UNICEF, 1980; [347] Women for Women, 1978; [348] Women for Women, 1979; [349] Women for Women, 1981; and [350] Women for Women 1983.

3.2.1.2   Household Relations

The complementary, symbiotic relations between married partners, which does indeed lead to a patriarchal overvaluation of the male role, but in which both normatively and economically, socially, sexually and reproductively mutual dependence exists, leads in praxis to the creation of a "household and conjugal community" with functional and structural consequences: the individual lives in a household ("domestic unit," *saṅgśā*) that, as a rule, has as its core a conjugal community-dyad including both sexes. This unit is frequently defined on the basis of (1) a common cooking place ("hearth group," *chulā*); (2) common meals ("eating unit," *khānā*); (3) common living quarters (separate room/house, *ghor*); and (4) a common farmstead ("homestead," "courtyard," *bāri*).

The major focus of this emic classification is centered on the, partially, *common utilization of income* ("income pooling"). Households are emically regarded as consumption and reproduction communities. For the production unit upon which this is based, there is no term. From this, one can conclude that whoever consumes independently does this on the basis of his own autonomous resource control. Whoever does not have his own resources must adapt himself to another consumption unit; i.e., he is neither separate (*pritak*), nor his own final decision instance as the head of a household is.

The unit comprising daily life and the economic and social activities is, thus, based on the nuclear family, or in some cases the "extended" *household unit*.

The cluster of relations that is frequently simply labeled "family," "household" and "family household" and may have varying degrees of extension in the form of distant relatives and members that are not related is a multi-functional, temporally variable entity. In this respect, no attempt will be made to define when one should speak of a family or a family household and what the "essence" of a household consists of. At this point, merely a brief description and characterization will be made. [172]

As a rule, married couples live together and form along with their unmarried children a primary unit. If a man has more than one wife, then the women have their own independent households – if possible – in which they provide for their own children and, at times, their husband. Married sons do not automatically have their own household, but can by all means still remain integrated for some time in their parents' household and then later become independent upon a solid economic basis. Thus, a household can consist of several married sons and their wives and children and the par-

---

172 With respect to this complex, see the elaboration of the aspect in Manig, ([247] 1990: p. 21 ff.) and the related discussions.

106

ents of the sons as well as unmarried daughters. Such large households can at times still continue to exist for some time after the death of the father, e.g., in order to commonly care for the mother or marry off sisters who are still single. Following the death of the mother, these family units generally break down into individual nuclear family segments with their own households. In rare cases, there can be as many as four generations included in the household unit. [173]

Households can include (1) distant relatives, sometimes members from the mother's or wife's line; (2) permanent labourers, farmhands, farmgirls and even private tutors and resident pupils, etc. (3) Divorced or widowed daughters and, in rare cases, sons can even return to their parents' household temporarily. Furthermore, (4) in the wake of a natural catastrophe, the household of one of the children or the parents can structurally be entirely absorbed in another household in order to then, following an improvement in the situation, go their own way once again. [174]

A household, however, must not necessarily be based on a complete nuclear family. On the contrary, a widower or widow, with or without children, can live alone and manage their own affairs by themselves. In rare cases, a bachelor may live separated from his parents and provide for himself. [175] At times, these rudimentary nuclei, however, are also extended along non-family lines.

Households consist in only approximately half of the cases of one nuclear family. In one-fourth of the cases, they consist of incomplete nuclear families. [176]

Households henceforth will be *defined as family-centred, more or less extended or reduced, multiple fusions of individuals.* The changes in the household membership over time, i.e. the dynamics in time and in the life cycle, further complicate this picture. A household that is without a housewife and spouse can within a short time become whole once again, and children can be born or die, sons can leave the household of their father after a fight or return to him, or the age of the parents and the necessity of providing for them may force a re-integration in the children's households. Household structures are subject in the course of time to changes in the personal and economic situation as a result of births and deaths, continual growth and decline. In this case once again, on the other hand, the individual

---

173 Cf. [225] Khuda, 1985. Also see the empirical findings in [147] Herbon, 1984: p. 44 ff.
174 Cf. Chapter 3.6.1.3, pages 207 ff.
175 This is more likely to be true in the case of "handicapped" men who, e.g., earn their own living as wage earners and who have difficulty to marry.
176 Cf., e.g. [147] Herbon, 1984: p. 47; [197] Jansen, 1983: p. 57 ff.; and [243] Luchesi, 1983: p. 34 ff.

age – especially in the case of an alliance of a married couple – is decisive. The resulting household is tied to the biological life cycle of the members: at first there is the young couple without children, but with their parents; next with children and with or without parents; then with parents-in-law and grandchildren and – depending upon the resource situation – sporadically, cyclically, or permanently extended by siblings and non-family members. [177]

The relationship between *the marriage partners* is brought about by the marriage and is subject to criteria of choice. The decision to marry is, however, only made in part by the married couple. Men have a greater potential to influence the decision than most of the very young girls, although women and men are, normatively seen, free and have the right to decide themselves. In reality, however, it is the men – i.e., the fathers, older brothers, and "uncles" – in both families who tie their own alliances by means of marrying off the girls, not only between the married couple, but rather between two family networks.

3.2.1.3   Kinship Relations

The relationships between a married couple is the interface that ties two kinship systems together, two patrilineal, agnate lines of decent ("clan," *guśṭhi, bangśo*). [178] The *patrilineal relationship* ties all of the male descendants together by tracing their kinship back to a common ancestor who, as a rule, existed a maximum of six to seven generations ago. This leads to a sense of solidarity that, however, gains in significance because this line of descent also establishes the main line of inheritance by means of which the key resource land is handed on over the generations. That is the reason (1) why the relatives reside close to each other either in the same or other nearby compounds (*bāri*) that have grown into neighbourhoods or hamlets (*pārās*). It is furthermore also the basis for (2) the practice of cultivating neighbouring fields within the boundaries of the village with implications of cooperation within the production sector. And, finally, this (3) is the basis of security. The "male community" is a physical "defensive unit" and a "solidarity community" in emergency situations.

Women, as new members of the husband's family, become simultaneously members of the patrilineal kinship group (*guśṭhi*). They still have rights, however, to inheritance, asylum and protection in their own kinship group.

---

177 In this respect, cf. [74] Cain, 1978; [197] Jansen, 1983: p. 59.; and [281] Rahman, 1986: p. 44 ff., who presents Shanin's mobility scheme.
178 Cf. [36] Arefeen, 1986: p. 54 ff.; [85] Chowdhury, 1982: p. 44; [147] Herbon, 1984: p. 74 ff.; [149] Herbon, 1988: p. 22 ff.; [197] Jansen, 1983; [243] Luchesi, 1983: p. 196; and [251] Mashreque, 1986.

The children are blood relations in both clans to which their parents belong (consanguineal related). Therefore, the maternal partrilineage plays an important role for them. Later, contact to other lines also comes to play on the basis of marriage and affinal relatives.

Fig. 26: **Schematic Presentation of the Multiple and Contingent Relations to Other Patriclans Through Women**

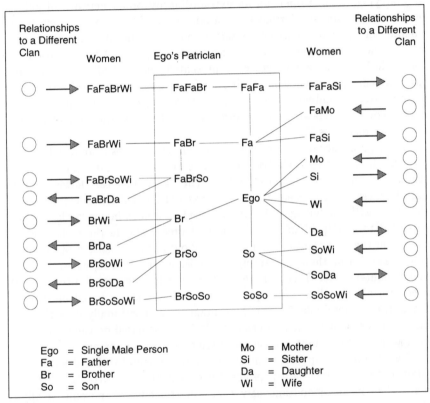

Source: the author.

Note: The figure presents in an exemplary and schematic way a section of the principally possible relations the *ego* has within his patriclan. Empirically, there will be more than one person for some categories such as brother (Br), uncle (FaBr), or son (So). As a rule, these males are married to at least one woman and, thus, maintain correlated relations to an entirely different patriclan. Daughters (Da) and sisters (Si) who marry into another patriclan and live there establish, thus, relations with an entire kinship group. This results in the fact that relationships through women bring with them a multitude of contacts.

109

The *affinal relation* opens up for both members of the married couple direct access to the network of relatives belonging to the partner. Indirectly – this will be gone into further later on (p. 208) once again – marriages of siblings, cousins and, later on, the children open up access to new networks of relatives.

In other words, whereas consanguineal relations are limited to matri and patriclan relations with a strong emotional and material "basis," [179] by marrying, women open up an extraordinarily broad network of affinal relations. The affinal relations allow a multitude of "relations." Each "new woman" in the clan opens up contact to another clan. And the marriages taking place there allow contact of the "second degree." Affinal relations in Bangladesh are characterized by, as presented schematically in Figure 26, their extreme contingency, i.e. their multifariousness, their broad scope, and their strategical influence, as well as their redundancy. That means that many people are related to one another several times on the basis of various levels and distances.[180]

The significance of relationships based on female lines is underestimated as a rule because these relatives do not live on the spot and most empirical studies are limited to the place studied. The significance can, however, perhaps be already recognized alone on the basis of the multistranded networks that exist *within* a "village." Relations based on women in one "village" that extended to a "depth" of three kinship "degrees" among the households – seen from the viewpoint of the male household head – consisted of relationships based on mothers amounting to 4.7 %; sisters, 12.2 %; wives, 12.4 %; and daughters 5 %. Together, thus, there was for the very limited spatial spectrum of one village [181] a percentage of relationships based on women amounting to nearly 35 %. This percentage grows continually if neighbouring villages are included, whereas the relationships based on the men in the village remains constant and becomes relatively less important.

The choice of a spouse is, hence, not only an emotional and normative affair, but rather essentially significant from a relationship strategical standpoint. This means, simultaneously, that a marriage is *not* an exclusive affair that only concerns the married couple, but rather a complex framework of relations and interactions among kinship groups with multiple interests.

---

179 The clan lives and resides together, cultivates the inherited land together, represents a protective and solidarity community and is emotionally closely tied on the basis of direct family interaction.

180 This extreme potential in relations has not been discussed to date by the usual phenomenological, normative and structurally oriented kinship studies.

181 The village comprised seven *paras* with 358 households.
   Cf. [147] Herbon, 1984: p. 74 ff.; p. 359, Table 7.

This has consequences for the type and frequency of divorces as "family interests" are also always involved.

Generally and normatively seen, the couple as a dyad forms (1) the nucleus of a combined kinship (consanguine and affinal) network of relations and (2) an operative unit, a living, reproduction, economic and security unit that, seen from a kinship-social point of view, is a family and, seen from an economic point of view, is a household and, under circumstances, a farm.

It should be kept in mind with respect to the situation in Bangladesh that the individual gains primarily within the framework of a bilateral marriage alliance access to the patriclan of the husband and/or patriclan of the wife. At the same time, each individual gains contact to the clan of the sisters-in-law, mothers and daughters-in-law and the clan of the spouse of the sisters, aunts and daughters who have been married off. The married couple forms here (1) an interface in the kinship network and (2) an interface in the daily life, economic and reproductive activities around which a further network of people consisting of children, relatives and non-family members forms a household and/or family.

In Bangladesh, there is an "extended" network of kinship-family relations for the individual that becomes broader and uniplexer with increasing "distance." Contact becomes increasingly sporadic with increasing distance, but it can still be activated: the closer the relations are, on the other hand, the more multiplex and frequent and important are the interactions. Daily interactions and transactions take place "on the spot" in the household, in the viri/patriclan and in the village. Exceptional interaction and transaction relations include people who live at a distance and are distantly related. Transaction, transport and information costs are, however, greater so that the relations are only activated sporadically and/or in the case of emergencies in order to mobilize resources. Extreme importance, however, is given to maintaining and supporting these relations – a fact which can be seen in the large number of distant relatives and familiar guests at "family" festivities.

The kinship and family relationships usually form in the case of landowning people a wider, and in the case of poorer people, a reduced network. The socio-economic network turns into a structural "framework" to which other relations can be "tied."

Figure 27 shows that the relationship net in the male line is different in its breadth if the number of members belonging to the clan and their households are taken as a criterion. The broad, large clans, however, are simultaneously, on the average, also those that have the most land. This shows, thus, a statistically positive correlation between the size of the clan, i.e. the size of the relationship network, and the per capita total landed prop-

111

Fig. 27:   **Relations Between Size of Clan and Average Landownership and Gross Cultivation Area per Capita**

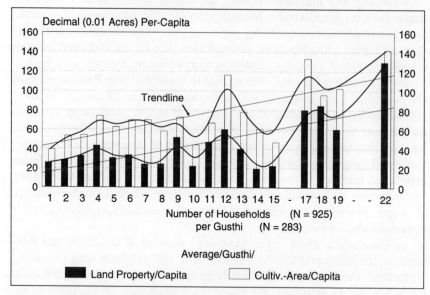

Source: The author's own surveys and calculations.
Note: For the numerical values, see Table 47 in the appendix.

erty, on the one hand, as well as the gross cropping area per capita. In the case of marriages between members of larger and, according to tendency, simultaneously prosperous clans there are, hence, new extensive potential opportunities to gain access to resources. Thus, for the prosperous – in comparison to the poorer or landless – household members the effect is geometrically growing resource-based networks. This results in generally (1) better access to resources and better than usual chances in life. In addition, there is a (2) security potential in crises because of socially differentiated security due to the greater *size* of the network – of people potentially obligated to help – and the implicit *volume* of resources. [182] [183]

---

182 With respect to the dispersion and significance of the basic endowment of various households within the same kinship group see: [197] Jansen, 1983: p. 34

183 The tendency in some Islamic societies for cousins (cross and parallel male and female cousin marriages) to marry only plays, according to my knowledge, a subordinate role in Bangladesh. These marriages are "functional" if an expansion of the kinship relationship network is considered to be less important than keeping the wealth, e.g., a trading enterprise, in the "family."

112

Kinship links are upgraded, expanded and supplemented with "cliental" or "functional" relations according to need. If there is a need for cliental and functional relations, the kinship "links" are "created." Thus, e.g., agreements concerning functional and clientelistic relations are clad in concepts and terms of kin relationships. Thus, e.g., "namesakes" and "blood brothers" develop quasi-kinship relationships. Interactors, in general, speak to each other using kinship titles very quickly: "big brother" (*bara bhāi*), "uncle" ("father's younger brother", *čāčā*), "big sister" (*āpā*), etc. Thus on the basis of the signals created by using kinship titles, normative roles and behavioural expectations are communicated and agreed upon within a very short time.

The utilization of "fictive" kinship roles and interaction definitions and concepts allows very rapid, frictionless and "diplomatic" communication by means of the cliental and functional relations expectations. [184]

3.2.1.4 Cliental Relations

Patronage, clientalism and factionalism characterize relations in which a "dependent" and "needy" person gains access to resources of a specific type and offers his labour, energy, loyalty and his allegiance as a reciprocal service.

As a rule, cliental relations are multiplexly organized and based on inequality in the disposition of resources. Access to land and the right of use are an essential motivation in Bangladesh for the cliental relations between landowners (*jamindār*) and tenants (*bargādār*) or farmhands (*kiśen, kāmlā*). [185] In these relations a right of use of the land and a partial right to the yield is transferred to the tenant and – only with respect to the latter right – to hired labourers. But the landlord receives a considerable share of the yield and gains socio-political loyality, backing and the willingness of the tenants and hired labourers to fight for him. In times of conflicts and threats from the side of the state and/or criminals, the tenants and hired labourers receive physical protection, and in emergencies they may receive help and credit from their landlord.

---

184 Cf. with respect to the complex of fictional relationships, among others, [36] Arefeen, 1986: p.91 f.; [40] Aziz, 1979: p. 79 ff.; [197] Jansen, 1983: p. 86; [243] Luchesi, 1983: p. 212 f.; [251] Mashreque, 1986: p. 102 f.

185 The description and valuation of the function and significance of cliental relations and the "inequality" and "inefficiencies" they cause and reinforce are found throughout the entire socio-economic literature on Bangladesh. Therefore, only a few publications will be mentioned here as examples: [37] Arens, Beurden, 1977; [67] BRAC, 1983; [68] BRAC, 1983; [85] Chowdhury, 1982: p. 51 ff.; [147] Herbon, 1984: p. 83 ff.; and [358] Zaidi, 1970.

The relation between non-land based employers (traders, etc.) and hired labourers in which employment and the obligation to look after the welfare of the other on the part of the employer are interwoven with the loyal performance of the hired labourer plays an increasing role in nonagricultural fields. These patron relations can be interwoven with those of a landlord as well as with regional and national politicians.

Politicians are frequently wealthier landlords and businessmen themselves who gain a clientele by promising to support their interests and by making anticipatory material "advances" in order to obtain access to resources at the local level, or to the national and international "development subsidies system." [186]

The details of the cliental interactions can not be dealt with here. The cliental network of relations ties the entire society together pyramidially. An important support are "obligations" that arise from the common birth place and/or kinship ties. In this case, too, the individual has once again a concentrically expanding network of relations to relatives and friends of relatives as well as his own friends. Or he has such a network of relations at least as a "goal perspective" of his actions. [187]

3.2.1.5 "Functional" Relations

Functional, goal-rational and "technical" *relations* play a minor role historically in rural Bangladesh, but are gaining significance as the goal-rationalization of "capitalistic" free enterprise and the administration gain importance. Independent of the kinship-cliental relations, there are issue-related interactions at the market, in the educational system and in the administration that do not necessarily run along the strands of the kinship-cliental relations. [188] In these cases, the attempt is frequently made to blend social behavioural expectations into the interaction by means of fictive kinship relations. This makes the relation subjectively more secure, calculable and satisfying.

---

186 Cf. acquisition strategies in Chapter 3.5, p. 185 ff.

187 I would like to point out the fact that cliental relations are not necessarily evaluated as *bad* from an emic standpoint – as they are sometimes considered by humanistic, socialistic and emancipatory Western perspectives – especially then when one has such relations at his disposal and needs them. Cliental relations are seldom questioned by those concerned, a fact that is interpreted by outsiders as a lack of an adequate consciousness. Frequently, however, the situation is such that criticism is supported by those involved if the relations *are not useful* to them. Otherwise, one needs and creates them. We, for example, also have family ties through marriage, connections, "buddy systems," lodges, etc.

188 Also see Chapter 3.5, p. 185 ff.

114

A number of "functional" relations result alone from the fact that one lives in the same place. Not all of the people living in a village are tied together by kinship or cliental relations. The geographical vicinity in a settlement leads to interaction. The neighbourhood (*pārā*), the village (*grām* or *moūzā*) and the local market (*hāt, bāzār*) are examples of such spatial units that are tied by neighbourly interactions and transactions and communication. This daily living together leads frequently to individual, private relations that, on the other hand, can be clientelistically or affinally "lined."

The religious community to which the men belong (*samāj, jāmāt*) is primarily geographically defined. One goes to the same mosque, prays together and participates in religious festivities together. Each and every Moslem can, and will, participate. Kinship and cliental ties are not a prerequisite, but frequently exist as to be expected in the case of the multiplex character of the network of social relations. The dimensions, thus, mix, whereby frequently one or the other aspect dominates in the relation.

3.2.1.6 Relationship Strategies

The individual, both with respect to women as well as men, thus has a large number of normative, culture-specific relationship forms at his disposal that are theoretically and empirically given contingent relationship elements, or that he can actively manipulate and use in order to increase the scope and quality of his network of relations by means of *social actions.* [189]

Consanguineous, affinal, fictive, or (only) terminological kinship with solidary, vertical-cliental, or purely functional quality form a concentric, extending network of relationships at whose centre is always the individual actor. The net is given in the case of the individual in its minimal form at his birth. With increasing age, it is then the concern of each individual, alone or with the help of already existing relations, to "make more of it," to increase the scope of his network of relations, to strengthen and complement it, or extend it by making it multiplexer and ensure its existence. The individual will also increasingly decide which goals he wants to achieve with his social actions: prestige and respect, resource control and acquisition, security on the basis of obligations and gaining rights, opening up access to existence niches, or the exploitation of dependents to his own advantage.

The notion that social relations in the form of dyadic interactions is the basis of extensive relationship systems, even the social system itself – with qualifying limitations –, seems at first to be strange. In actuality, empirically, groups of people always appear to exist in households, the neighbour-

---

189 As a rule, at all events, whereby social actions do not always have to be morally "valuable actions."

hood, village, even the overall society – structures, in other words. These corporative structures, which we perceive as entities, exist in actual fact as identity-giving reference points and as cognitive elements of order; however, they do not lead a "meta life," but rather are established and strengthened by the past and present interests of the single individuals. Social groups and units *fulfill* special *functions* that dynamically change, replace each other and dissolve, and they *are functions* in themselves. And the *interests* of the single individuals *are functions of the functioning* of the groups, which in itself, once again, depends on *individual interests*. Individuals establish groups and are determined by them, but at the same time social entities are only *constructions*.

With respect to Bangladesh, this means that the individual is a member of various groups by birth. Among these are the consanguineal kinship group and the settlement in which he grows up. He must, in the course of time, build up those relations that go beyond the scope of his position, his status and the group he belongs to himself. The specific goals and contexts for which he must have relations at his disposal in Bangladesh will be presented in the following sections. The fact should be kept in mind that an extensive consanguineal kinship network offers the individual a large potential on the basis of the quality of the implicit expectations and obligations and the quantitative scope of the network of relations. New settlers or people without any kinship line are, with respect to the potential, at a disadvantage. This results in compensatory strategies. As a rule, the individual will try to marry "favourably"; i.e., his family will usually try to find a partner who, among other things, essentially "brings" a "good family" with an extensive kinship group into the marriage. As both partners, however, have the same goal, as a rule it is the larger and more prosperous families and clans that are connected with other large clans, and the smaller who are connected with the smaller clans.

The *marriage strategies* of powerful clans are, hence, different from those of the smaller and newly settled clans. While larger and, for the most part, landowning clans are interested in increasing their control over land, the less powerful clans are also interested in the same thing, but their chances of obtaining their goal are much smaller.

Influential "families" attempt, therefore, to enter a marriage alliance with another landowning clan in another village. In order to keep the land in the family, as an alternative, they may also in rare cases marry a cousin (father's brother's/sister's child).

In the case of new settlers, who as a rule already have an affinal connection in the new village in order to gain a foothold there at all – even if it is only on the basis of a sister who married into the village –, there is great interest in establishing a "landed" marriage; however, the desire to find a partner in the *same* village is very strong. This contradicts the strategy that members of landowning clans follow. Generally they only find other adequate, landowning partners in *other* villages. These clans, which are usually "older" and "established," have as a rule an adequate and dense relationship network where they live so that they are more likely to orientate their contact outwards.

By means of the strategy of local marriages which is practised by the poorer and "newer" families, it is possible to form cliental alliances or solidary-"cartels" of the poor. These strategies are regulated in the end by the "price." The size of the dowry, bridal gift, morning gift and the expenditures for the festivities, as well as the "human capital" (educational qualifications and the family and kinship resource controls) are factors that are calculated and weighed against each other in, sometimes, very time consuming negotiations with graduated dates of payment. [190] Thus the marriage alliances are usually strata or class endogenous.

One's own marriage alliance, or that of a daughter or sister, opens up connections to other people and their resources. This, under certain circumstances, results in cliental potentials. On the basis of these relations, there are many opportunities for interactions, transactions and communication. These are prerequisites for either direct access to resources that belong to others, or indirect "further" ties. These relations will perhaps never be needed or "used," but one can in emergencies fall back on these relations. This will be referred to once again in Chapter 3.6.1.1, p. 200 ff.

The cliental relationship is not an end in itself, just as the solidary-neighbourly is not one. Their functions can be found either in the emotional-communicative area, or in the functional: access to resources and security in emergencies and times of crises. The functional significance of such relations makes clear that the relations in this case are goal-rational relations that take place within the framework of kinship or non-kinship contact whose *primary goal*, however, is access to and securing resources. This is the goal that motivates the individual actors to take up manifold kinship and non-kinship contacts and set them up so that one can depend on them. Without their material or security guaranteeing function, they soon lose their significance. The practical organization of these arrangements and the implied material transfer will be mentioned once again in Chapter 3.4, p. 143.

Summarizing, it possible is to say that as a rule the individual tries to

---

190 If payment is not made according to the agreement, banning the married partner or divorce are methods with which it is possible to apply pressure and consequences that are effective. Chasing after a dowry and the catastrophe of a divorce – for the woman – lead, under certain circumstances – to extremely tragic conditions.

enter further, or special, relations above and beyond the solidary community consisting of the patri and matriclans. Their purpose is to open up the chance to use resources, earn income and supply security beyond the existing connections and the normative-solidary implications. The objective the individual follows is to either put himself in a position to improve his material and social situation for himself and his closest household members, or to at least provide himself with security against the vicissitudes in life.

The social, relationship-strategic aspects of actions are not comprehensible without material dimensions. However, individual actions and interactions and collective actions are the preconditions and consequences of productive activities and, as will be seen later on in Chapter 3.4, exchange-strategic actions. The contingencies of the production system and the action-generating network of the production fields will be described in Chpater 3.3.

3.3 Production: Who Produces What, How and Why?

3.3.1 Contingencies of the Production System

Productive activities are the basis for earning physically necessary provisions. The agrarian economy in Bangladesh offers certain chances and implies some limitations for the production oriented activities of the individual people, or the groups they form – family household group, close kinship, village community, etc. The contingencies that exist in the production system and represent part of the framework for the activities of the individuals will be presented in the following section.

The presentation of the possible production-oriented activities in the agrarian economic system in Bangladesh is based on three abstractions.

1. The factors determining the social framework and network in which the individual finds himself and the dynamic interdependence between the social and the economic systems will not be described in detail at this point. Relationship structures, rights and obligations that are implied in the role concepts and social classes and conditions of production will be neglected at first; formally, they will be *treated as constant, concomitant conditions*. In Chapter 4, the attempt will be made to discover the dynamics of the conditions.

2. Furthermore, the task will not be to describe at this point how and whether the individual gains control or usage of the production resources that are implied here. To do so demands a discussion of the exchange and consume concepts which will follow in Chapter 3.4.

3. Finally, the household will be the focal point of attention here in its role as a family-based economic unit. For this, there are two correlating reasons. (1) Economic studies and national statistics are always based on the household/enterprise [191] as a survey, action and interest unit. (2) The practical implication of "pooling" resources, income and "provisions" leads to a – traditional – conception of the household as the relevant economic unit. Although this viewpoint is only valid under specific conditions, at this point the attempt will not be made to do away with it, but rather it should correspond to the data situation. Hence, the formal "crutch," the "household," will be used here as the unit to be studied. The fact must not be forgotten, however, that households are internally organized according to individual interests and that individual interests are by no means only satisfied in and by means of the household.

Here – to make it short – only true production-oriented activities carried out by individuals on the basis of their household unit will be isolated and discussed. The attempt will be made to establish the relevant possibilities for carrying out actions that are available to individual people and the living and household communities in which they live. In this chapter, the general "algorithym," the contingency of the system, will also be presented: (1) the "production" of land (land transformation), (2) plant production, (3) livestock production and (4) implement and consumer goods production. Far-reaching interdependencies will become clear in the following discussion.

---

191 The term *"household"* will in this context always comprise all of the members of the smallest economic unit with its multistranded activities (pluriactivities), resources and income. That does not include agriculture alone, but rather *all sectors*.

The term *"enterprise"* always comprises in this context a partial sector of the economic activities and resources of the members of the household, a production subsystem – agricultural or nonagricultural (e.g., trading or craftsman's enterprise) – in which individual, several, or all members of a household work full-time, or part-time, and, under certain conditions, with members of other households as partners or blue and white-collar employees in multifarious enterprise and earning combinations. The individual strategical activities are, hence, *"enterprises."*

When in the following *agricultural enterprises* are spoken of that are structured or occupied in such a manner or such a way, then this is a simplification that grew out of usage and the data situation. In reality, what is meant are the earning and income-oriented activities of individual people based on agricultural resources within a specific structural context.

Concrete areas of activities, however, extend beyond the enterprise. Seasonal or parallel pluriactivities or multiple employment on the part of individual or several members within and/or outside agriculture should be especially mentioned here (cf. Chapter 3.3.1.4, p. 134). This is an implication that should be continually kept in mind.

Fig. 28: Types of Soil and Land in Bangladesh

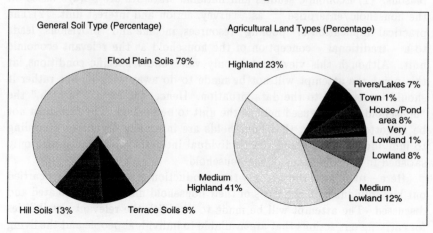

General Soil Type (Percentage)

Flood Plain Soils 79%

Hill Soils 13%   Terrace Soils 8%

Agricultural Land Types (Percentage)

Highland 23%

Rivers/Lakes 7%
Town 1%
House-/Pond area 8%
Very Lowland 1%
Lowland 8%

Medium Highland 41%

Medium Lowland 12%

Source: [124] Government, 1988: p. 7, Tab. 1.2; p. 9, Tab. 1.3.
Note: for the numerical values, see Table 48 in the appendix.

3.3.1.1 Land Transformation

Bangladesh has been an agrarian-culture based country since early times. The land has been used for agricultural purposes for a very long period. The production of plants, therefore, does not require primary land reclamation. The agrarian economy, which is based mainly on the production of rice, necessitates specific conditions for the soil and already existing agricultural land.

The key areas of Bangladesh are situated in an alluvial delta, an ancient settlement area. The soil quality is not homogenous, but rather varies according to the geological age of the alluvial soil and the sediment found there and varies in its degree of fertility. [192] This has been compiled in Figure 28. Not only the soil quality is important here, but rather also the type of land that ranges from "highland" (*ucho*) – that is not endangered by floods – to the regularly flooded "lowland" (*nichu*) areas and is varyingly suited as farmland, etc. The suitability depends, in addition to the flood danger, on sufficient moisture, the ability of the soil to retain water and its suitability as building land, etc.

In the central areas of Bangladesh every bit of land, with the exception

---

192 Cf. [35] Alim, 1982: pp. 53 ff.; [124] Government, 1988: p. 7, Tab. 1.2; p. 9, Tab. 1.3; and [138] Rashid, 1977: pp. 116 ff.

120

of a few hills, has already been under cultivation for generations. Since then, the entire land has been successively leveled to form very flat terraces in order to achieve an optimal distribution and utilization of the rain water. Merely those fields that are flooded annually by the rivers during the rainy season, on which generally only rice can be cultivated, are left in their "natural form." New alluvial land is gradualy terraced. [193]

The fields are usually leveled in the course of the preparation for cultivating rice. The soaked, muddy soil is leveled by means of a plough (*lāngal*) and harrow (*mai*) so that there are no depressions and the uneven places are leveled off. Movements of larger masses of earth are carried out with a type of hoe (*kadāl*). [194]

Earth movements still play a large role in the flood endangered delta: (1) when building houses because the houses frequently have to be built on pedestals of earth that have been piled up in order to prevent their being flooded and destroyed; (2) when constructing dikes within the scope of collective, publicly financed measures (Rural Works, Food-For-Work); and (3) when creating water ducts and canals for the irrigation facilities that are increasingly gaining importance. [195]

The land that is used for agricultural purposes, as far as it exists and is available and used for rain-fed and irrigated cultivation, is level and merely "repairs" have to be carried out. The chemical and physical soil quality varies greatly. Human endeavours steer the levelness and plough pan. The employment of artificial fertilizers and pesticides is gaining importance within the framework of the utilization of new seed varieties, especially during the winter period *boro*. Traditionally trust is placed in floods during the monsoon season to deposit sediment that delivers the necessary nutrients so that the land can be used permanently as well as to soften the soil, wash out salts and destroy harmful insects. Or in regions that are not flooded, measures to *maintain* the soil fertility are practised on the basis of rudimentary and primitive fertilization methods utilizing compost, waste and ashes before the rainy season begins.

The individual investments in soil meliorating and the maintenance of soil fertility vary, however, from region to region. The demands *traditional* rice varieties make on the soil fertility are minimal. Their capacity to take

---

193 Cf. with respect to this point and the following discussion, e.g., [138] Rashid, 1977: pp. 201 ff.

194 There are no studies available on these tasks, their frequency, their cost, etc.

195 There is no economic data on the individual farms regarding these tasks. Compilations and listings in the budget exist only with respect to the expenditures for public measures to create an infrastructure on the basis of job creation schemes. Cf., e.g., [110] FAO, 1986.

121

advantage of nutrients, however, is not bad. Hence, many different states of equilibrium are possible, and steps to meliorate the soil are carried out practically parallel to soil tillage in the present system.

In Figure 29, the land utilization structure is presented with respect to individual holding-size categories. [196] With the exception of the smallest holdings that consist practically of only the house, farmyard and garden, the relation between the size of the area used as farmland and other land remains nearly constant throughout all of the farm-size categories. The percentage of irrigated land among the total cropping area is minimally higher in the case of the middle-sized farms in comparison to the smaller and larger-sized farms. The area covered by the house and farmyard also increases absolutely with increasing size of the holding, but the relative percentage sinks.

The figure also clearly shows that the marginal holdings have a relatively high percentage of permanently cropped areas – as a rule planted with useful trees. These holdings can, on the average, utilize only just about two thirds of the land at their disposal for cropping, whereby the irrigated part of this land is relatively limited. This can be evidently traced back to the large percentage of permanent crops, or the vicinity to settled land.

These figures clearly show that, with the exception of the very smallest holdings, the proportions of the land-utilization forms and the utilization potential of all of the farm-size categories adjust themselves until they reach an "ideal scheme." There may be empirically strong deviations in individual cases, but on the national average, 1 acre holdings (small holdings) [197] deviate structurally only minimally from 10 acre-holdings. That supports the following hypothesis: (1) the pattern of utilization corresponds to the pattern of need. Their inner relations are, on the other hand, *inelastic throughout all of the non-marginal holding-size categories.* (2) The up to one-half acre-sized marginal holdings' pattern of utilization shows, in turn, that they represent *another "quality" of holdings.* These holdings have to utilize a larger percentage of the available land for non-cropping activities.

---

196 These statements refer to the gross cropped area, i.e. "...aggregated area of all temporary crops raised on a farm during the census year including the area under fruit trees (permanent crops) ..." ([125] Government, 1988: p. 21.)
Farmland is those areas of land that are really utilized by the farm/household, independent of the cropping intensity and tenure. "... all land which is used wholly or partly for agricultural purposes and is operated under single management by one person alone or with others, without regard to title, size or location." ([125] Government, 1988: p. 51.)

197 For purposes of simplicity, in the following I will use the terms "marginal holding" for households that have a house and garden (< 0.05 acres (5 dec.)); very small holdings (0.05 - 0.49 acre); small holdings (0.5 - 2.49 acres); middle-sized holdings (2.5 - 7.49 acres); and large holdings (7.5 < acres).

Fig. 29: Land Utilization According to Holding-size Category

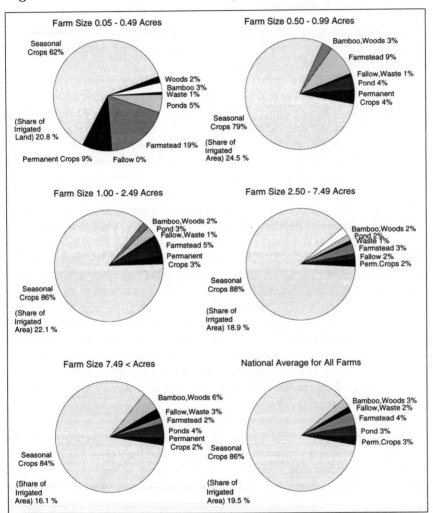

Source: [125] Government, 1988: pp. 139 ff.

Note: With respect to the absolute numerical values, see Table 49 in the appendix.

A tendency to utilize the land intensively for gardening and raising trees seems to be recognizable. [198]

3.3.1.2 Plant Production

The dominating product found in plant cultivation in Bangladesh is *rice* which is cultivated on three-fourths of the land used for cropping and represents a corresponding harvest volume. [199]

There is (still) an enormous abundance of traditional rice varieties that have been joined in recent years by a broad assortment of specially bred and adapted "high-yielding varieties." [200] As a rule, the rice is sown in seed beds and the young plants are transplanted to the fields when they reach a height of approximately 20 cm. Breeding the plants in seed beds saves land that can be used for other purposes, or prepared in the meantime. Thus, if need be, one can wait for the first rains of the monsoon and water the smaller seed beds by hand in the meantime. Furthermore, it is easier to care for and watch out for the young plants. Directly sown (broadcast seed) varieties are: (1) rice that grows in flooded areas (e.g., floating rice, swimming rice) and which, if need be, is harvested later from a boat; or (2) rice that grows on newly deposited alluvial soil. The production of rice (paddy, *dhān*) supplies the most important cereal for nutrition (rice, *chāul*) which is as a rule eaten boiled (*bhāt*) or baked to produce rice meal. The straw serves as raw fodder for cattle and buffalo and is occasionally used to roof the huts.

There are three rice cropping seasons that, furthermore, determine the entire cropping calendar: (1) summer rice *āuś* [201] that is traditionally planted during the pre-monsoon rains; (2) monsoon rice *āman* [202] which is planted exclusively at the beginning of the monsoon season; and (3) *boro* [203] which is planted in the flooded areas and irrigated during the dry winter season (post-monsoon). [204]

The obviously dominating role that rice plays in plant production has to be seen *relatively*. In addition to rice that is cultivated during the three cropping seasons in very many local varieties and varieties that have been altered through breeding, there is – in addition to wheat – a tremendous abundance of pulse crops, oil seeds, "market crops" such as jute and sugar

---

198 With respect to the utilization or cropping intensity, see Chapter 4.2.1.1, p. 243.
199 Cf. [121] Government, 1986: pp. 33 ff.; [138] Rashid, 1977: pp. 224 ff.
200 Cf. [138] Rashid, 1977: pp. 224 ff.
201 In the following, the most common spelling will be used, *Aus*.
202 In the following, the most common spelling will be used *Amon*.
203 The common way of writing the word is *Boro*.
204 Cf. with respect to rice cropping in Bangladesh among others, [35] Alim, 1982; [138] Rashid, 1977: pp. 224 ff.; and [121] Government, 1986: pp. 33 ff.

cane, [205] vegetables, spices, fodder and products that can be used as fuel.

Wheat is constantly gaining importance and is the second most important nutritional cereal following rice. There are traditional local varieties and adapted high-yielding varieties. The tremendous growth in wheat production can be traced to the increasing utilization of improved seed sown on larger areas and based on a growing attractiveness of baked wheat meal as a source of nutrition. [206]

Pulse crops are an important source of protein for human nutrition. Recently, the area used for cropping pulse crops has decreased. The supposition is that the areas that were used for these crops during the dry winter season are now used more intensively for wheat and *boro* rice. [207]

Oil seeds include varieties for producing edible oil and oil used for technical purposes. Plant fats and oil play an important nutritional-physiological role, it is true, but the need cannot be met by the domestic production in Bangladesh. Thus the percentage of imported oil is high. [208]

Jute is the main cash crop. It makes up three-fourths of the cash crop production and is primarily cropped for the purpose of obtaining cash. Other fiber plants that are produced for the purpose of selling them are: mesta, hemp and cotton, and as luxury crops: sugar cane, tobacco and betel nuts and leaves (*chupāri, pān*). [209]

Vegetables comprise a very large number of various cabbage varieties, roots and tubers, tree crops, green vegetables, tomatoes, etc. [210] They are differentiated from *spices* on the basis of their *nutritional value*. Classified in Bangladesh as spices are: onions, garlic, pepper pods (chili), coriander, anise, cumin, turmeric and ginger.

---

205 The official statistics define this product group as "cash crops" because they are almost exclusively produced for the market. The fact that all other field crops are also marketed to a large extent makes this categorization somewhat questionable.

206 Rice and wheat are complemented by an abundance of other cereals (millet) that are cropped on approximately 2 % of the cropping area. Among these are: *kāun* (Italian millet), *jāb* (barley), *cheena* (common millet), *bhuttā* (maize), *bājrā* (pearl millet) and *joār* (great millet).
Cf. [121] Government, 1986: pp. 45 ff. Also see [138] Rashid, 1977: p. 247, who also uses the Latin terms.

207 Cf. [121] Government, 1986: p. 48.
The most important pulse crops are: *keshāri, māsur, grām/cholā, māsh kālāi, mung, mātār, gari kālāi* and *ārhār.* Cf. [121] Government, 1986: pp. 52 ff.; and [138] Rashid, 1977: pp. 255 ff.

208 Cf. [121] Government, 1986: p. 57, and [138] Rashid, 1977: pp. 281 ff.
The most significant oil seeds are: sesame, linseed, rape, mustard (*sarser*), groundnut (*bādām*), soybeans, sunflower and castor.

209 Cf. [121] Government, 1986: pp. 65 ff., and [138] Rashid, 1977: pp. 290 ff.

210 For a compilation see [121] Government, 1986: pp. 73 ff., and [138] Rashid, 1977: pp. 264 ff.

Fodder crops for livestock production consist largely of rice straw, waste and by-products from food and market plant production and processing. Pastures and fodder cropping areas have become insignificant due to other utilizations of the fields. [211]

Firewood and material for fuel is very scarce. In addition to trees that are used to produce crops, furniture and building wood, there is hardly any pure firewood anymore. Thus, wood processing waste, roots and dry biomass derived from crops are used as fuel. [212]

Not all crops are cultivated in all of the regions of Bangladesh, on all types of land, in all mixtures and in every season. A complex cropping pattern and a cropping period that lasts 12 months with specific local characteristics leads in interaction with the other factors of the production system – soil quality, livestock production, etc. – to various land-use systems with specific combinations that have to be seen in the context of the farming system and holding size.

Figure 30 illustrates the quantitative significance of the various crops and the dependency of their combination on the size of the holding and the agricultural household. Particularly striking is the fact that in the case of the marginal holdings the utilization of the minimally sized areas for growing vegetable gardens and trees is predominant, as can be seen in Figure 31 on p. 129; however, with increasing size of the holdings – over all of the holding-size categories – another cropping pattern that is dominated by rice with stable cropping and land use *ratios* takes over very rapidly. The average utilization pattern of the smallest holdings varies only slightly from that of the largest holdings and, thus, the national average. There are also no differences in the mixture of the crops with respect to marketability. If there are holding-size differences in the market "dependence," they are not reflected in the cropping orientation of the holdings.

The introduction and increasing utilization of modern chemical inputs and the growing availability of water throughout the entire year, flood control and an increasing integration in the market, lead gradually to slow shifts within the cropping pattern. [213]

---

211 Cf. Table 49 in the appendix and the data on land that is not used for cropping purposes, as well as fallow land.
212 Jute stalks, rise straw, groundnut leaves and stems, roots from cereal plants and bamboo and foliage.
   For the significance of the production of the following useful trees and fruit varieties cf. [138] Rashid, 1977: p. 322: acacia atechu, betel nut, coconut, banana, mango, yak, pineapple, litchi, guavas, papayas, custard apples, citrus fruits, etc.
   With respect to the energy problem, cf. Chapter 3.1.4, pp. 89 ff.
213 Cf. [121] Government, 1986: p. 29, Tab.1; and [189] Jabbar, 1985.
   Cf. also Chapter 4.2.1.1, pp. 246 ff.

Fig. 30: Crop Ratio According to Holding-size Categories

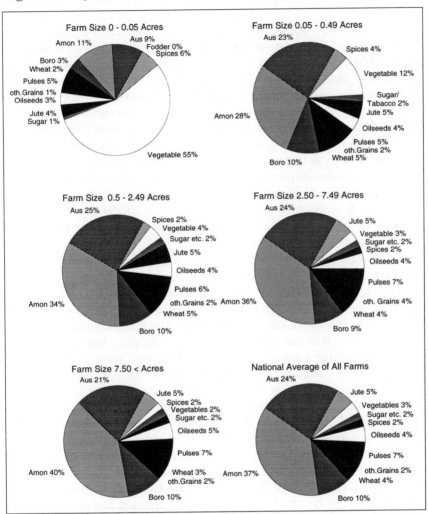

Source: [121] Government, 1986: p. 111.
Note: For the numerical values, see Table 50 in the appendix.

The average cropping intensity throughout the country is presently approximately 150 % to 170 %. In the case of smaller holdings, the intensity amounts to approximately 190 %: in the case of the larger holdings, it is about 150 %. [214] If it is not higher, this can be traced back to the facts that: (1) not every field can be cultivated the entire year round because, for example, it may be flooded for weeks at a time, or cannot be irrigated; (2) the three rice cropping seasons cannot be coordinated so that there is no overlapping. Concretely speaking, that means that in cases in which in winter irrigated Boro rice is cultivated, there is not enough time to harvest an Aus rice yield in time for the Amon rice in the monsoon season. (3) There are crops such as sugar cane and jute that need more than one season and, hence, prevent a fast succession of crops. (4) Frequently the inputs are not available on time or in large enough quantities, especially for cultivating high-yielding rice varieties, so that the fields lie fallow for a while. (5) The cropping intensity is higher in the case of the small holdings compared to the large holdings because the "pressure" on the resource land and the necessity of optimal utilization is greater. (6) There are seasonal labour-peaks and, sometimes, a shortage of labour that, e.g., in combination with liquidity bottlenecks, result in certain cultivating measures not being carried out due to work-organizational grounds.

The greater cropping intensity is not only evident when regarding the field crops, but also with respect to the crops raised at the level of gardening. The utilization of the rest, house and farmyard areas is an indicator of this fact. Figure 31 illustrates the overproportional significance of trees for the smallest and small holdings. Although the small holdings altogether only cultivate a minimal share of the overall farmland, they have nearly as many trees for the purpose of producing fruit and wood as the holdings belonging to the middle-sized holding categories (0.5 to 2.5 acres), which have a much larger share of land. The large holdings (2.5 to 7.5 acres) have only small numbers of trees compared to the middle-sized and small holdings. The largest holdings (large-scale landownership amounting to more than 7.5 acres) have overproportionally small numbers of trees.

This indicates the following facts: (1) smallest and small holdings utilize their land by cultivating an overproportional number of trees. Even without being able to estimate the relative productivity of the trees, this is an indication of the fact that they (2) use the farmyard and rest land more intensively. This can be explained by the fact, among other things, that (3) they have more labour for harvesting and cultivating tasks at their disposal and also (4) draw valuable additional income from this form of utilization that (5) is in all probability higher than that derived from field crops which frequently cannot be cropped on these usually elevated areas.

This brief sketch should make clear that – due to the multitude of tasks

---

214 Cf. Figure 63, p. 245.

Fig. 31: Number of Various Useful Tress in Relation to the Holding Area

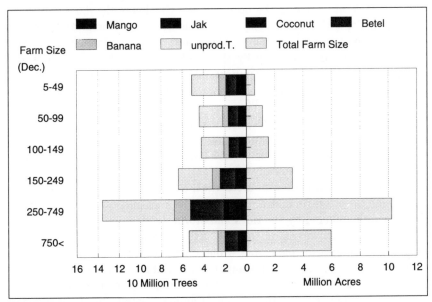

Source: [125] Government, 1988: p. 141, Tab. 1.
Note: For the numerical values, cf. Table 51 in the appendix.

that exist and are carried out in plant production and the conditions inherent in their coordination – a complex, manifold and interdependent plant production system exists. This is reflected in the seasonal crop rotation and the cropping intensity; in the interdependency between field and garden crops; and in the rotation between seasonal, annual and perennial plants.

It is necessary to clearly differentiate between the interdependent systems of land utilization based upon field crops, seasonal gardening of vegetables, the home garden based on mixed cultures which include all forms of tree and vegetable crops, the small plantations producing such crops as betel leaves (*pān*) and betel nut palm gardens (*chupāri*) and ponds that function as production systems for biomasses that are used to produce fish. The various systems which exist at the same time on the same tiny plot of land are ecologically interdependent and must be seen as being strongly interlinked and intertwined.

3.3.1.3   Livestock Production

Livestock production, including fish production, complements plant production. It is integrated in the farm system. Cattle are the most important large animals, while buffalo play a subordinate role. Horses and donkeys are rare. Small ruminants such as sheep and, in particular, goats are also important. Pigs are kept only by the Hindu and Christian minorities and are quantitatively of minimal importance. Poultry, such as chickens and ducks, are important, whereas one only seldom finds pigeons and geese as well as Chinese chickens, etc. [215]

In addition to these animals, one also finds fish that not only exist naturally in flowing waters and lagoons, but rather are also bred, fed and fished in the ponds that are used for several purposes. In some mangrove zones, raising shrimps is economically important. This takes place at the cost of capital-intensive cultivation of areas that, as a result of the radically dissipated mangrove forests that are cut down for this purpose, are ecologically extremely endangered by the tides and storm floods.

Cattle and buffalo are, on the one hand, indispensable in their function as draught animals for ploughing while, on the other hand, they represent a significant percentage of the draught power utilized in the rural transport system that is based on ox-drawn carts. Furthermore, the cows make a significant contribution to the supply of animal protein for the humans in their role as milk suppliers. The animals are as a rule only then used as a meat supply when, due to their age, the animals can no longer be used for other purposes. [216]

In addition to the integration of the animals as draught power on the farms, the animals also supply, in their role as "processors" of rice straw, manure that is utilized to a certain percentage in order to replenish the soil fertility. The manure, however, is mainly also utilized as fuel for cooking and as a binder when building the loam houses. Cattle and buffalo are, hence, integral components of plant cultivation, the transport system and the food and house economies. [217]

---

215 With respect to the importance of livestock keeping, see Helmrich's exemplary study on livestock keeping and utilization systems based on the example of a village [144] Helmrich, 1986; as well as, [119] Government, 1986; [118] Government, 1986; and [125] Government, 1988.

216 The exception are those, frequently beautiful animals, that are slaughtered at the occasion of the religious feast *Eid-ul-Azha* and, thus, are no longer available for breeding.

217 Cf. [138] Rashid, 1977: pp. 350 ff.
   For a study of the dynamics of the cattle population under the present agrarian conditions in six villages also see [156] Hermans, Udo, and Dawood, 1989.

Small ruminants, goats and sheep, are mainly utilized to "up-grade" usable plant biomasses and the human manpower on small farms. They serve, mainly, for the production of meat and are, within the scope of this utilization, at the same time relatively liquid and mobile "natural capital." [218]

Poultry is significant as a source of meat and eggs. The poultry runs around "freely" and consumes seeds, broken grain and kitchen wastes, as well as excrement. Furthermore, they exterminate harmful insects and their larva.

Fish are very important as sources of protein. The systematic breeding and feeding of fish is a well-known practice and carried out under certain circumstances. There are, however, regional differences in the abilities of the pond management. Pond fish raising opens up a large number of potentials which, however, cannot be taken advantage of due to the complicated communal property and utilization entitlements for the ponds. Since it is not possible to divide ponds or build fences in them in order to separate them into various parts, investments for spawn, feed, or pesticides are only then of interest if the collective made up of the owners works together, or a single individual receives the sole right of utilization. Since, however, there are frequently problems in this area, as a rule only the natural stock is fished and distributed according to a distribution key. This often signifies underutilization. Therefore, the yields from individually cultivated small ponds and pools – which are owned by either only one individual or a group of cooperating owners – are up to ten times as high per unit of area in comparison to the hectare-sized "lakes." [219]

Livestock keeping is gaining in absolute significance, although it is losing significance relatively in comparison to the general economic and demographic development. Thereby, the cattle and buffalo population, which is largely used as a source of draught power, seems to stagnate at a constant, absolute level, whereas small livestock and poultry are gaining an overproportional significance. [220]

The livestock intensity per unit of area varies extremely according to the diverse farm-size categories. With the exception of those households that have more or less no land at their disposal (up to 0.04 acres) and tie up their animals, which amount to an average of 3 animals per acre, the farms with an area consisting of up to one acre keep approximately 2 animals per household. In the case of the large farms, one finds approximately one large animal unit per acre. In the case of small ruminants and poultry, the

---

218 Cf. [138] Rashid, 1977: pp. 358 ff.
219 Cf. [115] Government, 1984.
220 In this context, also see the detailed discussion in Chapter 4.2.2.1 and, in particular, Table 19 p. 255.

situation is even more extreme. The figures have been compiled in Table 5.

Tab. 5:   Number of Animals per Unit of Area According to Holding-size Category, 1983/84

Holding-size Categories (Acres)	Large-Animals	Small-Animals	Poultry
	(Number per Acre)		
- 0.04	3.2	5.9	23.1
- 0.49	2.2	2.9	15.8
- 0.99	1.5	1.3	7.1
- 1.49	1.3	0.9	4.8
- 2.49	1.2	0.6	3.3
- 7.49	0.8	0.4	2.0
7.50 (	0.6	0.2	1.0

Source: [119] Government, 1986: p. 141, Tab. 1.1.

The practice of keeping cattle and buffalo correlates relatively close to the farm area, whereas keeping small ruminants and poultry is more independent of the size of the area and correlates more closely to the number of household members, i.e. to the available manpower. Figure 32 presents the relations.

It is obvious that in those households with smaller areas of farmland at their disposal, an overproportional number of large animals are kept. This can be explained by the following factors: (1) draught animal units cannot be divided. As a rule, a complete pair is necessary. (2) Cattle are used as transport animals in ox-cart enterprises that can be independent of the size of the land used for farming. (3) For the very small farms and households situated near the cities, the keeping of dairy cattle is gaining importance. (4) "Fattening" calves gains a specific significance for the capital formation of households that have little land although enough manpower at their disposal.

Despite this fact, there is a relatively close correlation between the number of large animal units and the farmland. The significance for cropping is, thus, clear.

Those households that are better endowed with land are relatively disinterested in small ruminants and poultry. For small, extremely small and marginal farms, keeping small animals is very important. These households obviously "invest" their manpower in the keeping and pasturing of small animals. The relative advantages of small ruminants, especially goats, lie (1) in their high reproduction rate; (2) in the small size of the animals which can use even minimal feed resources; (3) in their significance as a means of

Fig. 32: The Significance of Livestock Keeping for Various Holding-size Categories, 1983/84

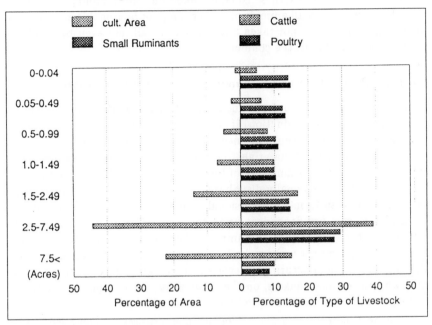

Source: [119] Government, 1986: p. 141, Tab. 1.1.

Note: For the numerical values, see Table 52 in the appendix. The figures refer to the percentage.

generating capital with greater mobility and good possibilities of liquidating; and (4) the good possibilities they offer to employ family members, in particular children, as manpower.

Small animals can be kept if (1) it is possible to utilize the household's *own* resources intensively and (2) if it is also possible to use *collective* resources. One's own land is hereby of secondary importance. That signifies that: (1) poultry runs around freely and also picks on the land of the neighbouring large farmers; and (2) communal grazing rights exist for the waysides and field boundaries, as well as for harvested fields (weeds, emerging seed and ratoon) and fallow land.

If limitations in these rights are not complied with – e.g., if grazing animals is not allowed on fields on which crops are grown and the crops must not be damaged – it gives rise to a large conflict potential. This leads,

133

e.g., to a "loss" of "boiling chickens" in the neighbour's pots and, under certain circumstances, to animal "prisons" from which it is expensive to bail the animals. Despite these facts, it should be kept in mind at this point that the keeping of small animals offers certain poor households an *economic niche* that, however, is not taken advantage of by all, not even by all of the poor households due to the conflict potential.

3.3.1.4   Production of Implements and Consumer Goods

Implements and consumer goods are produced by craftsmen (implement and consumer goods production) if specific craftsmanship skills and knowledge, as well as special tools, are necessary for their production.

Simple processing of materials to make implements and consumer goods takes place within the framework of the home. Since in this sphere the abilities and needs are unequally distributed, and at times one neighbour helps the other, the transition to professional activities are flowing. Whereas, for example, weavers are dependent upon the availability of a weaver's loom, a tinker at times only needs a hammer, pliers and charcoal, or a bamboo mat maker only needs a sharp knife. Weavers are usually found in fairly well-organized manufacturing enterprises, regionally concentrated and active, whereas cabinet-makers, on the other hand, travel around, if need be, and carry out work they are hired for.

The most important rural craftsmanship enterprises are complied in Figure 33 A. It presents the figures from a sample-survey and makes clear that all in all only approximately 6 % of all of the rural *households* are active in the craftsmanship sector, with or without an agricultural background. The most important craftsmanship occupations are the manufacturally organized weavers making up around 21 %; bamboo processing with 15 %; and fiber processing, mainly jute, with 7 %. Figure 33 B illustrates on the basis of the agricultural census (1983/84) the fact that members of the households carry out craftsmanship activities in only about 3 % of the households.

The number of rural/agricultural households that work in the craftsmanship production sector either as a main or sideline occupation is very small. For more than half of these households, the crafts are one of at least two economic "legs" they can stand on.

Figure 34 A clearly illustrates the fact that more than one-third of all of those households working in the crafts are indeed functionally landless and that much more than half cultivate farmland amounting to less than one acre; on the other hand, a considerable percentage of the households manage large farms in addition to their craftsmanship enterprises. Handicrafts and agriculture are, thus, at the level of the households not strictly

Fig. 33: Rural Craftsmen Enterprises, 1983/84

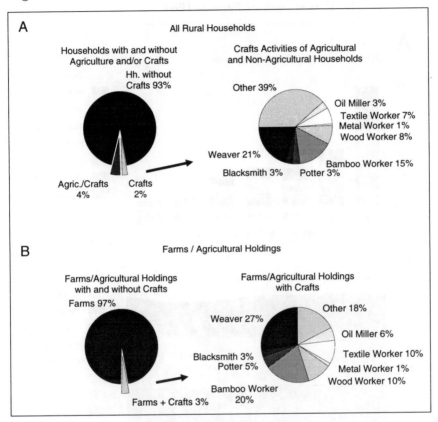

Source: A [125] Government, 1988: p. 433, Tab. 22,
   B [119] Government, 1986: pp. 61 ff., Tab. 26 and Tab. 28.
Note: For the numerical values, see Table 53 in the appendix.

segregated production sectors, but rather interwoven to a certain extent in those few households that are active at all in the handicrafts. However, an overproportional number of those households that work in the handicraft sector are landless or have only very little agricultural land at their disposal.

Figure 34 B illustrates the fact that the relative importance of the individual craftsmanship activities remains relatively constant throughout the individual holding-size categories. Striking differences can be established mainly in the case of smiths who, as a rule, do not run a farm as a second

Fig. 34: The Significance of Craftsmanship Production Within the Framework of Farms, 1984

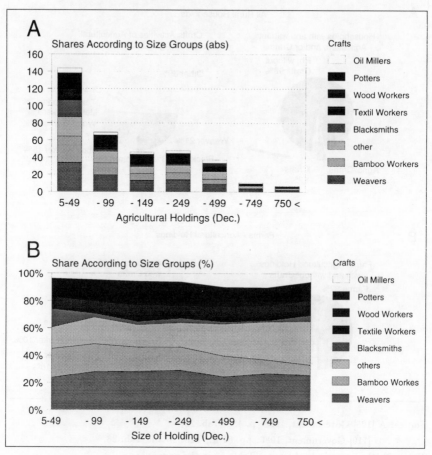

A

Shares According to Size Groups (abs)

Crafts
- Oil Millers
- Potters
- Wood Workers
- Textil Workers
- Blacksmiths
- other
- Bamboo Workers
- Weavers

Agricultural Holdings (Dec.)

B

Share According to Size Groups (%)

Crafts
- Oil Millers
- Potters
- Wood Workers
- Textile Workers
- Blacksmiths
- others
- Bamboo Workes
- Weavers

Size of Holding (Dec.)

Source: [125] Government, 1988: p. 433, Tab. 22.
Note: For the numerical values, see Table 54 in the appendix.

occupation. Those who work with bamboo, as a rule making mats, are also overproportionally represented among the household members of marginal or small farms. In contrast, members of larger agricultural households are *more likely* to be found in non-traditional handicrafts (the statistical residual category "others"): modern technical occupations (pump installer, pump technician, etc.) are to be counted among these.

136

The quantitatively significant weaver households, for example, can be both landless as well as relatively well-endowed with land. In this case there are evidently two categories: landowner households that have an adequate supply of production means in the form of land and looms at their disposal, and poor weavers who, if need be, work without any production means at their disposal.

The wide scope of handicraft products and the manifold uses for these products makes it seem inexpedient and inadequate to try to make a detailed categorization in implement and consumer goods production: smiths make both tools as well as cooking utensils; cabinet-makers make furniture, beams for the roofs, plows, etc., etc.

Handicraft skills, such as nearly all *women* possess – who however are not market or trade-oriented in their production, but rather household and subsistence oriented – are not recorded statistically. These skills, however, play an important role in the rural production system. For many jobs, manifold facets of special knowledge of the subject are necessary, no matter whether for working with loam (rough-casting, polishing, etc.), for mending clothing, processing the harvest (storage, drying, preparing), kitchen skills, all the way down to helping the men in their handicraft work, or taking care of the livestock on their own. Traditional jobs that the women have accepted or that are attributed to their role are only rarely included in statistics: they can hardly be assessed monetarily, and they are frequently "forgotten."

The literature available on this aspect is diametrically opposed to the economic importance of these household-internal, consume-oriented jobs that the women carry out on their own. The manifold home activities can, therefore, only be pointed out here. Processing the harvest appears to be quantitatively significant, in the sense of time spent working, in addition to the "reproductive activities" or taking care of the children and preparing food. The second threshing operation in the case of rice, parboiling it, drying, keeping it under surveillance, storing, husking, and cooking, as well as milking are jobs carried out by women. Furthermore, additional agricultural or garden yields have to be processed by the women. [221]

The activities carried out by *traders* also imply a number of productive activities that are, as a rule, statistically, empirically and, in many cases, also theoretically negated. "Unproductive (intermediate) trade" is not only responsible for the spatial movement and distribution, or collection of goods – for transport and marketing, in other words – but also for the value maintaining or upgrading activities such as packing, weighing and

---

221 Cf. for the "quantitative, and temporal" significance of these sectors, e.g., [83] Chen, 1986.
Furthermore, see the detailed discourse in [248] Martius-von Harder, 1978: pp. 96 ff.

measuring, sorting, storage, etc. In many cases it is also craftsmen, especially in the food processing sector, e.g., sugar baker, puffed-rice producers, maize roaster, etc., who help "market" their products as well as every agricultural producer who brings his produce directly to the market himself.

A description of these manifold craftsmanship, producing and processing activities that furnish many essential jobs as well as creating considerable additional value can only be indicated here and not gone into in detail. [222]

In summary, with respect to the handicraft production of implements and consumer goods, it should be kept in mind that the production activities are of relatively minor importance as *an independent, specialized* activity and enterprise. What has to be taken into consideration is, however, the significance of handicraft production as a supplementary and sideline for people working on farms. The household subsistence-oriented percentage of female handicraft production, which supplements the agricultural activities of the household community and supplies it with a reproductive basis, is wrongfully underestimated.

Thus, this supplies a production niche that (1) furnishes marginal or significant "income," whether by means of trading on the market, or present value gains and market value substitution. Simultaneously, they make it possible to (2) gainfully employ nonagricultural manpower and (3) to provide a functional basis for agricultural production, the distribution of produce and goods and their processing for consumption.

3.3.2 The Interconnectedness of the Production Sectors

The interdependence inherent in making available and furnishing certain volumes and quality of land, the plant production carried out on this land, the possibility of keeping livestock and the functional output of the implement and consumer goods production form an interdependent, seasonal and lifecycle and resource-dependent network of relations that lead to cyclic preperformances and subsequent utilization of one or the other area. The classical concepts of business/farm management regarding the manifold functional integration of branches opens up one's eyes to the rural production system and its interdependencies. What is important, however, is not only the functional interdependence, but rather the individual-strategical organization. The opportunities that are available to an individual in Bangladesh are essentially dependent upon the person's endowment with farmland, his

---

222 A detailed description of this complex field of nonagricultural activities can be found in [210] Kahrs, 1988; Kahrs, 1990 (in progress); [198] Jensen, 1983; [199] Jensen, 1987; [200] Jensen, Devnath, Das, 1984; and [201] Jensen, Paul, Devnath, Amin, 1983.

right to use rented land and the performance of those persons integrated in his economic community. The difference in the endowment with land leads to multiple and varying ways of organizing the "typical" production system and/or the production-strategical orientation of the household members. Thus, the individual "farm-size categories" demonstrate an – ideal typical – production strategical orientation they follow.

Marginal farms, which in principle only have a house garden at their disposal, do not use the land they have as farmland, but rather for planting fruit trees and other crop-yielding trees and cultivating vegetables. This can result in multi-stage and multi-seasonal as well as perennial mixed systems when, e.g., beans grow up a papaya tree which stands between betel nut palms. However, it is the members of such households with this type of farms who can only provide for themselves marginally off the land. If they cannot sell their manpower as hired labourers – a possibility that will be discussed in the following section – then they only have the possibility of taking up productive activities in household production, livestock keeping, handicrafts, or trade. This sector will also be treated in the following section.

The smallest farms – although they do indeed have a little land at their disposal that, however, does not suffice for them to exist from it alone – use their gardening land as a rule as intensively as the marginal farms in order to grow vegetables and try, at the same time, to also "produce" a little rice of their own, either for their own consumption, or to use as a "cash crop." These sales can, if need be, make it possible for them to buy larger amounts of another less expensive type of food.

The above-mentioned options available to the marginal farms, consisting of livestock and handicraft production, are relevant in this category as well. While it is still possible for the smallest farms to produce some of the plant biomass used for feed themselves, the marginal farms and the completely landless households are forced to use plant fodder resources that do not belong to them, but to which they have a right of access (communal utilization and grazing rights).

As a rule, these *small and smallest farms* use both their own fodder resources as well as communal resources. These consist of agricultural waste, plants growing on the waysides and the boundaries of the fields, as well as stubble pasture. Likewise, the "weeds" derived from weeding procedures can be used as fodder. Since this method of procuring fodder by means of intensive herding or weeding is extremely labour intensive, the opportunities are taken advantage of by (1) members of landless households and households with only very little land at their disposal whose utilization of "rests" is generally tolerated and (2) by households that are richly endowed with "cheap" manpower (low opportunity costs, e.g., children). In the case of

139

small-animal keepers, both factors are usually found together.

Large-animal keeping is of essential significance for *middle-sized and large farms* with respect to supplying the necessary draught animals for cultivating the fields. Their interest in small animals is relatively low since they (1) either have enough other more "productive" jobs for the family manpower; or (2) the children go to school (investments in human capital) and, hence, not enough manpower is available; or (3) the competition for marginal communal fodder resources that could cause conflicts is avoided. Nonetheless, small ruminants and poultry are also kept in these households, usually taken care of by women, children – insofar as they do not go to school – and hired hands ("permanent labourers"). The main interest and preference are given to the large animals. As a rule, the proportion between fodder basis within the farm and the draught animals is maintained. The principle of subsistence is the rule regarding fodder provision: fodder is only bought in extreme emergencies. The cattle and buffalo which provide draught power are integral components of the farm tillage system and household branch. Dairy cattle keeping and fattening calves can, however, be carried out above all by the poorer households, insofar as they succeed in maintaining sufficient rights of utilization and a secure fodder supply.

Livestock keeping, thus, takes place in an field of tension between the private and public fodder basis that itself is dependent upon the land disposition rights and the available manpower which is characterized by low performance and lacking alternative employment opportunities (children, older people and women).

The possibility of involvement in the craftsmanship sector demands either the utilization of what is produced within the household and farm itself, or an adequate demand for the product on the market outside the farm. Necessary are, in addition, adequate knowledge, skills and production equipment in order to produce goods of an adequate quality.

The engagement in this sector is particularly interesting for members of the landless households and those with little land at their disposal. People who are newly occupied in this sector have, however, to overcome the hurdles consisting of the necessary know-how and learning the required skills and the cost of procuring the necessary, more or less expensive production equipment.

Middle-sized farms tend to concentrate on the farm and cultivation of the crops. Garden and house production, the labourous keeping of small animals and the difficult engagement in nonagricultral sectors is, if possible, shifted in favour of intensive farming. This is dependent, however, not only upon the absolute endowment of the land, but rather also upon the available manpower among the household members, as well as on the yield situation.

Tab. 6:   Rural Job Fields with and without Pluriactivities in a Micro-region in the District of Bogra, 1986

Households Active in (N = 925)	Households Active in this Field (%)	Significance of the Side-line Activity per Field (%)
Agriculture	77.9	
Out of which:		100.0
Without Other Jobs		33.4
+ Paid Labour		32.5
+ Nonagri. Activity		28.6
+ Paid Labour + Nonagri.		5.5
Paid Labour	47.5	
Out of which:		100.0
Without Other Jobs		32.8
+ Agriculture		53.3
+ Nonagri. Activity		4.8
+ Agircul. + Nonagri.		9.1
Nonagricultural Job	29.7	
Out of which:		100.0
Without Other Jobs		2.9
+ Agriculture		74.9
+ Paid Labour		7.6
+ Agricul. + Nonagri.		14.5
Miscellaneous	3.3	

Source: Basic survey of the Bangladesh-Project + sample survey, compiled and calculated by F. Kahrs, Institute of Rural Development, 1990, cf. [211] Kahrs, 1991.

Frequently it is the *large farms* that have enough wealth at their disposal so that they have sufficient capital or can mobilize enough capital – without endangering the household or farm – with which to invest in "industrial" enterprises or urban trade activities. Under certain circumstances, the households also invest part of their wealth in political careers. This may lead to access to more production resources, or to an education for the children with further expected advantages.

Table 6 illustrates, partly in anticipation of the following section, the quantitative significance of nonagricultural activities carried out by members of rural households and the proportional relations. Whereas nearly 80 % of the 925 households in one surveyed region were engaged in some way in their own *agricultural* production – whereby farming, gardening and livestock keeping are not broken down –, at the same time nearly 50 % of

141

Tab. 7: Number of Households with Rural Nonagricultural Activities with and without Pluriactivities in the District of Bogra, 1986

Households with Non-agricultural Activities (N = 275):	Households in this Sector (N)	Significance of the Activities (%)
Only Handicrafts	102	37.1
Only Trade	112	40.7
Only Services	16	5.8
Handicrafts and Trade	27	9.8
Handicrafts and Services	8	2.9
Trade and Services	5	1.8
Handicrafts, Trade and Services	5	1.8
Total	275	100.0

Source: Sample survey, compiled and calculated by F. Kahrs, Institute of Rural Development, 1990.

Note: For details on the classification and theoretical findings and implications, see the study carried out by F. Kahrs at the Institute of Rural Development, 1990 (cf. [211] Kahrs, 1991).

the households are active as agricultural and nonagricultural wage laboureres and, overlapping, nearly 30 % in the field of nonagricultural independent activities. Table 7 breaks down the nonagricultural activities according to handicraft (production), trade and services, while ignoring agriculture and paid labour.

Summarizing, one can state that it is possible to clearly illustrate (1) which complex, interdependent network of functionally significant activities can be found with respect to production in rural Bangladesh; (2) which possibilities they can offer the individual and how the multiple production system they generate is organized; and (3) how the shortage of land leads to more intense utilization of the land, to strategic differentiation in the employment of manpower for the use of the land and to taking advantage of marginal niches in the nonagricultural production sector.

The description of the multiple productive activities already made clear the fact that a certain number of households earn their living in trade (the exchange of goods) with other households and from various paid jobs and services (the exchange of work and special know-how and skills). Agricultural production and product "marketing" are also dependent upon interaction and transactions with other households. These and further aspects of

142

exchange will be discussed in the following chapter: (1) land exchange, (2) manpower exchange, (3) capital exchange and (4) income exchange, as well as (5) the interdependence between these aspects.

3.4 Exchange: Who Buys and Sells What, How and from Whom and to Whom?

The endowment of the households forces the individual members living in them to use specific production and resource-utilization strategies, or makes it possible for them to use these. At the very latest when discussing the frequently deficient consume level that is reached by the individuals and their household and family communities, it will become clear that the *production resource utilization* strategies are not always successful. In this case, redistribution claims between people, households and classes become important, which for their part determine the distribution system of the overall society.

3.4.1 The Contingencies of Exchange

Before redistribution strategies can be carried out, those strategies are important with which the individual people try to exchange their individual or household resources: (1) in return for production resources and means that, up to this point, allow an optimal allocation and utilization of the resources at their disposal; (2) in return for consumer goods that directly serve the provision and reproduction of the people, e.g., food; and (3) in return for money that opens up unlimited possible decisions for the individual as long as the need is not acute. [223]

Such exchange relations – which are occasionally interdependent in a multitude of diverse ways in which giving and taking happens over an extended period of time in the form of long-term interaction – are themselves dependent (1) upon the network of relations that controls each individual and (2) upon the resources that he has "to offer." In the case of many resources, the purpose for utilizing them is not fixed a priori, and the act of exchanging and/or the implied interaction and transaction are always just part of a multiple, interdependent, material and immaterial process. Keeping this in mind, typical exchange interactions and relations will be *serparately* described in the following in a first step so that their mutual interdependence can be elaborated later on. These are the exchange of (1)

---

223 The term "exchange" implies in its most general form merely "give and take" and gaining and giving something away in exchange. This does not say whether the exchange is balanced, symmetrical, just, monetary, material, or the opposite. The criterion is merely that it, in the game-theory sense, achieves a "bartering result." Included are the concepts of gifts, purchasing and sales, fraud, appropriation, etc.

land by means of buying and selling it as well as various forms of tenancy (*exchange of land*), (2) labour for wages or on the basis of a two-way agreement (*exchange of labour*), (3) capital in the material form of production equipment and goods and in the form of credit (*exchange of capital*), as well as of, lastly, (4) various products and consumer goods (*exchange of income*).

3.4.1.1 Exchange of Land

The access, utilization and property rights to and in arable land are limited, and – as already mentioned – unequally distributed. The distribution of the rights of utilization and each person's initial endowment is historically and politically determined by the settlement of the area and is an individually, collectively and progressively or degressively ongoing dynamic process. [224]

Purchases and sales of land lead to the final and permanent transfer of *property rights*. *Tenancy* implies the temporary transfer of *specific utilization rights*. Every individual is interested in becoming his own landlord and owning his own house, i.e. in gaining disposition of land – also with respect to social position and materializing the desired religiously based life style. If this cannot be achieved on the basis of purchasing the desired objects, then tenancy is an acceptable second-best alternative.

The key mechanism for obtaining land is its transfer by means of *inheritance* - i.e., from the parents' generation to the descendants. The basic rule of the rights governing inheritance stipulate that sons and daughters inherit separately, but equally among the genders, whereby each son receives twice as large a share as a daughter after the widow has received one-eighth beforehand. Women generally renounce their rights to and utilization of their share of the land they inherit, although not always, because it (1) is frequently located in their father's distant village and (2) it preserves the right for them to return in case of divorce or becoming a widow. Each person inherits – insofar as it is available – a share of their parents' land and, hence, gains at this time at the latest a more or less sufficient resource basis. The increase in the number of people and, thus, heirs leads, however, generally from generation to generation to continually absolute smaller shares. Since the beginning of the 20th century, the number of people and, hence, heirs has grown fourfold. This has consequences that will be discussed in the following chapter on system dynamics.

State allocation of land within the framework of the allocation programme for "state land" (alluvial land, land for which no taxes were paid

---

224 The various forms of exchange and transactions will be presented in a first step. The consequences for the system and process will be discussed in Chapter 4.1.

over a certain amount of time) (*khās*) only plays a subordinate role. [225] Redistribution has not taken place to date within the framework of land reform, nor is it in sight. Furthermore, it is doubtful whether the effort would be justified because in the case of an – unrealistic – radical equal distribution on the basis of the 1978 census of landownership each household would have received 1.63 acres of land. Today it would probably only amount to about 1 acre. [226]

The usurpation of land by force is frequently described in village studies – i.e., it happens continually and everywhere – but a quantitative evaluation does not take place. The reason for such usurpation is, as a rule, ambiguous land titles. This happens, under certain circumstances, if (1) state *khās-land* is utilized on the basis of customary rights and then allocated to interested parties because they either pay higher bribes, or because they are allocated the land within the framework of a programme that they, as they are usually poor, cannot enforce. Forceful usurpation can also take place when (2) inheritance regulations or utilization rights of women are not clearly defined and this results in a conflict in the second or third generation, (3) invalid or fraudulent contracts are made and (4) the boundaries of the property are manipulated. [227]

The issue of such conflicts depends upon the existing and documented land titles, on the social and economic power position and "feelings of honour" (*izzāt*) of the involved parties who either try to enforce their will using every possible means – from falsifying documents, over physical brawls, to expensive court cases and murder – or who want to maintain the "good name" of their family and withhold themselves honourably from such actions. [228] In addition, the general conditions of social and political stability or unrest can also promote the tendency to use force to enforce interests and usurp land, or block it.

As a rule – except in the case of inheritance – transferring property titles takes place on the basis of *legal contracts*. The quantity of land that

---

225 Cf. on the "Land Redistribution Programme" [287] Rahman, Rahman, Islam, 1983.
226 For more details see [341] Wennergren, 1986: p. 78 f.
227 For the significance of arguments concerning land see, e.g.: [147] Herbon, 1984: p. 260 ff., p. 407, Tab. 88, and p. 409, Tab. 92, who shows that approximately 50 % of all of the serious conflicts in a village can be traced back to disputes involving land.
  See furthermore [197] Jansen, 1983: p. 215 ff., who describes individual cases and causes, as well as [37] Arens and Beurden, 1977: p. 140 ff.
228 [197] Jansen, 1983: p. 236.
  "We noted that as a mechanism for the transfer of land, the amount of land gained through disputes is small compared with the amount which is transferred through inheritance and sales." ([197] Jansen 1983: p. 236).

changes owners in this fashion is not registered in the national statistics, and empirical data from village studies in the form of "balances of land transfer" generally include the effects of the partitioning of the estate and the increase in the population as well as the transfers resulting from purchases and sales. [229]

The empirical data on a trend towards purchasing and selling land are partially contradictory. Herbon [230] registered the fact that during a period covering 1971 to 1980, approximately one-third of all of the households in one village had been involved in at least one land transaction, and the number of "winners" and "losers" was nearly balanced over all of the individual landownership-size categories.

In most of the other studies, a trend has been documented that shows that better situated landowners tend to purchase land from the poorer households. Jaim [231] reported that during the period from 1974 to 1979 (a period of crisis), the small farms (0 - 2 acres) sold in the end twice as much land as they purchased. In the case of middle-sized farms (2 - 4 acres), this relation was reversed. And in the case of the large farms (4 > acres), approximately eight times as much land was bought as sold, whereby this group, which represents only 11 % of the farms, was responsible for buying in absolute figures nearly half of all of the newly acquired land. Ahmed, [232] presents similar data by showing that during the period from 1972 to 1981, small farms tended to sell land, while the large farms evidently bought land. All in all, however, only 20 % of all of the households were involved in land transactions. Thereby it turned out at the same time that in one village in which irrigation technology had been introduced the middle-sized farms (3 - 5 acres) had taken over 50 % of the land that had been sold, while in a village without irrigation, it was the large farms (5 - 7 acres). In both villages, over 50 % of the total land that had been sold sold had been sold by small farms (< 1 acres).

Spinatsch [233] shows in that just under two-thirds of the households in a village he surveyed the situation with respect to the volume of the originally inherited land had worsened, whereby the necessity to sell was evidently *independent* of the size of the household or farm. [234] The general trend,

---

229 In the following Chapter 4.1, see the discussion on the development of village landownership and farmland conditions.
230 [147] Herbon, 1984: p. 158 and p. 372 f., Tab. 29 and Tab. 30.
231 [194] Jaim, 1985: p. 235.
232 [14] Ahmed, 1987: p. 11, Tab. II.
233 [322] Spinatsch, 1984: p. 244 f.
234 Cf. with respect to this complex of the dynamics of land purchases and sales also [38] Arn, 1986: p. 43 f., and [16] Ahmed, 1984: p. 73 ff. Ahmed compares the development of three samples in three villages that were developing (1) on the basis of the "Comilla

thus, seems to indicate a general loss of land among the landowner groups who own approximately 1 acre, and an increase among the groups with larger amounts of land. This, however, needs to be qualified. Two effects break this trend: (1) innovations based on irrigation technology raise (a) the yields and the economic stamina of the small farms because of higher profits and (b) the incomes of farmworker households who can, hence, buy one or the other plot of land. (2) External income (migrant workers, "foreign" workers) raise the financial power of the poorer households who can then, under certain circumstances, invest in land. [235]

Selling land is frequently the last means with which funds can be procured in order to satisfy consumer needs, [236] but it can definitely hit the more well-to-do as well.

The demand for land backed by purchasing power developes in connection with the dynamics of local production potentials that are dependent upon the introduction of technological innovations and the possibility of investing externally generated income in land. [237] The increases in land prices controls at the same time the height of the rent demanded. This is

Cooperatives," (2) the "Open Market Programme" and (3) without external support. In all three samples he registered a redistribution of the land in favour of the larger households. His methodological approach, however, was characterized by the general problem that affects all studies, namely that no real longitudinal-study data was utilized, and the effects of the population growth were not registered. The statements are indeed not false respecting their basic trend. The land purchase balances are based on memory: it is true that the probability that a landowner would forget such an important event as purchasing or selling land is very slight; however, it cannot be excluded, particularly in the case of large landowners. In addition there is also the fact that the willingness to supply information on such things that are closely connected with prestige varies to a great extent. There is a *strong tendency to be secretive about land sales*: this trend is more pronounced among the wealthy, prestige-oriented people and their households than among the poor. At times, the stressing of the severeness of the problem may also be a means of making claims on the researcher (indirectly, the government) or on the landlords.

The information on this topic must, in other words, be carefully interpreted, especially as the conditions seem to definitely vary or be diametrically opposed from village to village, from region to region and from period to period.

Cf. with respect to land transfers, e.g., also [21] Alam, 1983: p. 73 ff.

235 Cf. [38] Bhaduri, Rahman, and Arn, 1986, and the literature they analyzed. [16] Ahmed, 1984: p. 73 f., who unfortunately does not give any absolute values, clearly demonstrates that freely available and adequate means of production slow down the process in which land is sold (out).

236 Cf. [16] Ahmed, 1984: p. 68, who in addition to the population growth statistically registered "acute scarcity of consumption and production resources amongst vulnerable sections of poor farmers who are forced to sell land during critical times and thus become landless or nearly landless."

237 Cf. [16] Ahmed, 1984: p. 78 ff.

because the general increase in the value of the land due to increased productivity in the case of theoretical self-management raises the demands of the landlords, [238] just as they expect higher prices when selling land.

The general trend is that the increasing multitude of landless has less and less chance of buying land because the increases in the prices for land exceed by far the increases in the factor income from work alone - i.e., the percentage of capital among the total factor income has greatly increased. [239]

The permanent acquisition of land by means of purchasing it is only one possibility of "exchanging" the key production factor which, furthermore, in view of the increasing prices is continually more difficult for the poor and financially weak. The most significant form of gaining the right to use land is tenancy in all of its various forms and diverse conditions. These possibilities, however, are in the process of disappearing. [240]

Figure 35 illustrates the fact that the farmland used by small farms consists to nearly one-fourth of leased land (22.4 %), while the land used by the large farms includes merely up to one-tenth (9.9 %) leased land. *Sharecropping arrangements* (*bargā*) [241] are agreed upon for over 72 % of the total leased land that is cultivated. Thereby sharecropping on a fifty-fifty basis in which the yield is split equally and the tenant fincances the majority of the inputs (*bargādār*) is the most predominant form (64.5 %). In only rare cases does one find sharecropping conditions based on a 1/3 or 2/3 split, and in such cases complicated local conditions, special agreements, etc., are the reasons behind the arrangement.

Other forms of tenancy [242] such as fixed rent (*chāunia*), monetary leas-

---

238 Cf. [16] Ahmed, 1984: p. 80 f., who statistically demonstrated the correlation without elaborating the causality. Thus, contrary to his implications, the developments in the prices for land are *not causes* for the developments in the rent prices, but rather the general increase in soil productivity in many places is reflected in both the prices for land and rent. The situation is aggravated by the fact that the number of people and their demand for land is growing. It should be mentioned, however, that the prices are only relevant with respect to the demand of the well-to-do with respect to (rented) land, and not the absolute demand. And the demand on the part of the well-to-do has grown in real terms and caused the prices to explode.

239 The difference in the development of the demand for land on the part of those wealthy enough to pay for it and the need for land as a result of the increasing population pressure cannot be dealt with at this point. Furthermore, it will also not be possible to deal with the development of the market-integrated forms of farming that demand more capital, etc., and the question as to whether a political perspective is really involved in the subsistence-guaranteeing self-management of marginal farms can also not be treated in detail.

240 Cf. Chapter 4.1.4, p. 236.

241 The conditions and significance of the various forms of tenancy will be discussed in detail further on (p. 154).

242 Cf. footnote 241

ing, pledging (*bandak*), usufruct (*khāi khālāśi*) and other local and personal arrangements affect only about 27 % of the leased land and about 3 % of the farmland.

Figure 36, in which the relative percentage of the farmland is compiled respecting diverse individual holding-size categories, illustrates the relative percentages of farmland used under sharecropping agreements and the other tenancy arrangements. This makes above all clear the fact that it is the small farmers who cultivate a relatively large *relative percentage* of leased land on the basis of tenancy in general, and sharecropping in particular. Figure 36 shows that the *relative importance* of tenancy in its various forms does indeed decrease successively for small farms, then middle-sized farms and large farms. Figure 37, however, shows that the *absolute* area per farm in the case of sharecropping and other tenancy forms increases up to the size category of up to 5 acres and doubles thereby from size category to size category. Only in the size categories above that does the absolute percentage of leased land decrease again. Approximately two-thirds of the leased land is cultivated by farms belonging to the size category of 1.5 to 5.0 acres, and in each of these size categories, just under half of all of the farms are involved in tenancy arrangements. These are indications of the fact that the status of the tenants cannot necessarily be compared to that of being dependent because farmers who cultivate an area of 3 acres are certainly not "dependent" in the socio-political sense.

Various forms of tenancy have diverse economic and social implications which will be briefly sketched in the following discussion.

Sharecropping and yield splitting at a ratio of 1 : 1 is the dominant leasing arrangement that includes just under two-thirds of the tenancy relations. This "dominant" and "classical" form of tenancy has received a great deal of attention, whereby the implicit dependencies, on the one hand, and the economic inefficiency, on the other hand, were the focal points of attention. [243]

The basic principle of tenancy is based on the agreement that the landlord supplies land and the tenant his labour. As a rule, the tenants were expected to supply draught power and seed under the traditional low-input conditions. [244] If expensive modern inputs are utilized, there is a tendency

---

243 Cf. [100] Ellis, 1988.
244 Cf. with respect to the splitting ratios of inputs and yields, e.g., [147] Herbon, 1984: p. 149 ff., p. 368 f., Tab. 22, Tab. 23; [160] Hossain, 1979: p. 18 f.; [174] Husain, 1985: p. 26,f.; [213] Kashem, 1988: p. 52 ff.; [281] Rahman 1986: p. 160 ff.; and [322] Spinatsch, 1984: p. 199 ff.
On the general significance of transaction costs see, e.g., [72] Bössmann, 1982, and the literature cited there.

Fig. 35: Percentage of Farmland and Leased Land According to Type of Lease and Holding-size Category, 1983/84

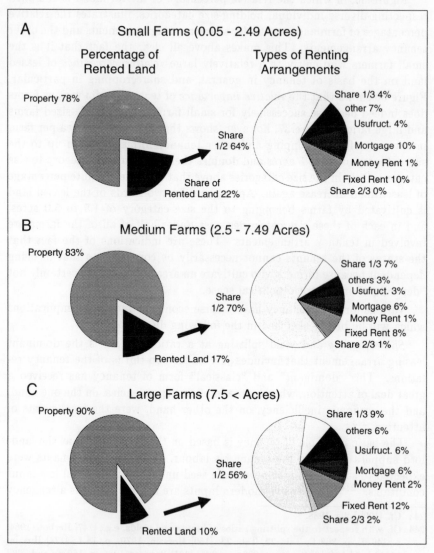

Source: [125] Government, 1988: p. 34 ff., Tab. 34, 35, 36; p. 339, Tab. 5.
Note: For the numerical values, see Table 55 in the appendix.

Fig. 36: Relative Percentages of Rented land among the Farm-land Cultivated by Tenants and All Other Farms According to Holding-size Category, 1983/84

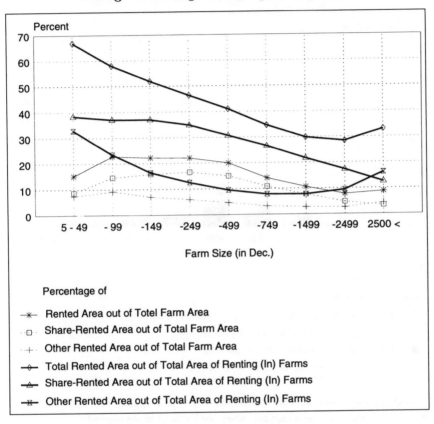

Source: Based on [125] Government, 1988: p. 139, Tab. 1; and p. 339, Tab. 5.
Note: For the numerical values, see Table 56 in the appendix.

to split the inputs. Basically, these are water, fertilizers and seed. Under the conditions of modern production, however, there are also an increasing number of basic changes in the tenancy arrangements in which (1) either land, labour and water are paid each at the rate of *one-third*, or (2) in which land and water are paid in an arrangement based on a *fixed percentage* oriented approximately on the thirds arrangement, and the tenant bears both the risk of loss as well as the chance of achieving a higher yield.

Fig. 37: Absolute Percentage of Leased Land Among the Land Utilized by Tenants and All Farms, According to Holding-size Category, 1983/1984

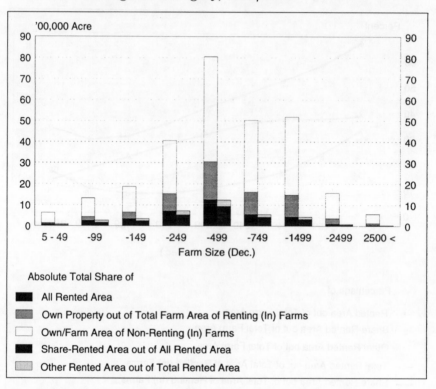

Source: [125] Government, 1988: p. 139, Tab. 1; and p. 339, Tab. 5.
Note: With respect to the numerical values, see Table 57 in the appendix.

As a rule, sharecropping arrangements that are not fixed in writing and, thus, for which there is no established right are valid for the period of one year. They can be prolonged each year. That can go on for more than 10, or even 20 years. This relative "insecurity with respect to tenancy" is regarded as the reason why investments in melioration and soil quality are not made, or not made to a great enough extent. The fifty-fifty ratio is also given the blame for the fact that the tenants employ the factors that he controls *suboptimally*. This is explained by the fact that for each factor employment that he makes, he receives only one-half of the increased yield (profit). In particular, the employment of additional manpower and expensive modern inputs that cost more than 50 % of the entire inputs is avoided. [245] The deficiency in productivity in such forms of farming increasingly results in (1) either the landlord sharing half of the expenses for modern inputs, (2) a transition to fixed rent arrangements being made, or (3) the factor percentages – in irrigated cultivation – being split in thirds (see above): (a) water and modern inputs, (b) land and (c) manpower and draught.

The importance of sharecropping seems to be decreasing, [246] but the trend towards decreasing importance has not been clearly established. It seems as if relations in which clear, fixed and, if the opportunity arises, monetary factor payments are possible are becoming more attractive. On the other hand, modern methods of farming demand in any case a higher, usually financial, contribution of the, sometimes, poor tenants who are frequently overtaxed and unattractive as tenants and, thus, are forced from the tenancy market.

The advantages of sharecropping for the sharecropper are (1) the fact that it supplies him with an opportunity to have *any land at all at his disposal* in view of a "land market" in which the demand has a tendency to be greater than the supply and, thus, gives the landlord a very strong market position. (2) The second advantage is the fact that *cash requirements are relatively low* and *factor payment does not have to be made until after the harvest has been brought in* when it is possible to make the payment out of the yield, and it is not necessary to take up credit. [247] (3) The risks in case of crop failure are split so that the rent can also be adjusted and decreased correspondingly.

The disadvantages of sharecropping are (1) that in the case of additional modern inputs a fifty-fifty sharing ratio must be agreed upon and institutionalized. This is not always successful and demands a long process of negotiating before it can be enforced. In order to do so, sharecropping has to be based on *economic deliberations*. It can be presumed that this is increasingly the case. In the case of purely feudal sharecropping relations in which socio-political dependency is their basis, structures arise that are in a normative-economic sense inefficient and in a normative social sense power structures that do not conform to modern ideals. (2) Compensation for

---

245 Cf. [7] Ahmad, 1984: p. 129 ff., who presents a discourse on this discussion, and [100] Ellis, 1988: p. 144 ff., who presents a general theoretical overview.

246 [147] Herbon, 1984: p. 370, Tab. 24.; [281] Rahman, 1986: p. 154 ff.; and [316] Siddiqui, 1982: p. 162 f.

247 The fact that the tenants may have to make considerable debts until the harvest is brought in so that they can (1) satisfy their consumer needs and (2) prepay limited inputs does not change the basic fact that at least the deferred payment of the rent is advantageous.

risks, long-term investments and skills are only rewarded to the amount of 50 %. On the other hand, they are the basic conditions that a sharecropper must meet in order to stand up to the conditions of hard competition in a limited land market.

The advantages and motivation for the sharecropper's landlord lie in the following facts: (1) he does not have to cultivate plots of land that are located a considerable distance away, which would constitute the risks of the harvest being stolen and high transport costs. (2) Primarily, there is hardly any need for capital. (3) It is possible to gain an income in kind from the land and be independent of the market without employing one's own manpower in agriculture. (4) It is not necessary to instruct and supervise the tenant's daily activities, which saves time.

Sharecropping is, in other words, also in Bangladesh not necessarily a semi-feudal venture, but rather it can arise on the basis of a specific combination of available factors and allocation needs that can definitely be optimal and expedient. In addition to landlord-feudal relations, there is also a large number of economically motivated sharecropping arrangements based on individual interests and correspondingly efficient resource allocation. Indeed it is in many cases the large landlords who lease land under the conditions of a sharecropping agreement, but these are also sometimes absentee landlords. In many cases, however, it is also the middle-sized and smaller farms which lease out land due to economic reasons. [248] Frequently social considerations are also the motivation for leasing land among relatives as sharecropping land. The parents secure, for example, their "old age pension" by leasing their land to their sons who work the land as sharecroppers. Bothers who look for employment as migrant labourers leave their land to be cultivated by their siblings who remain behind in return for a share of the harvest in order to guarantee their subsistence if they are unsuccessful in looking for work, etc., etc.

The advantages listed above cannot be achieved in every single case for both parties, particularly in the case of poor farmers who are confronted by a shortage in the means of production such as their own labour capacity, or efficient draught animals, or the will to enter an allegiance. In many cases, sharecropping is not interesting due to economic reasons, as has already been mentioned. Thus, each of the remaining forms of tenancy has its assets and comparative advantages.

1. *Cash tenancy* ("lease") [249] plays a marginal role and refers generally

---

248 Unfortunately there are no national statistics on this subject. Cf., however, [147] Herbon, 1984: p. 393, Tab. 66.

249 The difference between the various forms of tenancy is not always clear-cut: thus, among other things, "leasing" is used as a term for tenancy in general.

to pieces of land with buildings on them and monetary rent.

2. *Fixed rent* (*chāuniā*) means that a specific volume of rent in kind has to be paid after the harvest has been brought in. This arrangement is particularly interesting under the conditions of input-intensive farming (1) because it does not tie down any financial means that are needed for other inputs and (2) because the obligations can be calculated and the person farming the land is responsible for the risks and profits. This system can be found, under certain circumstances, during the irrigation season, while the same piece of land is either cultivated by the owner himself or sharecropped during the rainy season.

3. *Usufruct* (*khāi khālāsi*) is a functionally mixed system in which an acute financial means requirement in the case of the lessor fall together with a demand for land on the part of the lessee and is simultaneously accompanied by a high level of liquidity. Thus a sum of money is "lent," and payment as well as an implicitly agreed upon interest are paid back on the basis of a temporary limited transfer of the right to use a piece of land over a period covering several years. The annual remuneration can be regarded by the person renting the land as a form of an advance monetary payment. [250]

4. *Pledging* (*bandak*) basically serves the same goal as the "usufruct" regulations. In this case, however, only the interest and not the "loan" is paid back on the basis of a temporary transfer of the utilization of the land. This system, which has not been mentioned in the relevant literature in recent years, [251] can therefore lead to the fact that the loan is never paid back due to a lack of the production resource land. Thus the land that has been "pledged" cannot be reclaimed and may have to be sold following new loans. This system, however, is disappearing because, firstly, Islamic religious concepts do not allow this procedure and, secondly, the landlord who is in financial trouble can find better conditions.

In addition to these four essential, institutionalized tenancy arrangements, there are a number of individual and local special forms. Thus the "tenancy rates," the modalities of payment, the length of tenancy, the implicit additional or already earlier transacted transfers, performances and demands are very specific in each case and, furthermore, still dependent

---

The differentiation between leasing and credit relations is also frequently more of a theoretical undertaking because the factor that motivates one side may be to give up resources in exchange for land. The other side may need the rent payments pressingly in order to acquire production means. The exchange with its multiple interactions and transactions can always be regarded from several angles, and it always contains more than two components.

250 Inflation, discounting, compound interest and such considerations are not included here.

251 Cf. in this respect [245] Maloney, Ahmed, 1988: p. 48.

Fig. 38: Rent Balance According to Holding-size Category, 1983/84

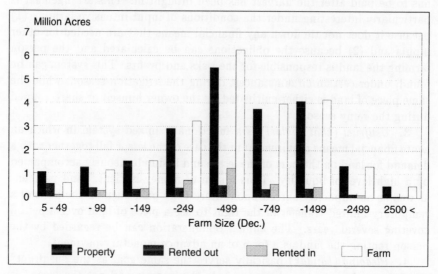

Source: [125] Government 1988: p. 139, Tab. 2.
Note: For the numerical values, see Table 59 in the appendix.

upon (1) employment alternatives, (2) cost of wages in the case of the alternative owner occupancy, (3) local power structures, etc.

People with farms belonging to all of the farm-size categories try to rent land under various conditions, whereby, however, the specific individual dependency upon additional rented land decreases with increasing size of the person's own land. This does not negate the possibility that local market power structures can lead to inequality and injustice, [252] but it does show that in the case of the arrangements multifarious individual interests find a more or less satisfactory balance. This balance can, under certain circumstances, appear to be irrational or inefficient on the basis of purely monetary, economic cost-benefit perspectives if land is transferred on the basis of usufruct and, simultaneously, the same piece of land is taken back under the conditions of sharecropping.

---

252 "Sharecroppers are often forced into debt, because their income from cultivation, after the landlord had deducted his share and more, was scarcely adequate for the family to survive on for the year. Since their landlords were also their creditors, debt bondage reinforced the dependency relationship of sharecropper and landlord." ([93] Cooper, 1983: p. 240).

As a matter of fact, however, it is difficult to judge the sharecropping arrangements because these relations are frequently found together along with other relations with the same person. Credit relations, protection and security, working relations and factional alliances that are carried on for years and sometimes even generations establish, under certain circumstances, a hierarchic, vertical and social, economic and political network between the landlord and tenant that encompasses much more than mere sharecropping relations. [253] On the other hand, the fact that (1) large and especially middle-sized farms also sharecrop significant absolute areas (as can be seen in Figure 37), and (2) small landlords also rent-out land (as can be seen in Figure 38) shows that, to a large extent, these arrangements are based on allocation-functional, economic benefit considerations. The tenancy balance presented in Figure 38 clearly shows that both small and large landowners hand over land to the middle-sized farmers. Hence, neither the "groups" of tenants nor the landlords can be regarded as being homogeneous.

3.4.1.2 Manpower Exchange

The exchange of manpower is implicit in tenancy arrangements, particularly in the case of sharecropping arrangements. The tenant supplies his manpower, which practically means that he "employs himself." This form of utilizing manpower on one's own farm on additionally rented land is very important for the majority of the small and smallest farms (cf. Figure 35 once again). Absolutely they have, however, only a small portion of the entire rented land available for farming at their disposal (cf. Figure 37). The category-size internal proportions between rented and own land, however, remain approximately constant when taking all farms into consideration (cf. Figure 36).

Rented land and the resulting possibility of self-employment has, however, also consequences respecting the labour market for "wage" earners. This is true both in the case of the rural areas as well as urban areas and with respect to the relative figure referring to employment opportunities and the level of the wages.

The percentage of those "mainly" employed in agriculture among the total national number of employees amounts at the time to approximately 56 %, and the percentage of those in rural areas who are mainly employed in nonagricultural jobs amount to approximately 32 %. [254]

---

253 Cf., e.g., [93] Cooper, 1983: p. 240; and [147] Herbon, 1984: p. 148 ff.
254 The percentages refer to the total number of those who are really active economically
     – 29,975,000 – and not to the total potential number of people amounting to about
     40 million. I.e., women and the housework they carry out is, as usual, unfortunately

Fig. 39: Index of Employment Relations, 1984/85

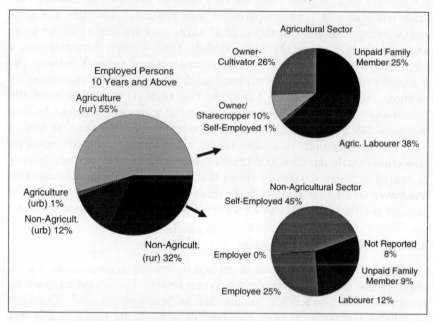

Source: [122] Government 1988: p 74, Tab. 20.
Note: For the numerical values, see Table 60 in the appendix.

The percentage of farmhands employed in the *agricultural sector* among the economically active population amounts to about one-third (38 %), which corresponds in principle to the number of landless households. Cultivation of the land in the form of cultivation of one's own land and/or rented land and in the form of purely directive activities (landlords who do not cultivate the land themselves) employs a second third. In addition, a fourth (25 %) of all of the people employed in agriculture consists of family members who lend a helping hand. [255]

In the *nonagricultural sector* in rural areas, the percentage of those who are "self-employed," including "employers," [256] among those active in this area is just under half (45 %). Dependently employed wage earners (*coolies*

---

neglected.

255 Family members that help on the farm are unfortunately only registered as "unpaid family workers."

256 The difference in the definition is unfortunately not elaborated upon in the statistics. A self-employed employer is evidently meant.

among others) and white-collar workers make up more than one-third (about 37 %), and the rest of those employed in this sector are made up of family workers who also work on the farm.

It is thus clear that in the rural areas of Bangladesh part, approximately *one third, of all of the job opportunities consist of nonagricultural jobs –* trade, handicrafts, services, administrative and wage work.

Tab. 8:   **Employment Status According to Gender in Rural Areas, 1984/85**

Economically Active Population People Over 10 Years of Age	Both Genders		Men		Women	
	in Thou.	(%)	in Thou.	(%)	in Thou.	(%)
Total Population	67213		34307		32906	
Rural Population Of These:	58394	100.0	29366	100.0	29028	100.0
Working	24946	42.7	22850	77.8	2096	7.2
On Leave	24	0.0	24	0.1	-	-
Housework	22241	38.1	93	0.3	22148	76.3
Schooling	8265	14.2	5023	17.1	3242	11.2
Unemployed	401	0.7	268	0.9	133	0.5
Retired	364	0.6	175	0.6	189	0.7
Ill, disabled	1135	1.9	454	1.5	681	2.3
Recipient of Transfer Remittances	1018	1.7	479	1.6	539	1.9

Source: [122] Government, 1988: p. 55, Tab. 11.

Table 8 discloses the type of employment with respect to people old enough to work who are 10 years of age or older. If one adds together the number of "employed" people, usually men, and the "houseworkers," usually women, then it becomes clear that approximately 80 % of the rural population – which makes up 85 % of the total population – is "economically active." The unemployed, elderly, the ill and welfare recipients, as well as those still receiving an education or training, make up approximately 20 %. The division of the economic activities in "houseworking" women and "employed" men also becomes clear.

Those people who are not in a position to work on their own farm or in handicrafts, trade, or services, have to sell their manpower, i.e. *work for wages* in the agricultural or nonagricultural sectors. Table 9 shows that

Tab. 9: Index Numbers on Employment Situation of Hired Labourers, 1984/85

	Number of People		Working Hours		Wage Sum (Tk)		Working Hours per Week	Day's Wage (Tk)
	Thou.	(%)	Thou.	(%)	Thou.	(%)		
Agricultural Paid Work:	6400	77.8						
Men	6280	76.3	343879	76.6	124360	71.9	55	20
Women	120	1.5	5729	1.3	1739	1.0	48	14
Non-Agricultural Paid Work:	* 1005	22.2						
Men	* 843	19.3	88441	19.7	44422	25.7	56	28
Women	* 162	2.9	11016	2.5	2381	1.4	47	11
Bangladesh	8228		449065		172902			

Source: [122] Government, 1988: p. 86 f. Tab. 28, Tab. 30.
Note: The values with asterix (*) refer to the rural areas / sector only.

paid jobs is a men's domain. There are some women, however, especially in the cities, who do work for wages. The percentage of women among those working for wages is, however, very small and amounts to only 4.4 % for all of Bangladesh and makes up merely 3.8 % of the working hours performed. It accounts for only 2.4 % of the received wages.

Men dominate in this sector of economic activities and this manner of earning an income. They work longer hours than the women, but also receive higher wages. The wages received by the men earning their living in the nonagricultural sector are about 40 % higher than those of the farmhands. It can be presumed that the data stating that the wages in the nonagricultural sector are so high applies to both the rural areas as well as the cities. That can be taken as an indication of the fact that (1) there is not too much land exodus as the wages – theoretically – would sink then in the cities; however, the cost of living is higher and marginal subsistence sources are rarer. This (2) also indicates the fact that people who do not find employment in the agricultural sector have, or had, a chance in the cities. As a result, (3) the wages for farmhands have not broken down completely because the farmhands are not totally dependent upon wage paying jobs in the agricultural sector, despite the large number of people looking for work, but rather have alternatives, even if they are limited. It can also, however, be (4) an indication of qualified, better paid or urban wages subsidized in

160

state-owned enterprises and administrative bodies.

In principle, all agricultural holdings have at some time a labour demand that exceeds the capacity of the family members. This demand for additional manpower is met as far as possible on the basis of the "labour market." Thereby, there are various institutionalized forms of work contracts.

1. *Neither directly nor monetarily compensated exchange and petitioned work (dhārā, gātā, māun-/māngun-kāmlā, shāhājo)* which is as a rule not statistically registered, but makes up approximately 5 % of the work carried out. [257]

2. *Permanent labourers integrated in the household (stāi kāmlā)* who are young people in general – boys and girls – that help the family in the function of helping hands.

3. *Permanent labourers tied to the holding* who, under certain circumstances, may be members of the clan who have a permanent right to a job and take over the function of foremen. They are preferably hired on a daily basis, but also have to be available. The wages that they receive are as a rule somewhat higher than the average wages. They are not integrated in the household of their employer and landlord, but rather have their own household and family.

4. *Farmhands hired according to demand (kāmlā)* who are hired for at least one, or possibly more days, or who are paid to carry out a specific task for a fixed wage (contract), or paid on the basis of contractual "piece" wages and work as a group with or without a foreman (*sardār*, labour leader).

Such job arrangements can also be discovered in the case of nonagricultural households, enterprises, and jobs, i.e. rice mill workers and coolies.

Figure 40 shows the differences in the significance of paid labour for the various holding-size categories. "Additionally hired" paid labour makes up approximately 20 % of the available labour on a small holding. The fact that the percentage of casual labourers amounts to 94 % of all hired labour shows that these holdings hire manpower mainly to meet seasonal labour peaks (rice transplantation, harvesting). The small holdings raise the available manpower that they have on their own by 20 % and create simultaneously 25 % of the job opportunities for labourers available on the "labour" market. [258]

In the case of middle-sized holdings, casual labourers make up approx-

---

257 Cf. [147] Herbon, 1984: p. 398, Tab. 72.
258 The interpretation of the figures and/or overestimating the quality of the data is a problem. As the need for manpower fluctuates greatly with the labour peaks and the survey covers just one week – retrospectively – and not the entire year, and as it is not known in which season or week the survey was carried out, the figures can serve at best as rough indicators.

Fig. 40: Type and Quantitative Significance of the Employed Labourers Respecting Various Holding-size Categories, 1983/84

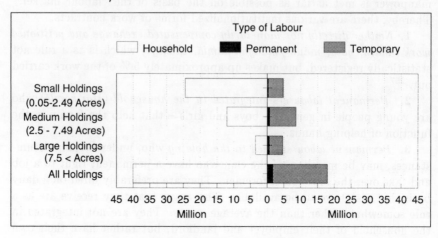

Source: [125] Government, 1988: p.25 and p. 144, Tab. 1.
Note: For the numerical values, see Table 61 in the appendix.

imately 90 % of the hired labourers. The volume of hired labour equals about three-fourths of the volume of family labour. All in all, this holding-size category – which comprises a total percentage of family labour of 70 % – creates nearly an additional 50 % of the available job opportunities for hired labourers.

In the case of large holdings, the percentage of permanent labourers among the hired labourers is rather high with 14 %. This is a proof of the fact that the holdings cannot be adequately farmed without additional permanent manpower. Thus for each five family labourers there is, on the average, one additional permanent worker. This decreases the relative percentage of casual workers to about 86 %. Although these holdings account for only about 9 % of the total economically active people, they supply one-fourth of all of the jobs. The volume of wage labour amounts to more than 130 % of the volume of the available family labourers.

It goes without saying that the large holdings supply a significant percentage of the employment opportunities. The quantitative importance of the middle-sized holdings is, however, striking. The significance of small holdings in their role as employers should also not be underestimated. At this point, it is not possible to discuss the economic consequences for the overall system. It should be pointed out, however, that the smallest holdings appear both as labour suppliers as well as labour employers, a phenomenon that can be found at all levels up to the middle-sized holdings on which, for example, the son may still not be the "manager" of the holding and, thus, complements his income by working for wages.

It should also be pointed out that the labour market, the level of the wages and the labour supply can shift so strongly due to changes in the cropping intensity that in the case of the small holdings, which have less financial means at their disposal, a shortage of labour can become noticeable in view of increasing wages, or at seasonal peaks. This can have repercussions on their system of farming.

In this chapter we saw that the holdings in all of the categories cultivate the land they have at their disposal partly with hired labour – the larger holdings more so than the small holdings – as well as selling family labour – the small more than the large. The manpower supply is directly inversely proportional to the supply of rented land. Hence the ability to employ one's self on one's own land – in particular on rented land – influences the necessity and the possibility of earning money as a wage earner. The interdependent shifts between job and employment sectors, between rural and urban areas, etc., will be treated in detail in Chapter 4.3.

3.4.1.3 Capital Exchange

In general there is a shortage of capital in Bangladesh (1) because traditionally the need for production resources other than land and labour has been relatively low and essentially limited to implements and draught animals and (2) because capital goods are usually tied to the farm and not timely and flexibly available. In addition, (3) the increasing need for financial means to purchase modern inputs such as seed, fertilizer and water and/or the necessary equipment for irrigation plays a role. This can be seen in the demand for "credit" that is not met by an adequate supply.

The demand for means in order to acquire productive agents is empirically strongly mixed with the demand for means for consumptive purposes. These means can appear in the form of cash, abstract rights of use with abstract or financial compensatory claims, or in the form of non-cash resources, i.e. in the form of production means. [259]

---

259 The discussion on capital exchange is found in the relevant literature as a rule under the rubric "credit." This has two problematic implications for the discussion, however, namely that (1) a mixture of credit for investments and production purposes, on the one hand, and consumptive, social purposes, on the other hand, is maintained and (2) that if the term credit is not limited to financial means but rather also generally

Due to formal and logical reasons inherent in the presentation, the investment-productive aspect of credit will be regarded here as part of capital exchange. The "consumptive" aspect [260] will be discussed under the rubric income exchange in the following chapter.

Non-cash resource "loans," i.e. the temporary lending of means of production (1) in return for payment (rent), (2) reciprocally, or (3) in return for qualitatively different material (e.g., services rendered) and immaterial (rights and allegiance) compensation are significant here as a form of capital exchange. They are sometimes neglected in the "credit" discussion. These aspects of the temporary transfer of capital and *capital exchange* are important within the framework of local production and reproduction.

A large number of people and households have a need for money or production means and, therefore, raise credit if possible. The so-called traditional or informal loans, i.e. private loans, are extremely important in Bangladesh. The significance of institutional loans, i.e. the lending of financial means that are more or less tied to a specific purpose by banks and cooperatives (BRDB), is limited.

The ratio of informal to institutional loans has, both with respect to the number of borrowers as well as the credit volume, shifted to a great extent in the direction of private loans. Figure 41 clearly shows that all of the socio-economic strata (in principle) can find and have access to institutional credit. Only a few people from poorer strata, however, receive merely a minimum percentage of the institutional loan volume. In contrast, 21 % of the large farmers take advantage of institutional credit. Over 90 % of the poorer people are faced by the necessity to borrow informal, private loans. But just under one-third of the wealthiest also borrow from informal sources. Figure 41 also shows that the percentage of loans borrowed from insti-

---

extended to include non-cash resources and rights, then if one continues to think consequently and precisely, each not immediately reciprocated transaction of any type of goods, services and rights, i.e. a hesitation in the return service or payment, is a form of credit. Furthermore, (3) a certain amount of time before the compensation takes place in both social and economic contexts is generally the rule, rather than the exception. Utilizing the term credit in this context is, hence, inoperable.

260 The form of dividing consumptive and investment-productive purposes is fundamentally questionable because consume, for example, as well as investments in labour and social expenditures can be investments in relationships that secure one's economic situation. The problem is generally recognized, and the division is made from the viewpoint of the individual, i.e. empirically, and is frequently irrelevant because it is a normal procedure to redirect, shift and make momentary changes in the utilization of resources and the purposes for utilizing them. The socio-economic interdependencies in the system of living and the directive contingencies do not allow, theoretically, this formal, analytical division. But for purposes of describing the phenomenon, it appears to be necessary.

164

Fig. 41: Strata Specific Percentages of the Borrowing Households and the Specific Relative Percentage of Institutional and Informal Credit Sources

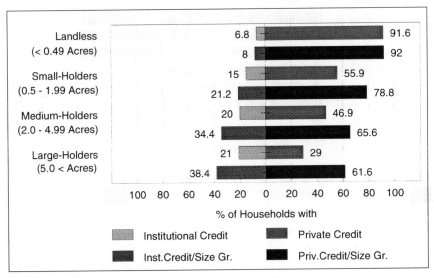

Source: [165] Hossain, 1988: p. 22, Tab. 3.

tutionalized sources increases with the size of the household's land endowment. The percentage of loans borrowed from private sources is indeed still larger in the case of those who are prosperous, but the relative percentage is lower. [261] Unfortunately I do not have any data on the absolute credit volume in Bangladesh. [262]

The survey on institutional credit indicates that not only the percentage of institutional loans is larger in the case of the wealthy than the poor, but rather that the specific credit volume is also larger. This is strongly correlated with the type of credit. Thus Herbon [263] showed that the large loans went to the large landowners within the framework of the BRDB-cooperatives. Special landless and women-oriented credit programmes were

---

261 [165] Hossain, 1988: p. 22, Tab. 3.
262 Credit belongs to the most difficult areas of research. The social stigmatization of the term "usurer," the Islamic prohibition not allowing interest and the individual status-oriented negation of debts make surveys in the field extremely difficult. I do not know of any surveys that analyze credit and debts according to social or economic strata.
263 [151] Herbon, 1988; [152] Herbon, 1988.

Fig. 42: Sources of Informal Credit

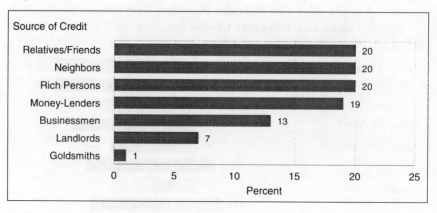

Source: [245] Maloney, Ahmed, 1988: p. 42, Tab. 4.

overproportionately represented, it is true, and granted to the, by definition, less prosperous members of the cooperatives. Short-term and limited
agrarian production loans were also relatively equally distributed among the
members of agrarian cooperatives. These members are primarily recruited
out of the stratum of middle-sized farmers. The really large loans were,
however, granted to the prosperous within the framework of the programme
to promote irrigation technology and – in contrast to the other loans – not
paid back.

Institutional loans are indeed given a great deal of attention within the
scope of development policy deliberations; [264] however, the informal private
credit relations are still of great importance. In contrast to the institutional loans, they are of particular significance in times of distress. They
are characterized by their *permanent and potential availability.* This is a big
difference when compared to the more likely sporadic and arbitrary character of institutional loans which are, it is true, comparatively inexpensive
with respect to other loans that yield interest. It is, however, difficult to
raise them.

Informal credit sources for the approximately 50-70 % of the people
who borrow money are widespread. Figure 42 shows that relatives, friends
and neighbours – overlapping groups – and well-to-do people in the villages

---

264 Cf. [13] Ahmad, 1983; [134] Haq, 1985; [151] Herbon, 1988; [152] Herbon, 1988; [167]
Hossain, 1984; [163] Hossain, 1984; [165] Hossain, 1988; [245] Maloney, Ahmed, 1988;
and [352] World Bank, 1983.

Fig. 43: Utilization of Informal Credit

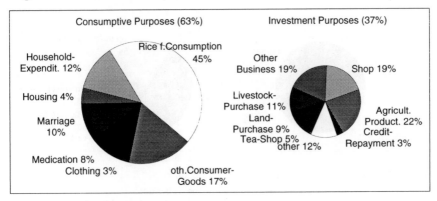

Source: [245] Maloney, Ahmed, 1988: p. 52, Tab. 5.
Note: For the numerical values, see Table 64 in the appendix.

grant about 60 % of the loans. Landlords and businessmen also grant loans – about 20 % – but at the same time they further their own economic interests. Professional money lenders were responsible for about a further fifth of the loans. The spectrum of the professional money lenders ranged from poor widows, who improve their insufficient livelihood by giving interest-yielding loans, to the landlord who has a large amount of cash at his disposal, all the way down to the classical "usurer." The local, regional and personal forms of these "informal" credit relations and systems vary, however, considerably. [265]

Consumptive purposes dominate as the reason for taking up a loan – independent of the source. Thus, as can be seen in Figure 43, about two-thirds of the loans, according to number and volume, are used for consumptive purposes, whereas approximately one-third are more likely to be used for investment purposes.

Of the two-thirds of the total *loans* that are more likely to be *used for consumption*, approximately three-fourths are utilized for subsistence, for food (rice), consumer goods and other household expenditures. "Unusual circumstances," weddings, medicine and clothing are the reasons for borrowing the final fourth of the loans used for consumptive purposes.

Investment loans are utilized in a broad spectrum of enterprises. One can also borrow "institutional" loans for purposes of plant production, busi-

---

265 Cf. [37] Arens, Beurden, 1977: p. 111 ff.; [147] Herbon, 1984: p. 173 ff.; [190] Jahangir, 1979: p. 135.; [197] Jansen, 1983: p. 95 ff.; and [322] Spinatsch, 1984: p. 144 ff.

Fig. 44: Credit Conditions: Collateral and Interest

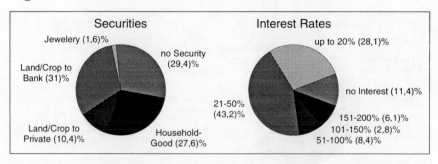

Source: [134] Haq, 1985: p. 25, Tab. 9; p. 27, Tab. 10.

Note: For the numerical values, see Table 66 in the appendix.

Banks and private parties accept land and crops as collateral for institutional and informal loans.

ness and purchasing livestock. Agricultural production (plant production and some livestock sectors) is, it would seem, not the most important "investment area" for the loans that are raised. As a rule, it is nonagricultural sales, trade, service and transport enterprises that are financed on the basis of loans. [266]

The *conditions* for the loans are every bit as diverse as the reasons for using them and the sources, as can be clearly seen in Figure 44. *Collateral* is necessary in most of the cases. Merely about one-third of the loans are granted without collateral, i.e. on the basis of trust. Two-thirds of the loans are granted against collateral by and to private parties. 30 % are granted against valuable everyday goods or the wife's jewelry. 10 % are "secured" on the basis of land. This form of collateral is *"khāi khālāsi,"* which is the transfer of usufruct for a limited amount of time in return for money,[267] or *"bondok,"* mortgaging land.

Loans and renting land flow into one another in those cases in which the utilization of land is used as collateral, interest and/or to pay back debts. Similarly, some loans are "underpaid," or not paid at all, but rather "paid" back in the form of work that is carried out, or by entering an allegiance

---

266 There are unfortunately no empirical studies available on sources, the flow of credit, purposes and conditions, as well as "yields" derived from credit. An extensive and detailed study would certainly disclose general allocation trends and implicit strategies and policies.

267 If regarded from another perspective, this is a form of land exchange, tenancy, not an exchange of capital.

with the lender. In such transactions, various services, services in return, rights, demands, obligations and forms of dependency are implied. These implications also play a role in the type and rate of interest.

Interest can be fixed and has to be paid back at a specific time, or unlimited, e.g., right after the harvest has been brought in, or later, in the form of money or payment in kind, with or without compound interest. Compound interest, it is true, is neither accepted nor are the people generally aware of its existence, but it does exist as a result of borrowing an interest yielding loan in order to redeem an older interest yielding loan. On the other hand, there are also agreements according to which the total rate of interest does not increase, even if repayment is prolonged. The nominal interest, in other words, does not necessarily reflect the real cost of the loan. There are, to put it short, nearly as many interest and payment conditions as there are loans.

The combinations of credit volume, source, collateral and terms of the loan are, however, not unlimited, but rather specific institutionalized credit and capital exchange arrangements have established themselves in the course of time that form a kind of normative framework. Maloney and Ahmed [268] mention the following. Some have already been discussed in connection with land and labour exchange.

1. *Khāi khālāsi* is a right to utilize land, a form of usufruct, in which the party granting the loan is allowed to use the land if the borrower has land at his disposal. The lender is allowed to use the land for a limited, agreed upon period of time (generally 7 years with possible prolongations) and the harvest is used each year to pay back part of the loan. The "loan" can be paid back prematurely, whereby the proportional *share* with respect to the residual term has to be paid back at the specific date. At times, the borrower continues to cultivate his own land as a sharecropper, which leads to a decrease in the lender's "return" and thus to an increase in the length of time necessary to redeem the loan, or to a smaller loan, etc.

2. *Kāṭ* is an arrangement according to which land is mortgaged and left at the borrowers disposal until the loan is paid back *without any interest*. Poor people who are not able to pay back their debts or are thus forced to borrow another loan wind up in a "negative spiral" and easily lose their land as a result. [269]

---

268 [245] Maloney, Ahmed, 1988: p. 49 ff.
269 This has been repeatedly mentioned in the relative literature on the subject. Cf. [245] Maloney, Ahmed, 1988: p. 48, who refer back to [351] Wood (Huq), 1975, who writes about this phenomenon with reference to Comilla. On the other hand, the following authors could *not* confirm the existence of this system: [37] Arens, Beurden, 1977; [38] Arn, 1986; and [147] Herbon, 1984.

3. *Bandhak* or *badhaki ṛin* means that land is "pledged," similar to the case of *khāi khālāsi* and *kāṭ*. In this system, however, in addition to paying the loan back by usage or redemption, interest has to be paid. This system does not necessarily imply, however, pledging the land itself, but rather that any valuable object can be pledged.

4. *Dādan* or *dhāndiyā sud* is a cash loan that is paid back in kind after the harvest has been brought in. As a rule, the debt is "paid" in unhusked rice following the harvest. In the nonagricultural sector, this system is also used by suppliers and traders who advance craftsmen capital and working material and receive their recompensation later in goods that the craftsmen produce.

5. *Hāulat, karja, karja hasānā* is a non-interest bearing small loan that is granted in emergencies by friends, relatives, neighbours and patrons in accordance with the rules of Islam. The borrower is morally and honourably obligated to pay back the debt on time.

6. *Rehān* is an official promissory note that can be drawn up between unrelated persons or people who are not socially close whereby land – similar to under the conditions of the *kāṭ* arrangement – is ceded, however "under one's hand and seal" and not on the basis of "trust and in good faith."

7. *Ṛin* is an interest bearing cash loan that has to be paid back in cash similar to ("institutional") bank and cooperative loans.

8. *Sāfkāula* is a sales contract for land that is permanently transferred to the hands of the creditor if the borrower does not pay back the loan. It is based on a document, the *firtināmā*, that the creditor signs in which he promises to return both the land and the sales document – the *sāfkāulā* – as soon as the debt is redeemed.

On the basis of the credit relations described up to this point, it is clear that in the case of these credit relations *usable* collateral is often supplied. The utilization of such collateral is, from this viewpoint, itself a goal of

---

The mechanism by which land is lost *is not based*, strictly speaking, *on a specific form of tenancy or credit*, but rather on the general principle that resource control and income do not suffice for a particular person to meet his own consumption needs and those of the other members of the household to a sufficient extent. Thus over a medium-length period of time the only way to procure the means of existence necessary in order to live is by selling or lending the production resources, by means of "living from one's substance" which, e.g., in earlier times led to the fact that children were sold and families indebted to work for the lender (this sometimes affected several generations), as well as to work as bonded labour, or to successively selling the family's land in order to pay back the debts. The negatively sanctioned *Kāṭ* system has, thus, been practically replaced by indirect mechanisms. Borrowing loans and selling land have been institutionally separated.

Cf. with respect to this negative spiral and the reactive "absorption strategies" Chapter 3.6.

economic interactions and transactions.

All of the capital transactions that have been discussed until now are based on the fact that one of the components of the exchange is *money*. At times, however, means of production are also lent in exchange for shares of the crop.

1. Lending *draught animals* signifies the lending of draught animals on a reciprocal basis, either an entire pair for the purpose of ploughing, or if two small farmers only have one animal each, in the form of a *pāti* arrangement. Both animals, thereby, are combined as a pair and can be used reciprocally. [270] This system of exchanging draught animals is complemented by an integral fodder exchange system and, under certain circumstances, also a work exchange system. These interactions can take place between people with the same rank with approximately the same farm structures, or between patronage-oriented landlords and their tenants. One also finds draught animal owners who plough other people's land in exchange for natural goods or monetary wages [271] and the exchange of draught animals – i.e., draught power exchange in reciprocal (*dhārā*) or rotating systems in which *more* than two partners are involved (*gātā*) – and labour parties (*māun*) – i.e., an analogue system based on an exchange of labour. [272]

The quantitative significance of the transactions with means of production and the resulting network of service flows can only be surmised. As these transactions are in kind and take place within the framework of an interlaced and decentralized market, the financial value cannot be ascertained. For the subsistence and existence-sustaining oriented small and smallest farmers, however, this nonmonetary exchange of production means and the resulting inner village equalization with respect to the means of production and the factor utilization potential is very important. [273]

2. *Animal sharing* (*ādi*) is a further form of an exchange of the means of production. As a rule, thereby, an animal – a head of cattle, buffalo, goat, sheep and more rarely chicken – is ceded to another person and their household members under the condition that yields derived from keeping the animal will be split in half. Lambs, calves and chicks are exchanged alternatively or partially; milk and eggs are usually kept by the person raising the animals; and increases in value resulting from the growth of the

---

270 Helmrich discovered that among 175 farmers, 40 owned only one draught animal and 7 three draught animals, which resulted in the fact that the small farmers have to unite if they want to plough their land. ([144] Helmrich, 1986: p. 366 f. and p. 461 f.)

271 Cf. [144] Helmrich, 1986: p. 367 ff., who registered the transactions on a monetary and in kind payment basis in connection with livestock keeping. Such interactions and transactions are unfortunately hardly empirically registerable and quantifiable.

272 Cf. [144] Helmrich, 1986: p. 462 ff.

273 Cf. [147] Herbon, 1984: p. 179 ff.

animals are split fifty-fifty after they are sold.

Animal sharing opens up the opportunity for a family that is endowed with sufficient labour, usually children, but without sufficient capital of its own to build up its own capital stock. As a rule, however, these forms of interaction are based on already existing relations, either family or friends, because trust is a fundamental aspect of such an arrangement. The relations between the partners are strengthened by such transactions. Generally, middle-sized holdings are involved which concentrate their resource utilization as far as possible on plant production and, hence, lease animals to other nearly landless households.

3. *Tree leasing* is a marginal form of transferring the right to dispose of capital, i.e. capital exchange, although it is very important for some households. The practice of seasonally ceding the rights to the tree crops in exchange for a share or money has not been described in the relevant litera- ture. In some areas of Bangladesh, however, there are, e.g., date-palm juice making specialists who rent a large number of date palms for the season and use them for economic purposes. [274]

4. The *leasing of ponds* takes place on the basis of analogous principles. The fact that they do not have the necessary equipment to catch fish, as well as a lack of the necessary technical knowledge, plus the relative low status of fishing and the multitude of interests among the owners are motives that encourage the owners or community of owners/heirs to "lease out" their ponds to be farmed, or to be fished empty.

3.4.1.4 Income Exchange

There are hardly any households in which the members succeed in sat- isfying all of their demand for consumer goods on the basis of their own production and their own means. In this section the following aspects will be discussed: (1) how the – ultimately more or less adequate – income which is available to the members of the household community at the end of all production and exchange processes can be converted and exchanged so that the *direct* consumer needs can be met; and (2) which are the interactive relations the people enter in order to procure goods and services which *they cannot produce themselves* for consumptive purposes.

Households have to fulfil certain conditions if they want to adequately procure the goods they require. Firstly (1) all of those households that want to and need to acquire external goods and services must have sufficient *"purchasing power"* at their disposal. (2) The direct exchange of goods plays

---

274 This statement is based on the author's own observations.

a subordinate role. Thus in the exchange process, the household's own more or less dispensable products and services must be traded in order to acquire that which it needs or wants to have – either mediated through the medium money, or by means of the direct exchange of natural goods.

Marketing products, "*selling*" one's services and manpower, or *exchanging* means of production and land and – in crises – *trading* inferior, inexpensive consumer goods for superior ones are the prerequisites for acquiring consumer goods because this is the only way the necessary means can be set free to supply the necessary "purchasing power." "Income" acquired in this manner can, if it takes the form of natural goods, be directly consumed if need be. If it exists in the form of money, the desired consumer goods can be procured if they are available. [275]

Marketing products is, next to the exchange of production factors, the key mechanism for acquiring income which, once again, can be used to satisfy consumer needs.

The marketing of agricultural products plays a key role in the rural areas of Bangladesh. All kinds of products are marketed. Most of the marketed products, however, are also used to meet the household's own needs. Cereal production (rice) is, measured on the "value added," the key product grown for the purpose of self-sufficiency by the producers, on the one hand, and in order to obtain income, on the other hand. Cereal production accounts for approximately two-thirds of the marketed products and the other plant products and livestock production for approximately one-sixth each. In order to compare this data and assess the ratios, the "production values" for the rural manufacturers and the "wages sums" for agricultural and nonagricultural labour have been included in Table 10. [276]

---

275 It will not be necessary to discuss the fundamental economic principles any further here. What is important to keep in mind is the fact that one of the basic intentions of the households in Bangladesh is to exchange products, services and rights for other products, services and rights. Prices regulate the supply and demand in the form of monetary values or opportunity costs.
  If production resources (land, manpower, or capital goods) are acquired, this has been discussed under the aspects of land, manpower and capital exchange (see above). In the case of income that is procured without the party receiving the income supplying its own "material" performance as, e.g., in the case of transfer income or acquisition income, the mechanisms behind the acquisition of this "income" will be discussed later in Chapter 3.5, p. 183.

276 Despite being aware that the figures have been derived from various sources and could be based on different calculating methods that were not disclosed, it is possible to make the following deliberations. (1) If one subtracts the wage totals for paid labour and hired labour amounting to approximately Tk 44 billion from the agricultural economy's net added value, then one has with the resulting figure of Tk 134 billion approximately the net value added derived from the totality of all

Tab. 10: Indicators of the Economic Significance of Various Rural Economic Sectors

Indicators	Mio. Tk
Creation of Value in the Agricultural "Sector" (1985/86 Prices in Million Tk) [a]	
Plant Production	147259
(Cereals)	(106871)
(Other)	(40388)
Livestock Production	32110
Total: Agriculture	**179369**
Production Value [b] **of Rural Small-scale Industry** (1983/4 in Million Tk) [c]	
Total: Small-scale Industry	**30992**
Total: [d]	**210361**
Sum of Wages [e] **Paid to Rural Workers** (1984 in Million Tk) [f]	
Agricultural Wages	44640
Nonagricultural Wages	9000
Total: Wages	**53640**

Source: [122] Government, 1988: p. 87, Tab. 36; [124] Government, 1988: p. 135, Tab 4.16; and [125] Government, 1988: p. 433, Tab. 22.

---

a   [124] Government, 1988: p. 135, Tab 4.16.
b   Monthly average values * 12 months * number of holdings.
c   [125] Government, 1988: p. 433, Tab. 22.
d   Agriculture (– agri. wages) + Small-scale Industry (– nonagri. wages) + (Wages). As wages have to be paid out of the value added in the agricultural "sector" and the production value in small-scale industry which, on the other hand, have to be created once again, the wage payment and income balance themselves out. Cf. also footnote 276, page 173.
e   Sum of day rate * 360 days.
f   [122] Government, 1988: p. 87, Tab. 36.

Manpower and manufactured products as well as various services have to be exchanged on the corresponding markets. With respect to agrarian

---

agricultural holdings, from which the family labour, own and rented land, and own and borrowed capital must be paid. (2) If one subtracts in addition the wage totals for nonagricultural jobs (which, however, include wages from the service sector) from the production value of the rural small-scale industries (cottage industries), then the value of circa Tk 22 billion makes up the sum out of which the rural manufacturers have to pay for all of their own production (own manpower) and working assets and means of production. Paid labour amounts to a total of about Tk 53 billion. (Cf. [122] Government, 1988: p 87, Tab. 36; [124] Government, 1988: p. 135, Tab. 4.16; and [125] Government, 1988: p. 433, Tab. 22.)

Fig. 45: Rice Marketing Balance According to Holding-size Category

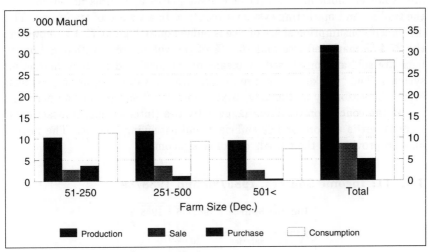

Source: [273] Quasem, 1987: p. 87 ff., Tabs. I ff.

Note: For the numerical values, see Table 65 in the appendix.
 Cf. also Table 67 for the per-capital supply of rice in the holding-size categories after the rice has been exchanged.

products in general, there are no quantitative and/or national data available. In addition to cereals, however, nearly all other plant products are produced for the market and only a small portion is used within the agricultural holding and household. In the case of rice, however, approximately 70 % is used for self-consumption and about 30 % of the total volume is sold. It should be pointed out, however, that Figure 45 shows that about 16 % of the produced rice is "bought" back so that only a net volume of about 11 % is marketed. This phenomenon is found among all of the holding and household categories.

The figure clearly shows furthermore that there are significant holding-size specific differences. Thus the small producers all in all have to purchase about 9 % of the rice they consume, whereas the middle-sized and large holdings market more than 20 % of the rice they produce. [277]

---

277 In reality, however, these values are probably too low because, as (1) Chowdhury, ([89] 1988: p. 107) argues, the marketable surplus has been registered at too low a volume in the case of the large holdings and (2) the surplus – with reference to the overall economy – would not suffice in view of the rice import quotas to supply the

It is not possible to present the complex and multistranded and inter-woven (produce) marketing system in this context. [278] Produce markets are, however, both in the form of market places as well as in the form of the trading and marketing system a reality with a wealth of traditions. The direct self-consumption share of rice is indeed quite high at 72.4 %; however, the 27.4 % marketed rice and 16.4 % of the volume of rice that is bought back are sold and purchased by means of the local and regional marketing systems. The "market" is even more important for other agrarian products, even if in seasonally and locally varying forms [279] and to varying degrees.

At the conclusion of all exchange activities (interactions, transactions), what is left is a more or less sufficient and satisfying income. The people have to provide for their needs out of this income.

Tab. 11: Income Sources, 1985/86 and 1988/89

Income Source	1985/86 (%)	1988/89 (%)
Wages / Salaries	20.08	6.79
Agriculture	39.55	38.31
Professions	2.90	0.35
Transfer Income	0.52	6.84
Rent	6.00	9.65
Businesses	14.91	14.97
Other Sources	16.36	23.09
Total	100.00	100.00

Source: [123] Government, 1988: p. 46, Tab. 1.08; [129] Government, 1991: p. 54, Tab. 1.08.

---

nonagricultural population.

278 Cf. in this respect in addition to [273] Quasem, 1987; [274] Quasem, 1988; [89] Chowdhury, 1988; and [285] Rahman, 1973; [145] Herbon, 1984; [144] Helmrich, 1986: p. 286 ff.; [96] Crow, 1989; and [319] Sikder, Elias, 1988.
One should also look at the Indian aspects in this context: [43] Balkrishnan, 1978; [44] Bardhan, 1080; [58] Bohle, 1983; [195] Jana, 1978; [252] Mellor, 1969; [305] Sarkar, 1981; and [339] Wanmali, 1985.

279 Cf. in this context, for example, as two of the few studies that attempt to quantify the importance of the marketing of agrarian products [319] Sikder, Elias, 1988, and [99] Elias, 1988: p. 75 ff. Sikder and Elias (1988: p. 5, Tab. 2.1) registered five different pulse crops with marketing shares between 44 % and 65 %, which indicates a marketing share of on the average more than 50 %. Pulses are still grown as classical basic foodstuffs for the purpose of self-consumption and are, if one considers the development in the overall production as a basis, uninteresting as marketable crops since the production seems to be stagnating.

Fig. 46: Percentage of Income Source According to Each Income Category, 1985/86 *

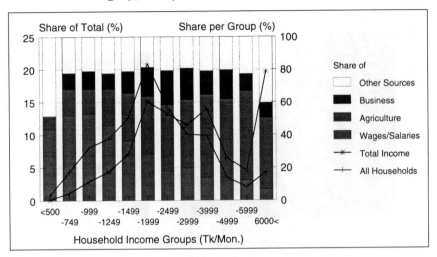

Source: [123] Government, 1988: p. 39, Tab. 1.01, and p. 46, Tab. 1.08.

Note: For the numerical values, see Table 68 in the appendix.
* This presentation is *not* based on the data from the "Household Expenditure Survey" 1988/89 ([129]) of 1991. The drastic differences between the material published in that statistical report and the data from 1985/85 cannot be explained. Thus. e.g., in 1988/89 the value of "other sources" of income is 23.1 % as against 16.4 % in 1985/86. On the other hand, the percentage of "wages & salaries" has shrunk from ca. 20 % to 6.8 %. Both are unrealistic. An explanation might be a change in the method of data analysis, which counts labourers' wages as a residual, "other" category.

The explanation which is offered in the report itself, i.e., that the situation of poverty has led to increased disinvestment and liquidation of savings is *not plausible* because (1) the real incomes strongly increased in the same period and, thus, there would not have been a need to fall back on buffers to such a degree; (2) the values oszillate erratically between the different income categories; and (3) the proportion of wage decrease is too dramatic in order to have taken place otherwise unnoticed. Both facts indicate methodological flaws which prohibit the use of these data. Cf. [129] Government, 1991: p. 54, Tab. 1.08 and p. 13.
Cf. Table 11, page 176.

Figure 46 and Table 11 present the sources of rural "income." Approximately 40 % is derived directly from agricultural production: about 20 % is made up of wages and salaries. 15 % is produced in businesses and 6 % rental values. The remaining 20 % is derived from more or less precisely

Fig. 47: Correlation between Household Income Level and Size of Landed Property

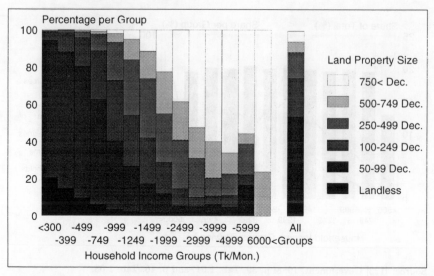

Source: [255] Muqtada, 1986: p. 58, Tab. A1.

Note: For the numerical values, see Table 69 in the appendix.

defined and attributable factors. [280]

Figure 46 illustrates furthermore the differentiation in the relative significance of the various income groups. Thus in the case of the group with low incomes (< Tk 1250), nearly 50 % of the income is derived from paid labour. The example of the groups with higher incomes (Tk 2000 <) shows that the income earned in agriculture makes up approximately 50 % of their total income. Income from businesses as well as other sources and transfer income seem to be constant over all of the groups.

Two thirds of all of the households (67.5 %) have a monthly household income between Tk 1250 and Tk 4000 and, likewise, a share of the total income amounting to two-thirds (65.1 %). The income groups above and below this have, however, (as naturally all in all on both sides of the mean) disproportional shares. This, though, does not say anything about the per capita income.

---

280 It can only be presumed that income derived from savings accounts or interest bearing loans is included here.

Fig. 48:   Relative Percentages of Purposes for Utilizing Income
           According to Rural Income Category, 1985/86 *

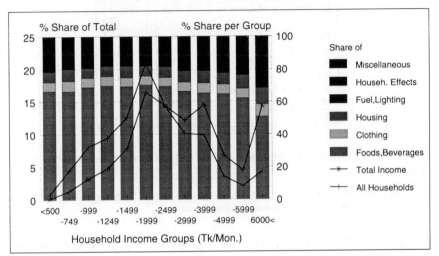

Source: [123] Government, 1988: p. 49, Tab. 1.11.

Note: For the numerical values, see Table 71 in the appendix.
    * See note to figure 46, page 177.

The households' income is derived – as has already been pointed out – to only about 40 % directly from agriculture. The fact that the correlation between cultivating land and income level is only relative can also be clearly seen in Figure 47. In this figure, the correlation between property size (indirectly approximately the size of the holding) and the level of the household income is presented. Thus one can see that there is indeed a correlation, but, on the other hand, the dispersion of the households that belong to *one* property size category can be clearly recognized over a wide range of income categories. Hence, other income sources (as Figure 46 shows), on the one hand, and the number of household members who also contribute income from other sources play a large and differentiating role here. [281]

The pooled income earned by various people from diverse sources which is available to be used is utilized for a variety of purposes: essentially for

---

281 The correlation between the number of income earners (indirectly the size of the household, in other words) and level of the household income is presented in Figures 16, p. 84 and 17, p. 85.

179

Tab. 12: Utilization of Income, 1985/86 and 1988/89

Utilization of Income [a]	1985/86 (%)	1988/89 (%)
Food	65.08	67.63
Clothing	5.91	5.62
Rent	7.36	8.01
Energy	8.97	5.88
Household Appliances	1.22	1.29
Miscellaneous	11.46	11.49
Total	100.00	100.00

Source: [123] Government, 1988: p. 49, Tab. 1.11; [129] Government, 1991; p. 57, Tab. 1.11.

a   Only that 99 % of the total expenditures that are used for consumption have been included here: 1 % must be used for taxes, etc.

subsistence. Table 12 shows that 65 % of all of the expenditures are used for food and the rest for clothing, housing and energy, among other things. Figure 48 demonstrates the fact that the percentage spent for food remains remarkably constant all the way up to the high income level groups. The same is true in the case of expenditures for clothing and housing. The amount spent for energy – for cooking – is overproportionately high in the case of the low income groups, however. The opposite is true in the case of expenditures for household appliances and "miscellaneous."

This list clearly shows that (1) despite its tremendous importance , agricultural production generates only about two-fifths of the rural income, and wage labour another fifth. This gives an indication of the (a) significance of the variety of income sources and (b) the *danger of overestimating* – with respect to its significance for income – agricultural production. Furthermore, (2) the fact is clear that income is very unequally distributed in the various income categories and that it is simultaneously an empirical and statistical problem to fix an adequate minimal limit for reproduction income. (3) Regional and urban/rural disparities as well as seasonal fluctuations were not taken into account here. [282]

282 The income data available in the national statistics are not broken down according to region, and an urban/rural comparison was not made here in order to save space.

3.4.2 Interdependencies in Exchange

Individual people attempt within the framework of the existing structures as members of their household to gain a better position with respect to production and income earning by exchanging that which is less important to them for things they desire.

With the exception of the final alienation of land, the other forms of exchanging land such as tenancy – the exchange of land for labour, capital and capital goods – and ultimately income serve to achieve a more efficient allocation and reallocation of resources for the purpose of supplying and providing better for one's self. The contingencies inherent in the exchange system have already been described in detail above. In the following, a few interdependencies will be pointed out once again.

1. The "markets" for rented land and labour are interdependent: if an adequate amount of leased land can be obtained, the family does not necessarily have to sell its manpower. If the land available to the farm is not sufficient to either supply employment for all of the family members nor achieve a minimal income, then manpower must be sold, or other forms of capital utilization have to be found and taken advantage of. Since, however, only 12 % of the land used for agricultural purposes is exchanged via the market for leased land and, on the other hand, the ratio of employed family labour and hired labour is approximately 2 to 1, the small holdings in particular are frequently faced by a dilemma between a very limited supply of expensive land, or no land available for tenancy and a saturated labour market. Thus small holdings are often only left with the possibility of (1) intensifying their land utilization by means of input-intensive farming methods, by utilizing the garden and tree culture potential for production for the purpose of selling the yield, or (2) by taking advantage of the opportunities available through intensive livestock production which is not dependent on land, as well as (3) by utilizing seasonal niches on the labour market that true wage labourers cannot exploit.

2. The exchange of means of production and capital is only then significant if the fundament of existing resources which are structurally determined, i.e. within the household or farm, are not equally available and can only be utilized inefficiently, i.e. are only available for a limited amount of time, e.g., seasonal deficits must be done away with. Either (1) the resources – which under the existing conditions cannot be utilized efficiently or in such a way that they bring an adequate yield – must be alienated, or (2) the attempt is made to use the available unused potentials more efficiently by complementing them with resources that have to be additionally obtained. Thereby the decision has to be made in accordance with the farm, the house-

181

hold and family capacities as to whether one (1) wants to relinquish money or income, or whether (2) one wants to obtain additional resources under various conditions in order to overcome bottlenecks and use them one's self, or whether (3) one wants to give away a certain type of resources in the course of concentrating and specializing activities in order to obtain another type. These general *allocation decisions* and the implicit and explicit *allocation strategies* can, however, hardly do away with fundamental deficits in the a priori given resource endowment unless one is "lucky." This aspect will be mentioned once again in the discussion of acquisition and physical reproduction strategies in the following chapter, Chapter 3.5.

3. The exchange of income likewise serves two goals: (1) to obtain productive resources and use yields, profits and means of existence that can be consumed or used consumptively for these, or (2) exchange a consumer good (real or money), e.g., wheat for rice, meat for bread, etc. Since allocation, reallocation, disposition and redisposition and investing and dropping an investment are both complex and contingent, it is only possible to summarize that such exchange, transactions and interactions take place in a distinct and detailed system of "markets." This aspect of exchange – the local, regional and national markets – is a sign of the ability and necessity of adapting the means that are available for various purposes to the desired goals and limited possibilities. [283] All in all, this results in a *regulation* within the disposition and demand structures as they exist for the individual and result from his activities.

Such a perspective implies, however, – abstractly, formally and as a model – a certain static-stable *equilibrium concept*. The exchange system in a comprehensive sense is, however, not static. Instead it is a *dynamic framework of conditions* that evolves with the transition in the production system, the population growth and the change in consumer demands, values, etc., as well as the overall social "conditions" and distribution structures. Furthermore, a purely static and equilibrium oriented approach, as will be used on formal grounds in the following sections, would hide the fact that critical situations caused by (1) natural catastrophes and the resulting crop failures, (2) disturbances in the market due to panic reactions that are not combated and (3) political unrest can influence and destabilize a balanced – even if poor and containing discrepancies – economic system to such an extent that hunger catastrophes are the result. The manner of dealing with the new chances and dangers resulting from the dynamic overall system will be treated in the following two chapters, 3.5 and 3.6.

---

283 The activities of individual participants in the markets within this marketing system will be treated in the following chapter, Chapter 3.5.1.1, p. 183.

3.5 Acquisition: Who Opens up Which New Opportunities for Himself, How and Why?

3.5.1 Contingencies of Acquisition Strategies - Possible Forms of Utilizing External Resources

Until now, the description of how sufficient income is secured by means of building up and mobilizing relations, by means of production in various sectors and by means of exchange implies a limited and local cosmos in which the actions take place, that of a "closed system." The criterion of direct individual control over the resource flow and the resource genesis was implied. These implications, however, are only permissible as the first formal step towards analysing the system of actions and the radius of the strategies.

In the following chapter, the attempt will be made to describe which potential strategies can be employed by the individual in Bangladesh in order to take advantage for himself of the resources in the regional, national and global system surrounding his "micro cosmos." The term acquisition is used here in order to illustrate the fact that the activities of the individual are strategically oriented towards gaining control over the resources that appear to be within his reach outside the house, village and family community and to acquire and take advantage of niches and opportunities. The term acquisition implies certain factor and income allocation strategies in order to gain access to "external" resources by means of exchange from within his "system." In other words, what is meant here is *not* interactive exchange with people, but rather exchange with anonymous, corporate and institutional "actors," the extension of the relation and resource access network and the expansion of the field of activities and contingencies.

Four – ideal type but *interdependent* – acquisition strategies can be mentioned which will be described in the following: (1) commerce (economic brokerage), (2) politics (political brokerage), (3) formal education (education) and (4) migration (upward, outward mobility).

3.5.1.1 Commerce

The flow of goods (production and consumer goods) in the rural areas of the country, as well as the flow of the agricultural products out of these regions onto the national and international markets – i.e., the market system in a broader sense – gives the individual and his household community the chance to acquire income. Specialized knowledge, contacts and access to resources (among other things, loans), as well as a certain transport capacity are the prerequisites that have to be fulfilled before one can become involved in commerce. Not everyone, however, has such resources at his disposal to

Tab. 13: Indicators of the Significance of Trade in the Rural Areas

Indicator: Significance of Commerce	Survey:			
	Bhuyan, Mandal a	Kahrs b	Herbon c	Government d e
As a Main Occupation (Percent of Holdings)	3	11	4	12,5 f
As a Part-time Occupation (Percent of Holdings)	22	4	2	-
For Income (Percent of Total Income)	2.8	-	-	14.9

Source: [55] Bhuyan, Mandal,1987; [211] Kahrs, 1991; [147] Herbon, 1984; [123] Government, 1988; and [122] Government, 1988.

a   [55]Bhuyan, Mandal, 1987, Village Survey;
b   Kahrs, 1990 (in progress), Village Survey;
c   [147] Herbon, 1984, Village Survey;
d   [123] Government, 1988, Rural Sector; and
e   [122] Government 1988.
f   Sales Workers.

the same extent, or in a sufficient amount. Involvement in the commercial sector, thus, opens up the chance for a number of people to earn at least part of their living and, if possible, to become prosperous.

No national data are available on the quantitative significance of commerce, neither with respect to the number of people involved in commerce, the time spent in and for the involvement in commerce, the volume of goods, nor the income earned in the sector.

Rough indicators can be derived from Table 13, whereby it is necessary to differentiate between the significance of commerce for the village population and its importance for the *rural* population. As many "full-time traders" no longer live in the villages themselves but rather in urban agglomerations, or have migrated there, the figures are not *representative for the overall economic* significance of commerce.

In Chapter 3.4.1.4 it was shown that approximately 30 % of the rice production is "marketed," ca. 16 % "flows back" into the rural households and the rest "flows off" into the macro system. It was also shown that about 55 % of the *pulses* are marketed. [284] In the case of *jute* and *sugar cane*, it is safe to assume that the market quota amounts to nearly 100 %.

284 Cf. footnote 279, p. 176.

Despite the fact that, to begin with, each individual producer of agricultural goods can market his products himself and thereby furnish by himself to a greater or lesser extent income-influencing services in the form of packing, storage and transport and obtaining market and price information, there are a large number of income-generating activities carried out by and for "commercial specialists."

Crow [285] sketched the rice marketing system [286] on the basis of the rice trade, and Sikder and Elias on the basis of the trade with pulses. [287]

In principle, it is possible to differentiate between four different market levels: (1) the inner village exchange – monetary or in kind, (2) marketing that takes place at the weekly market (hāt), (3) marketing at the urban (large) markets and (4) central markets and ties to international markets in the capital Dhaka. [288]

At these various levels of the system, there are *traders* with the corresponding capacity for the trade volumes in the form of capital, transport and storage capacities and the required access to the market. For the rural regions and the people involved there, however, contact to the nearest urban market is extremely important.

1. *Fāriā* are traders who buy and sell small amounts of goods in the villages, or sell goods at the local weekly markets to consumers, processors and middlemen. This function can be carried out by the producer/consumer

---

285 [96] Crow, 1989: p. 201 ff.
286 He assumes that there are three rice sectors that can be found in the rice trading field or "market":

- The normal, public rice trade on the market.

- The state rice distribution system, via which subsidized rations and payment in kind are distributed within the framework of the Food-for-Work programmes. On the other hand, the state also buys certain volumes of rice annually at guaranteed prices. (It is not possible to go further at this point into the subject of the state interventions in the grain market and the resulting tax, stabilizing and adjustment factors.)

- The natural transfer of rice that results from rent in kind (sharecropping, fixed rent – bargā, ādi, chāuniā) and the reimbursement of loans and interest in kind.

  The statements in the following refer to the "public" market segment.
287 The structure of the marketing channels is similar in the case of both products. Cf. [319] Sikder, Elias, 1988: p. 5; as well as [145] Herbon, 1984; and [285] Rahman, 1973: p. 67.
   I am not aware of any other studies regarding this aspect that have been carried out with respect to Bangladesh other than these two "marketing studies" so that it is not possible to make any detailed statements concerning regional differences or other products such as chilies, wheat, jute, sugar cane, oil seeds, etc.
288 Smuggling activities from Burma and into India that represent a special form of marketing activities will not be discussed here.

himself with the corresponding investment and risk, and he can, thus, take advantage of the margin of profit.

2. *Bepāri* are traders that have very large trading capacities and who are less active in the villages themselves. On the contrary, their activities take place at the local markets where they carry out large volumes of transactions. They are involved in both the marketing of agrarian products as well as in the function of intermediaries to processors (millers) and/or in the marketing of products that rural consumers are interested in.

3. *Āratdārs* are large wholesalers who have both large storage and transport capacities at their disposal, as well as the necessary capital in order to build up and maintain large stocks until the prices have reached a level that is attractive to the traders. *Āratdārs* are at the same time commissioner agents who store, manage and do commission business with goods belonging to others. Both functions, that of the wholesaler and that of the commission agent, can be carried out separately. One no longer, however, speaks of *āratdār*, but rather of "wholesalers" and "commission agents."

Rice and pulses are not only traded, but also processed, at least husked, and parboiled in the case of rice. The processing can be carried out either by individual people, or in automatic mills, in steps, or as a total process. The processors buy the amounts they need at the corresponding markets and sell them again there if the circumstances are such. Family enterprises which parboil rice buy, e.g., "paddy" from the farm, transport, store and process it, and finally market it husked at the weekly market. Or large millers buy from the *āratdār* and pass the milled product on to the *bepāris* who sell it to consumers at the markets and bazars. [289]

The activities of the traders working in the markets are extensive. They consist of collecting, transporting, storing and gathering information on prices, appointed dates, volumes, etc., and under certain circumstances in addition processing, as well as distribution at and over the various above-sketched levels of the marketing system. All of this is carried out for many different agricultural and handicraft products and consumer goods. These activities, the extent of which are dependent upon the individual's capital, knowledge of the market, credit worthiness and relations, as well as his personal performance, offer a large number of people the opportunity to earn income to varying degrees.

The income earned can merely reach the level of the income earned by casual workers in (1) the case of the "smallest" *fāriā* who carries his goods in baskets hanging from a yoke (*pār*). It can (2) in the case of the *bepāri* with

---

289 For a presentation of the flow of goods see, for example: [319] Sikder, Elias, 1988: p. 6, Figure 2.1; and [96] Crow, 1989: p. 204, Figure 1.

ox drawn carts be quite handsome. And (3) *āratdārs* in the bazaars in the cities who sometimes own a lorry can, without a doubt, be prosperous people. Their opportunities in life differ similarly. Large landowners attempt to take advantage of their "capitalistic" opportunities by means of such transactions (wholesaling, commission agencies, milling, processing and storing) and expand their enterprises and increase their incomes. *Fāriās* who may, for example, do trade with a small amount of vegetables, do so, on the other hand, in some cases only during the time of year in which they cannot find wage work and are forced to try and achieve a minimum profit and trade margin in order to earn an income. [290]

The minimal chances of establishing one's self as a trader in various sectors and at diverse levels of the market system are very unequally distributed. Hardly any substantiated studies exist on employment and income effects, trade margins and market power. The consequences of the attempts of the smallest traders to find a market niche and secure a minimum subsistence will be referred to once again in its function as a defensive and emergency strategy in Chapter 3.6.

The chance to enter trade is dependent, among other things, on the trader's relations. Relations are necessary in a double sense in the form of (1) *contact* with the corresponding trading partner, sources, or buyers and/or (2) *patronage* and *connections* to influential people in the cities. With respect to trade, the value of "influential patrons" in the cities, especially in the state and development administration, manifests itself when, for example, it is time to apply for trading licences for agricultural inputs and for state subsidized rice rations for state employees or the poor.

3.5.1.2 Politics

Gaining and taking advantage of political and administrative leader and power positions outside the village is a strategy with two goals: (1) gaining more recognition, influence and power, and as a consequence and frequently as a final goal, (2) gaining access to resources and increasing income.

The kinship and village social systems are clientelistically organized,

---

290 The efficiency and performance level of a market system which is structured in such a manner so that the individual and local economies are tied both together and with the national and international economic systems are evaluated very differently. Crow ([96] 1989) attempts to prove that it would be possible for wealthy, financially strong traders to influence the prices to their advantage – with a definite "exploitation effect." In doing so, he tries to refute the conclusions of all of the studies that have been carried out to date (with which I am unfamiliar or which are not available) which came to the conclusion "that food markets are highly competitive and surprisingly efficient." (Page 203)

whereby local leaders are characterized by above-average effective control of resources. The power and influence of the village clientelistic system can be based on the general control of a large amount of landed property. As a rule, however, the powerful people control external resources and make them, under certain circumstances, available to their clientele. In the case of these resources, they can be (see above) (1) trade capital and relations. Frequently, however, they are (2) state resources and services that are important and desired and meaningful to be able to take advantage of. Whereas people that are involved in trade earn their living on the basis of the flow of private resources and directing them, for the people in the political, administrative system it is important firstly to gain influence over state or external (general development organizations and non-government development organizations (NGO)) resource streams in order to take advantage of them (1) directly for *themselves* and (2) indirectly by means of the benefits that their clients receive from the recource streams who then support and vote for them. [291]

The benefits that can evolve for the individual "politician" by individually and privately gaining control of external and public resources is an important motivation for becoming politically active. The opportunity, however, is not available to everyone.

The preconditions to become effectively involved in politics are (1) a very good *resource endowment of one's own* that has accrued either on the basis of income from (a) extensive landed property, [292] or (b) commercial enterprises, [293] or from (c) public resources that have been successfully branched off and acquired. This means, concretely, that only either well-to-do *landlords* or *state protégés* (e.g., former "freedom fighters," police and army officers, or civil servants) who "purchase" their way if need be into the proper position (officers acquire landed property, etc.) have good starting chances. [294]

In order to find access to elected offices, however, the politicians have to have an (2) *effective and majority cliental basis* that is committed and motivated enough in order to carry through their candidates. The significance of (3) *troops of thugs* [295] for the politicians in higher positions should,

---

291 When sketching the relations in this manner, I am neither refuting the existence of individual good will, nor the honest, idealistic political involvement of individual politicians.
292 Cf. Table 74 in the appendix.
293 Cf. Table 14.
294 Cf. [19] Alam, 1976; and [135] Haq, 1976.
295 These thugs – *lāthiyāl* – are a traditional "institution." "Lathiyals' ... [are] strong arm men wielding bamboo rods or worse, and available for physical intimidation whenever necessary. ... Retaining 'lathiyals' is expensive." ([4] Adnan, 1976: p.129).

188

Tab. 14: Economic Characteristics of Local and Regional Political Leaders – Strategical Income Source Combinations

Level	Holding-size Category	Main Occupation			Total	
		Farming	Business	Other [a]	abs.	rel.
	(Decimal)	(N)				(%)
Union Parishad [b]						
Members [c]	0.0	2	2	-	4	3.0
	10 - 250	2	5	3	10	7.6
	251 - 750	21	12	6	39	29.5
	751 -1250	34	16	14	64	48.5
	2500<	9	2	4	15	11.4
	Total (N)	68	37	27	132	100.0
	(%)	51.5	28.0	20.5	100.0	100.0
Upazilla Parishad [d]	[e]					
Chairmen [f]	<500	2	6	5	13	11.5
	500 - 1000	11	4	8	23	20.4
	1000<	42	20	15	77	68.1
	Total (N)	55	30	28	113	
	(%)	48.7	26.5	24.8	100.0	100.0

Source: [283] Rahman, 1979: p. 99; and [281] Rahman, 1986: p. 213.

a   "Practice, service, teacher, others."
b   Comprises approximately 5 to 10 *mouzas*/villages.
c   [283] Rahman 1979: p. 19; cf. also [85] Chowdhury, 1982.
d   Corresponds approximately to a district.
e   Size of agricultural landed property plus an unspecified amount of land in urban regions.
f   [281] Rahman 1986: p. 312; income statements were not adopted as the data acquisition basis is not explained and there are no means of comparison.

however, not be underestimated.

In order to gain access to the positions in the "formal" leader system that is continually increasing in importance, i.e. in the local and regional politics and administration, a (4) *formal education* (as a minimum, reading and writing and, if possible, administrative, functional knowledge) is essential. It is now hardly possible to fill the positions efficiently and control the relationships and resources without having mastered the basic rules of "modern" social manners and formal administrative procedures and the ability to read documents, i.e. *leadership knowledge*. Local and regional leaders have, therefore, an above-average school education. [296]

296 It is not possible to go into the individual, empirical proof of qualifications (land, income, education, etc.) found among local leaders, Union and Upazila-Parishad

Tab. 15: Formal Degree of Education of Local and Regional Political Leaders

Education until School Year/Completed	Union Parishad Chairmen [a]		Union Parishad Chairmen [b]	
	Number (N)	Percent (%)	Number (N)	Percent (%)
- 5	14	4.3	-	15.9
- 8	57	17.6	-	-
- 10	101	31.2	-	25.9
SS-Certificate	77	23.8	-	24.2
HS-Certificate	30	5.3	-	24.2
B.A.	41	12.7	-	6.8
M.A.	4	1.2	-	3.0
Total	324	100.1	132	100.0

Source: [19] Alam, 1976: p. 7, Tab. 5; and [283] Rahman, 1979: p. 95.

a   [19] Alam, 1976: p. 7, Tab.5.
b   [283] Rahman, 1979: p. 95.

Gaining an "education," i.e. formal and functional qualifications, is thus the prerequisite for success in gaining access to the resources that can only be acquired by means of the administrative apparatus. Education, however, is also a key to other sectors of the "modern macro system."

members and chairmen in detail here (*pariśād* = Council). Likewise, it is not possible to demonstrate empirically in this context which strategies and tricks the individual politicians used in order to acquire public resources. Unfortunately it is also not possible to analyze the question of the leadership structures that arise in this manner and the consequences for the development efforts of international, national and voluntary organizations. Therefore, I would like to point out the following list of literature:
[4] Adnan, 1976; [84] Chowdhury, 1978: p. 109; [85] Chowdhury, 1982: p. 59 ff.; [147] Herbon, 1984: p. 287 ff.; [146] Herbon, 1984; [148] Herbon, 1987; [151] Herbon, 1988; [171] Huq, 1978: p. 16ff.; [191] Jahangir, 1981; [190] Jahangir, 1979: p. 240 ff.; [212] Karim, 1987; [261] Nebelung, 1988: p. 93 ff.; [283] Rahman, 1979; [278] Rahman, 1981; [324] Streefland et al., 1986; and [345] Westergaard, 1985: p. 130 ff.
In order to gain an overview of the structures of the state and development administrations *without* a specific analysis of the individual political structure and resource flow manipulation see, e.g.: [105] Faizullah, 1987; [185] Islam, 1979; [172] Huque, 1985; [173] Huque, 1988; [176] Hye, 1982; [179] Hye (ed.), 1985; and [317] Siddiqui, 1984.

3.5.1.3 Education

Education is primarily a privilege of the elite. It is indeed true that a primary education is principally available to quite a few children; however, the successive steps in the hierarchy of the educational system are open to only a few. The access to educational facilities is very unequally distributed. Even if one has doubts as to the value of a large portion of the contents of the curricula, i.e. its relevance for the questions in life faced by the rural population, education is – with the exception of socio-humanistic educational ideals – an important prerequisite to be able to take advantage of the chances in life that are offered by the "modern national system."

Before presenting the "educational strategies" and their relative social importance, the educational system will be briefly described here. The school system is based on British concepts and has been hardly restructured since colonial days. The first level are the primary schools that cover a span of five years. At the end of this time, the children have mastered the rudiments of reading and writing. [297] The secondary schools (high school) are based on the foundation of the education provided in the primary schools and cover a span of an additional three years (junior high school), or five years (senior high school). The school leaving certificate following the 10th grade is called the "Secondary School Certificate (SSC)." Grades 11 and 12 are called "intermediate college," and completed with the "Higher School Certificate (HSC)." A two year "college" education (Bachelor Degree Pass) or a three year "college" education (Bachelor Degree Honours) are the next possible steps. The universities offer a "masters" degree that can be achieved after three or more additional years. A doctor's degree can be earned at a few universities. [298]

A final evaluation of the potentials, deficits and dynamics in the educational system cannot be carried out here. The government has given the extension of primary education to the general public high priority, but at the same time, critically regarded past performance in this sector. [299] In reality, it seems as if – measured on the literacy rate and taking the population growth into consideration – the status quo has remained about the same. The number of illiterates (10 years and older) remained approximately the

---

297 The Bengali alphabet has just under sixty basic letters and over 200 combined letters which have to be learned. The relatively complicated (elite) alphabet makes it difficult to motivate adults to plague themselves with it within the framework of the literacy campaign. The written language itself and the very aesthetic-literary orientation of the educational concepts are neither relevant nor interesting for the rural population.

298 Cf. [307] Sattar, 1982: p. 13.

299 [116] Government, 1985: p. 335 ff.

same between 1974 and 1981, whereby a meager improvement of 2.6 % can only be traced back to a slightly improved percentage of girls and women. [300] While the relative number of illiterates still amounts to 75.4 % in the rural regions, in the cities the percentage amounts to about 53.4 %, whereby more women can now read and write here as well. [301]

Rural children are deprived as far as education is concerned. [302] With respect to the means that their parents make available, there is less interest in their education. Hence, the expenditures for education are minimal. Despite this fact, the percentage of the average monthly overall household expenditures amounting to 2.2 % in the cities is approximately double as high as the percentage made available by the rural households. In absolute figures, the rural expenditures for education amount to one-third of the urban. In the rural regions, the consensus seems to be that education is not as highly valued. Thereby, it is not clear whether this is the result of a lack of a *willingness* to spend means for education or – due to a want of schools – the lack of opportunities to receive a school education. [303]

There also seem to be, however, strata and occupational-specific differences in the rural regions. Figure 49 demonstrates [304] the occupational-group specific educational motivation.

The efforts the farmers undertake in order for their children to receive an education lie at approximately the level of the national average. Within the dismal overall educational situation, however, there are two extremes. Agricultural workers [305] place (1) evidently extremely little *value* in education, [306] and they are obviously also (2) forced to let their children *work*. The percentage of farmer's children who do not attend school and have to work instead is above-average. Not even 10 % of the children can go to

300 I am not in a position to make any judgement concerning rumors about falsified examinations, bribery, threats of violence and a sinking level of the examinations, but such rumours are quite frequent.
301 Cf. [123] Government, 1988: p. 170, Tab. 11.8; p. 171, Tab. 11.9.
302 Due to a lack of data, it is not possible to prove that they are disadvantaged with respect to educational *opportunities*, as one would be able to see on the basis of a state budget allocation. The Third Five Year Plan ([116] Government, 1985) does not stipulate the financial planning according to region or area.
303 Cf. with respect to the data: [123] Government, 1988: p. 91, Tab. 2.01; p. 125, Tab. 2.22.
304 The criteria for dividing the occupational groups into categories are extremely questionable and evidently unreasonable from a sociological standpoint. Since no better figures are available, however, the existing statistical material has to be used, even if it only indicates trends.
305 I presume that this occupational group is what is classified as "non-agriculture."
306 Many children, 67 %, "sit around"; i.e., they do not work – in the sense of the survey – and do not go to school.

Fig. 49: School Attendance of Children According to the Employment Satus of the Head of the Household in Rural Areas (Boys and Girls)

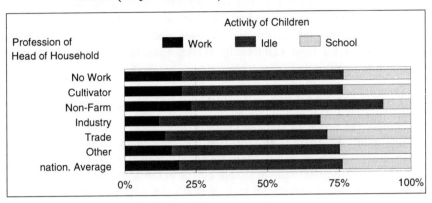

Source: [127] Government, 1985: p. 176, Tab. 11.14.
Note: For the numerical values, see Table 73 in the appendix.

school.

The other extreme group is that of the more likely qualified ("industrial") workers and, to a less extent, those in the commercial sector. In these groups, the degree to which the children have to work is *below average*. Thus the percentage of children who attend school is at about 30 % – *above average*. The fact that the expenditures for education are extremely dependent on the income [307] indicates, however, that the essential reason for a lack of education is not only the absence of schools and teachers in the rural regions, but rather can also be found in the income available to the households. Expenditures for education increase directly proportionally to income. Since modern and, sometimes, more attractive jobs are taken up in the vicinity of the cities and the educational opportunities are somewhat better there at the same time, there seems to be a correlation between the educational level and the urban environment.

Due to a want of better data, the discussion of the above-described trends will be cautiously concluded with the statement that the rural households perceive and take advantage of the educational opportunities in different ways. The relevance education has seems to be evaluated diversely. Important for the evaluation, however, are also the absence of schools and

---

307 Cf. [123] Government, 1988: p. 125, Tab. 2.22.

the poor condition of the existing schools with their inadequate supply of teachers. This all seems to indicate that *receiving a formal education is a strategy of prosperous, "outer" oriented families* who can, thus, support and demonstrate their own social and economic mobility. This, however, does not exclude the fact that individual – statistically unimportant for the mean value – mobile, but less prosperous, or even poor households try to create better chances for their children by taking advantage of the educational opportunities. [308]

3.5.1.4 Spatial Mobility – Land-Urban Centre Migration

Within the scope of the individual expansion of economic and socio-political relations, there is an increased necessity to spend time in cities or urban centres, or even move there. This strategy is used in order to (1) control the "resources made available by the external system," (23) expand the opportunities of earning an income that grow with increasing economic ties and (3) maintain the necessary and resulting relations. At times, a second dwelling is procured for occasional stays in the cities when business transactions have to be carried out, when it is necessary to negotiate with the bureaucracy, when it is necessary to participate in committee meetings, or also when it is necessary to supply a place for children to sleep who attend an institute of higher education in the city. Furthermore, buildings and property in the cities are capital investments outside the village. Thus a study carried out by the BIDS [309] in 1985 ascertained that approximately half of all of the Upazila-Parishad leaders owned property in the cities. [310]

This base in the cities leads in the long run to at least part of the family moving to the city and, if the case arises, *"absentee landlordism."* The farm is managed from the city. [311]

The well-to-do, educated, politically successful and dynamic families which succeed in acquiring and accumulating resources withdraw slowly from the rural environment. Another opportunity for the rural households are the relatively well-paid jobs in the Arab "oil countries" (Middle East).

---

308 There are no studies or statements on such transgeneration planning for Bangladesh as one knows it in Europe.

309 BIDS – Bangladesh Institute of Development Studies, quoted in [281] Rahman, 1986; p. 213, Tab. 8.4.

310 Unfortunately, the size of the pieces of property and the use of the property (a piece of land, storage, production facility, dwelling) are not specified. Furthermore, the term city is not defined.

311 Many urban dwellers who belong to the upper class still own landed property in the country and name their "native village" as their place of origin (*"bāri"*), even if they were born in the city and live there.

The required education and training and starting capital (for papers, "contacts," gratifications and trips) are prerequisites for taking up such a job. The money earned during the time spent abroad is sent, to a large extent, home and results in expenditures and investments that surpass the traditional scope. The effect can be a very rapid socio-economic ascent with the consequent new opportunities. [312]

Rural-urban mobility and the mobility to work in a foreign country are, thus, two significant components for acquiring "system external" resources and using them for one's own purposes. The significance of migration from one village to another within the same region or in another rural region has not been quantitatively established to date. There is, however, migration from economically deprived regions as well as regions that are dangerous for the people due to climatic reasons or because of natural catastrophes to villages that are not as endangered, or that have a somewhat more dynamic economic system due to the expansion of irrigated farming. Marriage is frequently used as a "stepping stone" for this type of *permanent* migration. The men try to marry women from the "good" regions and gain, as a result, the right to live in the parents-in-law's village and have, under exceptionally favourable circumstances, either the chance to inherit a piece of farmland through their wife, or even – if she is the sole heir – to take over an entire farm (*ghor jāmāi*). [313]

In this manner, [314] the individual search for a way to improve one's chances by changing the place of residence has led to a continual flow among the resettling population that has resulted in an intervillage and interregional equilibrium in the population and the disposition of resources.

Seasonal inner or interregional migrational work, as carried out by farm workers during the rice transplantation or harvesting seasons, leads for its part to a temporary unburdening of the own (worker) household and, on the other hand, to the utilization of work niches in other places. Caused by slight topological and hydrological as well as micro-climatic (local and regional) differences, the agricultural peaks – transplanting and harvesting

---

312 "Normally, only the rich farmers can send their sons abroad. They are the people who have money and education. Some middle and poor peasants have also gone abroad. But a significant portion of them have been cheated by the agents and have become paupers in the process. Some of the rich peasants, by sending one or two sons abroad have become the 'super rich.' " ([281] Rahman, 1986: p. 230.)

   I do not principally doubt the validity of this statement. However, Rahman does not mention his sources or proof so that the quantifications and qualifications that he implies seem at first glance to be based on rumors and do not allow conclusions to be drawn: e.g., the significance of economic "descent" as a result of being cheated.

313 Cf. in this respect [149] Herbon, 1988: p. 11 ff.

314 This has not been scientifically dealt with in the case of Bangladesh.

– vary from village to village and region to region. As these seasons are as a rule accompanied by labour-requirement peaks that cannot be met locally by the workers or family members living in the village, additional manpower is needed. The groups of itinerant workers from regions in which the peaks fall at an earlier or later date or where the wages are extremely low have their chance. These groups can, thus, sometimes be on the move for several weeks and "travel" with the season. The relatively high wages during this period are accompanied by low expenditures for living and are favourable for the family remaining at home.

The *land-city migration* that leads to a steady increase in the urban population and is found in particular among the young, relatively well-educated adults has resulted in a brain drain, a loss of the young, economically active and fertile people which results in both a burdening as well as a disburdening of the rural population that remains behind. [315]

The individual acquisition strategies and their socially differential, mutual synergetic and expansive effects will be summarized in the following.

3.5.2 Acquisition Strategies

A good, above-average income and wealth are – as is a well known fact – a good basis for improving one's situation by means of expansive strategies. Hence, in addition to (1) intensifying agriculture by means of input and capital intensive "modern farming methods," (2) entering the wholesale sector, (3) politics, (4) gaining an education and (5) opening up new chances through spatial mobility are key aspects.

A far above-average amount of landed property, experience and success in commerce, a higher education and/or political office are the prerequisites which individually, however best combined, create the basis for acquisition and accumulation. Whether and to which extent exploitation of others, pauperization and a dynamization of the system are accompanying phenomena will be discussed in Chapter 4.5.

An examination of the socio-economic situation and the endowment that politicians bring with them make it clear that they – on the average – display the following charateristics: they own large farms, are successful in trade and have received higher educations that allow them to gain such political offices. The conclusion, however, should not be drawn that only politicians fulfil these criteria. A political office is not the only way to acquire resources. Good trade relations, a position in the government apparatus – achieved on the basis of a good school or college record and perhaps through financial contributions to the right place – or working abroad are also possible means.

---

315 Cf. [216] Khan, 1982: p. 392 ff.

It should be clear here, however, that people with above average resource endowments have above-average chances in life and for acquiring further resources. This, however, does not by any means exclude the fact that people and families with less advantageous starting situations can "work their way up" by clever and effective measures and with corresponding perseverance and stamina.

In the next chapter, however, the attempt will be made to describe – in contrast – what people can do in order to combat a general or drastic deterioration in their situation.

3.6 Dealing with Crises: Who Overcomes which Crises, How and Why?

3.6.1 Contingencies of Strategies for Coping with Crises – Possible Forms of Limiting and Overcoming the Damage

Economic and social activities carried out by the individual and his closer and more distant social groups do not always lead to the result that was desired and aimed at. If an objective is not achieved, that means that adjustment "downwards" has to take place. Not every subjectively suboptimal result, however, is equally problematic. An unsuccessful acquisition and expansion strategy or a fluctuation in the harvest within a foreseeable scope do not necessarily have to be regarded right away as catastrophes.

Real catastrophes of varying gravity occur over and over in the normal economic process and the course of one's life. The extent, the duration and the consequences, however, differ greatly. Tentatively, catastrophes can be differentiated by whether they (1) are of a *predictable or unpredictable duration* and whether (2) their *occurrence* is somehow *predictable* ("foreseeable"). Furthermore, (3) the *size of the involved circle* is important – i.e., whether it is an individual, his family, the village community, or an entire region. In addition (4), *the gravity of the consequences* of the catastrophe – whether they are existential or only marginal consequences – for the individual and his social group, and (5) who they hit and what *material foundation and reserves* they have at their disposal.

In Bangladesh, three *catastrophic situations* can be basically defined in which the individual and those for whose welfare he is responsible are endangered: (1) individual blows of fate such as illness and death of the main income earner, [316] (2) extraordinary natural or social catastrophes that are

---

316 The significance of the individual fate and the individual consequences of catastrophes, illness, death and loss of one's wealth has seldom been dealt with in the relevant literature and, if so, then frequently more descriptively, more in the form of literature.

197

caused by storms, floods, and violent upheavals and war, as well as partial collapses of the market that hit many people at the same time [317] and (3) seasonal fluctuations in income that result in an income level that no longer allows the people to maintain their position. [318]

For more systematic studies, for example, see: [46] Beck, 1989; [76] Chambers, 1989; [157] Heyer, 1989; [214] Katona-Apte, 1988; [234] Lipton, 1983; [235] Lipton, 1983; [236] Lipton, 1983; [237] Lipton, 1988; [238] Lipton, 1988; [239] Lipton, 1988; [240] Lipton and Longhurst, 1988; [241] Longhurst, 1986; [242] Longhurst, Chambers, and Swift, 1986; and [325] Swift, 1989.

Regarding the problems that arise through individual illness, cf. for example: [70] BRAC, 1984; [97] Currey, 1981; and [267] Pryer, 1989.

317 The causes and consequences of such (macro) catastrophes that were the result of military actions and natural catastrophes between 1970 and 1975 in the form of the war of independence, hurricanes and floods, as well as the general economic (agrarian and industrial) depression, coup d'étas, and market collapses have been described and discussed in a few studies. Unfortunately, really substantiated data on the individual and collective *reactions* and *adaptions* to acute crises have hardly been treated, just as in the case of individual or collective recovery or mortality phenomena. This is evidently because there is (1) no data basis, statements of assets and liabilities and inventories that would make it possible to register the actual adjustment, i.e. *changes*. Furthermore, (2) during the crisis, normally only by chance is there the possibility of collecting data and recording the course of the crisis which is due, on the one hand, to the acute misery and, on the other hand, to the difficulty in organizing surveys ad hoc and (3) there are no follow-up studies of the same people and households. Long-term, anticipatory and perspective-oriented research and survey projects on the basis of panel studies could be a help in this context. However, neither researchers (individual career perspectives and project financing) nor the large institutions (timeliness of planning for financial acquisitions) seem to be prepared for such studies. Without going any further into the sociological research on the issue of crises, the following literature on this aspect should be mentioned:

[24] Alamgir, 1980; [25] Alamgir, 1981; [45] Basu, 1984; [70] BRAC, 1984; [88] Chowdhury, 1988; [91] Clay, 1985; [94] Crow, 1984; [97] Currey, 1981; [168] Hossain, Islam, and Saha, 1987; [254] Muqtada, 1981; [277] Rahaman, 1981; [296] Ravallion, 1987; and [312] Sen, 1982.

In this context, also see the studies on political and administrative implications of such crises and catastrophes:

[23] Alamgir, 1980; [25] Alamgir, 1981; [45] Basu, 1984; [47] Berry, 198; [91] Clay, 1985; [92] Clay, 1988; [95] Crow, 1987; [97] Currey, 1981; [98] Cuttler, 1985; and [312] Sen, 1982, and the following discussion, e.g., [294] Rangasami, 1985; [294] Rangasami, 1985; [295] Ravallion, 1982; and [296] Ravallion, 1987.

318 In this context, it is unfortunately impossible to go into the discussion that attempted to understand the strengthening mechanisms of market-price fluctuations and manipulations. It is likewise impossible to work out the conditions leading to and consequences of catastrophes in general.

Dealing with "catastrophic instabilities," i.e. emergency situations, has in some cases led to improved national and international policies and respective measures (observation, early warning systems, storage of provisions, regulating measures). It is not possible to deal with these aspects here.

These three types of incidents have diverse social consequences. If the victim of the catastrophe has the respective monetary and human capital reserves, e.g., a reliable network of relations, he can survive them without lasting negative consequences. In case he lives in subsistence reproduction conditions, however, the self-sufficiency basis can be so badly damaged that it is no longer possible to stabilize the situation one's self and can result in the middle or long run over a "negative dynamics spiral" to social and economic decline, i.e. impoverishment and morbidity increase. In the case of people who already live at the level of misery and poverty and no longer have any physiological or material power of resistance left, who – in other words – already live a miserable life, such catastrophes can destroy their existence.

However, no social stratum and no economic class is invulnerable to blows of fortune. The potential endangerment increases rapidly, though, with decreasing "assets," both in a structural-statistical as well as a temporal-dynamic sense.

In the following, the reactions and possibilities of adjustment available to an individual person and his household that were observed in Bangladesh will be presented. It will be partly necessary to do without statistical proof in this context because is does not exist. [319]

In the case of the action strategies that are described in the following sections, the attempt will be made to sketch principle reactions – cushioning reactions – that are "employed" in connection with crises successively, parallel, in anticipation, or reactively: (1) the *mobilization of existing reserves* if they are available; (2) *substitution* for that which is necessary, but not available and *compensation* for shortages; (3) *decreasing* the number of those *household members* that have a right to be supported; (4) *selling*

---

319 In addition to the lack of data, which are essentially very difficult to collect, (1) sometimes the reference data on a comparative or total population are missing, or (2) there is no information on the procedure that was used for the sample and how representative it is, so that it is impossible to evaluate the results quantitatively and make statements estimating the magnitude. (Cf. in this context the completely inadequate data with respect to its methodology that was submitted by [169] Hossain, 1987, for example).

What makes it even more difficult in view of the data situation is the fact that the behavioural and action patterns that are described in the relevant literature as "survival strategies" are not only found among the poor, but in nearly all socio-economic strata with gradual and temporal differences in significance. In other words, this is not just behaviour that is found among the poor alone, nor are these "survival strategies."

For this reason, I will not use the term *"survival strategies,"* but rather "cushioning," "parrying" or "coping strategies" because then the level of survival remains uncertain while the uniformity of the reactions and mechanisms appear more clearly.

production resources; (5) *overusing production resources*; and (6) *lumpen proletariat activities*.

3.6.1.1 Mobilization of Reserves

The liquidation and utilization of resources which are specially set aside for such crises [320] and used as a "buffer" is one of the first measures after a crisis has set in and been recognized. Savings, stores of grain, hoarded money, etc., assets that seem at first glance to be unproductive, are drawn upon. Strategies to mobilize loans and obligations come to play and are taken advantage of. Thereby, in the beginning this is nothing more than turning to reserves that are in someone else's hands and which one has a right to. [321] Social relations and networks are mobilized in the course of these efforts.

The results of these actions, i.e. the mobilization of reserves which can either be used directly for consume purposes or have to be exchanged once again before they can be taken advantage of, usually take place within the framework of the normal social and economic system, something that is not easy for outsiders to see, a fact that is sometimes intended. They are not recognizable to outsiders unless balances of the household endowments (assets and resources) are drawn up at various times. It is, however, difficult to interpret such balances. This is because the influences of crises have to be separated (1) from the effects of normal resource mobilization which takes place within the scope of the normal shifts following special allocation ideas of the decision makers in the households. They also have to be differentiated from the household mobility that takes place due to age such as when, for example, assets have to be mobilized so that a daughter can marry, or sons establish their own household or farm, or an "old-age pension" has to be paid, as well as (3) from seasonal fluctuations that lead to seasonally caused oscillations in the assets when consume remains constant.

Thus the act of putting aside such asset reserves and resource buffers in case of future crises is a "normal" activity carried out by people running a household, as well as *utilizing them* without harming the social standing

---

320 Cf. in this context: [68] BRAC, 1983; [70] BRAC, 1984; [88] Chowdhury, 1988; [214] Katona-Apte, 1988; [241] Longhurst, 1986; [277] Rahaman, 1981; and in a booklet from the IDS-*Bulletins*:
  [46] Beck, 1989; [76] Chambers, 1989; [157] Heyer, 1989; [267] Pryer, 1989; and [325] Swift, 1989.

321 The term "*exchange entitlements*" ([312] Sen, 1982) indicates this. The usage of the term "exchange," however, obscures the fact that this can be politically or normatively based "redistribution" claims within a cliental group that are *not* based on reciprocity, but rather on power.

and productivity of the economic unit. The (1) *more variable and crises vulnerable* the situation of the people is, (2) the *poorer and more existentially threatened* they are and (3) the *greater the risk involved in the productive or social investments* is, the larger the volume of those *assets that can be liquidated at any time* is in relation to the *relatively fixed productive assets* and the *circulating assets that have been lent.* [322]

Critical situations arise during the course of the realization of such strategies basically then if (1) the "buffer" is not adequate and sufficient, and (2) many other people have the same goal, either to mobilize their own resources for their own use, i.e. to stabilize their situation, or they do not want to give them to anyone else at the time because, for example, they have suffered crop losses themselves that they have to overcome. In this case, *secondary crises* arise if the markets collapse due to crises caused by surpluses of "buffer resources" while at the same time the demand for the articles or services is reduced because of a lack of purchasing power. This can be (1) a mass run on savings in banks (something that is better known in Europe) which can lead to a collapse of cooperatives, savings banks and finance markets. (2) A surplus of casual labour can arise in an attempt to compensate for crop damage, while at the same time the demand for labour drops because, e.g., a dry spell or floods reduce the need for cultivation measures or harvesting jobs. Furthermore, (3) there can be an excessive supply of (small) livestock – with consequently falling prices – while at the same time there is a shortage of food grain with corresponding price increases that can lead to a "paradoxical situation" in which meat is cheaper than bread.

Such market collapses, which fundamentally are merely system adequate adjustments to the current market situation, result in catastrophic *"crises cascades"* for the individual people who in this situation have to (1) mobilize their resources via the market and simultaneously (2) have to gain access to an additional supply through the market. On the one hand, "natural" crises – which are sometimes caused by "man" – [323] are aggravated,

---

322 This aspect of the relations between productive and security strategical saving of assets with the corresponding "access time and security" which frequently results in unproductive capital hoarding is, in my opinion, not taken sufficiently into account in discussions on the economic efficiency of employing resources. One of the consequences is that additional income is sometimes not utilized immediately productively or for consume purposes, but is used instead for "unproductive" increasing of the "buffers," which allows the lasting stability of the means of production and consume in the first place.

323 E.g., (1) dikes that break because they were either poorly built or maintained, which leads to severe catastrophes where they break; (2) the uncontrolled sinking of the local ground-water level; or (3) the cutting down of forests which results in slow microclimatic changes that, for their part, cause the land to become seasonally desert land

and on the other hand made even worse by "price collapses" for the things which those suffering from the situation have to summon up and offer and "price explosions" for the things which they need in which there is a short-age. [324] Small, individual crises are followed by an increasing secondary crisis consisting of a "price collapse" for the "buffer resources" if they hit many individuals at the same time, or are accompanied by a coincidental "oscillation in the system," or a natural catastrophe. This all affects poor people even more drastically because the "buffer resources" are frequently too valuable or useless for self-consumption or satisfying subsistence needs if the assets are in the form of livestock or money and gold, which is easy to hide and hoard, but difficult to mobilize (to eat). Apart from the fact that poor people generally have fewer such resources at their disposal, they are forced to offer and sell them at an earlier point in time, accept lower prices and may have to draw on their *production resources* at an earlier date and with the resulting more drastic consequences.

For other people, however, the mobilization and consumption of "buffer resources" does not mean right away that their "standard of living" will be affected or limited. By liquidating them, it is possible to maintain the past level of consumption and activities. This allows them to spare their own production resources, and if the circumstances allow it, even to "purchase" land and livestock from people who are in need. If the "buffer resources" start to run out, however, or no end can be seen to the crisis, or an end to the "buffer resources" is even anticipated, then a second behavioural or action strategy comes to play.

3.6.1.2 Substitution and Compensation

A second, and from time to time parallel and anticipative strategy, is *substitutions in consumer goods* and *compensation for experienced deficits* by means of "second-best" solutions. Thus, the people reduce expenditures and put off purchases until better times. Certain needs are postponed in the beginning. For example, (1) *wedding festivities* are either delayed until a later date, or have to be celebrated more frugally; (2) *the construction or repairing of housing* has to be postponed; (3) *investments* cannot be made at the time; and (4) *consumption has to be reduced* by those who neither

---

(in the north).

324 The term "price" is used here in its broadest sense, namely as an "indicator of expenditures" that have to be made in order to obtain goods or services. It also reflects "negotiating power situations." For example, cliental protective relations are "more expensive," interest on loans "increases," wages "sink," friendships become "more valuable," etc.

have the capacity nor plans to make expenditures at the time. [325]

A reduction in consumption can be recognized on the basis of the food supply, prices and consumption and nutritional standards. Currey [326] recorded in an empirical study carried out in two villages during the crisis and famine years 1972 - 1975, the fact that 500 out of 750 households ate rice less than once per day in the year 1975, i.e. reduced or had to reduce the *volume* of food intake. In addition, many households turned to emergency substitutes that would normally not be (not have to be) eaten such as the stems of banana trees, etc.

The reduction in the quantity and quality of the meals, not to speak of the supply of other basic subsistence needs, and the increase in the consumption of "wildly" growing food that is physiologically difficult to break down and absorb and, sometimes, toxic, but which at least alleviates hunger, as well as the increased intake of alkaloid, hunger relieving drugs (betel nuts and leaves, *chupāri-pān*) are (1) measures which have an immediate effect, (2) the final means one can turn to and (3) imply ruining one's health. This strategy may have to be adhered to until the physiological reproduction collapses and illness and death result at the next level of the catastrophe cascade. This happens when, e.g., a family loses its provider. [327]

In addition to the general reduction in consumption within a household, there is also – theoretically – the possibility of gender and age-specific refusals of food. This theoretical possibility of differentiated reactions within the household has hardly been described in the relevant literature on the subject. Maloney, Aziz and Sarkar [328] state that in interviews a number of cases of infanticide were reported. This was a result of the emergency situation in which the household found itself. The reasons that were mentioned were: the mother was not married (20), [329] poverty (14), neglect (8), handicaps (7), the stepfather hated the child (2) and the chance to remarry (1). Two-thirds of the children that had been "killed" were male. [330] It is not

---

325 The first three mechanisms and strategies for dealing with crises have not been described, as far as I know, in the case of Bangladesh. They are, however, empirically very important, but cannot be discovered without detailed breaking down of the household expenditures and disclosure of the household allocation strategies over longer periods of time. This problem complex is the topic of a dissertation that will be published by Ms Christa Räder within the framework of the Bangladesh project under the auspices of the Institute of Rural Development at the University of Göttingen.

326 [97] Currey, 1981.

327 Cf. [23] Alamgir, 1980: p. 157; and [97] Currey, 1981: p. 125.

328 [246] Maloney, Aziz, Sarkar, 1980: p. 248 f., Tab. 67, 68.

329 The absolute figures that were mentioned are given in parenthesis.

330 In this particular case, the child's gender, if it plays a role at all (as the number is small, this could be coincidence), does not seem to be advantageous for male children.

known whether, under certain circumstances, the neglect and underfeeding of the elderly who are sometimes sent (forced) to beg also leads to higher mortality among the elderly. [331]

In addition to these events, [332] it is possible to establish increased gender-specific mortality. A higher death rate among girls has been recorded that is believed to be the result of, as a rule, *unconscious* neglect of the girls over longer periods of time. There are, however, no socially or economically differentiated and gender-specific death statistics available so that the differences in the rationing of food within the households is not verifiable. [333]

Chen, Huq and D'Souza, however, discovered in their field studies unambiguously that: "The level of malnutrition among girls is substantially higher than among boys. This may be attributed at least in part to marked differences in the intra-family allocation of food between children of differing sexes. ... Overall, the observed pattern is consistent with the conclusion that in cases of family investment and consumption decisions, there is consistent and systematic discrimination against females in all age groups. The bias seems most pronounced among children and the very elderly." [334] However, they relativize this statement by pointing out the fact that there is a lack of panel data.

Chaudhury goes so far as to say on the basis of the analysis of his data: "The data do not support preference for sons in intra-family distribution

---

331 This topic is naturally very touchy and can hardly be "asked" about directly. It can only be "encircled" by means of carefully kept records of births and deaths, something that is impracticable. Direct, empirical observations that the author made make this appear to be desirable.

332 The causes of death are not known; however, due to a lack of sufficient food and neglect, the morbidity can increase so much that illness leads to death.

333 The documentation on the nutritional situation in Bangladesh is complex, confusing, incomplete and inconsistent. The International Centre for Diarrhoeal Disease Research, Bangladesh (ICDDR,B) undertook in Matlab Thana long-term observational studies, which in some cases lasted for years, on the complex of nutrition, health, fertility and mortality as well as influences of medical care and conception-controlling techniques. A few publications appeared in this context which presented preliminary findings, but which were inconsistent and, particularly with respect to the aspect which interests us here, not very conclusive and led to discussions. Therefore, one should take a look at the following studies that were not only written at the ICCDR,B but rather also at the Institute for Food Science, Dhaka University:
[41] Bairagi, Langsten, 1986; [52] Bhuiya, Wojtyniak, D'Souza, and Zimicki, 1986; [53] Bhuiya, Zimicki, and D'Souza, 1986; [78] Chaudhury, 1988; [86] Chowdhury, 1985; [87] Chowdhury, 1988; [81] Chen, Huq, and D'Souza, 1981; [141] Hassan, Huda, and Ahmad, 1985; [140] Hassan, and Ahmad, 1986; [226] Koenig, and D'Souza, 1986; and [300] Roy, Haider, 1988.
These studies, however, give no information on the specific consequences of the adjustment to food crises by reducing the intake of food.

334 [81] Chen, Huq, and D'Souza, 1981: p. 66.

for food when adjustment is made for different nutrient needs of boys and girls." [335]

The data, hence, allow a large number of explanations for the statistically established higher rate of mortality among women and girls. [336]

3.6.1.3 Decreasing the Number of Those Who Have a Right to Make Demands

The variations with respect to those consumers who have a right to make demands within various household communities in Bangladesh have not been the subject of specific studies to date. Therefore, such adjustments can only be ascertained indirectly.

The delaying or hindering of marriages during *times of crisis* has not been described. It is possible to observe the fact, however, that the festivities that accompany the marriage of a daughter and demand large expenditures are put off if unforeseen additional expenditures necessary to overcome a serious crisis arise, such as the illness of the head of the household or the loss of the house. [337] This does not mean that the marriage was not carried out quickly, for a single daughter is also a problem: she (1) has to be cared for and paid for and (2), as an "old maid," she damages the status of the family. The consequence of the reduction in the household's capacity is a smaller dowry and a not as favourable marriage for the girl – adjustment "downwards," which can basically hardly be verified. The household which is faced by serious difficulties is, however, rid of a "burden" and "obligation" once the daughter is married. The earner-consumer quota improves. [338]

---

335 [78] Chaudhury, 1988: p. 33.
336 At this point, the various explanations will not be discussed further. Causalities are obviously difficult to prove because long-term and individual factors work hand in hand and intensive adjacent studies would be necessary. Statistical correlations, however, lead to the supposition that the chances females have under the oppressive patriarchal conditions in Bangladesh are not as good as in the case of their male counterparts. The higher rate of mortality among females is a fact that at times is not unwelcome in a society in which daughters usually only cause expenditures.
    Cf., among others, for example: [226] Koenig, D'Souza, 1986; [52] Bhuiya, Wojtyniak, D'Souza and Zimicki, 1986; and [78] Chaudhury, 1988.
337 Here it is only possible to refer to my own observations. There was a flood in 1986 in the region in which I carried out my own field studies. Quite a few of the dwellings and farm buildings that were made of loam caved in. The expenditures for the new buildings were so high that a few households put off the marriages of their daughters that had been due to take place. The long-term consequences of such catastrophes could not be observed as the schedule for the research project was limited.
338 With respect to holding festivities, in other words marriage festivities under certain circumstances, one can observe adjustments to the seasonal income fluctuations. The time of the *amon* harvest (monsoon rice) when the stocks are full and monetary

Other *forms of excluding* "burdensome" members take place when (1) *young people leave* their parents house so that they do not have to share their *relatively* good wages with other members of the household, but rather, for example, keep them for their own nuclear family. Furthermore, (2) *elderly people* are sometimes *excluded* – especially if they have no children, or sons that only earn poorly – and may have to earn their living by begging, and (3) *children* are sometimes *handed over* to other families where they are raised as quasi children of the family. [339]

This adjusting of the size of the households in crisis situations, i.e. integrating or expelling household members, leads to two contradictory reactions. On the one hand, one can observe [340] that members of a household that has been hit by a catastrophe turn first to their relatives in their search for *"shelter"* and, thus, *the directly hit households reduce their number* and may even *dissolve* until the acute emergency situation is over. This leads, on the other hand, to an *increase* in the size of the households that take up those looking for shelter. This explains the paradox factor that during the crisis years 1972-1974, the average number of members in the households *increased* in comparison to the years 1960 and 1981, as is illustrated in Figure 50. The "hump" in the curve for 1973 towards more people per household, and hence larger households, is an indicator of this development.

Another regulative mechanism for controlling the size of the household is the *arrangement of the time for establishing a family* that as a *consequence* leads to the establishment of one's own new family. Table 16 shows that the age at which small farmers and landless men marry is more than one year older than in the case of well-to-do landowners. Two problems are "solved" by this: (1) the economically important manpower remains on the poorer farms, and (2) the time when the men have to take up the responsibilities involved in "consuming" women and children is delayed.

Table 16 further shows that the average marriage age for girls from prosperous families is older than in the case of poorer girls. That signifies that the "pressure" to marry off girls in order to "save" one more mouth is not as serious in these cases, with the exception of the still very young – socio-

---

income is available and the climate is dryer is the preferred season for marriages.

339 Giving children to brothers or sisters who may not have any children of their own is common. The children are raised in the other household.

This acceptance of "foster relations" should not be confused with "adoption" in which the children do not have any parents, i.e. have to be classified differently.

The abandoning of foundling children at the doors of orphanages is a sad thing. Usually the mothers are widowed, or have been expelled from the family, the children are half starved, sometimes they are already in a coma, and thus the mother who is forced to live in abject poverty has no other choice than this final desperate act.

340 The author's own empirical observations.

Fig. 50: Development Trends in the Number of Households and the People Living in Them According to Household Size, 1960, 1973, 1981 and 1988/89

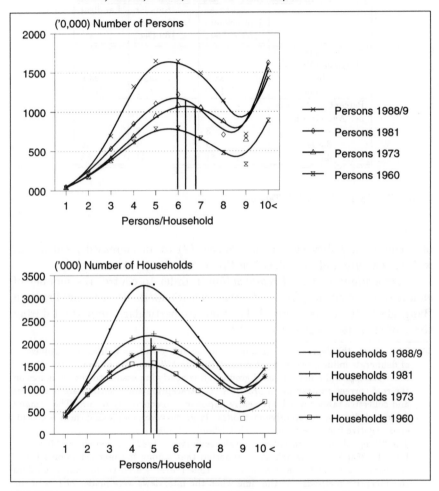

Source: [124] Government, 1988: p. 78 f. Tabs. 2.87 and 2.88; [129] Government, 1991:
p. 178, Tab 4.02.
Note: For the numerical values, see Table 75 in the appendix.

religiously determined – marrying age. The resulting larger differences in age between the spouses among poorer families leads – statistically – (as the table demonstrates) in the case of the women to (1) a greater probability

Tab. 16: Age at the Time of Marriage and Demise of Spouse According to Landed Property Category

	Larger Landowners 160 < Dec.	Smaller Landowners < 160 Dec.	Landless
Average Age at Marriage (Years)			
Men	21.9	23.2	23.0
Women	13.9	13.5	13.1
Percent of Widows per Age Group:			
<35	3	3	6
35-44	9	4	36
45<	41	41	58

Source: [74] Cain, 1978: p. 435, Tab. 3.

of becoming a widow earlier and, hence, (2) to an increased incidence of widows who are underprivileged in the poorer socio-economic strata.

Interventions in sexual reproduction in order to control the number of children, i.e. contraceptive and birth control methods, are employed in Bangladesh. It can be assumed that they are particularly important during times of crisis for those involved. [341]

---

341 The extent, the degree of social and economic differences, as well as the significance of deliberate influences – and not malnutrition and illness – are quite unclear. Due to socio-cultural and religious-moral grounds, it is nearly impossible to obtain figures on the real current contraception practices. Contraception and abortion are individual and collective taboos which are nearly impossible to concretely record. The demand for knowledge of contraceptive methods is large; however, employing them is considered negative from the fundamentalist-Islamic perspective.
The "Bangladesh Contraception Prevalence Survey – 1982" carried out by Mitra and Kamal ([253] Mitra, Kamal, 1985) reported that among the married women below 50 years of age, 33.4 % had at least one time ("ever") used traditional or modern contraceptive methods. At the time when the interviews were made, 24.1 % of the women and 29.5 % of the men reported during an interview of married couples that they used contraceptives ([253] Mitra, 1985: B14, Tab. 4.1).
As usual – for reasons that I cannot ascertain – all of this data has not been categorized according to socio-economic criteria. Perhaps this is due to the lack of sociological training among the more medically oriented population planning experts. It could also be that too much significance is placed on the individual education and attitudes. The formal degree of education of the mother, and in some cases of the men, is sometimes mentioned as an influential factor. However, this criterion is totally irrelevant with respect to 80 % of the rural population.

There is little information available on socially differentiated and, in particular, crisis-determined utilization of such birth control methods. It can be ascertained, nevertheless, (see Figure 24) that women living in poorer households give birth to fewer surviving children. Once born, however, the children have – on the average – approximately the same chances of survival in all of the socio-economic strata, with the exception of differences in gender. [342] With increasing age, however, evidently a socially differentiated mortality rate comes to play in the case of poorer people. [343]

Another possibility of adjusting the size of the household to correspond to the emergency situation is permanent, temporary, or seasonal *migration*. By (1) splitting up the household community and (2) the strategy of searching for and opening up new niches, the attempt is made to cope with the crisis. In addition to land-city migration, permanent land-land migration and seasonal land-land migration are important.

Next to relatively well-educated and active people who move to the cities, there is a large number of people who turn to the city as a last chance due to a permanent or acute emergency situation they are caught up in, or who seek shelter among their relatives in other villages and eventually settle there permanently because they see a better chance of stabilizing or improving their situation in the new environment. [344]

Household structures and household types are, hence, subject to the constant and acute necessity of adjusting to the situation. They react to the "pressures" more or less rapidly and openly. As a rule, *short-term* adjustment to crises is difficult on the basis of this method of regulating the

---

This is not the place to critically illuminate studies of population dynamics. The population "controllers" will only be able to fulfil their task halfway as long as sociological and economic-material aspects receive such little attention during the analyses of the causes of current reproduction behaviour. There are no figures on abortions – in normal times or times of crises. They are, however, carried out with local methods. One cause of a higher mortality rate among women and mothers is in all probability to be found in fatal abortion attempts. One fatal abortion attempt using poison took place during the time when I was carrying out my surveys in the field.

342 Cf. [74] Cain, 1978: p. 436, Tab. 3; and [321] Sohail, 1979: p. 71, Tab. 5 and p. 73, Tab. 6.
343 Cf. [74] Cain, 1978: p. 436.
344 In this context, see, for example, [269] Qadir, 1975; and with respect to the increase in the flow of those looking for help during times of crises: [254] Muqtada, 1981; [97] Currey, 1981; and [25] Alamgir, 1981: p. 131.
     The spatial mobility of the people and the preconditions and consequences of land-land migration have hardly been dealt with quantitatively by research. In reality, however, a large percentage of the rural households "give away" or "take up" members both permanently – within the framework of the normal family biological cycles – as well as temporarily – due to migration for the purpose of finding a job or escaping out of an emergency situation.

number of members. Households or people in a critical poverty situation or who live in a permanent crisis will try to adjust in this area in the near future, or over a longer period of time. One indicator is the correlation between household size and income. [345]

3.6.1.4 Alienation of Production Resources

The alienation of production resources is necessary for the members of a household if the members do not succeed in securing an acceptable standard of living for the remaining household members by means of short-term or long-term increases in production, using up assets, or excluding members.

The liquidation of the productive assets takes place, as a rule, over a longer period of time and insidiously. Important production factors such as land, draught animals and manpower are continually purchased and sold, i.e. exchanged, in normal adjustment processes. During acute crises, moveable productive assets such as, e.g., draught animals, are sold in a first step after other assets have already been exchanged and other resources already mobilized and exhausted. Family manpower that is otherwise only tied to the family's own farm is also offered on the labour market as wage labour. These measures can be introduced very quickly, even if they are faced by falling prices.

Land, as a rule, is more difficult to sell during acute crises. It takes time for the sale to take place, there has to be a demand backed by sufficient purchasing power and landed property is the final anchor for most of the people and is given up last. Thus land is frequently sold only after a period of time following catastrophes when the burden of paying back loans has become unbearable.

In the case of individual catastrophes, the consequences can be seen in a socio-economic descent in relation to other households within the village. In the case of large-scale catastrophes (floods, etc.), in addition to impoverishment of the smallest landowners and an increase in the number of landless, the fact also plays a role that land is bought up by outsiders who are still solvent and frequently come from the cities, or by large landowners and, thus, the village as a whole loses some of its control over the land.

The "land market," i.e. the significance of the permanent exchange of land, has already been described. The significance of land as a final reserve that is only reverted to in extreme emergencies cannot be stressed strongly enough. The overall resulting dynamics of landownership and the land market that can be caused by steady impoverishment and crises (or not), will

---

345 In this context, see Table 39, p. 323.

be taken up once again in Chapter 4.1.

3.6.1.5   Overusing Production Resources

The ruthless exploitation of the means of production is theoretically a strategy that can be employed in order to overcome an emergency situation. The possibility of *overusing* the means of production is presently still limited in Bangladesh; however, this aspect has not been studied nor assessed until now. *Manpower* can only be "overused" on the basis of too little time for rest and recuperation, or malnutrition, i.e. when the food intake does not correspond to the utilization of physical energy, or when the "reproduction of manpower" is no longer guaranteed by the recompensation paid for the manpower. The ruthless exploitation of physical strength that takes place sometimes and can be observed is due more to malnutrition and neglect rather than overwork, a factor that has the same consequences for those involved, but which are the result of two different causal complexes.

Draught animals can be overburdened. Inadequate feed and too little time for rest, particularly during working peaks, can lead to a general low level of performance, to an acute collapse and to too little intake and low calving rates in the case of cows.

The overutilization and destruction of the *soil* that is relevant in other ecological zones seems to be less important for central regions of Bangladesh. What is unclear is the significance and the extent of the permanent extraction of nutrients in both the rice fields as well as in the "highland" regions cultivated with bushes and gardens. In the flat and frequently terraced delta region, the danger of erosion is not as high. [346]

The overutilization of *water* can lead locally to negative consequences

---

346 I do not know of any studies that have dealt with the question of the long-term development of the soil fertility and possible questions of sustained soil utilization and production. Thus, it is only possible to state that six variables seem to contribute to the ecological stability of the soil to various extents: (1) sedimentation through floods; (2) deposition of nutrients through rain water; (3) restoration of nutrients by leaving biomasses on the fields and spreading compost and waste; (4) extraction of nutrients by removing biomasses, i.e. food and feed, and utilization of biomass as fuel and building material; (5) burdening through pesticides, ; and (6) burdening through poor water management (sinking of the water table and deforesting).
The significance of the individual factors and their interdependence over the course of time cannot be judged here.
As a result of ecological devastation, however, in the Himalayas there have been (1) flood waves that destroyed dikes and caused erosion damage along road embankments. Furthermore, (2) sand sedimentation also takes place that destroys the farmland, and (3) one finds direct erosion resulting from meandering rivers. This destruction can, however, be partially attributed to the land utilization system practised by the Bengali.

within a short period of time. (1) Intensive utilization of the ground water levels can sink the water table so drastically that the wells run dry. The utilization of water that contains a high mineral content (salt and iron were reported) can lead to soil destruction and yield losses. On the other hand, excessive and unqualified utilization of chemical inputs can have a direct negative effect upon humans if they absorb the chemicals over the drinking water. Since the hydrologic cycle is very short in Bangladesh, this can lead to local poisoning. The floods during the rainy season, however, dissipate the problem as the water washes it out. An acute danger of overutilization that results from individual predicaments does not seem to exist at the time. [347]

3.6.1.6 The Struggle for Survival

At times, people are unable to avoid a development that leads to their impoverishment, sometimes one that is spread over several generations and sometimes the result of catastrophes that cause or speed up the process. Finally, no assets, no land and no capital are available.

Those who are of healthy body and have the strength to work can sell their labour and, thus, as a rule earn their livelihood and support a small family at a miserable level. For abandoned women or widows and sick people, the situation can be much worse – a threat to life – because they are not strong enough to work, or they do not receive enough pay. At this point, the "inventiveness" of the individual is decisive as to whether he manages on the basis of whatever means he has left at his disposal – even if tricks and criminal offenses – to make a living. [348]

The *"survival strategies"* in the narrow sense that are described in the relevant literature on the subject still necessitate, as a rule, a minimum of social contact or resources and physical fitness. It is not necessary to stress here once again the fact that even with the existence of these pre-conditions, the living conditions are precarious, the physical reproduction is under certain circumstances not guaranteed and risky and can be ultimately endangered by a minimal catastrophe. But there are people in Bangladesh who have absolutely no chance and still try to survive. These are the beggars who consist of the old, the ill, cripples and sometimes their children. These are also the people that look for their last chance at traffic junctions,

---

347 These short statements have to suffice as I am not an expert in the field. The danger of general ecological overutilzation exists; however, that of individual, egocentric (due to a personal plight or profiteering) overutilization is not acute.

348 Persuasive examples that describe survival strategies in Bangladesh are, e.g.: [68] BRAC, 1983; [70] BRAC, 1984; [97] Currey, 1981; [214] Katona-Apte, 1988; and [267] Pryer, 1989.

bridges, landing places for fairies and in the cities. This is the group that dies in the streets in times of need. [349]

1. *Begging* is the final chance for completely uprooted people. One possibility of taking advantage of other resources is the utilization of common, collective resources (common property resources - CPR). However, this results in competition with everyone else. [350] Among other things, the following aspects and activities should be mentioned: gathering wild plants and herbs in the farmers' fields; utilization of "waste" such as processing what is left after threshing has been completed and picking up ears and corn from the fields after the main harvest has been brought in; fishing and trapping small fish in the irrigation channels and ponds; [351] collecting manure from the streets, paths, etc.; and tearing out stubble in the neighbouring fields, digging up tree stumps and bamboo roots; catching frogs; the nightly theft of rice or sweet potatoes; and the theft of food for immediate consumption. All of these activities are carried out. They are seldom described, however, and never quantified because they are basically marginal and split up over time and considered to be insignificant. The evaluation is correct in absolute dimensions, but not in the sense of a last chance that the poorest maintain for themselves.

2. *Accepting and asking for* help or social benefits such as *zākāt*, *fitrā* or *chāndā*, aid in the case of burials, or social welfare such as landowners giving a widow a place to live or supplying her with clothing and alms are further means of securing one's "nacked" existence. Hereby, in other words, claims to specific or general solidarity and patronage are formulated and realized. The transition to making claims for state aid such as food reduced in price or given away (rations - *reśian* and relief - *rilif*), which as a rule is distributed by local politicians who demonstrate their social convictions in this manner, fits without a gap directly into the traditional patronage expectations.

---

349 In December 1974, 700 unknown dead were found in the streets of Dhaka, an increase of several hundred percent in comparison to the month of July in the same year. Cf. [97] Currey, 1981: p. 123.
350 The term "common property resources" (CPR) does not refer only to public land, common pastures, etc. Instead, this term includes "rights of utilization" of certain resources. This consists, e.g., in the right to fish in rice fields or collect manure from cows outside the farm area. Sometimes the interested party has to ask for permission to use the resource, other times not. For certain goods, it is not permitted to refuse the right to use them. There are, in other words, established collective rules and rights governing the right of utilization which the poor and poorest people strive to take advantage of.
351 Systematic fishing with nets is generally no allowed unless the bodies of water belong to the state – Khāś-Land.

Assessment of the volumes of such – private – social welfare within a village came to about 5 % of the total village income. [352] The transitional borders between begging and asking for social welfare are flowing because the claims to social welfare can be supported by "demonstrations of wretchedness" and, on the other hand, beggars can be more or less aggressive and robust in their behaviour. Miserly households may wind up being insulted and threatened if they refuse to give alms or give only too little.

3. "*Outcast*" activities open up another niche. At times, these niches have their own sub-cultural dynamics. Criminality and prostitution are socially taboo and negatively sanctioned. But they offer some people a chance to survive. These activities, however, are not limited to the most wretched. Theft, robbery, kidnapping for ransom and prostitution are special activities carried out by "families" that, in certain cases, have a tradition. In some cases, however, these people emigrate to the urban marginal zones where they can avoid the control of traditional village communities or orthodox Mullahs. Imprisonment, which is very unhealthy in Bangladesh, and the very expensive measures that have to be taken to be freed from the hands of the police leave criminals who have been caught in such a miserable plight that there is nothing left to do other than carry out the next crime in order to have any income at all. At some point, the ends of the circle meet. [353]

3.6.2 Strategical Manipulations – Coping Strategies

Reactions to critical events and the anticipation of situations in which reacting becomes unavoidable play a large role in the action strategies of the rural population in Bangladesh. Avoiding and mitigating risk are strategical *orientations* which attempt to minimize *one's own part leading to the provocation of risks and resulting in them and their escalation*, as well as the consequences. Crises anticipating actions go beyond (additional) risk avoiding behaviour, however, and are reflected (1) in the organizational anticipation of a situation in which preventative measures have to be taken and (2) in the material and personal preparation for the possible event.

The liquidation of "buffer" assets, a measure that is dependent upon the socio-economic situation of the specific person and their household community, is an initial reaction to the individual or general crisis that has taken place. Cutting back expectations and needs, or substituting and putting

---

352 Cf. [147] Herbon, 1984: p. 199, p. 404 f., Tab. 83 and Tab. 84.

353 The fact that one lives a socially marginal existence does not mean, however, that this also coincides with a spatially marginal existence. On the contrary, such households that carry out such activities are spread throughout the villages and regions, are not recognizable for an outsider and have, hence, not been paid attention to by researchers.

them off for a time, i.e. various forms of "saving" (insofar as possible), take place parallel to the liquidation of assets, or take place additionally in the case of crises that last for longer periods of time. The same is valid in the case of attempts to influence and control the number of members in the household community who have the right to make demands on the household. In addition, at times overutilization may result and, as a consequence, a weakening of human and animal productivity. In the existing rice-ecology system in Bangladesh, irreparable damage as the result of individuals overtaxing nature will hardly take place as long as no chemicals are used. [354] Insofar as the effects of the crisis and its consequences cannot be met by liquidating "buffer" resources as well as all other possible available measures, productive exploitable resources (means of production) have to be liquidated. The intervention in the productive assets, however, is the beginning of a process of permanent damage. The productivity of the economic community decreases immediately and in the foreseeable future. An *absolute initial critical point in the crisis* has been reached when land, or all of the land, has to be sold in order to pay debts or buy food.

In this manner, a regressive spiral can begin for the household that does not even stop at landlessness and when the household has reached the level of having to work as farmhands. On the contrary, under the condition that the individual or household-community manpower is negatively influenced by illness, becoming crippled, or by death, then the *second absolute critical point in the crisis* has been reached. In addition to this, abject poverty and as a consequence hunger, more illness and death can be the outcome for the members of the household community.

Processes of decline can be cyclic (with regeneration phases), or cascading (accumulating) and take place over a short period of time, or over a long period of time (over generations). The present socio-economic stratification in the rural society in Bangladesh is, among other things, the result of such processes of decline which were individually "catastrophic" to varying degrees.

---

354 All of these questions of the lasting effects for the ecology have until now received only little attention. The pressure of the problem does not seem to have become that large. *Possibilities for ruthless individual exploitation of resources in order to guarantee, even if only for a short period of time, one's existence seem to hardly exist* if one ignores the basic problem of the shortages in the supply of the people themselves and the marginal possibility of overworking draught animals until they die. As long as the people do not have environmentally poisonous chemicals in any mentionable volumes at their disposal which can be used to increase the production for a short period of time and, thus, work as "last straws," people are the most dangerous and weakest link in the chain. Soil pollution could, however, have direct and extremely catastrophic effects due to the short hydrologic cycle.

The real, economic differences in the initial situation of the individual and the household, family and kinship community with which he is tied creates, however, at the same time different capacities to cope with crises, "the power of resistance."

A large farm household community will certainly be able to mobilize larger amounts and manifold resources in order to cope with the critical situation than a casual worker household with debts. Poorer strata are hit more quickly and harder by crises. The further "down" one is, the more rapidly the decent takes place in a crisis and the more difficult it is to recover and acquire reserves once again. It is clear that crises hit the lower socio-economic classes harder and, on the other hand, the upper classes can take advantage of chances more rapidly and efficiently. The consequences for these regressive and accumulative individual dynamics and the resulting system's dynamics will be the topic of the following chapter.

216

"The potential for increasing rural incomes through diffusion of the modern technology is substantial. ... Technological progress seems to have made a significant impact on alleviation of rural poverty."

Mahabub Hossain [355]

"It still remains uncertain whether the new agricultural technology introduced into Bangladesh will result in a higher production per capita being sustained ... [as] in the recent past. Continuing concern about the sustainability issue is not misplaced."

Mahammad Alauddin, Clem Tisdell [356]

4 Dynamics of Agrarian Structures [357]

4.1 The Development of the Village Conditions of Land Tenure

The present land tenure system in Bangladesh is the result of a long historical development whose fundamental driving force are the population dynamics and the changes in the system of rule. [358] National-statistical data on the land tenure conditions in the past were either not recorded, or were inadequate. Thus, either the representativeness of the random samples

---

355 [166] Hossain, 1988: p. 130.
356 [30] Alauddin, Tisdell, 1988: p. 57.
357 The following chapter is based on an analysis of statistical data under the aspect of the temporal dynamics and the interdependent determination of the consequences. As the material has been gathered and compiled from various published sources, there are at times small breaks in the argumentation when there is a lack of data. It is also difficult not to point out the fact that the material that has been used has methodological shortcomings (1) in order to explain interpretative deficits on my part, (2) in order to explain why I possibly evaluated certain pieces of information or trends differently than the original author himself, (3) in order to designate methodological criteria for generating scientific information in the future and (4) in order not to hide the fact that this is a *secondary analysis* that cannot generate any better data material than that found in the literature upon which it is based.
     This type of reasoning may seem difficult to follow to the reader; however, it seems to me to be only in this manner possible to (1) make use of and comment the manifold material from other authors, which is limited at the same time, and (2) to produce a theoretical and systems dynamic summary that transcends the informational content of the studies that have been carried out to date.
358 Cf., e.g., [59] Bose, 1986, p. 3 ff.; [229] Kuhnen, 1965; [298] Ray, Ray, 1973; and [323] Stepanek, 1978: p. 92 ff.

was not guaranteed, or it was not possible to compare the data due to differing criteria used to develop the categories. The agricultural census from 1960, [359] the Land Occupancy Survey from 1977 [360] and the agricultural census from 1983/4 [361] present a general, statistical picture of the developments in land tenure during the last 25 years (1960 to 1984). This has already been sketched in Chapter 2.3.6.

In the following four sections, therefore, an attempt will be made to gain an overview based on data obtained in panel surveys – for the most part village studies – on (1) the general causes and reasons for the transfer of land rights; (2) the "individual" socially differentiated land mobility; (3) the "collective," village dynamics of property distribution; and (4) the trends on the tenancy market with their consequences for the size of the farms.

4.1.1 Reasons and Causes for the Transfer of Land

The various forms of control and property and utilization rights with respect to land, as has already been described in Chapter 3.4.1.1, display diverse characteristics. The key mechanisms involved in the transfer of land from one person to another are (1) inheritance and presents made between the generations, i.e. land is handed over, and under certain circumstances, dispossession or allotments made by the state; (2) the selling of land; and (3) temporary transfers within the framework of various tenancy arrangements.

The transfer of land from one generation to the next leads in the course of time – and under the conditions of the present population growth rate – as well as the generally adhered to Islamic laws governing inheritance – the "real" distribution of the estate left by the person who passed away – to a *fragmentation* of the land. According to the statistical average, each person in the following generation receives less land than the members of the previous generation. In the future, the *per capita availability and distribution of land* is going to "worsen," as will be shown in the following.

Purchases and sales of land, individual acquisitions, or dispossession by the state are mechanisms that effect the specific individual disposition of land. The motivations for selling land are complex and vary. The major reason for the permanent transfer of land is, however, need. Illness, hunger and social obligations – e.g., the marriage of a daughter who has to be given a dowry – frequently force the one time only, or "creeping" successive selling of parcels of land. This process of impoverishment directly effects the resources of the specific person. On the other hand, in this manner a

---

359 [131] Government of Pakistan, 1962.
360 Cf. [196] Jannuzi, Peach, 1980.
361 [119] Government, 1986; [121] Government, 1986; and [125] Government, 1986.

few successful individuals are able to gain additional land and improve their endowment.

By gaining land on a permanent basis, it is possible to counter the process in which the per capita disposition of land continually decreases. The area of land owned by sons may indeed in accordance with their share be smaller than that owned by the fathers; however, one or the other son may be able to once again improve their individual land endowment by purchasing new land. On the average, however, each generation begins at a lower land endowment level. In addition, the forced selling of land due to a crisis leads to cumulative effects in a negative spiral.

The individual disposition of the individually available landed property is the framework in which its utilization for the purpose of farming can take place. By means of renting or leasing land, it is then possible to complement, to a greater or lesser extent, the property one owns by means of rented land. Renting out one's own land may under certain circumstances seem advantageous to the individual. Frequently, a "regrouping" of parcels may also take place if certain parcels are rented out while others that are more favourably located are leased. At the end of these dispositions, there are statistical, and often empirical deviations between the area under cultivation by the farm in comparison to the area owned. [362] The at any one time transferred farmland and the specific combination of rights of disposition of other parcels of land lead to complex tenancy and farm systems.

In the following, the disposition of land and the development up to the present conditions will be sketched in a first step. The resulting differentiated picture of the development of the rights to land and the disposition potential is the focal point of a number of publications and simultaneously the logical basis for studying the production activities.

4.1.2 The Mobility of Land and the Changes in the Size of Property

There are basically two ways for individual household communities to gain landed property: by inheritance and by purchasing land.[363] The initial en-

---

362 Cf. Chapter 3.4.1.1, p. 148 ff.
363 Methodological comment: *analysis of empirical processes.*
Most socio-economic empirical surveys can, as a rule, be made only once. Repetitions or panel surveys are generally not carried out. Thus, as a rule only analyses of the actual, real situation – i.e., for example, descriptions of specific distribution *structures* – are possible, but not however the development *direction* and the distribution *processes*. In order to make statements on the development trends despite this fact, the attempt is made as a rule to reconstruct past conditions and processes that have led to the present situation on the basis of memory and calculating back. In order to

dowment of each household is, as a rule, inherited. Frequently, however, the household is established before the inheritance is available so that either the first parcels of land owned by the household are purchased by the household, or the parents transfer shares of their property to the new household prematurely. In addition, a young man can simply lease land himself, even perhaps from his own parents.

Chaudhury [364] illustrates – see Figure 51 – the significance of the various manners of acquiring land. For the households that have little land, inheriting land is very important. Receiving land as a gift also plays a role, even if only a small one. This is because newly founded households are established at first without any land of their own and are, under certain circumstances, classified as "landless," but are later able to improve their situation and over the course of the years enhance their position by purchasing land or receiving it later by inheritance.

It is also clear that the significance of acquiring additional land increases with the size of the household's property. This is because (1) households with larger amounts of land tend to be endowed with more purchasing power, and (2) they are formed by older and larger households which as a rule, apart from their initial endowment that they inherited, have with the increasing "age" of the household only the possibility of purchasing additional land.

As no study is available on how the land left by the deceased is distributed among the various generations during the course of the years, this can merely be indirectly – statistically – deduced. The quadrupling of the population since the beginning of the century leads, ceteris paribus, to the conclusion that the average per capita inheritance that can be expected has been reduced to one-fourth. The initial situation of the new households, in other words, worsens form generation to generation.

do so, either a fixed point of reference is decided upon and, e.g., questions are asked referring to the status of landed property at that time, or the questions refer to the situation of the household at the time it was established. Both approaches imply more or less very large methodological problems: the statements and knowledge that is gained, however, is usually correct regarding the basic trend – even if not very precise and dependable – and more informative than theoretical deductions.

With respect to the equilibrium of land transfer and land mobility in Bangladesh, see among others: [14] Ahmed, 1987: p. 16, Tab. 5; [21] Alam. 1983: p. 74, Tab. 4.10; [79] Chaudhury, 1989: p. 161, Tab. 5.5 and 5.6; [147] Herbon, 1984: p. 224 ff. and p. 372, Tabs. 29 and 30; [322] Spinatsch, 1984: p. 222 ff., Tabs. 43, and 46 to 48; and [343] Westergaard, o.J.: p. 23 ff., Tab. 7. In particular see [49] Bhaduri, Rahman, Arn, 1986, whose conclusions and methodological concepts started a debate in the *Journal of Peasant Studies*. With respect to this debate, see: [50] Bhaduri, Rahman, Arn, 1988; [108] Feldman, McCarthy, 1987; [220] Khan, 1987; [264] Pandian, 1987; [265] Pandian, 1987; and [284] Rahmen, 1988.

364 [79] Chaudhury, 1989.

Land Acquired between 1969/70 and 1979 in a Village According to Manner of Acquisition and Property-size Category

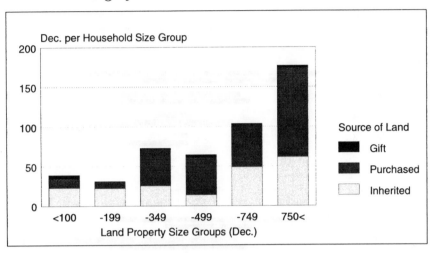

Source: [79] Chaudhury, 1989: Tab. 5.6.
Note: For the numerical values, see Table 72 in the appendix.

The improvement in the situation, i.e. the "re-ascent," therefore, usually has to be achieved on the basis of purchasing additional land. Ahmed recorded the purchases and sales of land in a study of two villages in Comilla for the period from 1972 until 1981. In the study, he contrasted the land transactions in the two villages. In one village, it is possible to cultivate the land on the basis of irrigation, and it is also possible to utilize the new forms of agricultural technology. In the other village, irrigation is not used, i.e. its productivity development is hampered, a factor which influences the land mobility.

The two figures 52 and 53 each illustrate the significance of the land transactions according to per capita household income and farm-size category. The following aspects become clear. [365]

---

365 The study has a methodological shortcoming which limits the interpretation of the data and makes it more difficult. Despite this fact, the material – as there are no better alternatives available – will be presented here. Ahmed recorded according to various criteria only the conditions of those households that took part in the transactions (purchasing and selling), but not the relative significance of these criteria within the parent unit, the village. Using this method, it is only possible to establish

Fig. 52: Purchases and Sales of Land between 1972 and 1981 in a Village without Irrigation According to Monthly per Capita Income of the Household and Farm-size Category

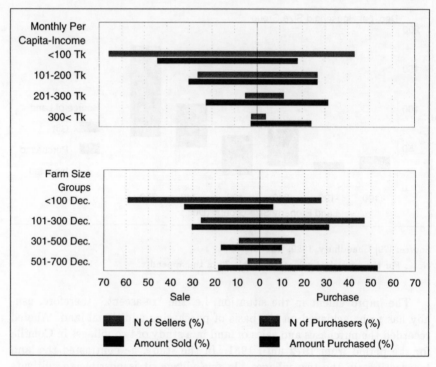

Source: [14] Ahmed, 1987: p. 11, Tab. 2: and p. 16, Tab. 5.
Note: For the numerical values, see Table 76 in the appendix.
Size of the total random sample = 300 households; households which sold land = 76 (25.3 %); and households which purchased land = 51 (17.0 %).
This data was acquired by means of questions pertaining to the past and can, therefore, not be regarded as absolute. Furthermore, Ahmed did not present data on the distribution of the group characteristics within the total population. The relative significance of the data can, therefore, not be evaluated.

1. Smaller *farms* make up the majority of those which sell land. The larger the farms are, the smaller the percentage of sellers. [366] If, however,

---

relative proportions and not absolute relations. Conclusions derived on the basis of such material can only be accepted with reservations.

366 It is not possible to say whether the percentages correspond to the parent unit.

Fig. 53: Purchases and Sales of Land between 1972 and 1981 in a Village with Irrigation According to Monthly per Capita Income of the Household and Farm-size Category

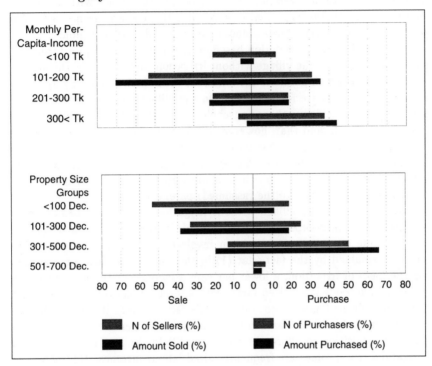

Source: [14] Ahmed, 1987: p. 11, Tab. 2; and p. 16, Tab. 5.
Note: For the numerical values, see Table 76 in the appendix.
Size of the random sample = 143 households; households which sold land = 15 (10.5 %); and households which purchased land = 16 (11.2 %).
Also see the note to Figure 53, p. 222.

land is sold, then the average areas sold are larger in the case of the larger farms.

2. Farms belonging to all of the size categories, however, also purchase land. The middle-sized and large farms are interested in and involved in purchasing land complementary to selling it. In the village without irrigation, it is specifically the middle-sized farms that are active in terms of figures. They are definitely interested in expanding the size of their farmland in order to increase their production while the level of technology remains constant.

In the village with irrigation, it is mainly the larger farms (300 - 500 dec.) that are both interested in purchasing land and have the purchasing power to do so.

3. Based on the amount of land, the *middle-sized to large farms* (100 - 500 dec.) are very involved in purchasing land in the village with irrigation. In the region without irrigation, however, it is the few large farms (500 - 700 dec.) which accumulate large amounts of farmland in this fashion.

4. According to the criterion based on the *monthly per capita income*, it is the households in the village without irrigation that belong to the higher-income groups which purchase the land that the households belonging to the low-income groups are forced to sell. In the village with irrigation, on the contrary, it is specifically those households that belong to the middle-income groups which sell land that, however, is bought by households belonging to all of the income groups. The amount of land per purchase remains nearly constant over all of the three higher-income groups. The highest-income groups, however, appear to purchase land overproportionally with a view to the (presumed) relation to the (assumed) parent unit.

5. Whereas in the village without irrigation, households belonging to the lower-income groups also purchase land, in the village with irrigation, such income groups are only seldom involved in such transactions. This can be explained by the fact that (1) in the case of the farming practised on the basis of irrigation, a lower per capita income for the household can be found alongside large-sized farms with a large amount of land (extended families). These families can, despite this fact, be very interested in purchasing land. Since land as a rule is relatively inexpensive, they are more likely in a position to afford the purchase. (2) In the agriculture based on irrigation, low incomes are frequently hired-labour incomes. Households in this socio-economic situation are, however, no longer represented in the dynamic high-price land market of the villages practising intensive cultivation of the land.

6. In the village with irrigation, the absolute farm size seems to be the determinante factor both for selling as well as purchasing land. Income is merely a "deduced variable." [367]

---

367 In the village with irrigation, a process of differentiation seems to be taking place: middle-sized to large farms are buying up the land that the small farms that are in financial difficulties are forced to sell. Simultaneously, however, households with middle-sized per capita incomes (Tk 100 - 200) also sell land. Without Ahmed having said so, it is possible to presume that a process of economic differentiation is taking place that is caused by the increased need for capital on the part of the farms practising intensive farming, on the one hand, and a demand on the part of the small farms that have the purchasing power. Unfortunately, the published material, the size of the sample and the theoretical interpretation of the data by Ahmed are rather

7. Finally, it is perhaps possible to summarize and say that (1) a more static form of agriculture without irrigation seems to bring about a process of polarization – according to the criterion of the distribution of property and farmland: smaller farms sell land, larger farms buy it up. (2) In the case of irrigated farming, which is probably also more dynamic, the smallest farms and the low-income groups tend to purchase land. The relative importance of large farms and the households with high per capita incomes also sinks. A demand backed by real purchasing power, on the one hand, but also the necessity to sell land, on the other hand, is concentrated in the middle-sized farms and income categories. As will be illustrated in Chapter 4.3.2, the farm workers' wages and incomes increase in the villages practising intensive irrigation farming so that the marginal landowners, who can also take up a job as a farmhand if need be, are confronted by less of a necessity to sell land.

Rahman [368] presents extensive material on land mobility based on his empirical survey of two villages covering the past period from 1951 to 1981 (1985). [369] In his presentation, however, he neither differentiates according to the type of acquisition or loss of land, nor the reasons that led to the land transaction.

The dynamics that households with diverse landownership statuses are faced by are presented in Figure 54. [370] The following statements can be derived on the basis of the survey. [371]

---

needy so that the deductions found here can only be understood as hypotheses that require further studies.

The need for research on the historical development and the socio-economic differential dynamics of the land market (purchasing/selling) becomes evident. It is certainly difficult to obtain such data; however, the theoretical conclusions that are frequently drawn up still need to be substantiated.

368 [279] Rahman, 1982, and [281] Rahman, 1986.
369 Rahman also based his survey on retrospective interviews studying the past land mobility. Thus there are uncertainties in the data in this case as well. The survey is made difficult by memory gaps as well as the fact that the subject of losses and gains in the form of land is very sensitive and the answers that are given are frequently either evasive or false.

The ideal case of a panel survey carried out in one and the same village at different times with large enough time intervals is not available for Bangladesh.

370 The villages were not selected on the basis of dichotomous characteristics (irrigated versus non-irrigated farming), but rather with the claim to being more or less representative.

See [281] Rahman, 1986: p. 265 ff.

371 Unfortunately, he does not supply any absolute figures. The problem in Rahmans's percentage data is that the population increase and, hence, the splitting up of inheritances, which is a significant force behind land transactions, has not been explicitly presented.

Fig. 54: Land Mobility in Two Villages, 1951 - 1981, According to Holding-size Category, Regarded Prospectively and Retrospectively

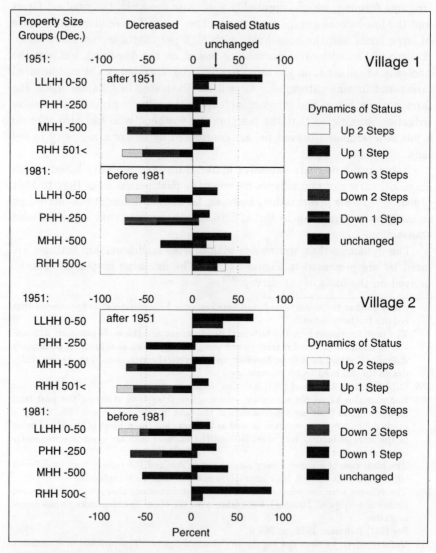

Source: [281] Rahman, 1986: p. 87, Tab. 3.5; and [281] Rahman, 1986: p. 88, Tab. 3.6.
Note: For the numerical values, see Table 77 in the appendix.

1. On the basis of 1951, one can state that since then only a small percentage of the households in both villages have succeeded in improving their situation significantly by means of acquiring land, i.e. moving up into a higher landownership category. Many households have, however, descended on the scale in the course of 30 years: some even from the wealthiest category down to that of being landless.

2. Of those that are (nearly) landless, approximately one-fourth to one-third were able to *improve* their position. [372] A descent is in principle hardly possible in this case.

3. The middle-sized farms (50 - 250 dec.) are strongly endangered by a descent in status. In village 1, approximately half of the households were able to maintain their status and, in some cases, improve it; however, the other half descended on the scale. In village 2, in this category (50 - 350 dec.), there were fewer who ascended on the scale, but at the same time there were more stable households.

4. In the category made up of the middle-sized and larger farms (250 - 500 dec. and 350 - 750 dec.), more than three-fourths of the households descended at least one category level and in some cases two, all the way down to landlessness. This took place in both villages. Only a small minority were able to ascend on the scale. The same is true in the case of the category consisting of the largest farms and the category directly below, but in a somewhat aggravated form.

5. As an *interim result*, one can state the fact that *the percentage of those descending the scale increases gravely the better the original position was*. The situation of the well-endowed households worsened to a much greater extent than that of the poor households. It should be mentioned, however, that the worsening of their situation usually still ends at a well-to-do level, whereas the landless can hardly end up in a worse situation.

6. Looking back from 1981, the majority of the households that were classified as belonging to the specific categories were recruited from households that had descended on the scale since 1951.

7. Those that were landless in 1981 and the middle-sized farm households (up to 250-350 dec.) were made up in both villages to about three-fourths by households that had descended on the scale.

8. In the larger farm-size categories, the percentage of households that was able to keep their position stable or even ascend the scale outweighs by far that percentage that was added on the basis of their having descended the scale.

---

372 This was, as has been illustrated in Fig. 51, partly on the basis of later inheritances or gifts. It is also possible under certain circumstances to acquire a piece of dry land and such.

9. The result of this interpretation can be described as the fact that the present (1981) members of specific holding-size and landownership categories probably already belonged with increasing holding-size to the category in 1951. That is to say, *only seldom does a household succeed in ascending the scale. Descent is the rule. The chance of ascending the scale increases with the size of the farm;* however, this can to no extent compensate for the pressure causing descent and the resulting decrease in the size of the farmland.

The above-presented discourse makes the following clear: the general process in which the farms are split up and the constant sales of land and, hence, the increase in the number of farms in the lower categories is the result of (1) the effect of the population growth and fragmentation of the estates left by the deceased and (2) of the increasing pressure to sell land the less one already has. For under such conditions, other emergency reserves are usually smaller. Thus, land is frequently the last form of security. The large landowners are particularly hit by the first effect: the households are on the average large, have more heirs and the fragmentation is graver in an absolute sense. The small households are hit by the second effect. In the case of the larger landowners, a rapid decrease in the average farm size is the consequence. The consequence for those households that are smaller and have little land, is a growing probability of losing their land in an emergency situation and becoming landless. The changes in income resulting from the transition in agrarian technology have, in this case, mitigating and hindering impacts, as will be discussed later in Chapter 4.4.3.

The process that has become visible on the basis of the above discourse can be characterized as follows: there is a general *drift* from fewer and larger to more and smaller farms. The number of farms increases while the volume of land remains constant. [373] An overproportional increase in landlessness takes place that can be described as land pauperization and that – theoretically – can lead to universal pauperization. The fact that this need not be the case will be illustrated in Chapter 4.4.

Discussions about the landownership conditions are frequently kindled by the inequality in the distribution of the property and the discrepancies in size. The fact is often assumed [374] that the large landowners "swallow" the small ones. This assumption is – regarded statistically – false.

Before the consequences of the decreases in the size of the farms and property will be discussed further, in the following section the absolute *shift* in ownership will be made clear, once again on the basis of differentiated

---

373 See, e.g., Figure 60, p. 238.
374 See the discussion in Chapter 2.2.

land distribution statistics according to ownership-size categories.

4.1.3 The Aggregated Dynamics of Landownership Distribution

In Figures 55 to 59, [375] the data that is presented is from surveys that studied the shifts in the landownership conditions over the course of several years. [376]

In order to illustrate the shifts, "trend curves" have been added. This simplifies the complicated shifts and makes them clearer. For three reasons the decision was made not to present the data in the form of Lorenz curves or calculate the Gini coefficients. (1) Data on the areas are not available in all cases, (2) these two operations conceal "structural" shifts and (3) they cover up the effects of the increase in the population. [377] The studies and data clearly show the following phenomena.

1. The households that have absolutely no land are increasing in number drastically. The initial basis, however, varies (ca. 3 % and 6 % in 1951 in Rahman's villages, and 17 % in 1951 in Siddiqui's). In the villages that

---

375 In order to make the presentations more or less uniform and because in several sources absolute figures are missing, percentages were used for the calculations. The oldest year forms the basis year for the percentage of the households per ownership-size category (= 100 %). The population growth leads on this basis to total percentage figures higher than 100. In this manner, not only percentage-wise, but also absolute shifts become evident.

376 Studies which record the land tenure in a village at several points in time are rare since historical material is only available in a few cases. Siddiqui ([316], 1982) presents in his study of a village both the number of households as well as the size of the areas found in various ownership-size categories for the years 1951, 1961 and 1977. Rahman ([281], 1986) even recorded the same type of data for the years 1951, 1972 and 1982 for two different villages. Schendel's ([309], 1981) data go back even further in time, but they only refer to the number of households per ownership-size category without recording the size of the area. He presents data on three villages for 1933, 1960 and 1977, as well as 1922, 1955, 1978 and 1894, 1960 and 1978. A few of the data collected by the author (Herbon) of a prospective study record data for 1980 and 1986, and the number of households with the individual land endowment.

377 I would like to present the wealth of material, although the structures and dynamics are partly repetitive. This is just the point that has to be shown in view of missing national data. On the basis of various villages and diverse methodological and conceptual procedures, however, it is possible to distill analogous characteristics for the structures and processes.

In this context, see once again the two Figures 12 and 13 on pages 67 and 68 in which the national data are presented.

Since the authors, under certain circumstances, themselves come to the statistical conclusion on the basis of the material presented here that the income conditions are becoming increasingly polarized and come to the political conclusion that in order to change these conditions radical political changes would be necessary, the presentation of this comprehensive data will serve to refute this popular opinion.

Fig. 55: Development in Size and Distribution of Landed Property in Village 1 – 1951, 1961 and 1977

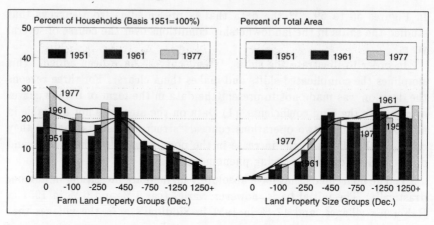

Source: [316] Siddiqui, 1982: p. 136 ff., Tabs. 4, 5 and 6.
Note: For the numerical values, see Table 78 in the appendix.

Fig. 56: Development in Size and Distribution of Landed Property in Village 2 – 1951, 1972 and 1981

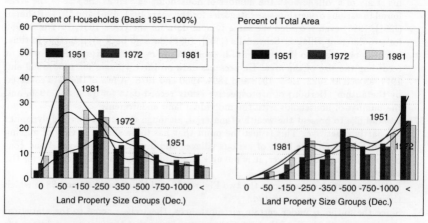

Source: [279] Rahman, 1982: p. 56, Tab. 2.a.
Note: For the numerical values, see Table 79 in the appendix.

Fig. 57: Development of Size and Distribution of Landed Property in Village 3 – 1951, 1972 and 1981

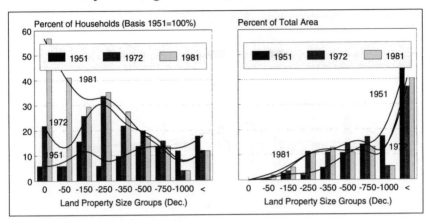

Source: [279] Rahman, 1982: p. 57, Tab. 2b.

Note: For the numerical values, see Table 80 in the appendix.

Fig. 58: Development in Size and Distribution of Landed Property in Village 4 – 1980 and 1986

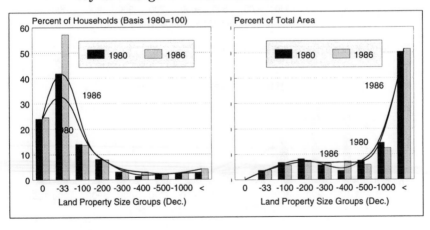

Source: the author's own unpublished survey.

Note: For the numerical values, see Table 81 in the appendix.

Fig. 59: Development in the Size and Distribution of Landed Property in Villages 5, 6 and 7 – 1894 to 1978

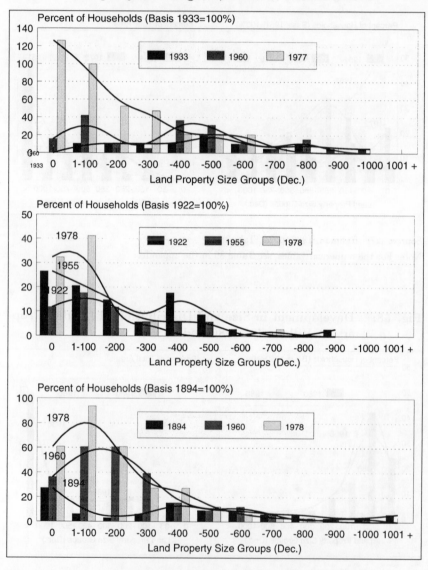

Source: [309] Schendel, 1981: p. 81, Tab. 2.11; p. 162, Tab. 3.13; and p. 231, Tab. 4.10.
Note: For the numerical values, see Table 82 in the appendix.

232

Schendel surveyed, landlessness was already very significant at the beginning of the 20th century.

2. The households with the most land at their disposal are losing significance both in number as well as in their "group"-specific area endowment, i.e. the absolute area that they control. In some cases, they are able to succeed in stabilizing their position. It is not possible to show land accumulation in the case of these households. In these ownership-size categories, the effects of fragmentation due to inheritance are especially marked. Evidently the households in these categories are only partly successful in combating the effects of fragmentation by means of acquiring additional land. Due to fragmentation caused by inheritance, many large holdings are reduced to middle-sized holdings.

3. It is possible to record a certain "middle-sized holding bulge" in all of the villages. Thus it can be seen that the larger holdings *tend* to lose land. Their number and the amount of land they have is decreasing. On the other hand, the percentage of land controlled by and the number of smaller and middle-sized owners is increasing. In the case of the smallest holdings, they sink once again – relatively – and then soar upwards extremely in the case of the completely landless.

4. The landownership structure shifts overall firstly in the direction of *more small* property units. The relative significance of the very large landowners is decreasing. Landlessness is increasing drastically and over-proportionally. However, a number of smaller and middle-sized holdings seem to be able to resist the downwards pull without, on the other hand, being able to improve their situation fundamentally. This seems to explain the "middle-sized holding bulge." In the case of the smallest landowners, the conditions seem to split: into landowners who succeed in maintaining or acquiring their small or middle-sized areas of farmland and, thus, remain in the "middle-sized holding bulge," and into landowners who lose most or all of their land in times of need and sink to the level of absolute or functional landlessness and, hence, contribute to the increase in the number of landless.

5. The population growth, measured on the number of households, leads basically to an increase in the number of landless and smallest landowners. That means, on the other hand, that the conditions for the landowners worsen more slowly than the population grows. That also means that the population growth is seen mainly in an overproportional increase in the number of landless households and people. Only a few households, i.e. their heads and members, manage to hold on to their landed property "against the tide."

In the discussion in Bangladesh on the development of the land tenure, four terms play a key role: concentration, polarization, persistence and differentiation.

Rahman, in particular, uses the terms concentration and differentiation, and Jahangir uses the terms differentiation, polarization and confrontation – both against the background of a Marxist interpretation: Rahman [378] argues on the basis of two village studies [379] that the percentage of land belonging to landowners in the lowest 60 % sank from 24.35 % in 1951 to 12.00 % in 1981 in his first village (here village 2), whereas the upper 10 % of the landowners increased their share from 34.81 % in 1951 to 47.85 % in 1981. He argues in the same manner with respect to his second village (here village 3) that the percentage belonging to the lower 60 % of the village households sank from 24.53 % in 1951 to 10.90 % in 1981, and the percentage of the upper 10 % increased from 29.69 % in 1951 to 35.81 % in 1981.

Using this argumentation as a basis, he comes to a misleading and, therefore, inadmissible conclusion without paying attention to the structural warps and complications and the population growth – in contrast to my interpretation and presentation of his data – and states that "...it may be summarized that *concentration* of land *in the hand of a few* has increased in both our study villages. Simultaneously a tremendous increase in the growth of landlessness was observed." [380]

If the term "*increasing concentration*" refers to an increase in the value of the Gini coefficients, the "coefficient of concentration," then the statement is indeed correct, but it says nothing. De facto, the distribution of landownership in his study villages, as in general in Bangladesh, is very *unequal*. That is *correct* and not new. That the landownership is *concentrated* "in the hands of a few" in the sense of *accumulation* is *false*. [381]

Ahmed [382] argues in a vein similar to that used by Rahman. The unequal distribution has been increasing, accordingly, in the villages he studied as well. Effects such as population growth and fragmentation due to inheritance remain unconsidered. [383] All in all, using the Gini coefficients as a basis for

---

378 [279] Rahman, 1982; [281] Rahman, 1986; and [284] Rahman, 1988.
379 The data from these two village studies were used in the past discourses. Interestingly, they were only used in the earliest publication: [279] Rahman, 1982. In his major publication – [281] Rahman, 1986 – they are only used in percentages. This is done for the purpose of a specific argumentation in which the negative overall trend is exposed. If one reverts to the absolute figures, however, as is done here, this leads to completely different conclusions. See the discourse here and in the following.
380 [281] Rahman, 1986: p. 114, my own italics.
381 The fact that the absolute figures are not presented in the publication in 1986, while at the same time the author comes to such conclusions, can only be caused by the ideological message the author wants to convey.
382 [16] Ahmed, 1984: p. 65 ff.
383 For a presentation of the distribution structures of landed property, as a rule in the form of Lorenz curves, see among others, [16] Ahmed, 1984: p. 74, Tab. 26; [21] Alam,

234

judging the character of the process and the structural conditions does not suffice. Concentration as a description of a state, i.e. inequality, is correct, but as a description of a process, the term is false. Jahangir's argumentation, which delivers hardly any relevant statistical material or empirical evidence, but who instead argues from a theoretical position, is situated at a similar (but more primitive) level. He states that, on the one hand, continually more farmers are becoming alienated from their means of production and that, on the other hand, the land is becoming *concentrated* in the hands of land speculators in alliance with external powers. Concentration in the sense meant here is difficult to prove empirically and cannot be proved on the basis of national statistics. And whether one classifies landowners and landless in antagonistic classes and, thus, proves in circular reasoning that there are divergencies is a theoretical-conceptual (ideological ?) problem and, thus, quite arbitrary.

In Chapter 4.1.2, in the presentation of the empirical findings on land mobility, the fact has already been established that the manifest development can be defined as a general *drift* towards smaller holdings and landlessness, i.e. that one could ceteris paribus speak of *pauperization*. This conclusion, however, is not imperative because alternative or additional income sources can help avoid pauperization.

Also the concept behind the term *persistence*, maintaining one's ownership status and the stabilization of one's position, becomes clear if one considers the fact that Ahmed's land purchasing and selling transactions in the village with irrigation concerned only ca. 11 % of the households and in the village without irrigation ca. 25 % [384] of the recorded households and that the others, in contrast, were obviously able to avoid such transactions. Figure 54 also shows clearly that despite a generally negative trend there are also a number of households that were able to maintain their position. *The better the basic endowment in land was and is, the greater was and is the chance of stabilizing the situation.*

The households that succeed, in other words, in "swimming against the tide" are particularly interesting from an individualistic viewpoint because they can (1) give indications as to special strategies, and (2) if they are neglected, there is the danger that they will be lost in statistical averages and thus encourage a simplified picture of the conditions. [385]

1983: p. 70, Tab. 4.8, Fig. 4.1; [147] Herbon, 1984: p. 224, Graphic 32; [159] Hoque, 1987: p. 183, Fig. 1; and [323] Stepanek, 1978: p. 99, Fig. 7.1. The value of the knowledge one can draw from them is, however, relatively limited.

384 [14] Ahmed, 1987: p. 24.

385 Unfortunately, the category of people who "successfully swim against the tide" is not particularly suitable as a category for an empirical study because the fact is evidently

The interpretation that the number of landless is enormous, even over-proportional, and increasing is correct, but it does not substantiate the argument that there is *concentration*. The implication is incorrect that land-lessness and striving to acquire land can be traced back to the rich. The implication is misleading that knowledge of the distribution of the "material basic resources," i.e. the distribution of the ownership rights for the "most important" means of production in an agrarian society – land – suffices to prognosticate the individual and collective development dynamics and chances. [386] Temporarily and in content limited rights of use of land in the form of tenancy are also of importance. The development and dynamics of tenancy will be discussed in the following section.

4.1.4 The Development and Dynamics of the Tenancy Market

A piece of land that has been acquired at one time is the basis upon which agricultural activities are carried out. Only about 1.4 % of all of the farms are true tenancy farms and make up merely 0.5 % of the total farmland. [387] However, many more households and farms attempt to increase their farm-land by renting additional land. They thus employ their able-bodied and willing household members who they have, in any case, at their disoposal and in this way they use their relatively fixed means of production more effi-ciently and/or generate more income. [388] The socio-economic differentiated significance of tenancy, i.e. of share tenancy and the other forms of tenancy,

---

difficult to establish. Real material endowments, which studies pay a great deal of attention to with respect to their distribution, are however limited in their ability to explain the facts and conditions. "The power to assert oneself" or "ability to sur-vive" and the strategies that lead to this success require increased attention because factors evidently intervene here that make projections on the basis of endowment distribution worthless and because in this case reasons for incalculable social and economic dynamics could be evidently found. At the *Institute of Rural Development* in Göttingen, a number of studies are being carried out that will attempt to help enlighten these aspects.

386 The criticism made by a few theoreticians of the land tenure system in Bangladesh and their methodological logic have been presented in such detail in this context because they made and published the fundamental suppositions that will have an influence on my following discourse and which characterize the viewpoint and inter-pretation of some other authors and have, until now, led to negative prognoses and socio-normative political stipulations. These "traditional" fundamental suppositions substantiate an own virtual reality that the social economists believe in that, on the one hand, has little to do with the virtual reality of the economy and the science of production and, on the other hand, even more so with the factual reality of the rural population.

387 [125] Government, 1988: p. 29.

388 See Figure 10.

has already been discussed in Chapter 3.4.1.1. Therefore, the attempt will be made here to, on the basis of the very sparse data and indicators, illustrate the changing significance of tenancy in the course of time, i.e. the dynamics of the tenancy market.

Tab. 17: Development in the Average Holding Size According to Farming Status from 1960 to 1983

Farming Status	Average Farm Size (Acres) In the Years			Magnitude of Change (1960 - 1983)
	1960	1977	1983	
Self-operator	3.12	3.71	2.13	-31.7 %
Owner-tenant	4.26	3.72	2.58	-39.4 %
Tenant only	2.42	2.54	0.91	-62.4 %
All Holdings	3.54	3.51	2.27	-35.9 %

Source: [125] Government, 1988: p. 29.

Figure 60 clearly illustrates the fact that, on the one hand, the total number of farms increased from 1960 to 1983/84 by about 50 %. On the other hand, however, the number of farms renting additional land has only increased relatively little, while the tenancy-only farms did not increase at all. The development in the percentages of land that farms renting additional land cultivated all in all – the percentage of land owned by these farms themselves is unfortunately not recorded separately in the sources – has decreased relatively.[389] Table 17 shows that not only the relative percentages of the types of ownership are decreasing, but rather also the average farm size:

The average decrease in the farm size is greatest among those holdings which are – at the lowest level – pure tenant holdings, followed by those holdings which lease additional land. It is clear that the average size of the holdings is becoming smaller overall; however, the tenant holdings are becoming smaller more rapidly. Thus one can establish the fact that in addition to the trend towards smaller holdings, self-management is increasing overproportionally. *The significance of tenancy* for increasing the amount of arable land operated is, in other words, *decreasing greatly.*

Figure 61 illustrates on the basis of data from two villages that (1) the significance of the percentage of land rented under tenancy agreements

---

389 With reference to the conditions in 1983/4, see Figures 11 and 12 on pages 67 ff.

Fig. 60: Development in the Number of Farms, Self-operator, Owner-tenant, or Tenant Only, 1960 to 1983/84

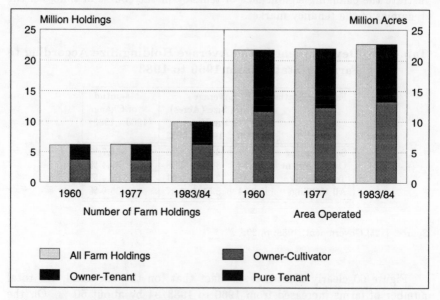

Source: [125] Government, 1988: p. 29.
Note: For the numerical values, see Table 83 in the appendix.
The sum of the values for self-management, owner-tenant and tenant only does not correspond to the total number of all farms with respect to the number of farms in 1960. This is due to a mistake in the source.

among the total area of village farmland fluctuates between 5 % and 20 %. The supply of land that can be leased to or from another party and the demand are decreasing. As the villages (due to the fact that fields are spread throughout the country-side and are intermingled with fields belonging to neighboring villages) do not form closed tenancy markets, the amount of land rented out does not correspond to the amount leased within one village.

Furthermore (2) the relative percentages of land leased or rented out in 1972 and 1981 was recorded for both villages. It is clear that the percentage of land rented out in both villages has decreased rapidly. The supply is dwindling. On the other hand, it can be seen (3) that the satisfied demand has increased. This contradiction can only be explained on the basis of methodological deficiences [390] because the *number* of holdings that lease additional

---

390 Rahman([281], 1986) presents in his study valuable material that is otherwise nowhere available. His presentation of descriptive data, however, is – as has al-

Change in the Significance of Tenancy in Two Villages
– The Development from 1972 to 1981

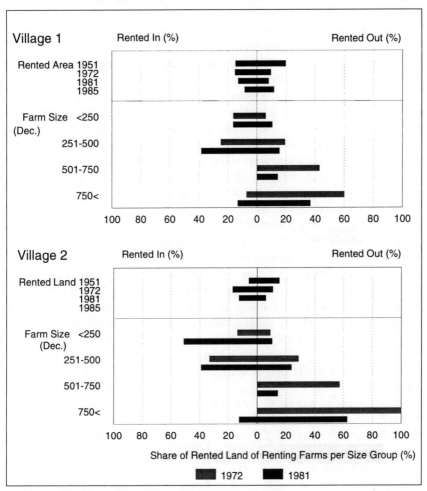

Source: [281] Rahman, 1986: p. 154, Tab. 6.1 and 6.2; and 1958, Tab. 6.4.

Note: For the numerical values, see Table 84 in the appendix.

ready been explained – carried out so that it is nearly only possible to interpret the data in his sense. Thus, in the case discussed here, the presentation of the tenancy market in percentages of land with respect to the overall percentage of each holding-size category without reference to the absolute distribution magnitude falling under land has obviously decreased more that the percentage of land they are able to rent. Thus, despite the decreasing overall amount of land available for tenancy, the *percentage* of land rented out or leased can *seemingly* increase for the specifically involved holdings. [391]

Summarizing, it is possible to make the following statements with respect to the dynamics of the tenancy market:

1. If the average size of the holdings decreases, the significance and the necessity of intensively cultivating one's available land by oneself increases.

2. That share of the land belonging to a holding that in the past could not be handled by the household members anymore and that was, therefore, rented out, has been reduced. This is particularly true in the case of the large holdings. In cases in which the size of the holdings decreases, the *rentable* land decreases *overproportionally*. On the other hand, under certain circumstances, the percentage of land that is "pledged" – which can be understood as a form of fixed rent – can be increased in order to meet the increasing need for capital resulting from more intensive cultivation. This has not been empirically clarified.

3. On the other hand, the reduced volume of the land owned by the holdings increases the demand for land that can be leased. Other economic effects such as increasing productivity per unit of area and the demand for increasing self-employment opportunities among the growing population increases the demand additionally. In the case of the transition to monetary rent (pledging the rights of usage), the demand of those households increases additionally that have solvent monetary means at their disposal (due to, among other things, income from jobs) and that want to satisfy part of their subsistence needs out of their own – more secure and prestigious – production.

4. A dwindling supply of land that can be rented out and an increased demand for land that can be leased leads to the theoretical postulate that the rent rates will increase. This could possibly be seen on the basis of a shift in the sharecropping conditions which would be independent of the possible simultaneous changes in the input-sharing conditions, or the intensity of the employment of inputs due to modern forms of production. This, however, has not been empirically substantiated. [392]

---

each category, or even overall village, limits the value of the data unnecessarily. The interpretation must, therefore be carried out with care. As other sources, however, are not available, it is necessary to use this one.

391 The data presented by Rahman is, hence, despite its importance, a lesson in how one should *not* present descriptive statistics.

392 I do not know of any study that proves that there has been a *shift* within a specific tenancy arrangement (institutional contract). Whether the *transition* from one type

5. In general, the trend seems to be for the *relative* significance of share-cropping to sink and the other forms of tenancy to increase. [393] Thereby, effects such as monetarization; a priori fixing of the tenancy rates; the reduction in long-term contracts; the expanding of short-term, one-season contracts; and the introduction of efficiency criteria when selecting the tenant play an increasing role.

6. The frequently postulated hindering of the increases in agricultural production and the increases in productivity caused by sharecropping seems to be dissolving. Land is only offered for rent if the landlord recognizes a profit that is higher than that which he can achieve by cultivating the land himself or by hiring workers to cultivate it for him. Self-management is becoming increasingly profitable. [394] The demand for land that can be leased only exists if, despite increases in cost, the tenant is still guaranteed a *satisfactory* share of the yield by increasing the productivity. [395]

It seems as if the dynamics of the tenancy market are based on two principles: (1) the choice of the tenant on the basis of the criterion efficiency because the rates themselves are subject to institutional limitations, and (2) reduction in the supply of rentable land because self-management is both more profitable and also necessary.

The former tenants or marginal owner-cultivators that were unable to survive in such a contracting and dynamic tenancy market, who in other words descended the scale to the status of "functional" or absolute landlessness, must take up alternative employment opportunities. The extent to which they are able to find such opportunities lies outside their control. Which consequences for the *employment situation* will result from the landownership and tenancy conditions that have been discussed until now will be elaborated in Chapter 4.3. In a first step, in Chapter 4.2, the dy-

---

of tenancy arrangement to another, e.g., from sharecropping to fixed rent, is accompanied by a relative or absolute increase in the rent rates is unknown. Diversification in the terms of the rent rates according to specific locations and types of land are known. As to how far the rates, however, can be attributed to free tenancy market price formation and not to institutional rigidity ("inefficiency"), which more likely leads to market contractions, is not known.

393 This is, unfortunately, not possible to establish on the basis of the sources available to me. This statement is founded, hence, on my own empirical observations. While the sinking importance of sharecropping is clearly evident, the significance of monetary and a priori fixed rent conditions, especially along with increasing input-intensive cultivation, has until now not been empirically studied. Theoretical deductions alone (increased rent rates) do not say much and are very speculative.

394 Cf. Chapter 4.4.1, specifically Figure 77 on p. 278.

395 I am not aware of any study that substantiates the dynamics of the tenancy market and the rent rates in Bangladesh. It has already been shown that the market is contracting.

namics of farming, production and productivity will be sketched as they result from the increasing importance of modern agrarian technology. The agrarian technological innovations cause the dynamics of the labour market.

4.2 The Development of the Agrarian Production

4.2.1 Dynamics of Cropping

The rice yields from 1970 to 1987 increased by about ca. 30 %. [396] Behind this general and statistically manifest development are, however, differential regional, local, individual and socio-economic dynamics. A comprehensive analysis of these conditions is not available; therefore, it is necessary to try to discover the type and significance of differential dynamics on the basis of indicative individual studies. [397]

In the following, (1) the changes in labour intensity, (2) the development of the yields and (3) the changes in the degree of self-sufficiency will be presented.

---

396 Cf. [124] Government, 1988: p. 175, Tab. 4.48; and [113] Government, 1979: p. 165, Tab. 4.30.

397 There are a number of studies in which specific cultural, technical or economic aspects of individual agrarian cultures are more or less analyzed and described in detail, frequently covering a few holdings, or one village, or the agricultural "sector." In this context, it does not seem meaningful to go into detail with respect to these aspects. Temporal, local and research specific aspects are so manifold and heterogeneous that the interpretation of these individual analyses as "pieces of a mosaic" would only present an extremely incomplete, partially useless picture full of gaps. Cf., e.g., [22] Alam, 1987; [66] Butler, 1988; [175] Hussain, Barman, and Elias, 1984; [258] Murshid, 1987; [271] Qazi, 1986; [313] Shahid, Herdt, 1982; [318] Sikdar, Banerjee, 1984; and [329] Uchida, 1986.

With respect to the question of the adoption of the techniques, see: [30] Alauddin, Tisdell, 1988; [17] Ahmed, 1983; [54] Bhuiyan, 1987; [55] Bhuiyan, Mandal, 1987; and [272] Quasem, 1982.

Regarding the question of appropriate technological innovations in agriculture and their effects (development conformable mechanization), see [249] Martius, 1977.

4.2.1.1   The Dynamics of the Cropping Intensity

The cropping intensity [398] increased on the average with respect to all holdings from 1960 to 1983/4 from 148 % to 171 %. Table 18 shows the development of the cropping intensity according to small, middle-sized and large holdings.

Tab. 18:   **Development of the Average Cropping Intensity According to Holding-size Category from 1960 to 1983/84**

Holding-size Category	Average Intensity in the Years		
	1960	1977	1983/4
Large Holdings	167	181	187
Middle-sized Holdings	152	168	171
Small Holdings	135	152	153
All Holdings	148	165	171

Source: [121] Government, 1986: p. 104.

The increase in production can be traced back to the facts that (1) the area used by agriculture was minimally expanded by making use of waste land, and (2) by controlling floods by means of damming in the river system, making increased cropping intensity possible. Simultaneously, (3) the irrigation possibilities improved and, thus, the possibility of using the land even during the dry season.

Figure 62 [399] illustrates the increase in the volume of irrigated farmland from approximately 7 % in 1961 to ca. 25 % in 1985. The increase itself was made possible by the introduction and utilization of motor-driven pumps that allowed the farmers to take advantage of the ground water. [400] To a

---

398   The definition of cropping intensity in Bangladesh, "intensity of cropping," is as follows: "Intensity of cropping represents the ratio between the total gross cropped area [total gross cropped area means the aggregated area of all temporary crops raised in the farm during the census year, including the area under fruit trees (permanent crops) ... [it] represents the aggregate area of the various crops raised in the same land of the farm during the census year] and the net sown area [net sown area is the cultivated farm area actually cropped during the census year regardless of the number of crops grown and it includes the area under temporary crops and permanent crops (fruit trees). It is the actual area or physical area under perennial or non-perennial crops.] expressed in percentage ... as follows: gross cropped area / net sown area * 100," ([125] Government, 1988: p. 21.).

399   Cf. in addition: [26] Alauddin, Tisdell, 1988: p. 55, Tab. 3.4; [164] Hossain, 1986: p. 41, Tab. 41; and [315] Shawkat Ali, 1982.

400   Cf. [153] Herbon, 1990, and the literature mentioned there.

Fig. 62: Development Trends in the Utilization of Modern Technological Innovations in Agriculture, 1961 - 1986

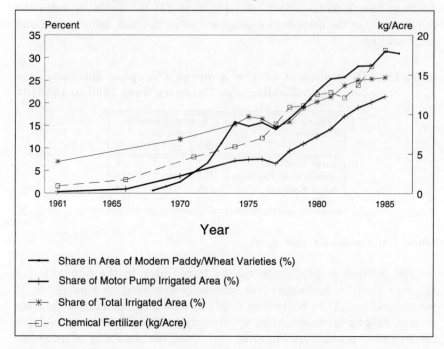

Source: [166] Hossain, 1988: p. 25, Tab. 6; p. 27, Tab. 7; p. 30, Tab. 8; and p. 31, Fig. 2.3.
Note: For the numerical values, see Table 85 in the appendix.

similar extent, the utilization of modern, high-yielding seed also took place – over 30 % at the time. The average utilization of artificial fertilizers also increased from 0 kg per acre to an average of more than 18 kg per acre. [401]

The growing absolute significance of modern fertilizer-seed-water technology becomes clear. [402] Its effects with respect to the agricultural yields

---

401 I have not discovered any study recording the really *utilized* volume. On the contrary, these statements are based on the figures on fertilizer *sales*, whereby the nearest conclusion is that the volumes of fertilizer that are distributed are also actually put to use.

As these indicators are only rough and the sources do not supply very much information, I will neglect product-specific, seasonally differentiated, regionally categorized information, as well as information on the types of fertilizer broken down according to the chemicals contained in them.

402 For the most comprehensive and recent studies on this topic, see [166] Hossain, 1988,

Fig. 63:   Specific Cropping Intensity According to Holding-size
and the Specific Percentages of Fertilized and Irrigated
Land

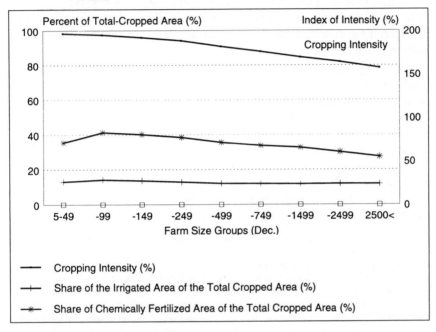

Source: [125] Government, 1988: p. 140 ff., Tab. 1.
Note: For the numerical values, see Table 86 in the appendix.

will be dealt with once more below.

The specific disposal of inputs dependent upon holding-size and the greater cropping intensity found among the larger holdings as well as the disadvantages for the smaller holdings that have been frequently discussed with respect to India are not applicable in the case of Bangladesh. On the contrary, it is rather the other way around. [403] Figure 63 [404] presents the holding-size specific cropping intensity, the percentage of irrigated land and the fertilized farmland. [405]

---

and [18] Ahmed, 1988: p. 76 ff.
403 For a theoretical presentation of the relation between holding-size and productivity and the importance of technical change, as well as an explanation of why small holdings are not necessarily disadvantaged, see: [48] Berry, Cline, 1979: p. 5 ff.
404 See in addition, [12] Ahmed, 1984: p. 30, Tab. 23.
405 The specific input intensity – volume of water and period of time available, for exam-

It is clear that in all three sectors, the smallest holdings do not in any way take the position of second place behind the largest holdings with respect to the utilization of modern inputs, but rather on the contrary lead in this field to a small extent. The relative financial expenditures for water that have to be paid specifically are, however, unknown. The volumes in the case of fertilizer, if fertilizer is applied, are minimally larger in the case of the small holdings than the large holdings. [406]

The adoption of modern technology by various sized holdings has been studied by Ali in a few villages. [407] It can also be seen here that the smaller holdings are more input-intensive oriented and that they use the land more intensively. Figure 64 illustrates the increases in the cropping intensity from 1950 to 1985 for four villages according to holding-size categories. [408] The following aspects are striking.

1. The greatest increases in the cropping intensity did not take place until the 70's. [409]

2. The smaller holdings seem to have tended to start working with the new technology somewhat earlier. [410]

---

ple – is, however, not shown as I do not have any figures pertaining to these factors at my disposal.

406 Cf. [12] Ahmed, 1984: p. 29, Tab. 22.

407 "The villages examined in this study are located in different agro-ecological settings. ... Each village is a representative case of the environmental and economic conditions in which the dominant type of agriculture is practiced. They vary from one another in terms of population density, type and degree of environmental constraints to agriculture, and the level of market and economic opportunities. ..." ([32] Ali, 1987: p. 51 f.)

Village No.	Agro-ecological Setting	State Measures
Village 1	flooded for long periods, low aridness	none
Village 2	aridness and saline soil	flood control
Village 3	aridness	none
Village 4	low aridness	Contract Growers Scheme
Village 5	low aridness	irrigation system
Village 6	floods, low aridness	none

[32] Ali 1987: p. 58, Tab. 1.2.

408 For reference to the general, national increases in the cropping intensity, see [164] Hossain, 1986: p. 47, Tab. 8: regarding the holding-size specific cropping intensity in 1978/79, see [289] Rahman, Ali, 1984: p. 44, Tab. 2.

409 This information is important because it shows that the "modernization" of the agricultural production and the visibility of its effects did not come about until the 80's. This explains why a large part of the socio-economic literature that is based on the results recorded in the 70's tend to have more negative perspectives.

410 This supposition is, however, very vague.

Fig. 64: Developments in the Cropping Intensity in Four Villages from 1950 to 1985

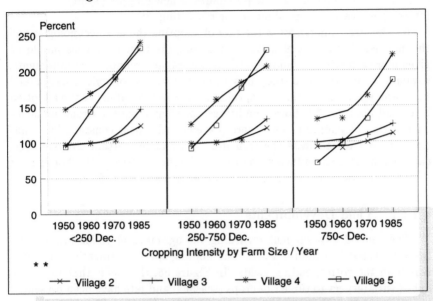

Source: [32] Ali, 1987: p. 207, Tab. 4.11; p. 277, Tab. 5.10; p. 341, Tab. 6.9; and p. 411, Tab. 7.10.

Note: For the numerical values, see Table 88 in the appendix.
Ali records the holding sizes in hectares. For the purpose of simplification, they are presented here in decimal (dec.) = 100th of an acre in order to be compatible with other presentations. For the purpose of making the data somewhat more easy to understand, the figures have been rounded off slightly. This does not seem to cause any significant loss of information.
* Village 1 and village 6 were not taken into consideration in this figure because Ali did not supply any data on them.

3. The smaller holdings adopted the new technology (increasingly since the 50's) at a slightly higher intensity level and continued to maintain this higher level of intensity over the last 25 years.

4. The adoption rates are independent of the holding size, but they definitely vary among the villages. Whereas all of the holdings in two of the four villages increased their cropping intensity at an early date, continually and radically in the period from 1950 until 1985, whereby the initial level did not significantly differ from the other surveyed villages, this was not true in the case of the other two. In these two villages, the increases in intensity were only moderate, and they basically did not take place until the 70's.

The reasons for this can be found in the greatly differing ecological and economic environments and the possibility of new cropping systems such as, for example, vegetable production for marketing. [411]

5. The large differences in the rate of adopting the new technologies and the increases in the cropping intensity among the various villages should be given more attention. In addition to the natural and economic environments, it would be important to study how the initial socio-economic situation and the power structures within the specific village system influence the adoption rates and abilities. [412] Local conditions apparently have a strong influence on the rate of adoption, and there are evidently local constellations that either hinder or facilitate the transition that, under certain circumstance, can have a stronger influence than the differences between the holdings or the social classes among the various households and their farms.

4.2.1.2 Yield Developments

The general development regarding the agricultural yields has already been discussed in Chapter 2.3.2. The holding-specific utilization of inputs results in the corresponding yields. In Figure 65, the yields that were produced with respect to three rice crops (seasons) and jute have been presented based on the data from an empirical field study. [413] Thereby, there are significant differences between the holding-size categories with respect to the yields achieved in the case of the *non*-intensively irrigated Amon and Aus rice varieties. This is also true regarding jute. In the case of input-intensive Boro rice crops, irrigated rice, the middle-sized holdings (about 4 acres) produce apparently higher yields per unit of area. Apart from the relative cautiousness necessary when interpreting the findings from a village study

---

411 Unfortunately, Ali did not present a comprehensive analysis of these "environmental influences." On the basis of such an analysis, one would have been able to ascertain which conditions were conducive to adopting the new technologies rapidly, and which factors, on the other hand, in the natural environment, in the infrastructure, or in the inner village social and political conditions were more likely to hinder such a transition.

412 Studies on village politics, structural and non-dynamic or ahistorical, as they usually are anyway, can indeed describe the local power and inequality structures, but cannot explain why – even though the village political situation always seems to be the same and be based on "clientalism" and "acquisition of farm labour and land" – such innovations are adopted and utilized in one village, while in others, on the other hand, they are only accepted to a limited extent, or not at all.

413 See in addition, [17] Ahmed, 1983: p. 132 ff., who did not discover any significant differences in the efficiency among the various holding sizes in cultivating high-yielding rice. Inefficient farmers, according to him, prefer not to crop these varieties at all.

Fig. 65: Output per Unit of Area for Rice and Jute According to Holding-size Category

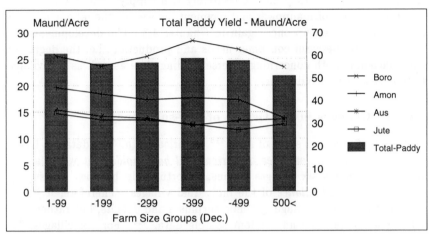

Source: [79] Chaudhury, 1989: p. 182.
Note: For the numerical values, see Table 87 in the appendix.

and the present quantitatively limited significance of Boro rice, this could prove to be an indication that the middle-sized holdings seem to be able to utilize the modern inputs more effectively. This shows once again that the small holdings are not only more input intensive, but that they also manage their holdings so that they receive higher yields. [414]

In connection with the findings in the last section in which the fact was established that namely the average holding size is constantly and rapidly decreasing, it can be – theoretically – deduced that the general *production increases are produced by the growing number of above-average input-intensive and profitable middle and small-sized holdings.* From this perspective, the predicament the poor farmers are faced by is responsible for their using the factors available to them optimally under the existing conditions and

---

414 The findings on the Boro yields – which appear to be highest in the case of the larger holdings that have the necessary financial means at their disposal – relativize this statement somewhat as larger holdings with a larger supply of capital are obviously in a more advantageous situation with respect to financing the required inputs.

Due to a lack of other sources, the question must be left open as to what extent such findings concerning yields can be transposed to the national level.

[17] Ahmed, 1983, comes to the quite clear-cut conclusion on the basis of his data, which are presented in Figure 76, p. 276, that the holdings with less than 250 dec. produce significantly higher *monetary* Boro and Amon yields per unit of area.

particularly successfully within the scope of the attempt to ensure their existence and subsistence. This is especially true with respect to the resource manpower, of which they have a relatively rich supply. The developments in the utilization of manpower and payment, as well as the labour productivity, will be taken up once again in Chapter 4.3. The development and the interaction between consumer needs and production, i.e. the degree of self-sufficiency, both concerning diverse holding-sizes as well as the village system, is a further indicator.

4.2.1.3 Changes in the Degree of Self-sufficiency

Figure 66 presents some of Ali's [415] empirical data. The data are based on stratified random samples of *agricultural households* that were carried out in each of his six villages. Thus, unfortunately he does not supply us with *an overall balance* of the individual villages. Therefore, it is *not* possible to ascertain village systemic surpluses and deficits, but rather only holding-size category and random sample data. [416] For six villages, [417] the development is presented that took place during the period from 1950 to 1985 with respect to the yields produced by the holdings belonging to the individual size categories in relation to the needs of the corresponding households. What is important here is not so much the absolute volume of the yields, but rather the question whether it is possible to supply the additional number of household and family members out of the holdings' own production. It should be mentioned here that the yields per unit of area and the cropping intensity in the case of the smaller holdings is higher, and the utilization of modern inputs seems to be more intensive.

1. The smaller holdings (up to ca. 250 dec.) evidently do not succeed (1) in meeting the household members' needs in rice to more than 50 % out of their own production. However, (2) the self-sufficiency capacity seems to have more or less stabilized after a period in which it worsened during the 50's. It can also be seen, however, that (3) the conditions are very different from village to village. Thus the self-sufficiency chances and development trends are by all means different for households in one and the same category in different villages, i.e. environments. That is to say (4) that under

---

415 [32] Ali, 1987.

416 Since, as is unfortunately also the case in other studies, there are no available data on the distribution of the holding-size categories in the sampled universe consisting of the entire village, the relative significance of the holding-size categories can neither be assessed, nor a weighting factor ascertained. Only on this basis would it have been possible to calculate the proportions of the balance within the villages.

417 With respect to village 6 (Shyampur), the village with the most difficult overall situation and trend, also see [33] Ali, 1987.

Fig. 66: **Development Trends in the Degrees of Rice Supply Derived from One's Own Production in Six Villages According to Holding-size Category for the Years 1950 to 1985**

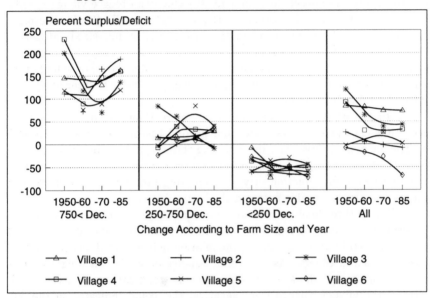

Source: [32] Ali, 1987: p. 144, Tab. 3.13; p. 212, Tab. 4.16; p. 280, Tab. 5.13; p. 346, Tab. 6.14; p. 415, Tab. 7.14; and p. 483, Tab. 8.13.

Notes: For the numerical values, see Table 89 in the appendix.
Village 6 is not represented in the largest holding-size category, (750 dec.).
Concerning the situation in the villages and a rough agro-ecological characterization, see footnote 407, p. 246, or [32] Ali, 1987: p. 51 ff.
Ali presents the holding sizes in hectares. For reasons of simplicity, they have been presented here in decimal (dec.) = 100th of an acre, as in other presentations. No significant loss of information seems to result from this practice.

the present conditions, it is not possible to make any prognoses as to the future on the basis of the holding size alone because both trends can be discovered signaling *village specific* improvements as well as a worsening of the situation. [418]

---

418 The causal factors are unfortunately not explicated. Thus, for example, (1) alternative employment opportunities may have led to an alleviation in the situation faced by the agricultural households, (2) the members succeeded in finding income sources in the off-farm rural sectors and (3) the intensity of cropping has increased, getting

2. In the case of the middle-sized holdings (ca. 250 - 750 dec.), it is possible to establish the fact that they (1) are evidently in a position to maintain their subsistence level and the trend is more or less stable, i.e. to produce approximately as many rice or "rice equivalent units" as they need in order to supply the household members. (2) One can observe village specific ascending and descending trends in this context as well. (3) The absolute marketable surpluses are small in the case of the middle-sized categories. That, however, does not exclude the fact that special crops are produced and marketed in order to purchase rice. Ali describes how households take advantage of their particular geographic locality in order to intensively produce vegetables for the market.

3. In the case of the large holdings (more than 750 dec.), it can be seen that (1) the surpluses above and beyond the amount needed for self-sufficiency more or less broke down during the 50's, did not begin to stabilize until the 60's, and only began to increase once again in the 70's. (2) This was due to the introduction of yield-increasing production procedures and inputs and the favourable area-member ratio.

4. For all three holding-size categories and in all six villages it is possible to recognize *a trend towards a decrease in the overall surplus*. While most of the villages still achieve a surplus, the relation between need and production has worsened in others. As no overall balance or statistical weighting factors are presented, the absolute development trend cannot be ascertained. Even if the village balance were negative, this could indicate, on the one hand, a deterioration in the living conditions, while on the other hand, non-agricultural income and the corresponding purchasing power could balance out this deficit by means of imports brought into the village.

In general, it is possible to say with respect to the dynamics of agricultural production, i.e. growth in the intensity on the basis of increased employment of modern inputs, and the developments in the yields in relation to the people who are *directly* dependent upon them that (1) there is a fragile balance between production and demand, between the increasing yields and the growing consumer demand volume that, among other things, is very dependent upon the local conditions. Furthermore, (2) despite high cropping intensity and yields, the favourable land/household-member relation shows its influence on the larger holdings in the sense that the absolute surpluses are larger than a (fictive) general demand level, and the absolute increases in yields exceed the internal growth in the consumer demand. (3) The six-village survey that was carried out by Ali shows that there is a

---

closer to gardening because of a growing settlement density, which transcends rice production and the yields and income that can be derived from it, etc.

trend for the surpluses to sink due to the households' own needs. National statistics show at the time that the development trends exhibit parallels. [419]

The developments in the agricultural production conditions is based fundamentally on two components: on the one hand, (1) the expansion in the areas cropped and the higher frequency of the utilization of the land per annum (area effect), and on the other hand, (2) the increases in the net-area productivity contribute to the growths in the yields. Both effects are interdependent and have positive reciprocal influences.

Jabbar [420] shows that while the cereal production is growing, at the same time other crops are decreasing in their relative importance. Thus, the land cultivated with various rice varieties and wheat is increasing at the cost of the non-cereal production. This has diverse negative impacts on the production and supply structure.

The effects of the increases in area contributed to the growth in production in the case of rice by ca. 36 %, or wheat by about 11 % (during the period 1967/70 to 1979/82). The increases in productivity amount in the case of rice to about 64 %, and wheat 3 %, and the interaction effects are per crop 4 % and 14 %. These increases in grain production may lead to problems for other products. [421]

The growing utilization of inputs in crop husbandry, the developments in the yields and the possible endangerment to the local self-sufficiency are, however, only partial aspects of the developments in agricultural production. In the following, the dynamics of further "agricultural" production sectors will be discussed.

4.2.2   Dynamics in Other Agrarian Production Sectors

The two leading forces in the present development in the agricultural sector are the growing number of people looking for employment and an income and the technological innovations. The pressure on the existing resources caused by the growing population is evidently partially compensated for by the effective utilization of modern technology based on innovations consist-

---

419 See the discussion in Chapter 2.3.2, and the presentation in Figure 4 on p. 56.
420 [189] Jabbar, 1986: p. 5.
421 The consequences of the replacement effects have not be discussed very much. Modern technology along with the corresponding productive varieties and the market demand, as well as the state promotional policies, seem to favour cereal production. Under favourable conditions, however, non-cereal production, which is more labour intensive and can under circumstances generate higher income, seems to have a good yield and income potential. There is an obvious need for research on the shifts in the cropping patterns and their consequences.
See in addition, [257] Murshed, 1983.

ing of fertilizer-seed-water within the field of cropping, particularly in the cereal production sector. The expansion of cereal production, however, implies dramatic changes in only *one* production sub-system. It has already been mentioned that there is strong competition among other farming activities and products. But even independent of the technological changes in farming, the population growth causes increasing demands on the other natural, economic and social resources and systems and leads to drastic changes in them. These changes have been only sporadically and unsystematically discussed in the relevant literature to date. That is why it is not possible to present a comprehensive picture of the dynamic interdependencies and effects here, but rather only a short list of *trend indicators* and a somewhat longer list of deficits in knowledge that have to be clarified.

In the following, the individual dynamics will be presented that are found in (1) livestock keeping, (2) gardening, (3) inland fishing and fish production in ponds, (4) the energy supply and (5) the overall dynamics in this sector.

4.2.2.1 The Dynamics of Livestock Keeping

The number of domestic animals in Bangladesh has been increasing steadily. That does not say anything about the development of the quality and performance of the animals. The existing data do not allow a conclusive judgment of the conditions that goes beyond pure figures. Table 19 presents the development in the number of large ruminants (cattle, buffalo), small ruminants (goats, sheep) and poultry.

The quantitatively most important species of animals are cattle, goats and poultry. Buffalo and sheep are quantitatively unimportant. The general development trend shows that the absolute number of cattle and goats has been increasing slightly and the absolute number of poultry greatly. [422] Calculated on the basis of the specific population figures, however, it is possible to establish a continual decrease in the figures per capita with the exception of poultry and goats.

1. The importance of large cattle, which are mostly used as draught and working animals, is tied to the number of agricultural holdings and the

---

[422] The problems involved in the census data can only be briefly touched upon here: (1) the number of animals fluctuates very strongly seasonally. Thus, cattle and buffalo are sold between the times when they are needed for ploughing, for example. Duck and chicken populations are subject to very strong seasonal fluctuations that are caused by the feed supply and the climatic burden. (2) The difference between the agricultural census and the random sample survey carried out in 1983/84 is so large that all of the figures appear to be questionable. (3) The quality of the primary surveys leaves a great deal to be desired, and that is naturally true in the case of other national statistics.

Tab. 19: Developments in the Number of Large and Small Ruminants and Poultry in Absolute Figures and per Capita of the Population from 1960 to 1983/84

Species	1960	1977 a	1983/4	1983/4 b	1960	1977 c	1983/4	1983/4 d
	Thousand				Per Capita of Population e			
Cattle	18961	20509	21495	21176	0.37	0.29	0.25	0.24
Buffalo	455	469	567	457	0.01	0.01	0.01	0.01
Goats	5660	8436	13558	8725	0.11	0.12	0.16	0.10
Sheep	477	508	667	490	0.01	0.01	0.01	0.01
Poultry	20096	53590	73713	78371	0.40	0.75	0.85	0.90

Source: [124] Government, 1988: p. 208, Tab. 4.86; p. 35, Tab. 2.6.

Note: Cf. also [119] Government, 1986: p. 53 ff., Tabs. 19, 22 and 24.
In the census from 1977, the poultry raising households/holdings were *not* included if they had less than 20 chickens and/or ducks, and/or no large animals or arable land.

a   Agricultural census data.
b   Random sample.
c   Agricultural census data.
d   Random sample.
e   In calculating the per capita data, the specific data for each of the years 1961, 1974 and 1981 were used: i.e., 50,840,000, 71,478,000 and 80,120,000.

internal feed basis. The population growth does not seem to influence this basic relationship. **2.** The small ruminants are particularly interesting for the small farmer household, and their number per capita of the population is increasing slightly according to the census. The animals are kept for the purpose of being sold, i.e. in order to generate income. A trend towards intensification of animal husbandry in this sector is indicated.

3. Analogous to goats and sheep, the same applies in the case of poultry. Poultry offers an income-effective – and at times labour intensive – employment opportunity for women and is relatively independent of the size of the land owned because it can run around freely. The numbers have grown enormously and the number of fowl per capita of the growing population seems to have about doubled between 1960 and 1983/84. Since poultry is an important source of protein (in some cases more for guests than for the household members themselves), the increase in the numbers seems to indicate an improvement in the protein supply nonetheless.

These general trends, however, do not say anything about the socio-economic *distribution* of livestock keeping as a source of work and food.

Fig. 67: Development Trends in Livestock Keeping in One Village in the District Noakhali according to Holding-size Category for the Years 1979 and 1984

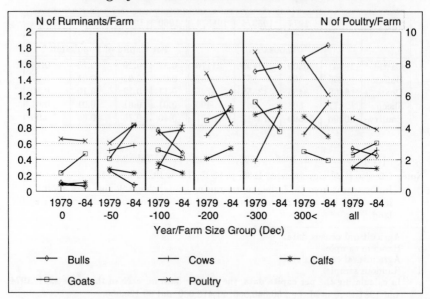

Source: [232] de Lasson, Dolberg, 1985: p. 342, Tab. 3.
Note: For the numerical values, see Table 90 in the appendix.

There are only a few studies on these aspects. In addition to Helmrich's [423] comprehensive and intensive structural analysis of the livestock keeping and production system in one village – which however only deduces development trends theoretically and does not substantiate them on the basis of empirical panel surveys – de Lasson and Dolberg [424] collected and compared data on livestock keeping in one village from 1979 and 1984. On the basis of these data, which however do not allow any long-term and general statements on trends as they were carried out too close in time, it is possible to deduce a few initial indicators referring to the current changes.

In Figure 67, the changes in the number of animals per holding have been presented for various holding-size categories for the two years 1979

---

423 [144] Helmrich, 1986. However, refer also to the discussion in Chapter 3.3.1.3 and the presentation in Figure 66, p. 251.
424 [232] de Lasson, Dolberg, 1985.

and 1984. [425]

Despite the short interval in time of only five years, a few trends concerning the village livestock keeping can be established. [426]

1. For households that have absolutely no land at their disposal, large animals – amounting to ca. 0.1 animals per household – play hardly any role. In individual cases, however, the animals represent a fortune. The significance of the number of cattle has not changed in any way. The number of poultry has also continued to remain at a very low level. The chances the landless have in the competition for feed resources that do not depend upon owning one's own land are not very good.

2. The significance of goat keeping has increased greatly for those households that are nearly landless and smaller holdings up to 200 decimal (the exception are the categories from 50 to 100 dec.), nevertheless. That is an indicator that points to an *intensification in the small animal production of the poorer households*. In this sector, the landless also seem to enforce their claims to collective, public feed resources.

3. The significance of oxen and young animals has *decreased* for the holdings up to approximately 100 decimal, whereas the importance of cows (multi-purpose cattle) has *slightly or greatly increased*. Oxen are only good for work, and young animals necessitate economically risky care and feeding activities which seem to interest poorer households less in comparison with goat keeping.

4. Larger holdings and households have increased their large animal stock all the way down the line. Merely in the case of poultry have there been decreases which de Lasson and Dolberg attribute to the failure of a poultry project. Thereby, however, the overproportional preference for *cows* becomes apparent, exactly as in the case of smaller holdings.

5. The larger holdings with over 200 decimal have decreased their stock of goats drastically.

6. Regarding the *entire village*, it was discovered that the number of young cattle nearly remained the same. This could signify that the village herds chiefly reproduce themselves. The number of oxen decreased to approximately the same extent as the cows increased, whereby a slight shift in cattle from smaller holdings to larger holdings took place. The number of goats increased by approximately 15 %. The slump in poultry, which

---

425 Whereas de Lasson and Dolberg presented absolute figures for 317 households in both years, I have converted the data to the specific number of households per category for each year. This was done in order to take into account the influences of the shifts that have taken place in the meantime in the number of households *between* the holding-size categories.

426 These statements naturally require long-term confirmation.

contradicted the national trend, [427] can be traced back to the failure of a poultry project and seems to have hit mainly larger holdings with large poultry stocks.

7. While the number of draught animals does not necessarily have to increase due to modern agricultural technology because the existing animals only have to be utilized and burdened better, the number of those animals is increasing that serve as important food and raw material suppliers. Thus the interest in keeping goats and poultry as sources of food and income and as a capital investment is obviously growing. Plant production seems in this context to increasingly produce by-products and, thus, create or augment resources that can be used especially by the poorer households after having been "processed in animals' stomachs." *Within small animal production, this aspect seems to be developing some dynamics of its own.*

8. The shift in the significance of animals that were used purely as a source of draught power and labour (oxen) in favour of multi-purpose cattle (cows) could, on the one hand, be an indicator of a decreasing demand for draught power on the holdings, which are growing smaller, and on the other hand, a decrease in the number of large animals per holding could be based on the fact that the trend is now for cattle to be used to fulfil as many functions as possible.

9. Summarizing, it can thus be stated that (1) small animals and poultry are very interesting for the poorer and smaller households and holdings. This is to be expected due to the limited land endowment, the methods of keeping the animals that demand intensive labour on the part of women and children and the positive income effects. (2) To the same extent that more poor people show interest in small-animal keeping, the prosperous withdraw from the livestock keeping sector. This could be an indication of the competition for resources, whereby the numerous poor obviously win. (3) Large animals are essentially draught animals and working animals and, therefore, of interest to farmers due to these qualities. However, there seems to be a trend to substitute smaller, versatile cows (multi-purpose cattle) for the stronger working oxen.

10. This indicates that the intensification in livestock keeping for the purpose of generating income and food is generally accelerated by households with little land at their disposal, but which are well-endowed with manpower. The interest seems, however, to be greater than the basis for feed or a demand for meat that is backed by available purchasing power. Both, however, appear to be expanding if one draws this conclusion from

---

427 Cf. Table 19, p. 255.

258

Fig. 68:   Development Trends in "Vegetable" Production from 1978 to 1987/88

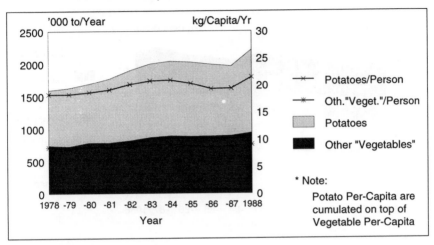

Source: [124] Government, 1988: p. 191, Tab. 4.67; [128] Government, 1990: p. 181,
        Tab. 58, and p. 79, Tab. 2.50; [130] Government, 1991: p. 17, Appendix B.
Note: For the numerical values, see Table 94 in the appendix.

the nation data. [428] This could be a consequence of the improved supply of feed for goats as the result of irrigated agriculture.

The development appears, briefly summarized, to improve the situation of the poor. The reasons have, however, to be looked for in the necessity the poor are faced by to make a living with whatever means are available.

4.2.2.2   The Dynamics of Gardening

Gardening is an economic activity that is interesting for two reasons: (1) because it can be a source of income, and (2) because an increasing amount of *gardening land* has evolved where earlier wasteland or rice fields existed as an increasing amount of land has been covered by farm buildings, courtyards and gardens due to the growing number of people and the housing this necessitates. Since the significance of the yields from gardening is as rule only appraised because it is very difficult to register the yields empirically, one should also be *extremely careful* when interpreting the meager (national) data.

---

428 Cf. Figure 5 in Chapter 2.3.2, p. 57.

Fig. 69:   Development Trends in "Fruit" Production from 1978 to 1987/88

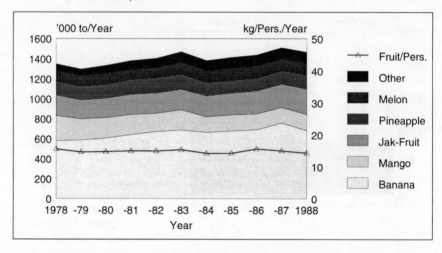

Source: [124] Government, 1988: p. 198, Tab. 4.74; [128] Government, 1990: p. 189, Tab. 4.65.
Note: For the numerical values, see Table 91 in the appendix.

Figure 68 shows the development trend in the yields with respect to potatoes and the sum of other "vegetables." It becomes clear that, again, yields (1) seem to be decreasing and (2) increases can be traced back mainly to the increased cultivation of potatoes. It can be seen that the per capita share of the yields has remained more or less constant. [429]

A similar picture is derived if one takes a look at the production of "fruit" that is presented in Figure 69.

1. The per capita availability of "fruit" decreases slightly. The total production increases only minimally. This growth can be traced mainly back to the expansion in many localities of banana trees which are easy to plant and grow relatively rapidly.

2. The one "classical" tree crop – mangos – exhibits sinking yields, probably because more and more of the large old trees are used for wood.

3. While taking the vagueness of the data into consideration, it would perhaps be possible to say that the production of fruit is increasing so little

---

429 The per capita calculation is based on the assumption of a *linear* growth from ca. 86.8 million people in 1978 to ca. 101.2 million in 1986. Due to the quality of the data, these figures are, in any case, only rough estimates.

that it will only be able to just about meet the increasing demand that results from the growing population, or not be able to quite come up to the present level.

In summary, it is possible to state regarding gardening, i.e. an indicative part of the "vegetable" and "fruit" production, that both are obviously more or less stagnating with respect to the factor per capita of the population. This may be due to the high percentage of self-sufficiency in the sector that limits both the supply and the demand. As both individual as well as state interest is primarily directed towards the production and supply of cereals as a staple produced by farming, gardening obviously leads an existence at a subsistence level. This is also reflected in the limited interest that is found on the part of research.

4.2.2.3 The Dynamics of Fishing and Fish Production

Fish is very popular, both as a protein supplier as well as food. The production and inland catch take place in rivers, canals, lagoons, ponds and pools and in the areas that are flooded during the rainy season. Fishing is carried out by professional fishers and is simultaneously a supplementary occupation for many households. Many of the poor own light fishing equipment (small nets, fish traps, rods) and take advantage of the right to fish in public waters during the monsoon season before the Amon harvest is brought in.

National statistical data on the production of fish are, as a result, rough estimates. No micro studies are available, and it would be difficult to generalize due to the very specific local conditions. The significance of fishing in public waters and fish production in private ponds remains, hence, in the dark.

Figure 70 presents the national data on inland fishing, despite the problematical quality of the data. According to this data, the catch decreased from 1972 to 1986 from approximately seven to six million tons per annum. The number of professional inland fishers increased during the same period of time from six hundred thousand to almost eight hundred thousand. [430]

The increase in the number of professional fishers has led to a drastic decrease in the catch per fisherman: due to the population growth, the catch

---

430 The development in coastal and deep-sea fishing as well as shrimp cultures will not be taken into consideration here because they represent structurally separate economic branches. It is indeed true that there are significant groups of the population that live from these activities and many people who live off this population; however, as they are not part of the rural-agrarian subsystem, it is not possible to consider this sector here, just as in the case of the urban-industrial sectors.

Fig. 70:   Development Trends in Inland Fish Production from 1972 to 1988/89

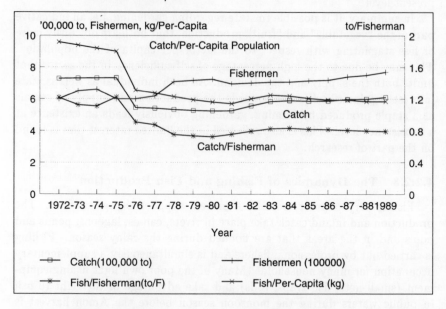

Source: [124] Government, 1988: p. 219, Tab. 4.106, and p. 220, Tab. 4.107; [128] Government, 1990: p. 206, Tab. 4.94, and p. 200, Tab. 4.95.
Note: For the numerical values, see Table 92 in the appendix.

per capita of the total population has decreased from just under 10 kg per year in 1972 to 6 kg per year in 1988/89.

The decreasing absolute catch, catch per fisherman and catch per capita of the population strongly indicate the possibility that the waters are being overfished, especially when more and more people exploit the resources and dynamite or poison are employed and when the fish eggs are collected in order to put them in ponds.

The significance that fishing and, in particular, *raising fish in ponds* has for the rural non-fisher population is unknown. The socio-differentiated utilization of the fish production and the fish ponds has evidently also not been studied. It is therefore necessary to state here that the fish ponds are economically an important supplementary factor for generating income and as a source of food and employment. The existing potentials seem to be very large, although this could not be substantiated. One problem faced by the private utilization of the ponds with systematic stocks is the rainy-season

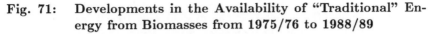

Fig. 71: Developments in the Availability of "Traditional" Energy from Biomasses from 1975/76 to 1988/89

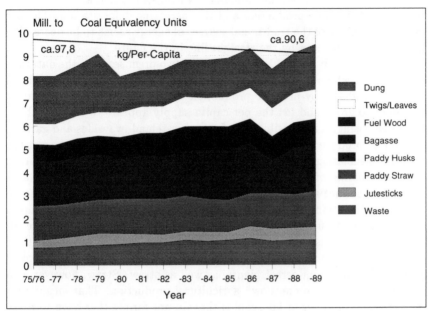

Source: [124] Government, 1988: p. 278, Tab. 6.5; [128] Government, 1990: p. 278,
Tab. 6.05.
Note: For the numerical values, see Table 93 in the appendix.

flooding of entire strips of land and the dammed in ponds. This can lead
to the loss of stocks that may be valuable and result in financial losses. A
second problem is the complex property laws and regulations that hinder
expanding private fish raising and cultures. [431]

4.2.2.4 The Dynamics of the Autochton-autonomous Energy Supply

The important sources of energy, particularly for cooking, are the types
of fuel that can be won from the local biomasses. Other sources of energy
exist in the cities and industries. The rural population's supply is, however,
determined by the locally available and "free" types of fuel.

Figure 71 demonstrates the national development in the availability of

---

431 In this context, see Chapter 3.3.1.3, p. 131.

"traditional" and rural sources of energy. The obtainable energy supply has been growing slightly, a fact that can evidently be traced back to the increased portions won from the biomasses (waste, straw) that are by-products of the expanding rice production and the increasing deforestation. The per capita availability of the traditional sources of energy seems to be decreasing slightly, as can be seen by the straight line in the figure.

Being extremely careful, one can develop two premises from the data: (1) it is not clear whether the energy demand can be met by the waste products from rice and the by-product production in the future if the population continues to grow; and (2) the per capita supply appears to be stagnating, if not decreasing. The possibilities of using wasteland, waysides and gardens in order to produce wood for fuel have not been fully exploited. As a result of an intensification in land utilization that is not based on cropping rice, a certain volume of material that can be used as fuel could be won as a by-product so that at least enough energy would be available to cook meals.

The distribution of the available sources of energy could develop into a problem in the future since, as can be clearly seen in Figure 22 on page 94, the poor households (based on the size of their holdings) already meet their energy needs to a large extent with "inferior" sources of energy such as waste, foliage and roots from cereal plants, as well as straw. Straw, however, can only be obtained from one's own agricultural production. That means that the increasing number of households that do not farm either have to make do with the "public" residues, purchase increasingly more expensive wood, or turn to the farmers for help who sometimes give them the rice straw for their usage. The consequences of a possible growing shortage of energy, energy distribution problems and energy cost have neither been the object of a study, nor can they be ascertained to date.

4.2.2.5 The Dynamics of "Subsidiary" Animal, Garden, Fish and Energy Production

Data from the national statistics record, on the average, *stable or slowly growing yield figures* in recent years in the production sectors livestock keeping, gardening and energy supply, with the exception of fishing. The production, calculated on the basis of the population, is stagnating or decreasing slightly, whereby the quality of the data is reason to be careful about further interpretations. Small animal production seems to be a positive exception. There are no differentiated panel-study data available except for this sector. The lack of locally specific, structurally dynamic and socially differentiated data makes the assessment of the potential and the micro-structural dynamics difficult.

264

As could be seen from the discussion of rice cropping, the holding size, the manpower supply by the household and its availability on the labour market, as well as specific local conditions, are important for local production increases and the profitable utilization and expansion of new niches. Not only the national production data, but especially information on individually successful utilization of niches as well as the dynamics of the local conditions allow one to make statements on the problems and potentials. There are still deficits in knowledge in this context.

The exploitation of niches by means of multiple utilization and cultivation of land and, as a result, the generation of "income" is only one of the individual opportunities if a farmer has land at his disposal. If, however, he cannot farm land, or if he does not have sufficient land at his disposal to secure his livelihood, he still has the possibility of selling his labour, of working for others and, hence, earning income. The labour market opportunities and the changes that are taking place in this sector will be discussed in the following section.

4.3 Labour Market Developments

The production factor labour, its employment and its payment have been discussed in Chapter 3.4.1.2 under the aspect of the exchange of manpower. The employment of human labour on one's own agricultural holding as well as on the holdings of others, or even outside agriculture, is subject to its own dynamics. The development trends with respect to the amount of payment, i.e. the trend towards income earned on other agricultural holdings and in non-agricultural enterprises, is decisive for assessing the development of the general welfare level of those people dependent upon selling their own labour. In the following section, an attempt will be made to discuss the consequences of the conditions under which income is earned.

The holding-size distribution and development as well as the changes in the cropping intensity and the input intensity and the development of the yields have to be seen in connection with the manpower endowment of the holdings and households – this has already been presented in Chapter 3.1.3 – and with (1) the general manpower demand that results from the new cropping patterns and cropping intensity and (2) the supply of labour on the market.

4.3.1 The Development in the Demand for and in the Employment of Manpower

As a result of the changes based on the new seed-fertilizer-water technological innovations, the plant production has led to an increased demand for manpower.

Tab. 20: Manpower Employment for Various Crops

Crop	Manpower Days per Acre and Year Sources:										
	1.	2.	3.	4,	5.	6.	7.	8.	9.	10.	11.
Aus - Local	77.9		60	46.2	56.6	60.2	56	64	-	-	66
Aus - HYV	92.4	60.4	86	75.7	62.2	75.3	79	68	71	98	80
B.Amon[a]	49.7	51.9	51	-	-	50.9	52	-	-	-	79
T.Amon[b] Local	53.1		55	54.7	62.4	59.1	53	66	-	-	62
T.Amon HYV	80.9	70.3	73	75.7	69.2	73.8	73	69	-	81	76
Boro - Local	72.5	82.6	83		70.2	75.4	83	85	-	120	82
Boro - HYV	109.7	96.4	103	68.8	87.2	-	88	117	125	162	113
Wheat - Local	-	-	42	36.4	-	39.2	-	38	-	-	-
Wheat - HYV	65.4	-	48	45.7	-	53.3	-	55	58	-	-
Jute	105.6	88.0	-	66.8	-	86.8	-	113	117	-	-
Sugarcane	275.5	-	-	111.3	-	193.4	-	144	150	-	-

Sources: [255] Muqtada, 1986: p. 66, Tab. 5.1:
1. Government of Bangladesh, Cost and Returns Survey for Bangladesh, 1978/79;
2. [219] Khan, Islam, Huq, 1981;
3. BARC/IFDC "Agricultural production, fertilizer use and equity considerations," 1982;
4. ADB Report;
5. [256] Muqtada, Alam, 1986; and
6. Mean calculation of Muqtada from columns 1 to 5
[166] Hossain, 1988: p. 44, Tab. 15;
7. ibid.;
[29] Alauddin, Mujeri, 1985: p.58, Tab. 2;
8. ibid. without irrigation;
9. ibid. with modern irrigation;
10. ibid. with traditional irrigation;
[21] Alam, 1983: p. 216, Tab. 8.7;
11. ibid.

---

a   B. Amon = Broadcast.
b   T. Amon = Transplanted.

Table 20 illustrates the data that has been published in the relevant

266

literature regarding the demand for manpower with respect to various crops. The ability to make statements on the basis of the data on the employment of labour concerning specific crops is limited, however, because the transition in the system of agricultural production does not merely consist of a traditional crop being exchanged for a modern variety. On the contrary, combinations of crops and their relations are changed as was, e.g., demonstrated on the basis of the relation between cereals and non-cereal crops. Thus, in the case of one crop, income and cropping area effects can ensue to the detriment of the others. What is important, therefore, is the overall balance for the holding or family – for example, the unit per area and/or labour productivity per annum. [432]

Ali [433] attempted in his empirical study to discover the developments in the employment of manpower in plant production for the period from 1950 to 1985 in six different villages for three holding-size categories. [434] Figure 72 shows that in three villages a slight, although not insignificant, intensification in manpower employment took place. The development in the other three villages was revolutionary: the number of labourers engaged in cultivation activities approximately *tripled.* In these villages, the effects of the improved infrastructure (protection against flooding, measures against salinity, etc.) and the new technology package were able to fully unfold. Furthermore, fundamental changes were undertaken in the cropping patterns towards more intensive cultivation practices, approaching forms of gardening. The absorption of manpower was particularly effective. It also became clear that the small holdings (less than 250 dec.) increased their labour employment in particular, independent of their initial situation and the overall constellation in the village.

Hossain [435] contrasted in his study holdings belonging to two separate theoretical ideal types of villages: villages in which traditional technology ("technological underdevelopment") dominated, and villages in which mod-

---

432 The complexity of the cropping, farm management and household systems (including its management), let alone their dynamics, have not (or hardly?) been the subject of study to my knowledge. There are indeed general models of rice-producing farming systems; however, they do hardly any justice to the specific conditions. A demonstration proving the relative advantages of *one* crop or *one* technological innovation is hardly of any help because the retroactive effects and synergisms cannot be recognized or conceptually overcome: to put it briefly, because the socio-economic systemic character is not done justice to. A greater need for research seems to exist here, particularly in the case of Bangladesh.

433 [32] Ali, 1987.

434 For a rough characterization of the villages see footnote 407, p. 246, or [32] Ali, 1987: p. 51 ff.

435 [166] Hossain, 1988.

Fig. 72: Development in the Employment of Manpower per Hectar and Year in 6 Villages from 1950 to 1985

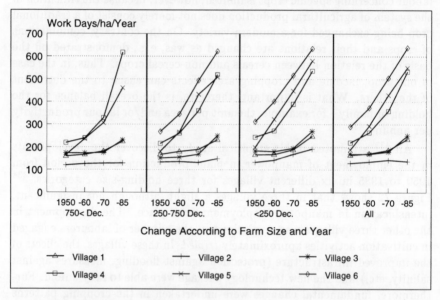

Source: [32] Ali, 1987: p. 142, Tab. 3.11; p. 210, Tab. 4.14; p. 279, Tab. 5.12; p. 344, Tab. 6.12; p. 413, Tab. 7.12; and p. 481, Tab. 8.11.
Note: For the numerical values, see Table 95 in the appendix.
Village 6 is not represented in the largest holding-size category (750 dec.).
With respect to the situation of the villages and an agro-ecological description, cf. footnote 407, p. 246, or [32] Ali, 1987: p. 51 ff.
Ali presents the holding size in hectares. For the purpose of simplicity, they are presented here in decimal (dec.) = 100th of an acre. In order to make the figures easier to read, they have been rounded off slightly. This does not seem to result in any significant loss of information.

ern technology had gained foot. [436]

---

436 This implies that *various stages of development exist simultaneously*. On this basis, it is possible to assume simultaneously two subsequent "system states" on the same one-dimensional time axis and then trace differences back to the influence of one or more defined variables and time. When observing individual variables, this may appear to be meaningful as a formal-methodological aid. If, however, one accepts the premise of multi-variable systems and the axiom that historical developments do not repeat themselves, then one recognizes the fact that one can indeed observe and isolate relevant variables, but not project calculations for the future.
If one does not carry out any panel studies, as is usually the case in empirical research, then this procedure is the only methodological possibility next to retrospective inter-

Fig. 73: Comparison of the Labour Employment and Labour Productivity in Villages with Diverse Technological Levels

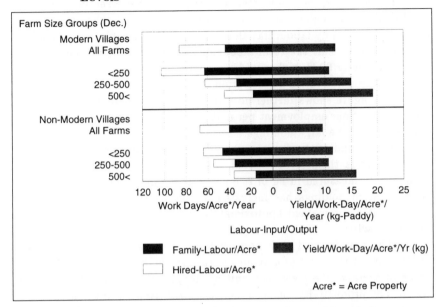

Source: [166] Hossain, 1988: p. 19, Tab. 2; p. 87, Tab. 42; and p. 105, Tab. 56.
Note: For the numerical values, see Table 96 in the appendix.
    The number of acres was calculated on the basis of *property owned*, as holding-size values were not published. Since on the average the share of land that is rented amounts to approximately 16 % and, as can be seen in Figures 36 and 37 on pages 151 and 152, it seems to be fairly proportionally distributed among all of the holding-size categories, this aid can evidently be used as an approximation.
    In order to calculate the labour productivity, the per acre yields for each ownership-size category were utilized as presented by [166] Hossain, 1988: p. 87, Tab. 42.
    */** The total value: yield/acer-day/acre/year for *all* holdings appears to also include all holdings under 50 dec., but the source does not specify this.

Figure 73 records the labour employment for holdings belonging to various size categories for the two village types isolated by Hossain according to family and hired labour. The contrast clearly illustrates the following aspects.

views and recording in order to construct "depths of focus in time." It must not be forgotten, however, that this is just a theoretical aid we are speaking of that merely – as in the case of most other indicators and data – produces approximate values and makes it possible to recognize trends.

1. The total-labour deployment per acre and year in "developed"-"modernized" villages amounts to approximately 27 % more than in "underdeveloped"-"non-modernized" villages.

2. Furthermore, the employment of hired labour has essentially increased considerably, particularly in the case of small holdings. The employment, absorption, of family labour has also increased considerably in this holding-size category so that the total labour deployment on these small holdings is approximately 60 % higher under modern conditions. This result corresponds in principle to Ali's description. [437]

3. The figure shows furthermore that independent of the level of technology, the labour employment per unit of area is twice as high on the small holdings as on the large holdings.

4. If one studies the average rice yields per hectare on the land owned by the farmers themselves [438] and year, then one finds that the labour productivity measured in kg of rice per year on all of the middle-sized and large, modern holdings has increased on the average. [439] On the small holdings, it has remained approximately the same. One can conclude the following factors.

5. The middle-sized and larger holdings were able to utilize the new technology *on the basis of a small increase in the employment of labour in order to increase the yields per unit of manpower,* i.e. the labour productivity. The productivity has also increased with respect to the area. Small holdings have *increased the productivity per unit of area greatly, accompanied by a considerable increase in the employment of family and hired labour without large changes in the labour productivity per person.* This signifies that while middle-sized to large holdings achieved increases in the output per unit of area, the small holdings were able to absorb labour effectively for the yield.

6. It becomes clear that, all in all, the employment of "self-employed" family labour does indeed increase; however, the increased labour demand is mainly met with hired labour. Hired labour, i.e. mainly landless, profit from the technological innovations through increased employment opportunities.

---

437 Cf. Figure 72, p. 268.

438 Hossain unfortunately did not publish the figures for the *farm areas,* but rather only the area of land owned by the farmer himself per holding-size category. The calculations of the yields per labourer and acre that are based on the tables that he published refer thus to the farmers' own land. The resulting values are inexact: however, they presumably reflect the *size relations* relatively well. For this reason, and because no other data are available, these data were used here.

439 Ali ([32] 1987) records lower yields per labourer per day than Hossain for his six survey villages, namely yields between 9.4 and 11.4 kg-rice.
This difference can unfortunately neither be explained nor resolved here.

These circumstances can also be clearly seen on the basis of Figure 74. It shows that [440] under modern technological conditions:

Fig. 74: **Comparison of the Working Time per Household Worker in Agricultural and Non-agricultural Occupations in Villages with Different Technological Levels**

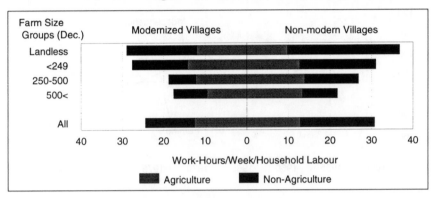

Source: [166] Hossain, 1988: p. 90, Tab. 44; and p. 94, Tab. 47.
Note: For the numerical values, see Table 97 in the appendix.

1. The large holdings reduce their employment of family labour in agricultural activities slightly, whereas the small holdings and landless become relatively more involved in agricultural tasks.

2. This goes along with a reduction in the amount of time invested in working in non-agricultural activities, as well as with the overall working time spent by members of small holdings and the landless. I.e. the individual worker *works all in all* really *less* in "modernized villages." In addition, due to the reduction in the overall working time, the members of the small holdings or landless households become *increasingly involved in agriculture.* This could be both an indication of an improved agricultural yield situation per unit of manpower and raised wages as well as signify an improvement in agricultural compared to non-agricultural wages and income.

4.3.2 Wage Developments

The developments in wages is a key indicator for judging the impact of technological innovations in agriculture, in particular on the situation of the poor. Without being able to deal with the entire complexity of the

---

440 Also see the findings recorded by [17] Ahmed, 1983: p. 142 f.

Fig. 75: Development Trends in Agricultural Real Wages, 1949-1989

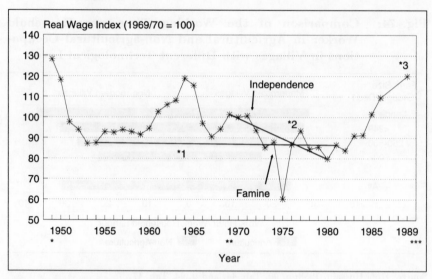

Source: [303] Samad, 1981: p. 202, Tab. 1a.; and [31] Alauddin, Tisdell, 1989: p. 565,
Tab. 2. [128] Government, 1990: p. 495, Tab. 10.35.
Note: For the numerical values, see Table 98 in the appendix.
*1 data from Boyce
*2 data from Muqtada
* to ** Source: Samad
** to * * * Source: Alauddin, Tisdell
* * * Estimate based on Government, 1990.

labour market here – seasonal and local fluctuations in the labour supply
and demand, the oscillations and social differentiation in the wages and the
labour, contract and payment conditions – an attempt will be made at this
point to sketch the general, that is the average, development in the level of
the real wages.

Figure 75 illustrates the relative improvements in the real wage level for
hired farm workers during the 80's. [441] The frequently proclaimed pauper-

---

441 Cf. in addition [90] Chowdhury, 1985: p. 21, Tab. 6.; [161] Hossain, 1984: p. 45, Fig. 3;
p. 57, Tab. A-2; [186] Islam, 1979: p. 394, Tab. 8; and [217] Khan, 1984: p. 190,
Tab. 8.1.
Furthermore [255] Muqtada, 1986: p. 57, Tab. 4.11, who carried out his study during the period 1970-1980 (at a time when the trend was negative), and [64] Boyce,
1989: p. 486, Tab. 1, who arrived at an average *decrease* in the real wages based on

ization process trend, which could be partially registered in the 70's, appears to have been broken. The increases in the real wages fall strikingly together with the impact of the new agrarian technology. This adoption of the technological package, on the other hand, took place together with the initiation by the cooperatives [442] and with a liberalization of the input market after they failed. Since the demand for manpower grew as a result of the adoption of the yield increasing technology, reciprocal effects and positive interdependencies seem to play a role here.

The changes in the demand for labour benefit the small holdings which have underemployed family labour who now, on the one hand, (1) find more possibilities for self-employment and (2), on the other hand, unburden the nonagricultural labour market to the advantage of the landless. The landless, in turn, find increased job opportunities both in agriculture as well as, partially, in nonagricultural sectors.

Modern technology has, where it was able to come to play, *increased the yields, absorbed manpower and raised the real wages.* This was clear in the case of *all of the holding-size categories and the landless.* The impact

---

the figures for 1953/4 to 1980/1 amounting to 1.63 %.

Also take a look at [21] Alam, 1983: p. 213 f., Tabs. 8.5 and 8.6, who found in two study villages during the period from 1955 - 1980 real wage increases (in rice equivalents, i.e. on the basis of *rice purchasing power*) for farmhands amounting to 41.5 % and 16.0 %. Despite this fact, he discovered sinking real wages that he calculated on the basis of the *official cost-of-living index.*

Here it becomes clear that the calculation procedure predetermines the evaluation of the trends – positive or negative. The length of time used as a basis for the evaluation appears likewise to be important.

Publications from the beginning of the 80's regularly record negative trends. More recent data clearly show minor upwards trends. It is not possible to do away with certain inconsistencies. Since the procedures for assessing the cost of living, the recording of wages for farmhands, the assessment of the basket of available commodities and the construction of the indexes seem to still be relatively unexplained, fundamental theoretical and development strategy deductions seem out of place, or at least such findings have to be treated with extreme care and caution.

Cf. [218] Khan, Hossain, 1989: p. 159, Tab. 7.6, who present other figures: for the period from 1971/72 to 1987/88, they recorded similar real wage developments, whereby following a phase in which the real wages sank, they have in the meantime once again reached the level of 1971/72.

442 As it is not the goal of this study to analyze the state agrarian and development policies and the individual promotion measures, but rather instead to establish the activity and system theoretical consequences of social dynamics, it is necessary to dispense with an analysis of measures and policies and point to the "application and development theory" literature.

For a brief description of the cooperatives in Bangladesh, see for example: [150] Herbon, 1988; [151] Herbon, 1988; and [152] Herbon, 1988, and the literature mentioned in these sources.

Tab. 21: Developments in the Agricultural Manpower Supply, Employment in Plant Production, Labour Productivity and Real Wages, 1950 - 1989/90

Indicators	1950 /51	1960 /61	1969 /70	1975 /76	1982 /83	1979 /80	1984 /85	1989 /90
			a			b		
Agricultural Labourers (Mill.)	10.18	12.36	14.19	15.15	14.82	15.0	16.0	17.0
Employment in Plant Production (Mill. Workdays)	1410	1506	1868	1848	2058	2093	2255	2480
Employment per Worker and Year (Workdays)	139	122	132	122	139	156	158	162
Yields in Plant Production per Labourer (Tk/Year)	4424	4454	4971	4597	5743	-	-	-
Labour Productivity (Tk per Workday)	31.92	36.54	37.76	37.67	41.42	-	-	-
Real Wages (Tk to 1975/76 Rice Prices)	-	18.17	10.76	8.82	9.80	8.1 c	10.3 d	-

Source: [161] Hossain, 1984: p. 43, Tab. 6 (1950 – 1982); [255] Muqtada, 1986: p. 67, Tab. 5.2; and p. 68, Tab. 5.3 (1979 – 1990 (Projection)).

a   [161] Hossain, 1984: p. 43, Tab. 6.
b   [255] Muqtada, 1986: p. 67, Tab. 5.2; and p. 68, Tab. 5.3.
c   Calculated on the basis of [31] Alauddin, Tisdell, 1989: p. 565, Tab. 2.
d   Calculated on the basis of [31] Alauddin, Tisdell, 1989: p. 565, Tab. 2.

and effects were not as strong everywhere, but in some cases they were revolutionary. There are large differences between the villages, [443] between the regions [444] and between the seasons. [445]

Thus empirically, one discovers a manifold and very complicated picture that, national statistically (with the corresponding delays in time), appears to be much simpler and less dramatic. Table 21 illustrates the national data. The following facts found in the data appear to be worthy of notice.

1. The increase in the number of agricultural workers and their contribution has lagged behind the increase in the population.

443 See [32] Ali, 1987.
444 Cf. [29] Alauddin, Mujeri, 1985; and [64] Boyce, 1989.
445 Cf. [169] Hossain, 1987; and [290] Rahman, 1981, whose methodology, however, has been so inadequately described that the data cannot be meaningfully utilized here.

2. The number of workdays per manpower is increasing slowly and steadily, a fact that has to be seen in connection with Hossain's finding that somewhat less work is carried out per day and person if, and because, the total labour demand increases, which leads to rising wages. This may result in workers being in a position to enforce better working conditions and shorter hours.

3. The real and monetary yields from plant production and the labour productivity are increasing slowly.

4. The real wages of the farmhands have been increasing in trend since the beginning of the 80's, which has implications for the situation of the poor that will be discussed later in Chapter 4.5.1.

Both the earnings from agricultural and nonagricultural self-employment as well as the earnings from agricultural and nonagricultural wage work seem to be increasing slowly. In the following section the general consequences for rural incomes will be discussed.

4.4 Developments in the Rural Income Conditions

The population development and the correlated slow fragmentation of the resource land, as well as the introduction of the new agricultural technologies and their coming into effect, have led via the dynamics of the land market, the production system and the labour conditions to a specific system of income distribution. Diverse interdependent components contribute to the income the household has at its disposal. An attempt will be made in the following sections to describe these components. This will take place against the background of the fundamental and general – not in every single case – overall stability of the rural income conditions in recent years as they have already been presented in Figure 9, page 64.

In the following sections, the significance of various factors for the income development trends will be presented: (1) holding size, (2) land utilization rights, (3) degree of modern technology and (4) multiple employment.

4.4.1 The Significance of Holding Size

The higher productivity of the small agricultural holdings has been substantiated in the case of Bangladesh. Ahmed points out in his study, which was carried out at the beginning of the 80's, [446] the income percentages regarding the important production factors for the small and large holdings (less than 250 dec. and more than 250 dec.) for the typical monsoon season Boro in

---

446 [17] Ahmed, 1983: p. 114, Tab. 6.3; and p. 116, Tab. 6.4.
   I am not aware of any more recent study supplying such data material.

275

Fig. 76: **Comparison of the Monetary Yields and Factor Compensation for Local (LV) and Modern (MV/HYV) Rice Varieties for the Boro and Amon Seasons According to Holding-size Category**

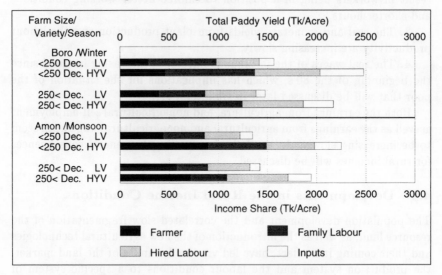

Source: [17] Ahmed, 1983: p. 114, Tab. 6.3; and p. 116, Tab. 6.4.

Note: For the numerical values, see Table 99 in the appendix.

winter, as well as for the monsoon rice season Amon. Figure 76 summarizes some of the findings and illustrates the relations.

1. It is clear that in the case of the high yielding varieties, the monetary yields per acre are about 50 % higher than those achieved by the local varieties. This is true both concerning large as well as small holdings. However, it should be mentioned that from the very beginning the level of the yield per unit of area is higher in the case of the small holdings. The input-intensive Boro season does indeed result all in all in slightly higher yields per unit of area, but the input expenditures are also higher. The factor farm manager per unit of land receives less remuneration during the Boro season. [447]

---

447 Ahmed subtracts the expenditures for variable inputs (water, seed and chemical inputs) and hired labour as well as the family labour that is assessed according to the market prices from the monetary yields. The income for the farm manager is, thus, the calculated rest left over after the other factors: disposition, land and fixed costs have to be paid, as well as rent, if the case arises. These are, however, not recorded by Ahmed. See in this context Figure 77.

2. Farm manager per unit of land and the payment for family labour bring summed up in the agricultural households *higher internal total factor incomes*. This is also true if, as is the case consistently, the expenditures (i.e. the right to receive payment) for hired labour and modern inputs increase.

3. Furthermore, it can be seen that (1) the expenditures or right to receive payment in the case of family and hired labour, taken together, are on the average higher in the case of the small holdings. Only a small portion of the increased expenditures is caused by the slightly higher wage costs that small farmers have to pay as a rule in comparison to the large landowners. [448] (2) The share of family labour is much higher in the case of the small holdings, which all in all use more manpower anyway, than in the case of the large holdings so that a larger portion of the (calculated) expenditures for household members remains in the household. Thus, despite the greater employment of manpower and the calculated right of payment for family labour, the "increased income" remains in the household. "Self-exploitation" is not an adequate term under these conditions. On the contrary, it would be better to speak of increasing "self-employment" and "self-acquisition."

4. The Amon season, with somewhat less of a demand for labour and inputs, is altogether the "more profitable" season. External inputs and services demand somewhat lower expenditures. In the case of small holdings, cropping high-yielding varieties during this season is particularly effective for the family income. While these households remain slightly behind the large holdings with respect to cultivating traditional and local varieties, they are successful – in the case of the studied holdings – in making use of the advantages of modern technology for themselves and, hence, increasing the internally available factor income overproportionally. The effects regarding hired labour are less positive during this season.

4.4.2 The Significance of Land Use Rights

Only approximately 15 % of the farmland is rented. The manifold, specifically Indian, discussions about the productivity inhibiting effects of sharecropping and the resulting poverty are, hence, relevant for only a small percentage of the farms and land. Figure 77 clearly shows on the basis of Ahmed's findings from the beginning of the 80's that:

1. Independent of the farming status, the yields per area are largest in winter. High yielding varieties are, in any case, profitable. Both the internal household factors (farm manager, land, family labour) and the externally

---

448 [166] Hossain, 1988: p. 100, Tab. 53.

Fig. 77: Comparison of the Monetary Yields and Factor Compensation for Local and Modern Rice Varieties for the Boro and Amon Seasons According to Farming Status

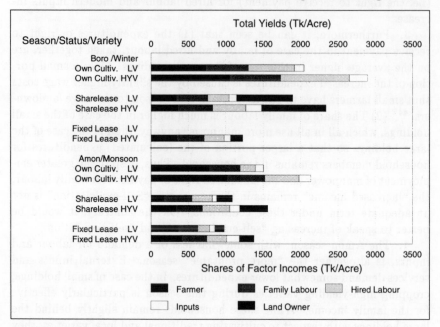

Source: [17] Ahmed, 1983: p. 109, Tab. 6.1; and p. 111, Tab. 6.2.
Note: For the numerical values, see Table 101 in the appendix.

hired manpower receive, seen absolutely, higher compensation if high yielding varieties are cropped.

2. Self-operated land results in higher profits than sharecropping or fixed rent, whereby the absolute profits from sharecropped land are greater than those from fixed rent. However, the share of the factor income that the farmer and his family receive is higher in the case of fixed rent and in times of the important monsoon-season (Amon). The landlord's share from sharecropping is higher so that the share is in absolute dimensions smaller in the case of the tenant and results in more profit for the landlord.

The data for the irrigated, input intensive Boro irrigation season does not suffice because in the studied region high yielding varieties are not cropped under the conditions of fixed rent. This, however, is only valid in the case of

278

the studies mentioned here from the years 1974/75. [449] New developments in the course of irrigated farming, which has since continued to grow in importance, result in fixed rent (*chāuniā*) gaining significance during the winter season when irrigation is employed and the inputs are high.

3. Compared to the potential profits that can be derived from operating a farm one's self, renting land out to be farmed by sharecroppers is unprofitable for landowners. The share of the harvest that the landlord receives is smaller than the share with which the factor farm operator/land is compensated with in the case of self-operation. This statement, however, is only true under the condition that, as Ahmed stated, hired labour and inputs are financed commonly and according to share, i.e. calculated according to share. This also means that the tenant may indeed prefinance such expenditures if need be, but that he can also demand recompensation for them after the harvest has been brought in. The usual reports in which, however, such detailed calculations are not presented are based on the *norm* according to which the tenant finances all of the inputs out of his share of the yield. [450]

4.4.3 The Significance of the Degree of Technological Modernization

Hossain [451] compares the effects of adopting or not adopting modern agricultural technology on the basis of data from the year 1982. [452] He does this

---

449 I have no economic analyses, profit and expenditure calculations, or such at my disposal, especially from more recent years. The analysis of the claims and titles as well as the share norms, as they are published as a rule, do not suffice to allow an economic evaluation, let alone an assessment of the profitability developments.
[166] Hossain, 1988, also only mentions in passing the significance of the property or farming status for the behaviour of the farmers with respect to adopting innovations in the context of modern technology, but does not deliver differentiated data on production, productivity and yields.

450 In this context, there is obviously a lack of precision that cannot be clarified in retrospect. In the case of traditional sharecropping and traditional farming methods, the matter is clear. The tenant supplies the manpower and draught power and traditional seed and receives half of the yield. The landlord supplies the land and, at times, also seed and receives the other half of the yield. In the course of the introduction of modern types of farming, however, one finds forms of financing in which each pays half, or one pays for the water and the other for fertilizer, etc. Theoretically, due to the increasing demand for leasable land, the tenancy conditions would have to worsen for the tenants.
There is a need for research in this context. Local and general economic conditions should be taken into consideration when doing so.

451 [166] Hossain, 1988.

452 2 x 317 households in 2 x 8 villages were included in the survey that were considered representative for various agro-ecological zones.
For a detailed description of the selection of villages and random sample as well as

Fig. 78: A Comparison of Agricultural and Nonagricultural Incomes According to Landed Property Size Category in "Modernized" and "Nonmodernized" Village Types

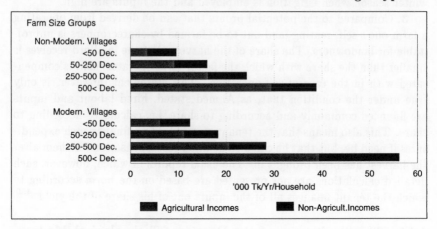

Source: [167] Hossain, 1988: p. 121, Tab. 65.

Note: For the numerical values, see Table 100 in the appendix.
Included in the survey were 2 x 317 households in 2 x 8 villages that were considered representative of various agro-ecological zones.
The group delimitations overlap in the source (250 dec.).

without the aid of holding-size or farming-status criteria. Figure 78 compares income effects of modern technology according to the "modernized" and "nonmodernized" village types. It is possible to draw a few conclusions on the basis of this data.

1. The *overall income level* of the households *in the "modernized" villages is much higher than in the "traditional"*. The agricultural income is essentially responsible for this. The shares are considerably higher for nearly all landed-property size categories. The relative differences (increases) are highest in the case of the small sizes. With respect to the absolute differences, the large holdings in the "developed"-"modernized" villages are way ahead of the "under-developed"-"nonmodernized" villages.

2. The nonagricultural income percentages for landless and small holdings were very significant in both village types, but they have not increased to the extent of the income from agriculture. They are in principle "constant" in both village types. The nonagricultural economic sector evidently has not (yet) increased in importance regarding wage incomes to the same

further methodological considerations, see [166] Hossain, 1988: p. 17 f. and Tab. 1.

extent as farming. The largest landed-property category in the "modern" villages is an exception. These *prosperous households have succeeded* in also *achieving a very high, absolute nonagricultural income percentage.* This will be mentioned again in connection with the presentation of the following figure.

3. *The income has increased for all of the households in the "modern" villages.* The absolute *differences* in income between the landless and the large landowners, however, have grown. In the beginning, this is not a problem because additionally available income can be invested and, thus, bring about further economic expansion with positive effects for wage income. Whether this is the case has neither been clarified in the relevant literature, nor empirically. The supposition that land is bought with it cannot be ignored. Empirically it is always possible to find prosperous, sometimes urban, land purchasers. The question as to what quantitative significance this has and whether the small farmers who are sometimes absolutely better situated (have to) sell land at all has not been conclusively clarified and can, therefore, not be judged here. Increasing land prices also absorb part of the purchasing power of the wealthy land buyers.

Figure 79 presents the average significance of the various agricultural and nonagricultural income sectors for the same villages and households that were surveyed by Hossain in a comparison of the two "development stages." The following aspects can be clearly recognized.

1. The *expanding income percentages originate* on the average among all of the households in the "modern" villages *from* plant production, essentially *rice production,* and from the increased services.

2. Whereas the increases in the income contribution derived from plant production, as was clearly illustrated by Figure 78, are divided according to farmland and own property, on the other hand, *it is the large landlords who earn the nonagricultural income growth in the service and trade sectors.* Unfortunately, Hossain does not describe how they do this. On the basis of other surveys, [453] it is possible to come to the conclusion that the large farmers take over the trading with modern inputs and the additionally produced rice. They have sufficient capital, ox carts, contacts in the key centers and, in some cases, "branches" in these centres.

3. The employment and income effects arising from the expansion of the trade and service sectors are not clear. The same is true in the case of the modernization effects that have taken place. It is possible that the surplus is drained off into unproductive areas, or it may be used for investment purposes that can have "catalytic" consequences, or may be "wasted" for

---

453 [211] Kahrs, 1991.

Fig. 79: **A Comparison of the Significance of Agricultural and Nonagricultural Incomes According to Income Source in "Modernized" and "Nonmodernized" Villages**

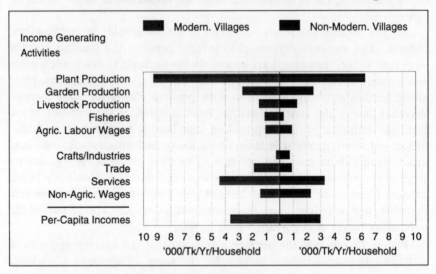

Source: [166] Hossain, 1988: p. 120, Tab. 64.

Note: For the numerical values, see Table 102 in the appendix.
For a description of the criteria used in selecting the villages, see footnote 452, p. 279.

consumption. This is not clear. Absolute growth in income and increasing absolute discrepancies alone cannot, in any case, lead to far-reaching conclusions.

4.4.4   The Significance of Multiple Employment

Multiple employment is an economic strategy practised by individuals and their households. It makes a very important contribution to stabilizing the living conditions. The economic significance of multiple employment is contrasted by the lack of scientific attention that has been paid to it. [454]

---

454 [6] Adnan, 1990: p. 127, found out in his study of village surveys that have been carried out to date in Bangladesh that: "It is hardly surprising that VS [village studies] tend to have much less information on non-agricultural sectors of the rural economy, given the preponderance of agriculture and its crop production subsector." It is only possible to agree with him when he writes: "This paucity of evidence has hampered our attempt to reconstruct trends in the non-agricultural sectors on par

Tab. 22: **The Significance of Multiple Employment and Earning Combinations in a Micro-region and in a Village in the District of Bogra, 1986**

Employment Sector	Micro-region [a] Percentage of Households (N = 925)	Village [b] Percentage of Persons (N = 620/ Hh = 376) [c]
		(%)
Agriculture Only	26.0	13.4
Wage Labour Only	15.6	36.3
Nonagriculture Only	0.9	21.8
Multiple Employment	57.5	28.6
Total	100.0	100.1

Source: [211] Kahrs, 1991: p. 44, Tab. 8; [147] Herbon, 1984: p. 43.

a   [211] Kahrs, 1991: p. 44, Tab. 8
b   [147] Herbon, 1984: p. 43.
c   This data excludes 4 people who were unemployed, 42 old people, 113 school children and 10 beggars. The data were not specifically collected for the purpose of studying multiple employment and have, therefore, to be interpreted cautiously in this context.

The research findings on the significance of multiple employment in Bangladesh are, in other words, sparse. On the basis of material that has already been presented here, it is possible to deduct a few statements. Table 22 illustrates on the basis of Table 6, p. 141 that of 925 households in one micro-region in the district of Bogra, 42.5 % of the households have members active in only one economic "sector" and 57.7 % in more than one sector who, hence, derive income from more than one sector. The village study shows a smaller percentage of multiple employment. The village, which is quite atypical, has such a high percentage of labourers ("proletarization" and degree of specialization) that the data on multiple employment – an aspect that was not specifically analyzed in the study upon which this is based and which lead to an under-representation of the seasonal sideline employment and such – surely represent too low a degree.

Ignoring the fact that percentage of multiple employment is considerably high in both cases, the agricultural economy is much less sectorally structured than the cagetgorical classification would imply.

The data presented by Hossain, [455] which are exhibited in Figure 79,

with agriculture." ([6] Adnan, 1990: p. 127.)
455 [166] Hossain, 1988.

p. 282, also clearly illustrate the income shares (of the average households) derived from nonagricultural occupations. Hossain's study did not pay any special attention to earning combination and multiple employment carried out by individuals and households. If, however, one assumes that in this case as well only about half of the households find employment in only one sector, the importance that the combination of earning sectors, the utilization of several niches and multiple employment have becomes clear. Since, however, neither detailed structure nor panel data are available, the significance of this aspect can only be vaguely pointed out here and hope placed in future analyses. [456]

In general, thus, it is possible to state, with respect to the diversity of niche utilization, spreading of risks and carrying out multiple anticylic and seasonal activities, as well as the combination of various opportunities for earning income, that this is an important aspect of rural society. It makes an important contribution to stabilizing the economic conditions and the individual chances without this being comprehensively quantified to date. It would be hardly possible to overestimate its importance – it seems – particularly under the aspects of the economic dynamics and securing the chances of the poorer sections of the population. In this context, there is a need for empirical and theoretical studies that go into more depth and further on the quantitative significance of multiple employment, on the dynamics of changing conditions in the agricultural economy and on its function as a buffer and basis of security for the poor.

The above discourse on higher wages, yields and agricultural incomes and multiple employment strategies is not relevant for all of the people in rural areas. Those who are landless, those who are unable to work and the people living in crucial areas do not, or still do not, participate in or profit from the present developments. It is necessary, in other words, to clarify the question as to the development of the situation among the poorer groups.

4.5 Developments in the Situation of the Poor

No empirical studies have been made that provide statements on the quantitative significance and changes in the conditions of the poor with the exception of an analysis on developments in poverty that was carried out at the micro-statistical level. A few studies deliver *status* descriptions, but they do

---

456 Cf. [211] Kahrs, 1991; [276] Räder, 1993; [259] Müller, 1993. As these are empirical studies, they will supply merely structure data and *not* panel data which could allow conclusions to be drawn on the changing significance of this aspect.
See in particular with respect to the complex of multiple employment in Asia [230] Kuhnen, 1987.

not make any fundamental and substantiated evaluations of the *development* trends. [457] National statistical data seem to substantiate the fact that there has been a general decrease in the "group" of people that would have to be characterized as being poor.

Studies which describe the situation of the poor and, in some cases, also make suggestions for measures to deal adequately with the problem indicate the complexity of the question. [458] Due to a lack of material it is only possible here to briefly outline on the basis of a few indicators how in the course of time the situation has changed, or how (1) "modernized" agricultural production and (2) other promotional measures seem to have worked. The scarcity of panel data, however, makes definitive statements a problem.

4.5.1 The Impact of Innovations in Agrarian Technology

Hossain [459] points out on the basis of various indices that the number of extremely poor seems to be drastically decreasing as a result of the technological innovations. Since when comparing his "traditional" with his "modern" villages, poverty seems to have halved in the latter, [460] it can be assumed that this is due to the production progress in the agricultural economy which has had indirect and positive consequences for the poor strata among the population.

Empirically the question has not been clarified whether below the surface of a statistically improving overall situation *"shifts"* are taking place among the members of the poorer groups, as well as the question of causal interde-

---

457 In this context, only development trends in the sense of statistics and systemic dynamics can be dealt with. The pressing individual situation will, of course, not be improved by statistical data. On the other hand, an analysis of the dynamics that lead to a general alleviation of poverty can by all means provide indications as to which type of *policy* has to be carried out in order to make these trends effective for as many individuals as possible. An evaluation of social and political dynamics cannot do without absolute statistical standards. The complexity of the individual conditions inherent in poverty and the possible strategies that can be used in dealing with poverty were described by [155] Herbon, 1992: p. 285 ff.

458 Cf., for example, [324] Streefland et al., 1986, and [169] Hossain, 1987, who – however – describes a methodologically completely inadequate and unsatisfactory, arbitrary random sample that with the exception of a few not exactly overwhelming qualitative insights does not allow quantitative dynamic evaluations.
Cf. in addition [261] Nebelungen who described the problems of poverty and approaches to change them on the basis of two non-government development organizations in Bangladesh.

459 [166] Hossain, 1988: p. 128 ff.; and p. 129, Tab. 70.

460 For a discussion on the poverty indicators and indices, see [166] Hossain, 1988: p. 128 ff.

pendence. *Landlessness*, for example, is *not* an adequate indicator as larger *landowners* may also belong to the groups of poor if one takes the household internal *per capita income* as a basis, for example. [461] On the other hand, not all of the landless are poor. The *dynamics* of poverty, causalities and, in particular, the *effects* of individual strategies are still largely unclear. The superficial phenomenon of the sinking importance of poverty must, therefore, be *positively* mentioned here without it being possible to clarify the complexity of the dynamics in detail.

4.5.2 Consequences of Additional Promotional Measures – Credit Programmes

In addition to the general agrarian policy there are a large number of projects, programmes and measures and policies in Bangladesh which cannot be dealt with further in this study and whose expressed goal is an alleviation of poverty, i.e. increasing the income of the poorer groups, among other things. Essential measures for reducing poverty are various types of credit programmes. Here is not the time and place to analyze the credit programmes and the institutions behind them. [462] Instead, the socio-economic *consequences* of the presently largest and most popular as well as best studied poverty-oriented credit programme will be described here, that of the *"Grameen Bank"* (village bank), in order to thus gain an impression of what socio-economic consequences such an approach had, and can still have.

The Grameen Bank is a credit and self-organization institute conceived for the rural poor. It arose on a private basis (Mohammad Yunus) and has, among other things, recently drawn interest to itself among academic and

---

461 [166] Hossain, 1988: p. 130, Tab. 71.
   Also see Table 1, p. 61, in which poverty is decreasing according to the national statistics based on the calorie supply.
462 Regarding the concepts of the various credit programmes (or alternative promotional measures) see, for example, [13] Ahmad, 1983: p. 29 ff., who described the concepts of the following programmes:

   • the Comilla Cooperatives,
   • the Integrated Rural Development Programme (IRDP),
   • the Taka Hundred Crore Credit Programme (100 Crore Programme),
   • the Rural Finance Experimental Project (RFEP),
   • the ASARRD Programme, and
   • the Grameen Bank Project (GBP, GB).

   Also compare [261] Nebelungen, 1988, who differentiates between the pure credit and the supervised credit programmes. Also see [152] Herbon, 1988, who presents empirical findings on the IRDP-Rural Poor Approach.

donor circles due to its success. [463] The impact of the Grameen Bank's credit programme on the income level of the poor has been empirically studied within the framework of studies carried out by the Bangladesh Institute of Development Studies (BIDS) by both Hossain [464] and Rahman. [465] [466] It is true that we are not dealing with *general social effects* and consequences here such as brought about by the changes which have been dealt with until now and were the result of agrarian technological innovations, but rather with *specific consequences of specific packages of measures.* Despite this fact, effects which were observed in individual project villages will be described here. This will clearly show that in addition to relatively positive effects arising from the changes in agriculture, there were other developments that took place and are still taking place which open up improved opportunities for the poor. They can be promoted by the state. This takes place mainly on the basis of the state making financial means available with which the poor can, despite the shortage of land, identify and take up a productive occupation outside agriculture which is, hence, independent of the need to have land at one's disposal and can secure a livelihood for them.

A number of Hossain's findings have been presented in Figure 80. The comparison between the households in a village in which the Grameen Bank granted loans and a "control" village shows the annual household incomes differentiated according to the criterion of landownership categories. Thereby it is not possible to differentiate between which specific sources the income was derived from, i.e. the fact is taken into account that it is not possible to empirically really impute the impact of the loans. However, it is clear that (1) in the village in which the poor landless and small farmers had more credit at their disposal, the average household incomes were somewhat higher than in the control village. It is furthermore clear that (2) in the Grameen Bank village the landless and those groups that have

---

463 With respect to the Grameen Bank, its concept, its organization and its success see, among others, [109] Fischer, 1983; [162] Hossain, 1984; [163] Hossain, 1984; [165] Hossain, 1988; [280] Rahman. 1986; [297] Ray, 1987; and [301] Sadeque, 1986.

464 [162] Hossain, 1984, and [165] Hossain, 1988, who endeavored to establish the effects on the basis of a target and a "control" group comparison.

465 [280] Rahman, 1986, who recorded the effects in a panel study (1982 - 1985).

466 These studies are interesting because they try to establish the *impact* of credit measures from the viewpoint of the "target" group and do not, as is usually the case, direct their attention solely to the philosophy, organizational efficiency and internal balance. This makes it possible to describe effects of a general socio-economic nature. For a presentation of the research methodology, choice of random samples and method of calculating, which were not always clear to me, it is necessary to refer to the recorded sources themselves. Here it is only possible to present a few significant findings.

Fig. 80: Comparison of the Annual Income of Households According to Landownership Categories between Households in a Grameen Bank Project Village and a Control Village

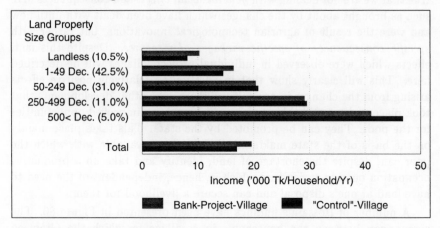

Source: [165] Hossain, 1988: p. 67, Tab. 39.
Note: For the numerical values, see Table 103 in the appendix.

little land at their disposal have absolutely and relatively higher incomes and (3) the prosperous households with large holdings have even somewhat smaller incomes. Hossain ascribes this to a "redistributive mechanism" without discussing or explaining it. Independent of this, however, he finds that the average household income in the bank village has "increased" by one-sixth due to the credit programme; i.e. stated more precisely, is relatively higher. [467]

Having land at one's own disposal has, however, only limited significance for the target group and their incomes. Figure 81 clearly illustrates that it was the nonagricultural income sources and those outside agriculture that were opened up by the financing opportunities. The figure illustrates the following effects clearly.

1. In the *share of income derived from agriculture*, the household groups show hardly any difference; i.e. the programme had neither a target group nor goal, nor (unintentional) effects in this context. Furthermore, in the case of the group consisting of the bank members, wage labour in the agricultural sector appears to be less important. It is doubtful, however, whether this is

---

467 [165] Hossain, 1988: p. 67.

288

Fig. 81: Comparison of the Income Sources of the Bank-project Participants and Non-participants and Control Village Households

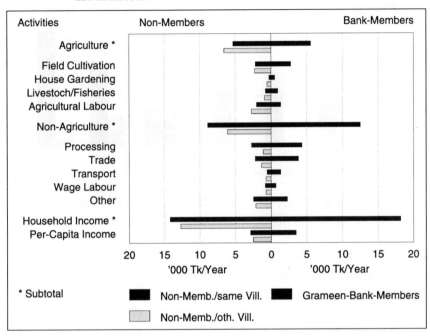

Source: [165] Hossain, 1988: p. 66, Tab. 38.

Note: For the numerical values, see Table 104 in the appendix.

due to the *impact* of the credit. [468]

2. Unequivocally, the income of the members of the Grameen Bank project – in comparison with the non-members in the same village or in the control village – is generated in the nonagricultural sector. [469] The processing and commerce sectors play a large role. It is obviously these two sectors that offer niches for the poorer and dynamic people if capital is made available.

---

468 As a rule, it is not the true farmhands that take up an occupation in the nonagricultural tertiary sector, but rather the smallest businessmen, craftsmen, etc., who from the very start are more interested in the credit opportunities and, hence, a certain self-selection among the bank project participant households takes place.

469 Both non-member groups were selected by the same criteria and correspondingly weighted.

Fig. 82: Chronological Comparison of the Income of the Bank-project Participating Households 1982 and 1985

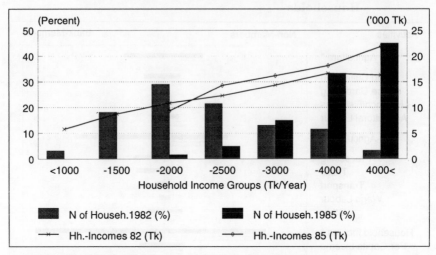

Source: [163] Hossain, 1984: p. 99, Tab. 5.3; and [280] Rahman, 1986: p. 26 f., Tab. 3.2.
Note: For the numerical values, see Table 105 in the appendix.

On the basis of Hossain's data [470] from 1982, in 1985 Rahman [471] studied 60 comparable households that were not identical. Some of his findings are presented in Figure 82. In this case as well, this time in a chronological comparison (+ participant group comparison), it could be seen that (1) the households that had credit at their diposal [472] were able to increase their income during this period of time by on the average 53 %, [473] whereby the households belonging to the lowest income category had "ascended the scale" in the meantime. [474] Hossain also registered income increases for the very brief period from 1980 (before the members joined the project) to 1982 of 32 % (on a constant price basis). [475]

One result of the credit programme is, accordingly, the fact that with respect to the poverty situation the access to and disposition of credit have spectacular effects on the incomes of those who possess knowledge but have

---

470 [163] Hossain, 1984.
471 [280] Rahman, 1986.
472 Calculated on the basis of constant prices.
473 For the figures, see Table 105 on page 368 in the appendix.
474 [280] Rahman, 1986: p. 24 f., Tab. 3.1.
475 [163] Hossain, 1984: p. 96, Tab. 5.1.

only very limited resources at their disposal and who, thus, receive the benefit of such offers. Until now, that was only a small group. [476]

Hossain also established the fact that another *result* of the improved income situation, in addition to the employment alternatives themselves, is that the labour market was unburdened by the reduction in the supply of manpower due to increased self-employment, a fact that proved to be a positive external factor for non-members/loan borrowers, [477] i.e. *the wages paid to the farmhands have increased in three years by approximately 19 % annually.*

In summary, it can be said that *in addition to the agricultural dynamics, the limited approaches for providing credit,* especially for the poorer sections of the population, showed *additional effects* (increases in income and self-employment which generated income) and *positive indirect effects* (a shortage of wage labour and resulting higher wages). The positive economic effects have – and this is of particular interest – positive consequences on the income and living situation of the poorer and weaker members of the society who were not able to take advantage of the credit programme themselves This led to further positive impacts.

It is also conceivable that in villages and regions in which the agrarian technological innovations and the new credit institutional organizations develop at the same time, positive reciprocal effects unfold between the increasing demand for goods and services and the increase in the job opportunities, as well as an improvement in the income sitaution. [478]

Apart from the reciprocal effects in the economic sector, however, reciprocal effects resulting from the changing social and political conditions are also conceivable. Deliberations on the change in the socio-political organization of rural society are the subject of the following section.

4.6   On Change in the Social and Political Organization

Economic and social change have left their mark on the social and political conditions in the rural regions. Concrete and, at the same time, fundamental changes which conform to general trends and not only local conditions are,

---

476 For a fundamental analysis and evaluation of the Grameen Bank Project with respect to the financed *activities*, the productivity, etc., see [163] Hossain, 1984: p. 129 ff.; and [280] Rahman, 1986: p. 79 ff.

477 [165] Hossain, 1988: p. 66, who bases his statement on a working paper written by Rahman that I have not been able to obtain.

478 Unfortunately it is not possible to carry out a holistic analysis of the expenditures, yields and results due to a shortage of data and due to a lack of general impact.

however, difficult to establish and substantiate. [479]

The growing importance of the "outside" relations, the economic and political alliances between local figures with higher incomes and urban – commercial and administrative – partners, patrons and institutions, has already been pointed out. [480] The increasing commitment on the part of those who achieve large growth in their income as a result of the new agrarian technologies in the commercial and service sectors has also already been mentioned. Naturally, the growing and improved transport network, the improved opportunities in means of transportation and communications and information should also be mentioned. Geographical mobility and the existing educational opportunities have led to an "opening up" of the confined village world.

Legislative measures such as doing away with the *Zamindari* system in 1950; political developments such as the struggle for independence, coups d'états and government and party "changeovers" and "elections"; administrative reorganization such as the (attempt) to introduce "grassroots democracies," to create cooperatives and institutions; and *grām śarkār* [481] and *upazilla* decentralization have led to "change." [482] The "aggregate effects" of many individual, coordinated and uncoordinated, effective and ineffective, state and private development projects, programmes and concepts should also not be neglected. All of these elements have essentially led to two developments.

1. The awareness has grown that the *world can be changed*, that *power, not fate*, is important, that various concepts can reign and one can sometimes *"choose"* between them, even if it has not necessarily resulted in "revolutionary actions." [483]

---

479 Westergaard ([345], 1985) describes the interdependence between the state and elite military structures and local village political and regional conditions in her study. The interdependence between these levels is frequently discussed in the context of the dependence theory discussion on control, carrying out and benefiting from the development measures. Cf., for example, [261] Nebelungen, 1988; [322] Spinatsch, 1984; [337] Vylder, 1988; [146] Herbon, 1984; and [148] Herbon, 1987.

480 See Chapter 4.4.3, p. 281 f. and Chapter 3.5.1, p. 183.

481 *Grām śarkār* = village government.

482 The multitude and diversity and chronological development of the concepts, approaches and policies cannot be presented within the framework of this study. Therefore, it is necessary to point out the following publications, among others: [28] Alamgir (ed.), 1981; [105] Faizullah, 1987; [173] Huque, 1988; [317] Siddiqui (ed.), 1984; and [345] Westergaard, 1985.

483 Many foreigners who despair at the poverty and distress, or "cocktail revolutionaries," dream of "revolutionary actions." The landless demonstrate their minimal autonomy in much more subtle and effective ways that can only be observed from the "worm's-eye view" of the villager and require patience on the part of the researcher.

2. Alternative organization forms, conflict forms and power poles did indeed arise. [484]

Ahmed [485] mentions the following changes in the rural socio-political conditions.

1. The extremely rigid, traditional status hierarchy was undermined by modern education and secular, worldly views. This can be seen, for example, by the fact that respect and an equivalent status position can be more easily *gained* or improved and that they are no longer essentially *designated* to the family landownership status, i.e. predetermined. [486]

2. Traditional concepts of status and virtue regarding economic activities have changed and become less rigid due to the growth in commerce, crafts and services. The necessity to take up jobs that forced the job-seekers to ignore their own social preferences but allowed them to find a niche has certainly also played a role.

3. The general horizon has expanded beyond the village. The embedment in the national administrative and economic system and a certain dependence with respect to resources that are derived from outside (agricul-

---

484 It is difficult to substantiate this with literature. The key perspective among the social scientists when studying the political, institutional conditions is to demonstrate how antisocial, commercial, feudalistic and traditional the local power structures are and that they, therefore, must be abolished. This is certainly true to a large extent. This attitude, however, overlooks the perspective that can perceive the sublime, cultural-specific changes that by all means have long-term drastic consequences. This is the aspect that plays a role here!

There is no lack of studies on the social organization and the socio-economic situation of the people in the villages. Village studies implicate or explicate the relevance of the social conditions for the development chances for the economy, the people, or the entire society, or for adequate measures that correspond to the target groups, allow participation and, in some cases, are "revolutionary." Nearly all of the studies are based on the implied or explicit supposition that (1) the conditions are worsening because of the overall social and demographic dynamics, and (2) the measures introducing technological innovations in the agrarian sector under the existing conditions and inequality aggravate the income disparities and the poverty.

Whereas economic change has been comprehensively dealt with and deliberations on the *induction* of change in the power structures carried out, the *consequences* and *dynamics* of what has already taken place – also as a result of external intervention – are hardly dealt with. This is surely partially due to methodological problems. While it is possible to grasp the material basis and the rights to production means with the help of direct or indirect observation over specific periods of time, it is empirically extremely difficult to grasp the change in socio-organizational conditions if one wants to *empirically substantiate* the findings and not *deduce them theoretically* on the basis of dogma. This would necessitate the long-term, repetitive studies that have been called for at another point in this study.

485 [15] Ahmed, 1985: p. 182 ff.

486 Cf. [146] Herbon, 1984; [147] Herbon, 1984: p. 83 ff. and p. 103 f.; and [212] Karim, 1987: p. 235.

tural inputs, development funds, etc.) as well as the increasing value placed in "modern" consumer goods lead to the development of an expanded perception and need horizon. [487]

4. Kinship relations are still important. This can already be recognized by its vital significance within the framework of "relationship strategies." However, there seems to be increased individual striving based on an increase in systemic alternatives (contingencies) that aims at increasing the chances individuals have of becoming independent and autonomous. Alam [488] points out the fact that kinship relations are decreasing relatively in importance in comparison to other forms of relations that are growing in number.

5. The struggle for independence gave birth to a class and generation of fighters and politically engaged young people who, without a doubt, found themselves confronting the traditional village patriarchs and "large landowners" and forced that circle to exercise "social caution."

Based on Karim, [489] it is possible to add the following changes.

6. The establishment of "modern" formal institutions such as cooperatives, *gram sarkar*, etc, has led to the creation of new positions in new, parallel power hierarchies with new qualifications. The "competition" between these structures and the people involved in them has questioned the old structures, and their significance has become, in part, relativized. Educated leaders had better chances in the – at times – more formal positions that were based on external contacts. Since, however, education is still frequently a privilege of the more prosperous, the social and economic background of the new leaders did, without a doubt, not differ greatly from that of the older leaders.

7. Education and the access to modern state, administrative leadership knowledge makes it also possible for other families, which do not necessarily belong to the old "large" landowner class, to gain admission to respected, influential and lucrative positions. Since these people are also status and prestige conscious and strive for power, they are often faced by the necessity to build up a clientele of their own by means of incentives and promises: this clientele wants to see its wishes fulfilled and can sometimes enforce them by means of elections. [490]

8. The party system, even if it is strongly factional and regionally organized, opens up election alternatives in the villages and to the poor. [491] Thus

---

487 Cf. [212] Karim, 1987.
488 [20] Alam, 1986: p. 163.
489 [212] Karim, 1987.
490 With respect to "qualifications" for leaders, see for example [147] Herbon, 1984: p. 306 f.
491 Naturally not in the case of the presidential elections. These elections are organized

the more formal power positions that the leaders have cannot in principle be guaranteed permanently. [492]

Alam [493] finally points out the following facts.

9. There is a growing number of people who keep out of the political faction struggles in the village and the wrangling for followers because (1) there is no convincing leader; [494] (2) there is a conscious rejection of squabbling and jockeying among the factions; and (3) they do not see what use it brings. These households are increasingly becoming a power factor in themselves because they can influence elections and determine the winner on the basis of their numbers alone.

The above observations make it clear that the researcher's perception and description of local power structures, or inequality, nepotism, control of resources and of normative and formal regulations are in themselves not able to ascertain changes, quantify them, or substantiate them.

Socio-economic dependence structures are gradually being dissolved such as sharecropping relations or, due to the shortage of labour supply and lacking geographical mobility, the establishment of patronage relations. Formal institutions, mobility and need, as well as striving for success have *resulted in openings and generated alternatives* (even if limited and still completely unsatisfactory); allow hope for a loosening up of the structural rigidity; and, in the course of the further developing demands, flexibility. It is to be expected that these processes have their own dynamics that have not fully unfolded which will find their structural "expression" in a manner which cannot be prognostisized. The opportunity to elect a leader at all, or the possibilitiy of *not* voting, to effectively *sabotage* or *contest* decisions in court, or even defend one's self physically, limits and relativizes the authority and power of the ruling village leaders. The significance of the *possibility* of electing the leader who promises the most, or offers and achieves the most, is a change that can only be properly estimated against the background of the total dependency in earlier times. [495]

---

at another level. But some of the local rulers are forced to face real elections and public criticism.

492 Cf. [343] Westergaard, 1980: p. 42; and [345] Westergaard, 1985: p. 145 ff.

493 [20] Alam, 1986: p. 162.

494 This also corresponds to my own observations. However, (1) a *possibility* presents itself here which is possibly based on improved economic independence; (2) followers are only relevant in *crises* anyway, and until then one upholds all possibilities in all directions; and, furthermore, (3) *independence* and autonomy, being one's "own boss," is a social ideal that one expresses when the opportunity and necessity are there.

495 The ideal concept of a totally participative democracy is a standard that is surely used in order to help justify in another way why the consciousness of mankind still

These minimal shifts in power put in some cases the "herd of voters" in a position to tilt the scales in their favour. In the case of individual dependent tenants, for example, this is less likely. Along with an increasing number of farm workers and the decreasing significance of sharecropping, it is obvious that the "proletarian" consciousness and collective actions will gain importance. This should be empirically studied and tested.

Such socio-political changes and processes require, however, a great deal of time and imply many setbacks. Conflicts concerning the formation of village governments (*gram sarkar*) in 1980, the avoidance of dependency spirals etc., are indicators of a hardly recognizable transition in the social conditions. If one avoids a dichotomous and dialectic as well as short-term and ahistorical viewpoint, it is clear that social and political conditions are caught up in a slow transition consisting of progress and setbacks. *This transition is characterized essentially by an increase in the individual and collective alternatives (contingencies).* One can also say that there are "markets" for followers, obligations, etc. People can choose between leaders, parties and – only sometimes – between two evils. [496]

These fundamental changes, however, have until now neither fully unfolded nor fully come to play. It is plausible, however, that (1) factors necessitating the state to decentralize; the (2) increasing need for the state, party and military rule to legitimize itself; (3) a sleeping consciousness of power among the poor; and (4) a certain easing in the poverty as a result of agricultural economic progress is gradually leading to political dynamics of their own which – considered in historical time dimensions – can bring about fundamental changes. It is not possible to make a prognosis as to how these changes will be. It has been shown here, however, that changes have already taken place that are difficult to substantiate and quantify, but which are nevertheless real.

---

needs to be helped in its development.

496 One must not believe in the illusion that the opportunity to vote will automatically do away with corruption, nepotism, hunger for power, etc. On the contrary, it can without a doubt result in short-term or medium-term increases in these phenomena. The question as to whether this always has to mean that it is to the detriment of the clientele can certainly be answered more competently by many an Asian.

"At the heart of ... this study lies a fusion of conviction and theoretical perspective that individuals matter, and that even the poorest individual, singly and/or in groups, can overcome the constraints of the economy, geography and history. He can take effective steps to cope with poverty, and deftly utilize even a minimum of opportunity to work for progressively higher living standards."

Jayanta Kumar Ray [497]

"The goal [of an analysis of organized complexity] is not to make a detailed prognosis of future behaviour, but rather a prognosis of behavioural patterns..., the functional contexts, problem figurations, and development lines. This knowledge increases the probability of bringing about or hindering certain things or results."

Helmut Willke [498]

5 Conclusion: Individual and Systemic Dynamics

5.1 The Development Dynamics in Rural Bangladesh

The population growth *rate* in Bangladesh has remained nearly constant since the beginning of the century, a fact that has led to exponentially growing population *figures*. It is impossible for this self-accelerating development to continue in the future. [499] These catastrophic trends in the population development and the current average wretched living standard of the population are the framework conditions within which the development process that will be discussed here has to take place. It must be stated, however, with respect to the reasons for these conditions and the historical processes that led to this situation and to the complex influences that still exist that

---

497 [297] Jayanta Kumar Ray, 1987: p. 4.
498 [346] Willke, 1987: p. 136.
499 As extremely problematic could also prove to be the presently emerging development in the global climate which – observed linearly – will lead to a medium-term raising of the sea level and, thus, horrendous consequences for the densely populated country. Contrary developments are, indeed, recognizable and conceivable, but it is doubtful whether it will still be possible to avert a total ecological disaster due to the long time lags. Even a change for the good would imply a slight rise in the sea level for Bangladesh.

at present the trends are stable despite the growing population because the economic development appears to be keeping up with the population development. Indeed no more, but also no less. The causes are summarized in the following points.

1. Landed property is being fragmented and spilt up among continually more households. Many households and families are completely losing their access to land. Fundamental land accumulation is not taking place. On the contrary, the large holdings, the landed property, is being divided up.

2. The existing production methods which integrate farming, essentially rice cropping; livestock keeping; fish husbandry in ponds; gardening; the domestic economy; and commerce, crafts and wage labour are subject to the population pressure and are in a process of continual development. Niches open up and are immediately – relatively efficiently – occupied. The interdependence between the sectors leads to immediate consequences and adaption in all of the sectors if something changes in any one of them.

3. Individuals are increasingly forced to take advantage of formerly unknown or not utilized niches and potentials in order to, thus, secure their existence and livelihood. On the other hand, pluriactivities allow individuals or members of the households or villages and regions to take advantage of a complex and many-faceted network of chances, securities and benefits that lead to a multi-stability of the system and an historically singular, inherent dynamic.

4. In this situation, the introduction of modern agricultural technology with its greater yield potentials and greater demands for inputs and labour has led to a sudden increase in innovations that has been strengthened by the gradual improvements in the irrigation and transportation infrastructures. The growing population has also led to a strengthening of the significance of the urban economy, the industrial sector and corresponding promotional policies.

5. The people living in and on the holdings, which are on the average decreasing in size, have recognized the chances that result from the possibility of utilizing the new cereal varieties, modern inputs, irrigation and the possibility of employing their manpower to increase the productivity, yields and income.

6. The pressure on the resources due to the demands of continually more people, on the one hand, and to the continually (on the average) smaller holdings, on the other hand, leads specifically in the case of the "endangered existences" to the necessity of making use of innovations. Thus, the members of smaller holdings have obviously, on the average, taken up the new technological possibilities more quickly and understood how to achieve higher yields per unit of area and employ their manpower increasingly and

298

productively on their own holdings. This (1) opened up additional employment opportunities for wage workers and, simultaneously, (2) unburdened the wage-labour supply market by decreasing the necessity to earn one's living outside one's own holding. In other words, we are faced by a *paradox situation* in which the holdings produce, even while becoming smaller, in synergetic combination with the technological innovations overproportional increases in the yields and efficiency.

7. The improved economic situation of smaller holdings as well as in villages and regions in which modern technological and, thus, institutional and organizational innovations (cooperatives, irrigation perimeter groups) were effective resulted in their *"crises resistance"* becoming improved. Hence, the income expectations were satisfied to a greater extent. *"Buffer resources"* can be accumulated and set aside. Thus in emergency situations, increased means are available that can be liquidated. The pressure to sell land is reduced.

8. The households with relatively large holdings invest their income derived from agriculture outside agriculture and in supplementary commercial, transport and service enterprises and open up, thus, the opportunity to establish and intensify economic cycles that unfold their own dynamics independent of agricultural production and can influence agriculture. The employment and income effects generated in this manner are largely unknown.

9. The landless and those who have little land at their disposal have the opportunity in situations in which the demand for manpower increases, as it is presently doing, to improve their income and working conditions. The growth in the demand for manpower appears at the moment to surpass the growth in the labour supply due to the population growth.

10. The current development is based on increases in the yields and efficiency that became possible as a result of the gradual adoption of modern technology in rice and wheat growing. The non-cereal production sectors do not seem to have developed dynamics of their own yet. On the contrary, increases in the yields in these sectors can be traced back to *more people* while the productivity remains the same and the autopoietic ties between the individual production systems are stimulated when changes take place in another sector. Therefore, with respect to these supplementary production systems, it should be mentioned with caution that (1) they partially *increase only just parallel to the population growth*, and (2) *no specific inherent dynamics* can be observed in these sectors which for their part could lead to synergetic effects in the overall system.

11. Whereas garden and energy production appear to be (at least merely) stagnating and are obviously not sending out any economic impulses, although they are currently evidently in a position to meet the population's "subsistence" needs, the situation in livestock production appears to be more hopeful. However, it is only possible to make restricted statements on the distribution of the resources here, or the rights of use.

12. The number of animals that are significant as food or raw material suppliers is increasing. Thus, the interest among the poorer households in keeping goats and poultry is evidently growing. They are interested in them as a source of food as well as for the purpose of gaining income and as a capital investment. Agricultural plant production seems to also increasingly generate supplementary products and, hence, set free or increase resources that can be utilized by the poorer households after being "processed in the animals' stomachs."

13. The provision of "external rescources," usually loans, can specifically promote the poorer people's productive utilization of niches – and does this in some cases – in agricultural sectors that are too painstaking for the prosperous (gardening and growing fruit, raising fish in ponds, small-livestock keeping, special production areas such as mulberry leaves for silkworms and raising bees, etc.). These niches are, however, not necessarily to be found only in agricultural production. Service sectors that are situated in the production chain before and after the agricultural production sector and services in connection with consumer goods are gaining importance. This results in an increase in income effective self-employment and, in addition, to a general, slightly growing demand for wage labourers. This unburdens the wage-labour supply market. This also has an additional positive impact on the wage-based income of the landless.

14. The current effect of the increase in agricultural production is a decrease in the pressure on the available resources. Depending upon how long this situation will be maintained and how the other rural and urban economic sectors develop, this episode will turn into a process that can maintain itself and increase the systemic contingencies and can bring about synergetic effects – but that must not necessarily be the case!

15. The regional and local conditions change for the better or worse, depending on the existing resources and potentials. While some villages and regions become poor, the income level sometimes increases in a revolutionary manner in others. Whereas a few villages are purely agriculturally oriented, isolated with respect to transportation and "stagnate" socio-politically in traditional structures, in other villages employment outside the agricultural sector, increases in the agricultural production and the development of the horticulture, fish raising and crafts sectors lead to employment and income effects which until now have resulted in radical structural changes. In some cases, these dynamic poles attract, on the other hand, people from deprived

300

regions: a fact which results in an unburdening in those regions. On a small-scale level, a multitude of synergetic effects can be observed which have as of yet not appeared as macro phenomena and whose consequences cannot be ascertained if one assumes a gradual and general spreading of these effects.

16. The systemic opportunities and the multifarious alternatives that open up to individual people and, to a limited extent, to the landless, poor and deprived generate their own prerequisites. The resulting conditions lead to developments whose consequences are not predictable because they are *not linear*.

17. The driving force behind the development is the million-wise, intelligent and diligent search for opportunities to earn an income, to improve one's chances, to live up to the ideal of the head of a family or a family member and to improve one's conditions as far as possible to one's own advantage. Among these are the absorption of new information, adoption of innovations, relativizing traditional concepts and rules, as well as solidarity with, but also exploitation of the weaknesses and hardships of others. The reason for the success of individual, common and aggregated strategies for securing existences are only partially known. To know them would open up the way to a better understanding of the opportunities a society bears inherent in itself. This, however, does not permit *any possibility to make prognoses* as to which of the – to some extent – still unknown opportunities will take place in which form, or which new problems will turn up, or which will become worse unexpectedly.

18. Bangladesh's development is not merely an example of the difficulty involved in eliminating hindrances for development and an example of the existence of inequality and inflexibility in the state, institutional and power structures. Bangladesh is also an example of the difficulty involved in making prophecies concerning social developments and as to which results the multifarious attempts to make the best of one's individual situation will produce.

19. The general trends have to be positively judged with respect to the indicators for the development in employment in the agricultural production sector, the real wages and the labour productivity, as they indicate a certain stability with a trend towards improvement. The overall *result* is indeed not overwhelming, but the trend is positive. If one takes, although the success of the new technologies could already have locally matured, the production and productivity growth rates that have been achieved in some cases as a standard, [500] enormous growth rates would be possible at the national level

---

[500] In other words, not the results from comparisons between countries or experimental stations.

in the agricultural economic sector. [501] The superficial, "placid" picture obscures the fact that the present development is an *aggregate effect*. Underneath the "surface" of this development, extremely dynamic processes are taking place: the living situation is worsening rapidly, stabilizing itself, or improving, or is semi-revolutionary. Behind all of this, many individuals with their multifarious goals and interests are "hidden" who are the driving force behind the exploration for and exploitation of niches in their pursuit of the goal of improving their chances. These are the people who look for and need innovations.

20. The macro-statistical "hidden" dynamics in the agrarian sector have various consequences: [502]

a. The decrease in the size of the holdings that are commonly available to the household members for their utilization increases the demands the people make on the soil to such an extent that each and every available opportunity for intensifying and raising the production and productivity is exploited, insofar as this is possible within the existing socio-economic framework conditions – which are politically determined – "within the situation itself." Furthermore, it is possible to predict that nonagricultural activities and jobs outside the agricultural sector will gain in importance and increasingly develop their own dynamics.

b. The creation and establishment of factor markets is – with respect to inputs and capital – a political question. The current regime has opened up some new opportunities by means of an "open market" policy. [503] With respect to land and manpower, this is principally a process with inherent dynamics, i.e. population dynamics, and a distribution policy process that can be stablilized (alleviated) but not controlled by means of state intervention, e.g., Food-For-Work. Indicators for the accelerating effects of the population growth and the self-regulating dynamics of the technological and market dynamics have been supplied by Boyce and Alauddin/Tisdell who

---

501 Unfortunately, it is difficult to recognize why there are such large local disparities, for as a rule the socio-political conditions are superficially quite similar. I am not aware of any study which has investigated what influence local socio-political conditions and economic inequality have on the adoption of innovations.

502 They will be *hypothetically* formulated in the following. They can hardly be substantiated as, until now, they have only partially been the subject of research and academic interest. This is evidently due to various personal, academic and political reasons. A lack of panel study data as well as the acceptance and utilization of a system-theoretical paradigm can be mentioned here.

503 One has to mention, however, the fact that the introduction of innovations through *cooperatives* created the incentive gradually that led to the demand for and utilization of modern technologies.

definitively anticipate negative effects as well. [504]

Summarizing, it is possible to sketch the recent development trends as follows: on the basis of economically and socially indubitably unequal conditions and technological innovations, the distribution of the resources has led as a result of the constant population growth rates to conditions under which currently the chances in life are becoming stabilized at an impoverished level and one that gains time. The question remains unanswered, however, whether and for how long the innovations and their positive effects will accompany the population growth and/or whether effects will emerge that have unforeseeable and unplannable consequences that could lead to completely new conditions. In this respect, a few final theoretical deliberations will be presented in the following section.

5.2 The Significance of Non-linear Development Dynamics and Their Effects

5.2.1 The Complexity of Systemic Processes

As a rule, discourses on Banladesh's development are based on deliberations in which many variable social conditions are conceived of as "remaining constant." In reality, however, all of the variables in a social system are naturally tied in a dynamic, interactive relationship to one another. Differences in the property or holding sizes (and the analytical distribution in categories) do indeed exist; however, their quantitative, relative and absolute significance shifts as a result of the absolute increase in the population, the fragmentation due to inheritance and situations that can result for some of the population sectors as a result of individual or natural catastrophes. That is to say, in this particular case there is a "paradox effect." The positive

---

504 Cf. [64] Boyce, 1989: p. 480 f., who mentions the possible institutional hindrances for adequate (system) reactions to the population pressure.

Cf. [31] Alauddin, Tisdell, 1989: e.g., p. 567, who regard the extreme seasonal wage fluctuations as a danger, despite the higher average real wages, because it is not always possible to compensate for periodic debts by means of adequate accumulation, or because collective reserves and security are no longer effective, especially with respect to the poor, due to increasing individual disposition of these resources.

Cf. in addition, [26] Alauddin, Tisdell, 1988, who bring up the question as to what extent modern agricultural technology, on the one hand, and the further growing population, on the other hand, can be embedded in a sustaining equilibrium system. This question is largely unanswered. This is because, on the one hand, (1) the ecological-demographic question of sustainability has for a long time *not* been the focus of interest and (2) the theoretical groundwork and empirical data for researching such complex systems' dynamics either does not exist, or is unkown.

For more advanced general and theoretical deliberations see [143] Hayami, Ruttan, 1985: specifically, p. 73 ff.

or negative effects of technological innovations that affect households that have little land at their disposal are additionally strengthened by their own increment. The result of this "paradox" synergetic effect is simultaneously once again the consequence of and precondition for the social absorption ability respecting innovations, the development need for further technological innovations and social-organizational innovations. It cannot be denied that there is a danger that the privation could become so marked that innovations and investments could no longer be paid for and, as a result, the privation would become even worse. Economic and social disparities could be so disruptive that the socio-economic structures would be destroyed faster and hindered more than they could be built up and improved. Finally, natural resources could be overexploited, destroyed and squandered and the shrinking resource basis could decimate the innovation capacity. There are many *dangers*. There are, however, also *potentials* that have in some cases become visible in this study without it having been possible to deal with the technological and organizational details. (1) It is possible that the average incomes will increase and become stabilized – including the wage income of the landless – to such an extent that they will be able, as is presently the case, to develop a better "catastrophe resistance." (2) There is the possibility that social organizational forms, e.g., cooperatives, clubs, unions, parties, etc., will evolve that make income and distribution demands and bring about the appropriate stabilizing effects if their demand increases the production. (3) It is possible that an improved utilization of the natural resources (water, climate, soil) as well as their supplementation with modern, conserving and appropriate inputs will open up further bases for existence.

The list of the dangers and potentials could be continued for a long time, as well as speculations as to if and how they could come about. *The empirical data basis and the theoretical preunderstanding of the significance and the interdependencies between many variables as well as the derived theoretical concepts (models) of temporal, process centred dynamics are, however, limited.* Therefore, an attempt will be made in the following section (with all possible caution and modesty and awareness of the limited horizon in which statements can be made despite the broad approach) to give a brief, summarizing evaluation of the rural socio-economic dynamics and, thus, of the individual chances.

5.2.2 Systemic Contingencies and Synergisms

The increase in the population in Bangladesh has caused pressure on the existing resources that – assuming that the conditions are static – consists, among other things, in the fact that the existing land is being distributed

304

among more and more people, the holdings are on the average smaller, less land is available for tenancy and the job opportunities have to serve for more people. Both the structure of the resource utilization as well as the distribution of the rights of utilization have changed under the pressure of the growing population and the multitude of ways individual people try to make the best of the situation for themselves. Presuming the simplified and problematic supposition that continually more people in Bangladesh have to share a resource basis that remains essentially static, there are three implied types of fundamental *prognoses* (speculations) on the future development trends that can be found in the relevant literature:

1. An *involutionary process* will take place. That means that continually more people will secure their existence in the same way without this resulting fundamentally in a basis giving birth to inherent dynamics in the development of material welfare. The system "marks time" while continually more people have to participate: "change without change."

2. A *polarization* will take place because a few people or classes maintain their situation in life more or less by "force" and let the others sink into a condition of absolute destitution with a high rate of mortality, etc: "below poverty level equilibrium trap." The power structures hinder better distribution and utilization of the resources and stabilize themselves by means of downward trends between antagonistic classes in the areas of power and affluence. The antagonism between the classes is the result of poverty.

3. *Evolutionary inherent dynamics* will evolve that, driven by destitution and the battle for survival on the one hand and the development of innovations on the other, "build up" new "system's qualities" and contingent system conditions in which new "emerging qualities" in the economic and social systems arise on the basis of synergetic effects.

The supposition that the resource basis will remain constant is naturally neither fundamentally accepted and acceptable, nor realistic. Since the *natural* resource basis, particularly land, will hardly improve per se, an improvement in the potentials can only be achieved on the basis of innovations and technological, organizational and institutional changes. The three above-described concepts of social development trends under the present conditions caused by the population pressure present themselves in multifarious varieties before the background of the conceivable consequences of innovations with their negative, neutral and/or positive reciprocal and feedback effects.

The *theoretical complexity* and the feasible dynamic developments and their consequences increase correlating to the more variable influencing factors that are included in the theoretical analysis. Thus the deliberations become more complex if one keeps in mind the fact that (1) involutionary, polarizing and evolutionary as well as revolutionary and catastrophic dynamics can exist in the same society simultaneously in various sectors, or are part of one another and can merge and that (2) these general dynamics have sectoral, temporal, regional, local and individual effects and do not only always move in opposing directions, are not always contradictory and antagonistic at diverse levels, but rather that they can strengthen and build themselves up reciprocally.

These theoretical deliberations on the *fundamental openness and complexity of multifarious individually induced systemic dynamics as well as the incalculable synergisms, emerging and capsizing effects (catastrophes) make it clear that statements on the future of the society in Bangladesh are, in principle, speculative and will remain so* because (1) in accordance with the choice and weighting of the initial conditions and the influencing factors, the (perceived) development trends are predetermined and because (2) the interdependencies are not constant and equal and, thus, non-linear – unexpected and inconceivable – development trends may take place, and will in all probability.

Policies that legitimize themselves on the basis of social system prognoses legitimize themselves ideologically. As every type of political decision, however, requires projections and perspectives, an ideological orientation is unavoidable. The assertation, nonetheless, that it is possible to derive ideological orientations on the basis of "scientific knowledge of the laws governing the movements" has been, I hope, clearly refuted here. The demand for socio-political and economic measures that are oriented towards maintaining and increasing the individual's chances in life is, however, very large. A scientific explanation for this is not necessary.

5.3   Guidelines for a Development Policy Concept

The reader will have noticed that in this study no guidelines for specific policies, programmes, measures, or government strategies have been drawn up. Furthermore, the impossibility of making prognoses has been theoretically postulated. [505] Secondly, allegations made elsewhere in the field of political science with respect to negative "laws of development" have been refuted. The actions-oriented reader will, therefore, at this point at the latest ask what practical consequences he can draw from it all, in particular in the case of Bangladesh. What is the result of the deliberations.

With utmost caution, it is possible now to propose a few hypotheses concerning development theory in the light of the individualistic, systems theoretical paradigm that has been used here. These hypotheses can, however,

---

505 Cf. [155] Herbon, 1992: p. 69 ff.

only serve as starting points and impulses and should not be misunderstood as dogmas.

1. Development signifies comprehensive societal (economic, social and cultural) change in the direction of greater social differentiation and attempts to achieve and improve the chances for more and more people. Societies are systems of great complexity with long histories and manifold and interdependent inherent dynamics. This fact has to be taken into account by means of increased "systems thinking." "Systems thinking means thinking in correlations. Only this can prevent a part being taken for the whole, or the conclusion that a change in one aspect leads linearly to a change in the whole." In particular, it is important to avoid the fallacy "that increasing efficiency (or an increase in inefficiency) in one specific part or a specific function within the system increases (or lessens) the efficiency of the system..." [506] On the contrary, it has turned out that in complex systems the interactions and reciprocal effects between various levels and components are not simple, linear, additive and causal, but rather discontinuous, nonlinear, contra intuitive, irreversible, positively and negatively reciprocal, etc. Above all, there are hardly any clear and isolatable cause-effect relations! This insight has, admittedly, (development) policy consequences.

2. When planning and carrying out measures, it is necessary to be careful when using the means to achieve these goals. Those who are politically and executively active must be conscious of the following facts:

- They are intervening in complex, multistable and adaptive relations that have until now opened up certain chances to the individual for his existence, even if they are only miserable.

- They legitimize themselves in the light of goals that could prove to be a mistake and unrealistic.

3. The fact that the existence of the individual is presently endangered and that the goals on the way to improvement can consist of removing hindrances of all kinds does not justify each and any political measure. The criterion here is not the *establishment* of the positive or negative effects of a measure, nor the *meaningful legitimation* of a policy, but rather the *real effects* on the individual. Balancing the positive effects for the general public and the negative effects for the individual (social contra individual costs) against each other is unequivocally a decision that is based on values and cannot be used definitively to legitimize a measure, nor does it allow certainty in the matter that can be substantiated scientifically and, thus, also

---

506 [346] Willke, 1987: p. 133.

serve as a legitimation for the measure. Surely there is no one who would not acknowledge these platitude-like statements and insights. What has to be demonstrated here, however, is the fact that neither the concept presented here, nor any other, contains liberation from political and ethical constraints to legitimize the targeted goals and the measures that are carried out. On the contrary, what has to be made clear is the fact that an understanding of the complexity of the world would instead give rise to political caution. The danger of simple and radical solutions and cures is sometimes strengthened by the "tendency to despair at the complexity."

4. Political measures whose goals are specifically the influencing, changing and directing of certain conditions have, if any at all, manifold consequences and reciprocal and secondary effects. The unintentional "secondary effects" can be positive or negative (usually both) and, furthermore, frequently become the "major effect." Just as it is true that cause-effect relations can no longer be specified or anticipated, the same is true in the case of cost-benefit relations.

Concretely, that means that more or less elaborate, specific measures can seldom achieve the goals politics and the administration have set without problems. On the contrary, a multistranded feedback of information is necessary that can within a short time give information on consequences and the contingent negative secondary effects which, thus, allows a partial revision. That means, preliminary political measures necessitate, on the one hand, an effective control of the course of events and effects that is not limited to project-internal efficiencies, but rather systemic interdependencies and, in some cases, "the overall effects." On the other hand, they demand and imply cautious and "held back" (low-key, small-scale, low-input and long-term) intervention.

5. The complexity and flexibility of the living conditions and the relative success of the struggle of the people in Bangladesh to survive and secure their existence and who understand within their context how to uphold their chances as well as their tremendous achievements in the field of self-reproduction and reproducing the system make it clear that more attention should be paid to individual and collective self-reproduction and self-reference. That is to say that the insight is necessary that these people are indeed subjected to the conditions individually, but that they by means of their mainfold activities collectively achieve more than many planners and politicians. In other words, it is time to rethink. That is to say, it is not the politicians that create and shape the society. On the contrary, they can at best promote and control endogenous and autonomously induced processes (developments). Political control can never simulate and surpass the complex process of social self-control and individual dynamics. It can, however, promote the ability to do so and increase the degree of systemic freedom.

What does that signify for Bangladesh?

6. The promotion of modern agricultural technology based on fertilizer-seed-water led, among other things, along with medical progress to an enormous acceleration in the societal dynamics. Following a rapid increase in the population at the beginning of the century, the same development took place with respect to cereal production. At present, thus, a dynamic-expansive equilibrium has been achieved. The present situation, however, will not remain stable from a long-term point of view. The political maxim will, therefore, have to be to create a stable condition for the two "factors" production and man; i.e., it will have to slow down the population growth and continue to increase the production of food. This, however, is not the place to sketch the entire potential development policy measure catalogue that would be necessary to achieve this. Accepting the supposition that there are manifold individual and societal (systemic) regulatory mechanisms, the task will have to be to create more opportunities for the individual people to aid them in organizing and helping themselves. It is not specific activities that are necessary, but rather what has to be increased is the degree of freedom the individual actors have.

The millions of experiences that the people in Bangladesh have gone through and the success that they have achieved create a potential that has to be taken better advantage of, i.e. to be mobilized. The – *normative* – conclusion must be, therefore, that it will be necessary *to develop and carry out policies and programmes which increase the individual alternatives in the form of resources and information. The expansion of systemic contingencies may put the people in Bangladesh in a position to find solutions for the pressing problems – which in some cases are still to come – individually and, perhaps, collectively.* The present dynamic state of equilibrium will help gain some time for this process to take place.

Such an approach should, and would, increase the specific individual ability to search for niches and make use of them and lead, with certainty, via synergetic effects to new emerging conditions. The precondition for this is, however, "systems thinking" and a "slowed down" concept of policies and projects. In order, moreover, to substantiate these normative statements, concrete policy and project analyses would be necessary which, however, can no longer be presented here. There is still a lot to do.

Appendix

Tab. 23: Population Growth 1901 – 1989 + Three Projections for the Year 2000

Year	Population Figures Census Data		
1901	28,927,800		
1911	31,555,060		
1921	33,254,100		
1931	35,604,170		
1941	41,997,300		
1951	44,165,740		
1961	55,222,660		
1974	76,398,000		
1981	89,912,000		
1985	[a] 97,144,000		
1990	[b] 107,992,940		

	Projections as of 1980		
	+ Projection1	+ Projection 2	Projection 3
1985	[c] 100,054,000	100,468,000	100,200,000
1990	112,865,000	113,005,000	111,300,000
1995	127,086,000	126,341,000	121,999,000
2000	142,141,000	139,693,000	131,695,000

Source: [114] Government, 1984: p. 33, Tab. 1; p. 144, Tab. 10; [126] Government, 1988: p. 62, Tab. 3.25 and Tab. 3.26; [130] Government, 1991: p. 4.

a   Estimated value.
b   Adjusted value.
c   The figure 100,100,000 presented in [126] Government, 1988: p. 62, Tab. 3.26 seems
     to be more plausible.

310

Tab. 24: Development in the Areas Cropped with Rice, 1960/61
- 1988/89

Year	Amon	Aus	Boro	Reis
	Thou. Acres			
1960/61 [a]	14579	6425	988	21993
1961/62	14085	5931	988	21004
1962/63	14332	6178	988	21499
1963/64	14579	6672	988	22240
1964/65	15074	6672	988	22734
1965/66	14823	7413	988	23228
1966/67	14085	6919	1482	22487
1967/68	14823	8155	1482	24463
1968/69	14332	7664	1977	23970
1969/70	14823	8402	2224	25452
1970/71	14332	7908	2471	24711
1971/72	13344	7413	2224	22981
1972/73	14085	7166	2471	23723
1973/74 [b]	14133	7681	2595	24409
1974/75	13469	7857	2871	24097
1975/76	14236	8452	2837	25525
1976/77	14355	7952	2112	24418
1977/78	14261	7814	2703	24779
1978/79	14347	7995	2649	24992
1979/80	14761	7504	2839	25104
1980/81	14918	7689	2867	25474
1981/82	14854	7774	3219	25874
1982/83	14812	7805	3542	26159
1983/84	14845	7765	3463	26064
1984/85	14112	7260	3891	25263
1985/86	14876	7031	3789	25696
1986/87	14958	7176	4082	26217
1987/88 [c]	13816	6891	4800	25507
1988/89	12606	6644	6026	25565

Source: [124] Government, 1988: p. 180; [128] Government, 1990: p. 169, Tab. 4.46; [80] Chen, 1975: p. 205 Tab. 3.

a   For the data from 1960/61 to 1973/74 see [80] Chen, 1975: p. 205 Tab. 3.
b   For the data from 1973/74 to 1986/87 see [124] Government, 1988: p. 180.
c   For the data of 1987/88 and 1988/89 see [128] Government, 1990: p. 169, Tab. 4.46.

Tab. 25: Developments in Rice Production, 1960/61 - 1988/89

Year	Cereals [a]	Amon	Aus	Boro [b]	Rice [c]
		Thou. Tons			
1950/51	-	-	-	-	6200
1951/52	-	-	-	-	5900
1952/53	-	-	-	-	6160
1953/54	-	-	-	-	7010
1954/55	-	-	-	-	6420
1955/56	-	-	-	-	5420
1956/57	-	-	-	-	7100
1957/58	-	-	-	-	6490
1958/59	-	-	-	-	5840
1959/60	-	-	-	-	7260
1960/61	9704	-	-	-	8350
1961/62	9657	-	-	-	8330
1962/63	8915	-	-	-	7670
1963/64	10658	-	-	-	10200
1964/65	10537	-	-	-	9430
1965/66	10536	-	-	-	9400
1966/67	9634	-	-	-	9200
1967/68	11230	-	-	-	10440
1968/69	11438	-	-	-	9990
1969/70	12110	-	-	-	10550
1970/71	11255	-	-	-	-
1971/72	10046	-	-	-	-
1972/73	10186	-	-	-	-
1973/74	12020	6699	2802	2230	11721
1974/75	12308	6000	2859	2250	11109
1975/76	-	7045	3230	2286	12561
1976/77	-	6906	3011	1650	11566
1977/78	-	7422	3104	2239	12736
1978/79	-	7429	3288	1929	12647
1979/80	-	7303	2809	2427	12539
1980/81	-	7837	3237	2588	13662
1981/82	-	7095	3218	2102	13415
1982/83	-	7483	3018	3490	13991
1983/84	-	7811	3171	3297	14279
1984/85	-	7805	2739	3847	14391
1985/86	-	8407	2738	3613	14803
1986/87	-	8136	3080	3947	15163
1987/88 [d]	-	7690	2993	4731	15414
1988/89	-	6857	2856	5831	15544

Source: see the footnotes.

a   [80] Chen, 1975: p. 204, Tab. 1.
b   [124] Government, 1988: p. 180.
c   The values for the period from 1950/51 to 1969/70 have been taken from [190] Jahangir, 1979: p. 169, Tab. 28 (quoted from Alamgir, Berlage, 1973). The values from 1973/74 on were taken from [124] Government, 1988: p. 180.
d   1987/88 and 1988/89 from [128] Government 1990: p. 169, Tab. 4.46.

Tab. 26: Developments in the Rice Yields per Capita and Acre, 1951 - 1989

Year	Rice Yields		Year	Rice Yields	
	Per Acre + Year (Kg.) [a]	Per Capita + Year (Kg.) [b]	[c]	Per Acre + Year (Kg.)	Per Capita + Year (Kg.)
1951	-	140	1971	455	157
1952	-	130	1972	437	137
1953	-	133	1973	429	136
1954	-	148	1974	460	164
1955	-	132	1975	490	151
1956	-	109	1976	470	165
1957	-	140	1977	470	148
1958	-	125	1978	520	159
1959	-	110	1979	510	153
1960	-	134	1980	500	148
1961	441	151	1981	530	157
1962	460	145	1982	520	150
1963	415	129	1983	530	153
1964	479	166	1984	550	152
1965	463	148	1885	570	150
1966	453	143	1986	580	151
1967	428	135	1987	580	151
1968	459	149	1988	504	150
1969	477	138	1989	593	149
1970	476	142			

Source: [124] Government, 1988: p. 180; [128] Government, 1990: p. 169, Tab. 4.46; [80] Chen, 1975: p. 204, Tab. 1 and p. 205, Tab. 3; [190] Jahangir, 1979: p. 169, Tab. 28.

a   The values from 1961 to 1973 were calculated on the basis of [80] Chen, 1975: p. 204, Tab. 1 (overall data on cereal production, including wheat) and the data supplied by [80] Chen, 1975: p. 205, Tab. 3 (number of acres of rice per year). The resulting figure is incorrect and should be regarded and understood as an approximate evaluation.

b   The values for the period from 1951 to 1970 were calculated on the basis of [190] Jahangir, 1979: p. 169, Tab. 28, and those from 1961 to 1973 on the basis of [80] Chen, 1975: p. 204, Tab. 1 (cereal) and the population figures from [114] Government, 1984: p. 31, Tab. 1 for 1961 and 1974 (linearly extrapolated). In other words, the figures are relatively inexact.

c   The values of 1988 and 1989 are from [128] Government 1990: p. 169, Tab. 4.46.

Tab. 27: Per Capita Availability of Food, 1960/1 - 1988/9

Year	Edible Cereals	Legumes	Meat	Milk
		(%)		
1960/61 [a]	102	-	-	-
1961/62	96	-	-	-
1962/63	94	-	-	-
1963/64	104	-	-	-
1964/65	95	-	-	-
1965/66	95	-	-	-
1966/67	87	-	-	-
1967/68	98	-	-	-
1968/69	97	-	-	-
1969/70	101	-	-	-
1970/71	80	-	-	-
1971/72	85	-	-	-
1972/73	101	-	-	-
1973/74	100	-	-	-
1974/75 [b]	100	100	100	100
1975/76 [c]	106.6	96.6	100.0	99.5
1976/77	96.5	98.3	100.2	98.6
1977/78	105.0	101.7	100.4	99.5
1978/79	102.7	94.9	100.6	96.7
1979/80	107.4	86.4	100.8	96.2
1980/81	101.8	83.1	192.8	78.2
1981/82	106.7	79.7	170.6	72.5
1982/83	108.7	81.4	174.3	80.1
1983/84	108.6	74.6	184.8	82.5
1984/85	110.2	71.2	180.8	91.9
1985/86 [d]	108.6	69.5	216.1	88.6
1986/87	108.6	69.5	216.1	88.6
1987/88	108.6	69.5	216.1	88.6
1988/89	108.6	69.5	216.1	88.6

Source: [124] Government, 1988: p. 617, [128] Government 1990: p. 611, Tab. 14.01 [80]
Chen, 1975: p. 208, Tab. 4.

a   [80] Chen, 1975: p. 208, Tab. 4.
b   Basis Year 1974/75 = 100 %.
c   [124] Government, 1988: p. 617.
d   [128] Government 1990: p. 611, Tab. 14.01.

Tab. 28: Developments in the per Capita Intake of Food, 1962-1988/89

Source (Gr./Day)	1962-64 [a]	1975/76 [b]	1981/82 [c]	1988/89 [d]
Grain	536.9	523.0	487.9	499.8
Animal Products	77.4	44.0	44.0	68.8
Other Plant Products	246.4	240.3	232.6	[e] 300.2
Total	840.7	807.3	764.5	868.8

Source: [342] Wennergren, Antholt, Whitaker, 1984: p. 21; [18] Ahmed, 1988: p. 46; [129] Government, 1991: p. 21, Tab. 4.8.

a   According to [342] Wennergren, Antholt, Whitaker, 1984: p. 21, who base their data on the *Nutrition Survey of Rural Bangladesh: 1975-76*. [18] Ahmed, 1988: p. 46, reports somewhat higher figures.
b   [342] Wennergren, Antholt, Whitaker, 1984: p. 21, and [18] Ahmed, 1988: p. 46.
c   [18] Ahmed, 1988: p. 46.
d   [129] Government, 1991: p. 21, Tab. 4.8.
e   Including Miscellaneous = 63.6 gr.

Tab. 29: Developments in the per Capita Intake of Nutrients, 1962-1988/89

Nutrients	1962-64 [a]	1975/76 [b]	1981/82 [c]	1982-86 [d]	1988/89 [e]
Calories	2251.0	2094.0 [f]	2031.0	2021.5	2215.3
Protein (Gr.)	57.5	58.5 [g]	52.5	52.1	63.7
Fat (Gr.)	17.7	12.2	38.6	39.7	-
Carbohydrates (Gr.)	476.0	439.0	394.8 [h]	-	-

Source: [342] Wennergren et al., 1984: p. 21; [124] Government, 1988: p. 630; [126] Government, 1988: p. 286; [129] Government, 1991: p. 22, Tab. 4.9A and Tab. 4.9B.

a   [342] Wennergren et al., 1984: p. 21.
b   [342] Wennergren et al., 1984: p. 21.
c   [124] Government, 1988: p. 630.
d   [124] Government, 1988: p. 630.
e   [129] Government, 1991: p. 22, Tab. 4.9A and Tab. 4.9B.
f   [126] Government, 1988: p. 286, reports lower values.
g   [126] Government, 1988: p. 286, reports lower values.
h   [126] Government, 1988: p. 286.

Tab. 30: Developments in Rural Food Consumption per Capita, 1962-64 - 1981/82 and 1973/74 - 1988/89

Year[a]	Rice	Wheat	Other Cereals	Animal Products	Roots, Tubers	Vegetables	Other Plant Products
	(Gr./Day/Pers.)						
1962-64	511.6	16.3	17.9	56.5	80.6	142.0	61.1
1975/76	493.0	29.0	1.0	44.0	52.3	125.7	62.3
1981/82	451.0	31.0	6.0	44.0	62.7	120.1	49.8

Year[b]	Rice	Wheat	Pulse Crops	Vegetables	Milk	Meat/ Poultry	Fisch
	(Gr./Day/Pers.)						
1973/74	354.0	84.7	21.1	89.1	27.4	4.9	25.6
1976/77	329.4	48.7	13.0	102.0	15.9	3.5	18.7
1981/82	403.8	54.4	12.0	122.0	16.2	3.9	26.9
1983/84	420.2	62.8	25.9	104.7	22.6	6.8	28.5
1985/86	453.7	51.3	18.3	141.0	24.3	7.0	34.7
1985/86 [c]	453.7	51.3	18.3	141.0	24.3	7.0	34.7

Source: [123] Government, 1988: p. 20, Tab. 20; [139] Hassan, Ahmad, 1984: p. 146 ff., Tabs. 2, 3, 5, 6; [129] Government, 1991: p. 21, Tab. 4.8.

a   [139] Hassan, Ahmad, 1984: p. 146 ff., Tabs. 2, 3, 5, 6.
b   [123] Government, 1988: p. 20, Tab. 20.
c   [129] Government, 1991: p. 21, Tab. 4.8

Tab. 31: Percentage of Expenditures Used for Food

| Monthly Per Capita Income of the House- holds in Tk | Percent of House- holds | Monthly Percentage of Expenditures for [a] | | | | | Percent of Total Income |
| | | Cereals | Pulse Crops | Fish | Meat | Vegetables | |
		(%)					
<200	4.59	47.44	2.3	4.3	1.0	6.3	74.9
−249	6.90	47.80	2.3	4.4	1.1	6.3	75.8
−299	10.35	46.15	2.5	4.7	1.7	6.1	75.6
−349	11.32	43.77	2.5	5.2	1.6	6.4	74.3
−399	11.28	41.45	2.6	5.2	1.7	6.1	71.6
−449	9.59	38.49	2.6	5.9	2.2	6.4	71.5
−499	7.89	35.38	2.8	6.3	2.6	6.2	70.1
−599	12.55	33.73	2.5	6.3	2.6	6.2	68.3
−699	7.31	30.83	2.6	6.8	2.6	6.0	65.5
−799	5.02	27.97	2.3	5.9	2.6	5.2	59.6
−899	3.21	26.02	2.4	6.4	3.1	5.8	61.4
−999	2.67	25.13	2.1	5.9	4.0	5.3	59.2
1000 <	7.28	17.61	4.1	5.6	1.9	4.5	50.3
Total	100.0	33.11	2.4	5.7	3.6	5.8	-

Source: [129] Government, 1991: p. 65, Tab. 1.14.

a   Monthly percentage of expenditures according to per capita income groups (in Tk) in the year 1988/89. The percentages were calculated on the basis of the data in [128] Government, 1990: p. 65, Tab. 1.14. In this source, the data regarding food were set at 100 %. It refers to the relative percentage of expenditures for food from the overall expenditures.

317

Tab. 32: Wage Developments, 1963/64 - 1988/89

Year	Agri-culture a	Fishing b	Rural Small Indus-try c	Textile Indus-try d	Jute Indus-try e	Modern Indus-try f	Con-struc-tion g	Natio-nal Wages h
			(Tk/Day) at 1973/74 prices					
1963/64	9.81	9.25	7.64	-	-	-	-	-
1969/70	7.59	9.69	6.59	10.28	10.10	12.08	8.74	-
1973/74	6.96	5.23	5.03	5.53	7.81	6.23	7.10	-
1978/79	6.48	5.88	5.73	6.23	5.45	6.30	7.70	-
1979/80	6.26	7.63	5.94	6.37	5.76	5.75	7.42	-
1980/81	6.53	8.57	6.49	6.63	6.49	6.06	7.59	-
1981/82	5.90	8.23	5.95	5.59	5.82	6.03	7.20	-
1982/83	6.13	7.73	5.89	5.62	5.47	5.74	6.38	-
1983/84	6.15	6.74	7.89	5.73	5.54	5.98	7.71	6.15
1984/85	-	-	-	-	-	-	-	5.88
1985/86	-	-	-	-	-	-	-	6.95
1986/87	-	-	-	-	-	-	-	7.00
1987/88	-	-	-	-	-	-	-	7.30
1988/89	-	-	-	-	-	-	-	7.45

Source: [355] World Bank, 1985: Annex I, Tab. 5 and Tab.6; [126] Government, 1988: p. 249, Tab. 11.08; [128] Government, 1990: p. 495, Tab. 10.35.

a   [355] World Bank, 1985: Annex I, Tab. 5.
b   [355] World Bank, 1985: Annex I, Tab. 5.
c   [355] World Bank, 1985: Annex I, Tab. 5.
d   [355] World Bank, 1985: Annex I, Tab. 6.
e   [355] World Bank, 1985: Annex I, Tab. 6.
f   [355] World Bank, 1985: Annex I, Tab. 6.
g   [355] World Bank, 1985: Annex I, Tab. 6.
h   Own calculations based on [126] Government, 1988: p. 249 and [128] Government, 1990: p. 495, Tab. 10.35.

Tab. 33: Developments in the per Capita Incomes, 1973/74 - 1988/89

Year	Rural Per Capita Incomes [a]	National Per Capita Incomes [a]
	(Tk/Mon.)	(Tk/Mon.)
1973/74 [b]	552	640
1974/75	552	649
1975/76	603	694
1976/77	586	689
1977/78	621	722
1978/79	622	732
1979/80	621	742
1980/81	647	759
1981/82	636	748
1982/83	645	750
1983/84	658	763
1984/85 [c]	-	-
1985/86	861	1026
1986/87	-	-
1987/88	-	-
1988/89	953	1140

Source: [355] World Bank, 1985: Annex I, Tab. 9; [129] Government, 1991: p. 18, Tab. 4.5

a   Calculated on the basis of the gross domestic product at 1972/73 prices and the national population figures.
b   [355] World Bank, 1985: Annex I, Tab. 9.
c   Calculated on the basis of [129] Government, 1991: p. 18, Tab. 4.5.

Tab. 34: Developments in Income Distribution, 1963/64 - 1988/89

Percentage Population	Percentage of Income						
	1963/64	1868/69	1973/74	1981/82	1983/84	1985/86 [a]	1988/89 [b]
<10 %	3.3	5.0	2.4	2.8	2.9	2.8	2.6
11-20 %	5.2	5.4	4.8	4.3	4.4	4.2	4.0
21-30 %	5.3	5.4	5.8	5.3	5.5	5.1	5.0
31-40 %	5.8	7.8	6.5	6.4	6.5	6.0	5.9
41-50 %	8.3	8.3	7.1	7.5	7.5	7.0	7.0
51-60 %	8.3	8.3	8.0	8.7	8.7	8.1	8.1
61-70 %	10.0	11.2	9.8	10.3	10.1	9.5	9.6
71-80 %	11.8	11.6	13.5	12.3	11.8	11.3	11.6
81-90 %	15.0	11.6	16.1	15.7	14.8	14.6	15.2
91< %	27.0	25.4	26.4	26.7	27.9	31.5	31.0
Total	100.0	100.0	100.0	100.0	100.0	100.0	100.0

Source: [288] Rahman, 1988: p. 1010; [123] Government, 1988: p. 33, Tab. 1; [129] Government, 1991: p. 32, Tab. 6.1.

a   [123] Government, 1988: p. 33, Tab. 1
b   [129] Government, 1991: p. 32, Tab. 6.1.

319

Tab. 35: Distribution of Landed Property, 1978

Landownership Size Category (Acres)	Percentage of Households	Area
	(%)	
0	14.69	-
< 1	44.68	8.33
1-2	15.21	12.78
2-3	8.69	12.28
3-4	5.16	10.29
4-5	3.08	7.93
5-6	2.11	6.61
6-7	1.44	5.40
7-8	0.92	3.98
8-9	0.79	3.86
9-10	0.58	3.06
10-11	0.51	3.05
11-12	0.32	2.14
12-13	0.30	2.17
13-14	0.22	1.69
14-15	0.16	1.37
15 <	0.16	15.07

Source: [196] Jannuzi, Peach, 1980: p. 19.

Tab. 36: Developments in the Number of Holdings and the Percentage of Cultivated Area per Holding-size Category, 1960 - 1988/89

Holding-size Categories (Acres) [a]	Number of Holdings					Area per Holding-size Category			
	1960	1968	1974	1983/4	1988/9	1968	1968	1974	1983/4
					(%)				
<0.5	13	12	32	24	44	1	1	2	3
0.5 –1.0	11	13	9	16	13	2	3	3	5
1.0 –2.5	27	32	25	30	23	13	17	19	21
2.5 –5.0	26	26	22	18	14	26	30	34	28
5.0 –7.5	12	9	7	7	4	19	18	19	18
7.5 –12.5	7	5	3	4	2	19	15	13	18
12.5<	4	3	1	1	1	20	16	11	8
Total	100	100	100	100	100	100	100	100	100

Source: [125] Government, 1988: p. 139; [129] Government, 1991: p. 141, Tab. 3.02; [7] Ahmad, 1984: p. 30 (quoted, Alamgir, 1975).

a   The sizes for the years 1960 to 1974 are unfortunately not exactly defined, but rather overlap. They have been defined for 1983/84 and 1988/89 so that the second value is no longer included, e.g., >0.49 and not >0.50 acres.

Tab. 37: Developments in Manpower Figures, 1961 - 1985/6

Recorded Year [a]	Agriculture, Forestry, Fishing	Nonagricultural Jobs [b]	Total Population	Manpower [c]	"Not"-Workers [d]
	In Thousands		In Millions		
1961	14676	2767	55.2	16.9	38.3
1974	15838	4681	76.4	21.9	54.5
1981	15401	10506	89.9	25.9	64.0
1983/4	16448	11528	95.2	28.5	66.7
1985/6 [e]	17478	13084	101.6	30.9	70.5

Source: [120] Government, 1986: p. 23, Tab. 1 and p. 33, Tab. 1A; [128] Government, 1990: p. 97 f., Tabs. 3.01 and 3.02.

a   The manpower figures from [120] Government, 1986: p. 33, Tab. 1A, do not coincide with the total number of workers in columns 2 and 3 which were taken from [120] Government, 1986: p. 23, Tab. 1.
b   "Professional, technical, administrative, managerial, clerical workers, sales, services, production, transportation workers, and not adequately defined."
c   "Employed population, unemployed population."
d   "Housewifes, other inactive persons, children 0 to 9 years."
e   [128] Government, 1990: p. 97 f., Tabs. 3.01 and 3.02.

Tab. 38: **Average Number of Wage Earners (Head of Household and Others) and the Specific Contributions to the Income of Rural Households, 1988/89**

Household Income Category (Tk/Mon.)	Number of Earners		Income Contributions of	
	Household Heads	Family Members	Household Heads	Family Members
	Average (N)		Average Tk/Mon.	
<750	0.75	0.17	529.4	27.8
- 999	0.92	0.15	841.5	39.3
- 1249	0.90	0.24	1058.9	60.2
- 1499	0.95	0.31	1282.7	89.5
- 1999	0.92	0.47	1599.3	145.4
- 2499	0.93	0.56	2035.2	202.9
- 2999	0.94	0.72	2494.4	243.3
- 3999	0.94	0.97	3085.0	345.0
- 4999	0.94	1.08	3963.1	483.5
- 5999	0.93	1.17	4682.6	788.3
- 6999	0.93	1.40	5680.5	740.2
- 7999	0.92	1.48	6227.2	1306.7
- 8999	0.92	2.60	7429.4	1130.6
- 9999	0.96	2.40	8992.4	525.8
- 12499	1.00	1.70	9362.7	1745.0
12500<	0.89	2.13	15993.7	4064.1

Source: [129] Government, 1991: p. 48, Tab. 1.02.

Tab. 39: Average Number of Household Members and the Ratio of Consumers to Earners and the Height of the Average Total and per Capita Income of Rural Households, 1988/89

Household Income Category (Tk/Mon.)	Number of Household Members	Ratio Consumer/ Earner	Household Income	Household Income per Capita
	Average (N)		Average Tk/Mon.	
<750	2.6	2.9	557.1	214.3
- 999	3.4	3.1	880.8	259.1
- 1249	4.0	3.5	1127.0	281.7
- 1499	4.4	3.5	1372.2	311.9
- 1999	4.9	3.5	1744.7	356.1
- 2499	5.5	3.7	2238.1	406.9
- 2999	6.2	3.7	2737.7	441.6
- 3999	6.7	3.5	3430.0	511.9
- 4999	7.4	3.6	4446.6	600.9
- 5999	8.0	3.8	5471.0	683.9
- 6999	8.5	3.6	6420.7	755.4
- 7999	8.8	3.7	7534.0	856.1
- 8999	10.3	2.9	8560.0	831.1
- 9999	10.7	3.2	9518.3	889.6
- 12499	11.6	4.3	11107.7	957.6
12500<	9.9	3.6	19657.4	1985.6

Source: [129] Government, 1991: p. 48, Tab. 1.02.

Tab. 40: Absolute and Relative Percentages of Family Members and Other Persons Among the Total Number of Members of Rural Households, 1988/89

Household Income Categories (Tk/Mon.)	Percent of Households	Number of Family Members	Number of Non-family Members	Relative Percentage of Family Members	Relative Percentage of Non-family Members
	(%)	(N) in Household		(%) According to Income Category	
<750	4.2	2.53	0.07	1.9	0.06
- 999	6.9	3.34	0.05	4.2	0.06
- 1249	9.4	3.87	0.09	6.6	0.16
- 1499	9.8	4.88	0.11	7.6	0.19
- 1999	18.3	4.70	0.24	15.6	0.78
- 2499	14.5	5.18	0.36	13.6	0.93
- 2999	9.7	5.67	0.53	10.0	0.93
- 3999	12.2	5.99	0.73	13.2	1.62
- 4999	5.9	6.25	1.16	6.7	1.25
- 5999	3.0	6.08	1.93	3.3	1.04
- 6999	1.9	6.88	1.59	2.4	0.55
- 7999	1.3	6.35	2.46	1.4	0.56
- 8999	0.8	7.20	3.13	1.0	0.45
- 9999	0.5	7.35	3.35	0.7	0.32
-.12499	0.5	7.85	3.80	0.7	0.36
12500<	1.0	6.95	2.92	1.2	0.53
Total	100.0	-	-	100.0	

Source: [129] Government, 1991: p. 47 f., Tabs. 1.02, 1.03.

Tab. 41: Food Consumption per Capita and Household Type - 1982

Household Type [a]	Cereals	Legumes	Roots Tubers	Vegetables	Meat	Fish	Milk Products	Fat, Oil, Others
	(Gr./Pers./Day)							
Type A = Not Taxes	460	5	53	125	4	18	8	37
Type B = Low Taxes	470	6	71	117	2	21	12	43
Type C = Normal Taxes	491	8	63	96	7	24	17	39
Type D = High Taxes	541	13	65	139	7	29	28	45
All	488	8	63	120	5	23	15	40

Source: [139] Hassan, Ahmad, 1984: p. 146, Tab. 1.

---

a "In rural Bangladesh populations are classified into four groups A, B, C, and D. (In the authors' opinion.) The A group are the poorest, most certainly landless and are not required to pay any local tax. The B group are a little bit better off and pay a token tax. The C group may be regarded as a rural middleclass and pay an appreciable amount of tax. The D group are the richest and pay the highest proportion of tax." ([139] Hassan, Ahmad 1984: p. 144.)

Tab. 42: The Nutritional Condition of Children According to Household Income Category

Income Category (Tk)	Children 1 - 59 Months				Children 60 - 144 Months			
	Above-/ Normal	Slight	Moderate	Drastic	Above-/ Normal	Slight	Moderate	Drastic
		Malnutrition				Malnutrtion		
	(%)				(%)			
> 2000	40.0	32.2	20.0	7.7	54.5	28.6	10.7	6.2
- 4999	37.0	29.7	20.4	10.7	43.2	35.8	15.7	5.5
- 9999	42.5	28.1	20.2	9.3	43.3	36.0	14.2	4.5
- 20000	48.3	27.8	17.1	6.7	49.9	33.1	14.9	2.2
20000 <	45.4	34.0	14.4	6.2	53.0	28.7	14.6	3.7

Sources: [356] Weltbank, 1985: p. 77, Tab. 2.06 and p. 80, Tab. 2.10.

Tab. 43: Non-food Biomass Winning and Utilization Balance According to Socio-economic Household Category

Socio-economic Category	Produc-tion	Procure-ment (Net)	Issue (Net)	Building Material	Ferti-lizer	Fodder	Loss	Fuel
	GJ/Household/Year							
Farmhand Household 0 - 1.5 Acre	11.5	14.6	-	3.9	-	1.9	0.8	19.6
Holdings 1.5 - 5 Acre	42.8	7.5	-	5.1	6.0	7.4	2.9	28.9
Holdings 5 - 10 Acre	107.0	-	11.8	11.5	19.4	22.3	6.2	36.1
Holdings 10< Acre	205.3	-	47.7	21.8	42.4	40.0	10.4	43.2
Holdings	424.5	-	114.7	38.2	94.3	93.6	19.7	64.1
Other Households	34.3	20.1	-	1.7	-	-	-	52.7

Source: [215] Kennes, Parikh, Stolwijk, 1984: p. 231. Tab. 7.

Tab. 44: Percentage of Traditional Energy Won from Biomasses According to Holding-size Category

Holding Size (Acre)	Wood	Branches	Bamboo	Waste, Straw, Manure	Twigs, Leaves	Total
	(GJ/per-Capita/Year)					
0 - 1	0.51	0.65	0.38	2.24	1.63	5.41
1 - 2	0.36	0.83	0.48	1.87	1.54	5.08
2 - 3	0.51	0.68	0.51	1.87	1.28	4.85
3 - 4	0.41	0.76	0.41	1.66	1.08	4.32
4 - 5	0.57	0.66	0.36	1.57	1.07	4.23
5 - 6	0.78	0.71	0.48	1.39	1.03	4.39
6 - 7	0.59	0.68	0.50	1.58	0.79	4.14
7 <	0.82	0.95	0.35	0.94	0.75	3.81
all [a]	0.54	0.74	0.42	1.80	1.32	4.82

Source: [183] Islam, 1984: p. 68, Tab. 5.

a   Weighted average.

Tab. 45: **Women and Men's Desire to Have Children, Depent on the Number of Already Existing Sons and Daughters**

Number of Living Sons	Stated *No* Desire for More Sons (%) of Interviewed		Number of Living Daughters	Stated *No* Desire to Have More Daughters (%) of Interviewed	
	Men	Women		Men	Women
1	14	22	1	22	29
2	46	51	2	51	60
3	69	63	3	63	66
4	71	71	4	71	76
5	77	77	5	77	70
6	76	69	6	69	91
7	83	84	7	84	83

Source: [246] Maloney, Aziz, Sarkar, 1980: p. 311, Tab. 36.

Tab. 46: **Number of Births per Woman According to Landownership-size Category and Age of the Woman**

Land-ownership-size Category (Dec.)	Age of Mother (in Years)				All (N = 2825)
	<24	25-34	45-44	45<	
<20	2.1	3.3	5.2	6.7	4.5
20-49	1.0	3.1	5.0	6.8	4.9
50-99	2.9	3.0	5.4	6.3	4.6
100-299	3.3	3.6	5.3	6.9	5.3
300-499	3.0	4.3	5.2	7.3	6.0
500-999	5.5	4.0	6.5	8.5	6.7
1000-1999	6.7	4.4	6.5	7.4	6.4
2000-2999	-	5.4	6.6	7.0	6.4
<4000	[a] (5.0)	(4.0)	(10.3)	(11.0)	7.5

Source: [246] Maloney, Aziz, Sarkar, 1980: p. 316, Tab. 41.

---

a   The figures in parenthesis are based on very few cases.

Tab. 47: Ratio: Kinship Group Size and Disposition of Land Resources per Capita of Kinship Group Members

Number of Households (N = 925) per Kinship Group (Gusthi)	Number of Gustis	Number of Persons	Average Land	Gross Cropping Area (in Dec.)
		Per Gusthi-size Category	Per Capita and	
	120	650	25.9	39.2
2	49	424	28.5	53.5
3	32	438	32.7	54.2
4	19	353	43.3	73.9
5	18	467	30.5	62.6
6	10	317	33.5	69.8
7	6	202	24.2	69.9
8	7	279	24.5	58.3
9	5	205	51.8	72.7
10	3	158	22.1	44.2
11	1	31	47.2	66.9
12	3	205	60.3	116.5
13	2	121	40.1	78.2
14	1	68	19.5	60.6
15	2	125	22.5	46.8
-	-	-	-	-
17	1	77	80.4	133.3
18	1	85	84.9	95.8
19	2	192	60.4	102.6
-	-	-	-	-
22	1	120	129.6	141.8
Total	283	4397	-	-

Source: the author's own data material.

Tab. 48: Types of Soil in Bangladesh

Type of Soil	(Thousand Ha.)	(%)
Alluvial Soil	113895	79
Hilly Land	18079	13
Old Soil	12025	8
Total	143999	100
Type of Land		
Highland	33220	23
Mid-level Highland	59075	41
Mid-level Lowland	17543	12
Lowland	10958	8
Deep Lowland	2158	1
Farm and Pond Areas	10847	8
Municipal Areas	791	1
Bodies of Water	9405	7
Total	1433997	100

Source: [124] Government 1988: p. 7, Tab. 1.2; [124] Government 1988: p. 9, Tab. 1.3.

Tab. 49: Significance of Land Use for Various Agricultural Holding-size Categories, 1983/84

Type of Use [a]	Holdings in the Holding-size Categories (Dec.)					National Average
	5 - 49	50 - 99	100 - 249	250 - 749	750 ⟨	
	Thou. Acres					
Cultivated Area	363.7	892.6	4120.0	8996.3	5124.0	19496.6
Permanent Crops	50.35	48.8	126.7	225.3	146.1	597.2
Fallow Land	2.37	3.3	18.1	61.8	58.9	144.4
Total Arable Area	416.3	944.7	4264.8	9283.4	5329.0	20238.2
Of This: Irrigated	86.4	231.9	941.7	1754.5	859.4	3938.9
in %	20.8	24.5	22.1	18.9	16.1	19.5
Not Cultivated Area Of This:	172.9	187.5	488.7	935.2	621.4	2435.7
House and Farmstead	110.5	101.4	246.2	298.4	104.2	856.7
Ponds, Pools, Excavations	30.6	43.0	138.4	181.9	247.4	741.3
Arable Waste Land	4.3	7.7	20.9	102.5	110.7	256.1
Bamboo Plantations	16.2	21.3	65.1	122.4	70.1	295.1
Copses	11.3	14.1	32.1	130.0	273.5	286.5

Source: [125] Government, 1988: p. 139 ff., Tab 1.

---

a   Plots under 5 dec. are not recorded.

329

Tab. 50: **Significance of the Cropping Pattern for Various Agricultural Holding-size Categories, 1983/84**

Crop	Holdings in Holding-size Categories					National Total
	0 - 0.05	0.05 - 0.49	0.50 - 2.49	2.50 - 7.49	7.50<	
	Acres					
Aus	4717	180589	2296322	3640210	1582569	7684407
Amon	5609	194765	3138810	5608292	3016556	11964030
Boro	1762	56791	932901	1353452	784341	3138268
Wheat	820	36553	436760	594794	253627	1322554
Other Cereals	363	11824	159943	633646	128761	542408
Pulses	2700	32558	538033	1018619	540439	2132658
Oil Plants	1791	24862	384304	679765	345649	1437172
Jute	1837	35404	506644	838691	364180	1750756
Sugar etc.	443	13224	203326	304724	173325	644502
Vegetables	28195	80458	393695	458941	177114	1134403
Spices	3046	28429	228301	322849	142318	724944
Wood/Fodder	78	595	7240	17102	12850	37896
Gross						
Cropped Area	51381	685053	9180524	15105313	7521728	32544000
Cropping						
Intensity	368	192	187	171	153	171

Source: [121] Government, 1986: p. 111.

Tab. 51: **Distribution of the Most Important Fruit Trees According to Holding-size Category, 1983/84**

Holding-size Category (Acres)	Productive Trees					Non-productive Trees
	Mango Trees	Jackfruit Trees	Coconut Palms	Betel Nut Palms	Banana Trees	
	In Thousands					
0.05 - 0.49	4923.4	2072.7	2165.4	9971.0	6368.2	25500.7
- 0.99	3735.2	1971.5	1857.2	9525.3	5013.3	22102.5
- 1.49	3266.8	2065.2	1738.3	9489.6	4579.7	21139.6
- 2.49	4999.6	2785.8	2723.9	14319.8	7205.4	32034.5
- 7.49	9616.7	6840.8	5019.8	31175.3	15242.2	67894.8
7.50 <	3549.3	2929.9	1876.8	12159.0	6435.9	26950.9
Total	30091.0	18664.9	15381.4	86640.0	44844.7	195623.0

Source: [125] Government, 1988: p. 141, Tab. 1.

Tab. 52: Significance of Livestock Keeping for Various Agricultural Holding-size Categories, 1983/84

Holding-size Category (Acres)	Farm Area	Number of Households	Large Animals	Small Animals	Poultry
			(%)		
- 0.04	1.5	27.3	5.0	14.2	14.9
- 0.49	2.7	17.5	6.2	12.5	13.3
- 0.99	5.0	12.9	8.0	10.4	11.1
- 1.49	6.9	9.7	9.8	9.8	10.3
- 2.49	14.0	12.1	16.8	14.2	14.6
- 7.49	44.4	18.0	39.2	29.3	27.5
7.50 (	22.5	3.6	14.9	9.7	8.3
Total	100.0	100.0	100.0	100.0	100.0

Source: [119] Government, 1986: p. 81, Tab. 1.1.

Tab. 53: Rural Handicraft Enterprises, 1983/84

Housholds or Enterprises	Households [b]	Farms [a]
	(%)	
Without Handicrafts	93.2	97.0
With Handicrafts	2.4	3.0
Handicrafts Only	4.3	
Total	100.0	100.0
Handicraftsmen		
Weavers	21	27
Smiths	3	3
Potters	3	5
Bambooworkers	15	20
Woodworkers	8	10
Metal Founder	1	1
Spinning	7	10
Oil Mills	3	6
Others	39	18
Total of All Craftsmen	100	100

Source: [125] Government, 1988: p. 433, Tab. 22; [119] Government, 1986: p. 61 ff., Tab. 26 and Tab. 28.

---

a   Sample survey findings.
b   Census findings.

Tab. 54: Significance of Handicraft Production Within the Framework of Farms, 1986

Farm Size Categories (Dec.)	Weaver	Bam-boo-work	Other	Smith	Fiber-work	Wood-work	Pottery	Oil Mill
	In Thousands							
5 - 49	33.9	30.5	22.5	19.4	13.0	12.3	6.6	5.4
- 99	19.4	14.1	13.5	2.0	6.1	7.7	3.2	3.2
- 149	13.1	8.2	7.6	1.1	5.6	5.1	2.9	2.6
- 249	14.0	8.1	8.5	1.6	4.4	6.1	2.2	2,9
- 499	9.1	5.7	8.7	0.6	4.1	3.5	1.8	3.7
- 749	2.9	1.1	3.0	0.1	1.2	1.0	0.4	1.1
750 ⟨	1.7	0.5	2.1	0.3	0.7	0.5	0.4	0.4
Total	94.1	68.2	65.9	25.1	35.1	36.2	17.5	19.3
	(%)							
5 - 49	23.6	21.2	15.7	13.5	9.1	8.6	4.6	3.8
- 99	28.0	20.4	19.5	2.9	8.8	11.1	4.6	4.6
- 149	28.4	17.7	16.5	2.4	12.1	11.0	6.3	5.6
- 249	29.3	16.9	17.8	3.3	9.2	12.8	4.6	6.1
- 499	24.5	15.3	23.4	1.6	11.0	9.4	4.8	9.9
- 749	24.6	10.2	27.8	0.9	11.1	9.3	3.7	10.2
750 ⟨	25.8	7.6	31.8	3.9	10.6	7.6	6.1	6.1
Total	26.0	18.9	18.2	6.9	9.7	10.0	4.8	5.3

Source: [123] Government, 1988: p. 46, Tab. 1.08 and p. 49, Tab. 1.11; [125] Government, 1988: 433, Tab.22.

Tab. 55: Percentage of Leased Land and Various Tenacy Forms Among the Farm and Leased Areas According to Holding-size Category, 1983/84

Percentage of	Small Holdings (0.05 - 2.49 Acres)	Middle-sized Holdings (2.5 - 7.49 Acres)	Large Holdings (7.5 Acres <)
		%	
Own Land	78	83	90
Leased Land [a]	22	17	10
Of This:			
Sharecropping [b] 1/3	4	7	9
1/2	64	70	56
2/3	0	1	2
Fixed Rent [c]	10	8	12
Lease [d]	1	1	2
Usufruct [e]	4	3	6
Pledging [f]	10	6	6
Other [g]	7	3	6

Source: [125] Government, 1988: p. 34 ff., Tab. 34, Tab. 35, Tab. 36 and p. 339, Tab. 5.

---

a   The statistics supply only very inexact data. Entries obviously overlap, etc. These figures are, therefore, only approximations.
b   "Sharecropping" – bargā.
c   "Fixed rent / amount" - chāuniā, in money or in kind.
d   "Lease"' - monthly or annual payment of the lease.
e   "Usufructury mortgage" - khāi khālāsi, payment in the form of temporally limited utilization.
f   "Mortgage"' - bandak, transfer of property until the loan and intererst have been paid back.
g   Not specified, possibly mortgaged by banks; the official statistics does not supply any information.

Tab. 56: Relative Percentage of Leased Areas among Land Farmed by Sharecroppers and all Other Farms According to Holding-size Categories, 1983/84

Holding-size Category (Dec.)	Percentage of					
	Total Leased Areas	Share-cropping Areas	Otherwise Leased Areas	Total Leased Areas	Share-cropping Areas	Other-wise - Leased Areas
	Among the Total Farm Areas			Among the Farm Areas of Farms Leasing Land		
	(%)					
5 - 49	15.2	8.7	7.5	66.8	38.4	32.9
50 - 99	22.8	14.6	9.2	58.0	37.1	23.5
100 - 149	22.2	15.8	7.0	51.9	37.0	16.4
150 - 249	22.0	16.6	5.9	46.4	34.9	12.5
250 - 499	20.0	15.0	4.6	41.0	30.7	9.5
500 - 749	14.1	10.8	3.2	34.6	26.6	7.8
750 - 1499	10.6	7.7	2.7	29.8	21.7	7.7
1500 - 2499	7.8	4.7	2.6	28.4	17.3	9.4
2500 <	8.8	3.3	4.3	33.0	12.6	16.1
Total	100.0	100.0	100.0	100.0	100.0	100.0

Source: [125] Government, 1988: p. 139. Tab. 1 and p. 339, Tab. 5.

Note: The data from the two tables that were used here are unfortunately not consistent. They have been used and exhibited here despite this fact because they (1) can supply a general overview of the *dimensions*, and (2) the deviations do not appear to be too serious.

Tab. 57: Absolute Percentages of the Leased Areas Among Land of Farms Leasing Land and All Farms According to Holding-size Categories, 1983/1984

Holding-size Categories (In Dec.)	Farm Area of Farms That Do Not Lease [a]	Farm Area of Farms That Lease [b]	Areas under General Tenancy [c]	Areas under Share-cropping [d]	Areas under Other Tenancy [e]
			(in Thousand Acres)		
5 - 49	455.0	134.2	89.7	51.5	44.1
50 - 99	689.5	445.7	258.4	165.2	104.6
100 - 149	886.5	662.5	343.8	245.2	108.8
150 - 249	1697.9	1536.6	712.5	535.8	192.2
250 - 499	3197.1	3050.5	1251.0	936.9	290.1
500 - 749	2352.5	1618.5	560.6	430.0	127.0
750 - 1499	2679.2	1472.2	439.1	319.2	113.8
1500 - 2499	957.1	359.5	102.2	62.1	33.9
2500 <	353.8	128.2	42.3	16.1	20.7
Total	13268.6	9407.9	3799.6	2762.0	1035.2

Source: [125] Government, 1988: p. 139, Tab. 1 and p. 339, Tab. 5.

Note: The data from the two tables that were used here are unfortunately not consistent. They have been used and exhibited here despite this fact because they (1) can present and general overview of the *dimensions*, and (2) the deviations do not appear to be too serious.

a   [125] Government, 1988: p. 139, Tab. 1.
b   [125] Government, 1988: p. 139, Tab. 1.
c   [125] Government, 1988: p. 139, Tab. 1.
d   [125] Government, 1988: p. 339, Tab. 5.
e   [125] Government, 1988: p. 339, Tab. 5.

Tab. 58: Number and Percentages of Land Leased by Sharcrop-
ping Farms and Farms Leasing Land Under Other Conditions According to Holding-size Categories

Type of Lease	Small Holdings < e 2.50 Acres		Middle-sized Holdings 2.50 - 7.49 Acres		Large Holdings 7.50 < Acres		% Holdings	
	N of Farms	% of Area	N of Farms	% of Area	N of Farms	% of Area	N of Farms	% of Area
	(%)							
All Holdings Of These [a]:	70	29	25	45	5	26	100	100
Sharecropping	62	35	33	50	5	14	26	12
Other Tenancy Forms	66	41	28	40	6	19	14	5

Source: [125] Government, 1988: p. 34 ff. Tab. p. 34, Tab. p. 35 and Tab. p. 36.

---

a   All of the holdings equal 100 % in each case.

Tab. 59: Tenancy Review According to Holding-size Categories, 1983/84

Holding-size Categories (In Dec.)	Own Land	Leased Out Land	Leased Land	Farm Area [a]
		(In Thou. Acres)		
5 - 49	1055.7	556.9	90.1	589.2
50 - 99	1261.3	388.1	258.4	1132.2
100 - 149	1532.5	327.3	343.5	1549.0
150 - 249	2910.8	390.0	712.2	3234.5
250 - 499	5505.3	511.1	1252.1	6247.6
500 - 749	3751.1	342.5	562.0	3971.0
750 - 1499	4086.0	376.1	441.5	4151.4
1500 - 2499	1341.3	130.5	103.6	1316.6
2500 <	487.4	47.8	42.7	482.0
Total	21929.9	3070.3	3806.1	22673.5

Source: [125] Government, 1988: p. 293, Tab. 2.

---

a   Original data.
Own land − leased out + leased area is not identical with the original data on the farm area in column 5 which is probably due to mistakes in rounding off in the source.

Tab. 60: Employment Indices, 1984/85

Employed (Older than 10 Years) In:	Number of Economically Active Persons		
	(In Thousands)	(%)	
Total / All	29975	100	100
Agriculture, Urban Areas	336	1	
Agriculture, Rural Areas	16374	55	
Of These:			100
Owner-occupancy	4176		26
Owner-occupancy + Leasing	1630		10
Self-employed	242		1
Farmhand	6200		38
Family Members Helping on Farm	4040		25
Nonagricultural, Urban Areas	3671	12	
Nonagricultural, Rural Areas	8594	32	
Of These:			100
Self-employed	3871		45
Employer	42		0
White-collar Employee	2171		25
Worker	1005		12
Family Members Helping in Enterprise	799		9
No Data	706		8

Source: [122] Government, 1988: p. 74, Tab. 20.

Tab. 61: Type and Quantitative Significance of the Employed Wage Labourers for the Various Holding-size Categories

Holding-size Category	Small Holdings 5-249 Dec.		Middle-sized Holdings 250-749 Dec.		Large Holdings 750< Dec.		All Holdings	
	Thou.	(%)	Thou.	(%)	Thou.	(%)	Thou.	(%)
Economically Active Persons 10> Years	24459.0	61.1	12081.1	30.2	3511.3	8.8	40051.8	100.0
Permanent [a] Labourers								
- In the - Household	155.9	3.3	472.3	5.5	419.1	9.0	1047.1	5.0
- Separated	134.5	2.8	275.0	3.2	233.1	5.0	642.6	3.6
Temporary [b] Labourers	4468.7	93.9	7856.9	91.3	3986.7	85.8	16306.	90.6
All Wage Labourers	4759.1	100.0	8604.2	100.0	4638.9	100.0	18002.2	100.0
As % of the Household Labourers		19.5		72.2		132.1		44.9
As % of the Holding-size Category		26.4		47.8		25.8		100.0
Employees with an Impact on Income [c]	11546.1	47.2	5736.6	47.5	1686.6	48.0	18969.3	47.4

Source: [125] Government, 1988: p. 144, Tab. 1.

Source of the footnotes: [125] Government, 1988: p. 25.

---

a   "Permanent workers are those workers who are engaged in the holding for farm work for half or more than half the period of the total annual working days. These are further sub-divided into other non-related members of the household and not members of the household..."

b   "Temporary workers are those who work on the farm for a period of less than half of the total working period. The workers engaged on a daily basis are also included here."

c   "The occupation from which income in cash or kind is derived is called gainful occupation, while the occupation which does not give monetary benefit is termed as non-gainful occupation."

Tab. 62: Number of Borrowers and Percentage of Institutional and Private Loans According to Holding-size Category

Holding-size Category [a]	Landless (< 0.49 Acres)	Small Farmers (0.5-1.99 Acres)	Middle Farmers (2.0-4.99 Acres)	Large Farmers 5.0< Acres)
	(%)			
Percentage of Households With Loans from				
Institutions	6.8	15.0	20.0	21.0
Private Persons	91.6	55.9	46.9	29.0
Of All Households				
Percentage of Total Volume Of Loans Received from				
Institutions	8.0	21.2	34.4	38.4
Private Persons	92.0	78.8	65.6	61.6

Source: [165] Hossain, 1988: p. 22, Tab. 3.

a   Basis = 640 Households, in 16 villages.

Tab. 63: Sources of Informal (Private, Traditional) Credit

(N = 10 Credit/Village Studies) [a] Source of Private Credit:	Share (%)
Relatives and Friends	20
Neighbours	20
Prosperous Persons	20
Prof. Money Lenders	19
Goldsmiths	1
Businessmen	13
Share-landlords	7
Total	100

Source: [245] Maloney, Ahmed, 1988: p. 42, Tab. 4.

a   See the presentation and discussion in [240] Maloney, Ahmed, 1988: p. 41 ff.

Tab. 64: Utilization of Informal (Private, Traditional) Credit

Utilization of Private Credit: [a]	Share (%)	Share (%)
Consumptive Purposes:	63	
Rice for Consumption		45
Other Consumer Goods		17
Household Expenditures		12
Housing		4
Wedding		10
Medicine		8
Clothing		3
Total		100
Investment Purposes:	37	
Plant Production		22
Shop		19
Other Business		19
Buying Animals		11
Buying Land		9
Tea Shop		5
Other		12
Paying Back Loan		3
Total		100

Source: [245] Maloney, Ahmed, 1988: p. 52, Tab. 5.

a   On the basis of a study covering four villages.

Tab. 65: Rice Sales Balance According to Holding-size Categories

Holding-size Categories (In Dec.)	Total Production	Total Sales	Total Repurchases	Total Availability
	(In Maund = ca. 40kg)			
51 - 250	10329	2696	3644	11277
251 - 500	11705	3548	1123	9290
501 <	9430	2438	385	7377
All/Total [a]	31464	8682	5152	27952

Source: [273] Quasem, 1987: p. 87 ff., Tabs. I and ff.

a   Also see [89] Chowdhury, 1988; and [274] Quasem, 1988.
   N = 496 Households, 446 agricultural holdings, in 16 villages in 1982.

Tab. 66: Loan Conditions: Security and Interest

	Share (%) [a]	Share (%) [b]
Security for All Loans		
Without Security	29.4	
Land or Crops to Bank	31.0	
Land or Crops to Private	10.4	
Household Appliances	27.6	
Jewelry	1.6	
Total	100.0	
Interest on All Loans		
No Interest	11.4	60
Up to 20 %	28.1	ca. 17
21 - 50 %	43.2	
51 - 100 %	8.4	ca. 16
101 - 150 %	2.8	
150 - 200 %	6.1	ca. 6
Total	100	100

Source: [134] Haq, 1985: p. 25, Tab. 9 and p. 27, Tab. 10; [147] Herbon, 1984: p. 337, Tab. 37.

a   Haq's data are based on a survey of 200 households, and Herbon's are based on a survey covering 358 households, of which 231 borrowed loans.

b   These data were taken over and changed by [147] Herbon, 1984: p. 377, Tab. 37. They are not completely compatible because different categorization and evidently also assessment methods (compound interest) were chosen. Important in this context is the large percentage of small loans for which no interest is demanded. They are, however, frequently considered not to be important enough to be mentioned in interviews.

Tab. 67: Net Availability of Rice According to Holding-size Categories

Holding-size Categories (In Dec.)	Persons per Holding	Number of Producing Holdings	Number of Marketing Holdings	Per Capita Production of Rice (In Maund)	Per Capita Availability of Rice (In Maund)
51 - 250	5.9	282	187	6.2 [a]	6.8
251 - 500	8.1	114	97	12.7	10.0
501 <	11.2	50	42	16.8	13.2
All/total [b]	6.5	446	327	10.8	9.6

Source: [273] Quasem, 1987: p. 87 ff., Tabs. I and ff.

a   Quasem recorded the figure 5.2 here which he probably arived at by including landless households.

b   N = 496 households, 446 agricultural holdings, in 16 villages in 1982.

Tab. 68: Share of Rural Income Source According to Income Category 1985 - 86

Income Category (Household/ Monat/Tk)	Share of House- holds	Share of Total Income	Wages and Saleries	Share of Agricultural Income	Business Income	Other [a] Income
			the Income Group among the total Income of the Individual Groups [b]			
			(%)			
< 500	0.8	0.1	43.5	8.0	0.0	48.5
- 749	4.4	1.1	51.9	16.0	10.0	22.1
- 999	8.0	2.9	53.0	15.1	11.0	20.9
- 1249	9.4	4.3	45.4	22.8	9.6	22.2
- 1499	12.5	7.1	36.4	29.1	13.4	21.1
- 1999	20.9	15.1	28.6	34.7	18.0	18.7
- 2499	14.2	13.2	18.1	40.3	21.0	20.6
- 2999	10.1	11.5	19.7	41.6	19.4	19.3
- 3999	9.8	14.0	13.9	50.6	14.6	20.9
- 4999	3.5	6.5	11.5	50.2	18.0	20.3
- 5999	2.0	4.5	12.1	54.7	10.4	22.8
6000 <	4.3	19.7	6.8	43.4	9.3	40.5
Total	100.0	100.0				

Source: [123] Government, 1988: p. 39, Tab. 1.01 and p. 46, Tab. 1.08.

a   Rent, transfer income, etc., are included here without being specified.
b   Slight deviations from the disaggregated data in the source can be traced back to mistakes made when rounding off the figures.

Tab. 69: Correlation Between the Volume of the Household Income and the Amount of Land Owned

Monthly Household Income Category (Tk)	Land-less < 49 Dec.	50 - 99 Dec.	100 - 249 Dec.	250 - 499 Dec.	500 - 749 Dec.	750 < Dec.
	(%)					
< 300	20.5	73.8	4.7	0.4	0.3	0.3
- 399	14.6	73.4	10.3	1.3	0.3	0.1
- 499	9.8	70.4	15.6	3.1	0.7	0.3
- 749	6.4	56.2	26.3	8.9	1.4	0.7
- 999	3.4	36.9	32.5	20.4	4.6	1.9
- 1249	2.4	24.1	27.7	29.7	11.0	5.0
- 1499	1.7	15.8	24.7	31.7	14.6	11.4
- 1999	1.7	10.3	17.0	25.9	22.6	22.3
- 2499	0.3	5.1	9.4	26.0	20.6	38.5
- 2999		5.3	4.7	21.2	16.5	52.3
- 3999	1.6	4.7	4.7	9.4	19.7	59.8
- 4999		4.5	6.8	11.4	11.3	65.9
- 5999		16.7	5.5	16.7	5.5	55.6
6000 <					23.8	76.2
Average	7.0	46.3	20.9	13.7	5.6	5.7

Source: [255] Muqtada, 1986: p. 58, Tab. A1.

Tab. 70: Main Occupation of Local and Regional Political Leaders

Employment	Union Parishad Chairmen [a]		Upazila Parishad Chairmen [b]	
	Number (N)	(%)	Number (N)	(%)
Farming	104	32.1	58	45.7
Business	13	4.0	37	29.1
Combination	207	63.8	32	25.2
Total	324	100.0	127	100.0

Sources: [19] Alam, 1976: p. 6, Tab. 4; [281] Rahman, 1986: p. 213.

a   [19] Alam, 1976: p. 6, Tab. 4.
b   [281] Rahman, 1986: p. 213.

Tab. 71: Relative Percentages Represented by the Purposes for Utilizing Income According to Rural Income Category 1985/86

Income Category (Household/ Month/Tk)	Share of House- holds	Share of the Total Expen- ditures	Food	Cloths	Housing	Fuel	House- hold Goods	Others
					Share of the Income Groups among the Total Expenditures of the Individual Groups (%)			
< 500	0.8	0.1	66.7	5.5	6.6	17.0	0.4	3.8
− 749	4.4	1.3	66.6	6.4	7.2	14.4	0.6	4.8
− 999	8.0	3.2	69.1	5.7	6.0	13.5	0.5	5.1
− 1249	9.4	4.7	70.0	5.7	6.2	12.2	0.6	5.2
− 1499	12.5	7.8	69.5	5.3	7.0	11.1	0.6	6.4
− 1999	20.9	16.4	70.5	5.5	6.0	10.3	0.7	7.0
− 2499	14.2	14.3	69.6	5.3	6.8	9.4	1.1	8.7
− 2999	10.1	12.1	66.4	5.6	6.9	8.7	1.3	11.1
− 3999	9.8	14.5	65.3	6.2	7.5	7.7	1.1	12.2
− 4999	3.5	6.8	64.7	5.9	7.1	7.8	1.3	13.1
− 5999	2.0	4.5	61.9	6.0	8.3	6.7	1.6	15.4
6999 <	4.3	14.3	50.7	7.5	10.1	5.9	2.6	23.4
Total	100.0	100.0	100.0	100.0	100.0	100.0	100.0	100.0

Source: [123] Government, 1988: p. 49, Tab. 1.11.

Tab. 72: Land Acquisition per Household between 1969/70 and 1979 in One Village According to the Type of Acquisition and Property-size Category

Property- size Categories (Dec)	Land Given As a Present	Inherited Land	Purchased Land
	Per Household and Size Category (Dec.)		
< 100	4.2	12.1	25.0
100-199	-	8.9	22.4
200-349	0.4	47.0	25.5
350-499	3.6	47.5	13.9
500-749	-	54.9	49.0
750 <	2.6	112.7	61.6

Source: [79] Chaudhury, 1989: p. Tab. 5.6.

Tab. 73: School Attendance of Children According to the Employment Status of the Head of the Household in Rural Areas (Boys and Girls), 1985

School Attendance of the Child	Employment Status of the Head of the Household						National Average
	Unemployed	Farmer	Not Active in Agriculture	Industry	Commerce	Other	
	(%)						
No School Attendance, But Job	20.26	20.09	23.41	12.05	14.19	16.43	19.19
No School Attendance, No Job	56.42	56.24	67.00	56.49	56.74	58.81	57.74
School Attendance	23.31	23.66	9.57	31.45	29.06	24.75	24.05
Total	100.0	100.0	100.0	100.0	100.0	100.0	100.0

Source: [127] Government, 1985: p. 176, Tab. 11.14.

Tab. 74: Size of Holdings of Local and Regional Political Leaders

Holding Size in Decimal a	Number (N)	Percent (%)	Holding Size in Decimal b	Number (N)	Percent (%)
<100	-	-	<10	4	3.0
100 - 200	21	6.5	10 - 250	10	7.6
201 - 300	27	8.3	251 - 750	39	29.5
301 - 400	35	10.8	751 - 1250	35	26.5
401 - 500	53	16.4	1251 - 2500	29	22.0
501 - 1000	127	39.2	2500<	15	11.4
1000<	62	18.8			
Total	324	100.0	Total	132	100.0

Sources: [19] Alam, 1976: p. 5, Tab. 2; [283] Rahman, 1979: p. 96.

a   [19] Alam, 1976: p. 5, Tab. 2.
b   [283] Rahman, 1979: p. 96.

Tab. 75: Development Trends in the Number of Households in Bangladesh and the Persons Living in Them According to Household Size, 1960, 1973, 1981, 1988/89

Number of Household Members	Number of Households			
	1960	1973	1981	1988/89
1	411317	385107	479464	381198
2	855527	870043	1126760	1147222
3	1272009	1360058	1768764	2315847
4	1544855	1732450	2119889	3308414
5	1564569	1903091	2211955	3297107
6	1322642	1811195	2031234	2740048
7	951490	1512188	1640300	2136555
8	696582	1101999	1178190	1429060
9	336148	716255	786493	793525
10<	704367	1263062	1441799	1239893
Number of Household Members	Number of Persons			
	1960	1973	1981	1988/89
1	411317	385107	479464	381198
2	1737744	1780086	2253520	2294444
3	3816027	4080174	5306292	6947541
4	6179420	6929800	8479556	13233656
5	7822845	9515455	11059780	16485535
6	7935858	10867170	12187400	16440288
7	6660430	10585320	10482100	14955885
8	4772656	8815992	7078437	11432480
9	3295332	6446295	6880133	7141725
10<	8894178	15287400	16222530	14309639

Source: [124] Government, 1988: p. 78 f. Tabs. 2.87 and 2.88; [129] Government, 1991: p. 178, Tab. 4.02.

347

Tab. 76: Land Purchases and Sales Between 1972 and 1981 in a Village Without and a Village With Irrigation According to the Monthly per Capita Income of the Household and Holding-size Category

Village 1: Without Irrigation				
Monthly per Capita Income of the Household (Tk)	Number of Sellers	Amount Sold	Number of Buyers	Amount Bought
		(%)		
< 100	65.8	44.2	43.1	17.9
101-200	26.3	30.3	26.7	26.7
201-300	5.3	22.7	11.8	31.4
300 <	2.6	2.8	3.9	24.0
Total	100.0	100.0	100.0	100.0
Holding-size Category (Dec.)				
< 100	59.2	33.8	27.5	6.0
101-200	26.3	30.4	47.0	31.0
201-300	9.2	17.3	15.7	10.0
300 <	5.3	18.5	9.8	53.0
Total	100.0	100.0	100.0	100.0
Village 2: With Irrigation				
Monthly per Capita Income of the Household (Tk)	Number of Sellers	Amount Sold	Number of Buyers	Amount Bought
		(%)		
< 100	20.0	5.5	12.5	1.3
101-200	53.3	70.3	31.2	35.6
201-300	20.0	21.8	18.8	19.2
300 <	6.7	2.4	37.5	43.9
Total	100.0	100.0	100.0	100.0
Holding-size Category (Dec.)				
< 100	53.3	41.6	18.8	10.9
101-200	33.3	38.5	25.0	18.7
201-300	13.4	19.9	50.0	66.1
300 <	0.0	0.0	6.2	4.3
Total	100.0	100.0	100.0	100.0

Source: [14] Ahmed, 1987: p. 11, Tab. 2 and p. 6, Tab. 5.

Note: The data were collected on the basis of questions concerning the past and, therefore, are certainly not absolute. Ahmed also does not present a categorization of the group characteristics within the parent population. The relative significance of the data can, thus, not be ascertained.

Tab. 77: Land Mobility in Two Villages Between 1951 and 1981 According to Holding-size Category Prospectively and Retrospectively Viewed

Land-ownership Size Category (Dec.)	Unchanged	Property Status					Total
		Descent			Ascent		
		1 Level	2 Level	3 Level	1 Level	2 Level	
		(%)					
Village 1							
1951							
0-50	75.8				17.2	6.8	100.0
51-250	26.5	61.2			8.2	4.1	100.0
251-500	18.4	45.0	26.6		10.0		100.0
501 <	22.6	14.3	40.4	22.5			100.0
1981							
0-50	27.0	36.5	19.5	17.0			100.0
51-250	18.6	38.7	35.6		7.1		100.0
251-500	42.3	34.6			15.4	7.7	100.0
501 <	63.6				27.4	9.0	100.0
Village 2							
1951							
0-50	66.7				33.3	0.0	100.0
51-350	46.5	50.0			3.5	0.0	100.0
351-750	24.0	60.0	12.0		4.0		100.0
751 <	18.0	20.5	43.5	18.0			100.0
1981							
0-50	20.0	46.7	10.0	23.0			100.0
51-350	27.0	31.3	35.6		6.3		100.0
351-750	40.0	53:4			6.6	0.0	100.0
751 <	87.5				12.5	0.0	100.0

Source: [281] Rahman, 1986: p. 87, Tab. 3.5 and p. 88, Tab. 3.6.

Tab. 78: Developments in the Landownership Size and Distribution Conditions, Village 1, 1951, 1961, 1977

Landowner-ship Size Category (Arable Land) (Dec.)	Number of Households			Percentage of Land		
	1951	1961	1977	1951	1961	1977
	(%)					
0	17.0	22.2	30.4	0.7	1.0	0.9
< 100	15.6	19.2	21.4	3.3	4.9	5.0
101 - 250	14.1	17.8	25.2	5.9	9.7	13.5
251 - 450	23.7	22.2	19.3	21.3	22.3	20.4
451 - 750	12.6	11.1	8.1	19.1	19.0	14.9
751 - 1250	11.1	9.0	7.4	25.4	22.7	20.6
1250 <	5.9	4.4	3.7	24.1	20.4	24.6
Total	100.0	105.9	115.5	99.8	100.0	99.9

Source: [316] Siddiqui, 1982: p. 136 ff., Tabs. 4, 5, 6.

Tab. 79: Developments in the Landownership Size and Distribution Conditions, Village 2, 1951, 1972, 1981

Landowner-ship Size Category (Dec.)	Number of Households			Perentage of Land		
	1951	1972	1981	1951	1972	1981
	(%)					
0	2.9	5.8	8.7	-	-	-
< 50	10.9	32.6	50.7	0.3	2.7	3.1
51 - 150	10.1	18.8	26.8	2.1	5.9	8.6
151 - 250	18.8	26.8	23.9	8.8	16.4	15.3
251 - 350	11.6	13.0	4.3	7.9	11.8	8.1
351 - 500	19.6	13.0	10.1	20.0	16.6	14.4
501 - 750	9.4	5.1	5.1	13.2	10.0	10.2
751 - 1000	7.2	5.1	6.5	14.4	13.2	18.4
1001 <	9.4	5.1	4.3	33.2	23.3	21.7
Total	99.9	125.3	140.4	99.9	99.9	99.9

Source: [279] Rahmen, 1982: p. 56, Tab. 2.a.

Tab. 80: Developments in the Landownership Size and Distribution Conditions, Village 3, 1951, 1972, 1981

Landowner-ship Size Category (Dec.)	Number of Households 1951	1972	1981	Percentage of Land 1951	1972	1981
	(%)					
0	5.9	21.8	56.9	-	-	-
< 50	5.9	5.9	41.2	0.4	0.3	1.9
51 - 150	15.7	25.8	29.4	2.7	3.6	5.0
151 - 250	5.9	33.6	35.3	2.0	11.3	10.8
251 - 350	9.8	21.8	27.5	4.9	10.8	12.8
351 - 500	13.7	19.9	17.6	10.7	14.6	10.9
501 - 750	13.7	15.9	13.7	14.0	17.0	13.0
751 - 1000	11.8	4.0	3.9	17.2	5.4	5.3
1001 <	17.6	11.9	11.8	47.9	36.9	40.3
Total	100.0	160.6	237.3	99.8	99.9	100.0

Source: [279] Rahman, 1982: p. 57, Tab. 2b.

Tab. 81: Developments in the Landownership Size and Distribution Conditions, Village 4, 1980, 1986

Landowner-ship Size Category (Dec.)	Number of Households 1980	1986	Percentage of Land 1980	1986
	(%)			
0	24.0	24.6	-	-
< 33	41.9	57.2	3.6	3.8
34 - 100	14.0	13.7	6.7	5.7
101 - 200	8.1	7.8	8.2	7.5
201 - 300	3.1	3.7	5.7	6.3
301 - 400	1.4	3.1	3.5	7.1
401 - 500	2.2	1.9	7.5	5.8
501 - 1000	2.5	2.5	14.5	12.4
1001 <	2.8	4.2	50.3	51.4
Total	100.0	118.7	100.0	100.0

Source: the author's own findings, unpublished survey and calculations.

Tab. 82: Developments in the Landownership Size and Distrib-
         tuion Conditions in Villages 5, 6, 7, 1894 to 1978

Landowner-ship Size Category (Dec.)	Number of Households								
	Village 5			Village 6			Village 7		
	1933	1960	1977	1922	1955	1978	1894	1960	1978
	(%)								
0	10.5	15.6	126.3	26.5	11.8	32.3	27.3	36.3	60.8
< 100	10.5	42.0	99.9	20.6	17.6	41.2	6.1	60.6	93.8
101 -200	10.5	10.6	52.5	14.7	11.8	2.9	3.0	60.6	60.8
201 - 300	10.5	5.2	47.4	5.8	5.9	5.9	6.1	39.3	27.3
301 - 400	21.1	36.8	20.9	17.7	5.9	-	15.2	15.2	27.3
401 - 500	10.5	31.6	20.9	8.8	5.9	-	9.1	9.1	12.0
501 - 600	5.3	10.6	20.9	2.9	-	-	9.1	12,0	6.2
601 - 700	10.5	5.2	5.1	-	-	2.9	6.1	6.1	2.9
701 - 800	5.3	15.8	-	-	-	-	6.1	-	2.9
801 - 900	5.3	-	-	2.9	-	-	3.0	2.9	-
901 - 1000	-	-	-	-	-	-	3.0	3.9	-
1001 <	-	-	-	-	-	-	6.1	-	-
Total	100.0	173.0	393.9	99.9	59.9	82.3	100.2	246.0	294.4

Source: [309] Schendel, 1981: p. 81, Tab. 2.11, p. 162, Tab. 3.13 and p. 231, Tab. 4.10.

Tab. 83: Developments in the Number of Holdings Which Culti-
         vate the Land Themselves, Lease Additional Land and
         Lease Land Only, 1960 to 1983/84

Operating Status	Number of Farms			Farm Area		
	1960 [a]	1977	1983/4	1960	1977	1983/4
	(Mio.)			(Mio. Acres)		
Owner-operator	3731	3646	6239	11654	12286	13266
Owner/Tenant	2380	2575	3593	9830	9585	9284
Tenant	100	35	134	242	89	124
All Holdings	6139	6256	9972	21726	21960	22674

Source: [125] Government, 1988: p. 29.

a   In the case of the number of holdings in 1960, the total – which consisted of owner-
    operators, farmers leasing additional land and farmers who are tenants only – does
    not correspond to the total number of holdings. This is due to a mistake in the
    source.

Tab. 84:   Changes in the Importance of Tenancy in Two Villages
          – The Development from 1972 to 1981

Village 1	Owner-tenancy				Owner-tenancy			
Year	1951	1972	1981	1985	1951	1972	1981	1985
				%				
Share of Leased Land	14.80	15.22	13.00	8.47	19.78	9.60	8.03	11.64
Holding-size Category (Dec.)								
< 250	-	16.38	16.44	-	-	6.09	10.52	-
250 - 500	-	25.00	38.46	-	-	19.23	15.38	-
501 - 750	-	-	-	-	-	42.85	14.24	-
750 <	-	7.14	13.33	-	-	60.00	36.66	-
Village 2				%				
Share of Leased Land	5.84	17.20	12.78	-	15.29	10.81	5.93	-
Holding-size Category (Dec.)								
< 250	-	13.81	51.21	-	-	9.09	10.34	-
250 - 500	-	33.33	39.13	-	-	28.57	23.80	-
501 - 750	-	-	-	-	-	57.14	14.28	-
750 <	-	-	12.50	-	-	100.00	62.50	-

Source: [281] Rahman, 1986: p. 154, Tab. 6.1 and 6.2; p. 158, Tab. 6.4.

Tab. 85: Development Trends in the Utilization of Modern Agricultural Engineering Innovations, 1961 - 1986

Year	Percentage of Land Planted with Modern Rice/Wheat Varieties	Percentage of Land Irrigated with Modern Pumps	Percentage of the Total Irrigated Land	Volume of Spread Fertilizer
	%			(kg/Acre)
1961	-	0.3	7.0	0.9
1962	-	-	-	-
1963	-	-	-	-
1964	-	-	-	-
1965	-	-	-	-
1966	-	0.9	-	1.7
1967	-	-	-	-
1968	0.6	-	-	-
1969	1.5	-	-	-
1970	2.5	3.0	12.0	-
1971	4.6	-	-	4.6
1972	6.7	-	-	-
1973	11.1	-	-	-
1974	15.8	7.2	15.3	5.9
1975	14.9	7.5	17.0	-
1976	15.7	7.6	16.5	7.0
1977	14.2	6.6	14.7	8.8
1978	16.6	9.4	15.8	10.9
1979	19.4	11.0	18.9	11.1
1980	22.7	12.6	20.3	12.5
1981	25.4	14.3	21.4	12.8
1982	25.8	17.1	23.9	12.1
1983	28.2	19.0	25.1	13.7
1984	28.3	20.2	25.4	16.1
1985	31.5	21.5	25.7	18.1
1986	31.0	-	-	-

Source: [166] Hossain, 1988: p. 25, Tab. 6, p. 27, Tab. 7, p. 30, Tab. 8 and p. 31, Fig. 2, 3.

Tab. 86: Holding-size Specific Cropping Intensity and the Specific Percentage of Fertilized and Irrigated Land

Holding-size Category (Dec.)	Cropping Intensity	Percentage of Irrigated Land Among the Gross Cropping Area	Percentage of Chemically Fertilized Land Among the Gross Cropping Area
		%	
5 - 49	196.6	13.07	35.46
50 - 99	196.0	14.20	41.23
100 - 149	192.0	13.66	40.15
150 - 249	188.3	12.88	38.51
250 - 499	181.6	12.02	35.54
500 - 749	175.8	11.88	33.76
750 - 1499	169.3	11.72	32.63
1500 - 2499	163.9	11.89	30.06
2500 <	157.1	11.79	27.35

Source: [125] Government, 1988: p. 140 ff., Tab. 1.

Tab. 87: Output per Unit of Area for Rice and Jute According to Holding-size Category

Holding-size Category (Dec.)	Boro	Amon	Aus	Jute	Rice Total
	Maund/Acres				
1 - 99	25.60	19.55	15.41	14.73	60.56
100 - 199	23.63	18.37	14.19	13.52	56.19
200 - 299	25.49	17.30	13.82	13.50	56.61
300 - 399	28.45	17.65	12.49	12.68	58.59
400 - 499	26.79	17.28	13.35	11.58	57.42
500 <	23.44	13.83	13.62	12.71	50.89

Source: [79] Chaudhury, 1989: p. 182.

Tab. 88: Developments in the Cropping Intensity in Four Villages from 1950 to 1985

Holding-size Category (Dec.)	Village	Cropping Intensity			
		1950	1960	1970	1985
< 250	2	97.4	99.4	103.2	123.3
	3	96.9	99.4	102.2	146.5
	4	146.6	168.8	188.9	240.0
	5	94.1	143.3	192.3	231.6
250 - 750	2	98.0	99.4	102.4	119.0
	3	98.0	98.9	102.5	131.7
	4	124.9	159.6	183.2	205.6
	5	91.0	123.2	205.6	227.8
750 <	2	92.9	91.0	99.5	111.4
	3	99.0	101.4	109.1	124.5
	4	131.4	132.2	164.3	221.3
	5	70.0	98.0	131.9	186.0

Source: [32] Ali, 1987: p. 207, Tab. 4.11, p. 277, Tab. 5.10, p. 41, Tab. 6.9 and p. 411, Tab. 7.10.
Note: Ali recorded the holding-sizes in hectars. For purposes of simplicity, they have been transposed here into decimal (Dec.) = 100th of an acre, as in the other presentations. In order to make the data more easy to read, they have been rounded off slightly. This does not seem to cause any significant loss of information.
Villages 1 and 6 were not included since Ali did not supply any information on them.

Tab. 89:   Development Trends in the Rice Demand Coverage out of the Farmers' Own Production in Six Villages According to Holding-size Categories for the Years from 1950 to 1985

Holding-size Category (Dec.)	Village	Portion/Degree of Self-sufficiency in % of Demand			
		1950	1960	1970	1985
750 <	1	145.8	146.6	130.4	162.3
	2	111.2	71.9	165.2	187.3
	3	200.7	117.6	70.1	136.5
	4	230.9	89.3	146.7	160.0
	5	118.0	75.8	88.7	118.9
	6	-	-	-	-
250 - 750	1	14.0	17.0	15.6	28.5
	2	16.0	0.4	17.7	-5.6
	3	83.7	61.5	15.0	-9.2
	4	-6.8	39.1	33.0	-30.2
	5	-3.1	40.1	84.1	40.0
	6	-23.8	8.0	8.3	38.4
< 250	1	-7.6	-72.6	-47.4	-45.5
	2	-61.1	-57.9	-67.0	-66.5
	3	-33.0	-67.5	-53.8	-60.8
	4	-36.8	-47.4	-49.5	-51.5
	5	-59.2	-35.7	-29.0	-43.9
	6	-35.7	-41.8	-51.6	-72.5
All	1	84.2	82.3	74.0	73.3
	2	26.3	4.9	-2.2	-8.1
	3	120.0	64.3	38.9	43.1
	4	92.4	30.1	27.2	32.2
	5	-2.6	7.6	26.1	2.1
	6	-8.0	-17.6	-27.0	-68.2

Source: [32] Ali, 1987: p. 144, Tab. 3.13; p. 212, Tab. 4.16; p. 280, Tab. 5.13; p. 346, Tab. 6.14; p. 415, Tab. 7.14; p. 483, Tab. 8.13.
Note: Village 6 is not represented in the largest holding-size catgegory (750 dec.).
For a description of the villages and their setting and a rough agro-ecological outline, see footnote 407, p. 246, or [32] Ali, 1987: p. 51 ff.
Ali presents the holding sizes in hectares. For purposes of simplicity, they have been presented here in decimals, (dec.) = 100th of an acre, as in the other presentations. In order to make the data more legible, they have been slightly rounded off. This does not seem to cause any significant loss of information.

Tab. 90: **Development Trends in Livestock Keeping in a Village in the District of Noakhali According to Holding-size Category for the Years 1979 and 1984**

Holding-size Category (Dec.)	Oxen 1979	Oxen 1984	Cows 1979	Cows 1984	Calves 1979	Calves 1984	Goats 1979	Goats 1984	Poultry 1979	Poultry 1984
					(N per Holding)					
0	0.11	0.06	0.08	0.07	0.09	0.11	0.23	0.47	3.29	3.16
1 - 50	0.26	0.08	0.51	0.58	0.28	0.23	0.41	0.83	3.03	4.17
51 - 100	0.77	0.48	0.29	0.83	0.35	0.23	0.52	0.42	3.65	3.87
101 - 200	1.16	1.24	0.70	1.07	0.41	0.54	0.89	1.02	7.39	4.24
201 - 300	1.50	1.56	0.38	1.00	0.96	1.06	1.12	0.75	8.73	5.94
300 <	1.67	1.83	0.72	1.11	0.64	0.69	0.50	0.39	8.28	6.06
All	0.54	0.45	0.32	0.52	0.30	0.29	0.46	0.61	4.59	3.89

Source: [232] de Lasson, Dolberg, 1985: p. 342, Tab. 3.

Tab. 91: **Development Trends in "Fruit" Production from 1978 to 1988**

Year	Bananas	Mangos	Jack-fruit	Pineapple	Melons	Other	"Fruit" p/Capita
			Thou. Tons				Kg/Year
1978	580	251	203	141	110	64	15.54
1979	587	211	190	137	109	63	14.62
1980	606	204	165	140	114	75	14.76
1981	642	200	201	151	99	89	14.99
1982	673	181	204	153	101	93	14.95
1983	688	201	205	154	120	102	15.34
1984	664	156	208	134	121	100	14.23
1985	679	160	218	130	122	106	14.24
1986	691	159	229	128	124	108	15.60
1987	759	155	235	133	120	109	15.00
1988	684	160	254	145	116	108	14.30

Source: [124] Government, 1988: p. 198, Tab. 4.74; [128] Government, 1990: p. 189, Tab. 4.65.

Tab. 92: Development Trends in Domestic Fish Production from 1972 to 1988/89

Year	Catch	Fisher	Fish per Fisher	Fish per Capita of Population
	Hundert Thou. Tons	Hundert Thou. N	Tons	Kg
1972	7.29	6.0	1.21	9.59
1973	7.31	6.5	1.12	9.40
1974	7.32	6.6	1.11	9.20
1975	7.33	6.0	1.22	9.00
1976	5.45	6.0	0.91	6.55
1977	5.41	6.2	0.87	6.36
1978	5.33	7.1	0.75	6.14
1979	5.27	7.2	0.74	5.94
1980	5.27	7.2	0.73	3.80
1981	5.25	6.9	0.72	5.69
1982	5.56	7.0	0.75	6.01
1983	5.83	7.1	0.79	6.23
1984	5.89	7.1	0.83	6.18
1985	5.86	7.1	0.83	6.03
1986	5.87	7.2	0.82	5.93
1987	5.97	7.4	0.81	5.93
1988	5.99	7.5	0.80	5.84
1989	6.10	7.7	0.79	5.84

Source: [124] Government, 1988: p. 219, Tab. 4.106 and p. 220, Tab. 4.107. [128] Government, 1990: p. 206, Tab. 4.94 and p. 207, Tab. 4.95.

Tab. 93: Developments in the Availability of "Traditional" Energy Won from Biomasses from 1975/6 to 1988/89

Year	Waste	Jute Sticks	Rice Straw	Rice Husks	Bag-asse	Fire-wood	Twigs, Leaves	Manure	Total p/Capita
			Hundert Thou. Tons of Hard-coal Units						Kg
1975/76	742	316	1498	1968	389	297	895	2034	97.8
1976/77	755	382	1449	1871	423	602	911	2049	-
1977/78	817	426	1458	1968	452	328	986	2139	-
1978/79	852	574	1462	1968	436	339	1028	2486	-
1979/80	891	466	1498	1713	580	360	1076	1530	-
1980/81	949	387	1520	1867	572	381	1145	1555	-
1981/82	953	364	1537	1832	619	381	1150	1576	-
1982/83	1058	382	1550	1911	635	424	1277	1582	-
1983/84	1009	410	1430	2108	603	407	1219	1626	-
1984/85	1053	363	1379	2142	581	435	1270	1670	-
1985/86	1125	541	1415	2177	581	435	1343	1677	91.8
1986/87	1009	541	1536	1408	602	425	1220	1677	-
1987/88	1056	526	1440	1975	628	475	1270	1807	-
1988/89	1056	570	1556	2022	602	475	1270	1927	90.6

Source: [124] Government, 1988: p. 278, Tab. 6.5; [128] Government, 1990: p. 278, Tab. 6.05.

Tab. 94: Development Trends in "Vegetable" Production from 1978 to 1988

Year	Potatoes	Other Vegetables	Potatoes	Other Vegetables
	Thou. Tons		Kg/Capita/Year	
1978	849	740	9.8	8.5
1979	895	728	10.1	8.2
1980	903	785	10.0	8.7
1981	983	783	10.7	8.5
1982	1078	816	11.5	8.7
1983	1131	863	11.8	9.0
1984	1148	888	11.8	9.1
1985	1141	879	11.5	8.8
1986	1103	883	11.1	8.9
1987	1069	891	10.6	8.8
1988	1276	936	12.4	9.1

Source: [124] Government, 1988: p. 191, Tab. 4.67; [128] Government, 1990: p. 181, Tab. 4.58, p. 79, Tab. 2.50; [130] Government, 1991: p. 17, Appendix B.

Tab. 95: Developments in the Employment of Manpower per Hectare and Year in Six Villages from 1950 to 1985

Holding-size Category (Dec.)	Village	Work Days/Ha./Year			
		1950	1960	1970	1985
750 <	1	160	167	182	225
	2	120	126	128	129
	3	174	173	176	231
	4	219	239	328	617
	5	166	236	306	461
	6	-	-	-	-
250 - 750	1	168	181	190	232
	2	134	136	132	149
	3	152	156	169	250
	4	216	261	360	519
	5	182	266	432	509
	6	268	345	494	622
< 250	1	167	168	189	248
	2	133	142	169	192
	3	184	181	195	270
	4	244	272	389	536
	5	199	322	447	580
	6	312	401	516	634
All	1	165	172	187	235
	2	129	135	143	137
	3	170	170	180	250
	4	220	264	359	533
	5	189	293	429	550
	6	290	373	505	638

Source: [32] Ali, 1987: p. 142, Tab. 3.11; p. 210, Tab. 4.14; p. 279, Tab. 5.12; p. 344, Tab. 6.12; p. 413, Tab. 7.12; and p. 481, Tab. 8.11.
Note: Village 6 is not represented in the largest holding-size category (750 Dec.).
For a description of the villages and their setting and a rough agro-ecological outline, see footnote 407, p. 246, or [32] Ali, 1987: p. 51 ff.
Ali presents the holding sizes in hectares. For the purposes of simplicity, they have been presented here in decimals (dec.) = 100th of an acre. In order to make the data somewhat more legible, they have been slightly rounded off. This does not seem to be connected with any significant loss of information.

Tab. 96: Comparison of Manpower Employment and Labour Productivity in Villages with Diverse Technological Levels

Holding-size Category (Dec.)	Family Worker – MP-Days / Acres of Own Land	Hired Worker – MP-Days / Acres of Own Land	Yield / MP-Day / Acres/Year In Kg Rice Units
Modern Villages			
All	43.6	42.2	12.0
50 - 250	62.7	39.5	10.8
250 - 500	33.0	29.3	15.0
500 <	17.8	26.8	19.2
Unmodern Villages			
All	40.2	27.1	9.5
50 - 250	46.6	17.5	11.4
250 - 500	35.1	19.7	10.6
500 <	15.8	20.0	15.9

Source: [166] Hossain, 1988: p. 19, Tab. 2; p. 87, Tab. 42; and p. 105, Tab. 56.

Tab. 97: Comparison of the Working Time per Household Manpower Unit in Agricultural and Nonagricultural Occupations in Villages with Diverse Technological levels

Holding-size Category (Dec.)	Modern Villages		Unmodern Villages	
	Agricultural	Non-agricultural	Agricultural	Non-agricultural
	(Working Hours/Weeks/Household Labour)			
Landless	12.00	17.00	9.83	26.88
< 249	14.20	13.43	12.73	18.30
250 - 500	12.31	6.46	13.89	12.98
500 <	9.53	8.06	13.39	8.35
All	12.53	11.89	12.86	17.85

Source: [166] Hossain, 1988: p. 90, Tab. 44 and p. 94, Tab. 47.

Tab. 98: Development Trends in Agricultural Real Wages from 1949 to 1985

Year	Real Wage Index, Basis Food Purchasing Power	Real Wage Index, Statistical Market Basket	Year	Real Wage Index, Basis Food Purchasing Power	Real Wage Index Statistical Market Basket
1949	-	128.3	1970	2.96	100.0
1950	3.25	118.2	1971	2.96	100.7
1951	2.89	97.6	1972	2.77	93.6
1952	2.78	93.9	1973	2.53	85.3
1953	2.58	87.2	1974	2.60	87.9
1954	2.59	87.5	1975	1.78	60.2
1955	2.75	92.9	1976	2.57	86.7
1956	2.74	92.6	1977	2.76	93.4
1957	2.78	93.9	1978	2.30	84.6
1958	2.75	92.9	1979	2.53	85.5
1959	2.71	91.6	1980	2.36	79.7
1960	2.80	94.6	1981	2.36	86.6
1961	3.04	102.7	1982	2.48	83.8
1962	3.14	106.1	1983	2.69	91.0
1963	3.20	108.1	1984	2.70	91.2
1964	3.52	118.9	1985	3.00	101.5
1965	3.42	115.5	1986	3.24	109.5
1966	2.87	97.0	1987	-	-
1967	2.68	90.5	1988	-	-
1968	2.79	94.3	1989	-	120.0 [a]
1969	3.00	101.3			
1970	2.96	100.0			

Source: [303] Samad, 1981: p. 202, Tab. 1a.; [31] Alauddin, Tisdell, 1989: p. 565, Tab. 2; and [128] Government, 1990: p. 495, Tab. 10.35.

a   Estimate based on [128] Government, 1990: p. 495, Tab. 10.35.

Tab. 99: Comparison of the Monetarily Appraised Yields and the Factor Remuneration for Local (LV) and Modern (MV/HYV) Rice Varieties for the Boro and the Amon Seasons According to Holding-size Category

Season	Holding Size (Dec.)	Variety	Income Share			
			Farm Manager	Family Labour Unit	Hired Labour Unit	Inputs
			Tk/Acre			
Boro/						
Winter	< 250	LV	287	694	436	148
		HYV	459	912	663	442
	250 <	LV	396	471	517	93
		HYV	693	552	619	305
Amon/						
Monsoon	< 250	LV	435	426	361	127
		HYV	897	592	489	272
	250 <	LV	576	317	429	101
		HYV	716	373	619	237

Source: [17] Ahmed, 1983: p. 114, Tab. 6.3 and p. 116, Tab. 6.4.

Tab. 100: Comparison of the Agricultural and Nonagricultural Income According to Landownership Category in "Modernized" and "Non-modernized" Village Type

Holding-size Category (Dec.)	Agricultural Income	Nonagricultural Income
	Thou. Tk/Year/Household	
Non-modern Villages		
< 50	3549	6036
50 - 250	9201	6819
250 - 500	16190	8119
500 <	29437	9372
Modern Villages		
< 50	6151	6264
50 - 250	11234	7071
250 - 500	20685	7610
500 <	39425	16721

Source: [167] Hossain, 1988: p. 121, Tab. 65.

Note: 2 x 317 households in 2 x 8 villages which are considered representative for various agro-ecological zones were included in the survey.

Tab. 101: Comparison of the Monetarily Appraised Yields and the Factor Remuneration for Local (LV) and Modern (MV/HYV) Rice Varieties for the Boro and Amon Seasons According to Status of the Farmer

Season	Status of the Farmer	Variety	Income Share				
			Farm Manager	Family Labour Unit	Hired Labour Unit	Inputs	Land-lord
			Tk/Acre				
Boro/ Winter	Owner-cultivator	LV	729	572	616	128	-
		HYV	1051	681	915	250	-
	Owner-cum tenancy	LV	336	424	284	101	750
		HYV	358	467	443	209	859
	Fixed Tenancy	LV	-	-	-	-	-
		HYV	348	364	268	86	162
Amon/ Monsoon	Owner-cultivator	LV	777	416	203	108	-
		HYV	1016	506	459	155	-
	Owner-cum-tenancy	LV	169	379	271	59	212
		HYV	331	356	368	134	373
	Fixed Tenancy	LV	362	265	158	70	125
		HYV	411	337	266	170	195

Source: [17] Ahmed, 1983: p. 109, Tab. 6.1 and p. 111, Tab. 6.2.

366

Tab. 102: Comparison of the Significance of Agricultural and Nonagricultural Income Sources in "Modernized" and "Non-modernized" Village Types

Occupations	Average Incomes from Occupations	
	in Modernized Villages	in Non-modernized Villages
	Tk/Household/Year	
Plant Production	9265	6258
Garden Production	2730	2465
Livestock Keeping	1511	1272
Fishing	1099	287
Farmhand Wages	1039	896
Handicrafts/Industry	268	726
Commerce	1889	886
Services	4417	3268
Nonagricultural Wages	1420	2271
Per Capita Household Income	3626	2961

Source: [166] Hossain, 1988: p. 120, Tab. 64.

Note: For a description of the choice of villages (criteria), see footnote 452, p. 279.

Tab. 103: Comparison of the Households' Annual Income Sources According to Landownership-size Categories of the Households in a Project Village of the Grameen Bank and an Own Control Village

Landownership-size Categories (Dec.)	Random Sample Proportions (%)	Income in	
		Bank-Projekt Village	"Control" Village
		Thou. Tk/Household/Year	
Landless	10.5	10256	8090
1 - 49	42.5	16381	14553
50 - 249	31.0	20349	20809
250 - 499	11.0	29110	29549
500 <	5.0	41074	46776
All	100.0	19603	16970

Sources: [163] Hossain, 1984: p. 99, Tab. 5.3; and [280] Rahman, 1986: p. 26 f, Tab. 3.2.

Tab. 104: Comparison of the Income Sources of the Bank-Project Participants, the Non-participants and "Control' ' Village Households

Income Sources	Non-members in Grameen Bank Village	Control Village	Members of the Grameen Bank
	Tk/Household/Year		
Agriculture (Total)	5323	6577	5606
Farming	2199	2312	2783
House Garden	306	567	512
Livestock/Fishing	788	928	9412
Farm Work	2031	2770	1371
Non-agricultural (Total)	8881	61128	12528
Processing	2753	1119	4355
Commerce	2234	1369	3859
Transport	572	765	1352
Wage Labour	826	738	670
Other	2496	2158	2292
Household Income (Total)	14204	12696	18134
Per Capita Income	2900	2523	3524

Source: [165] Hossain, 1988: p. 66, Tab. 38.

Tab. 105: Comparison of the Height of the Incomes of the Bank-project Participant Households in 1982 and 1985

Income Category (Tk)	Number of Households 1982	1985	Total Income 1982	1985
	(%)		Tk/Household/Year	
< 1000	3.2	-	5796	-
1001 - 1500	18.2	-	8750	-
1501 - 2000	29.1	1.7	10867	9350
2001 - 2500	21.5	5.0	12292	14308
2501 - 3000	13.1	15.0	14356	16189
3001 - 4000	11.6	33.3	16650	18152
4000 <	3.4	45.0	16310	21831
Total	100.0	100.0		
Average			11950	19171

Sources: [163] Hossain, 1984: p. 99, Tab. 5.3; and [280] Rahman, 1986: p. 26 f, Tab. 3.2.

References

1 **Abdullah, T.** Women in rice farming systems in Bangladesh and how technology programmes can reach them, in: IRRI (International Rice Research Institute), Women in rice farming, Aldershot and Vermont, **1985**

2 **Abdullah, T.A.**; Village women as I saw them, BARD Comilla, **1976**

3 **Abdullah, T.A., Zeidenstein, S.A.**; Finding ways to learn about rural women: Experiences from a pilot project in Bangladesh, Report No.44, The Ford Foundation, Dacca, **1976**

4 **Adnan, S.** Land, power and violence in Barisal villages, *Political Economy*, Vol.2, No.1, p. 125-132, **1976**

5 **Adnan, S.** An annotated bibliography of village studies and related literature on Bangladesh & West Bengal, Report commissioned by The Bangladesh Academy of Rural Development (Draft), Chittagong, **1988**

6 **Adnan, S.** Annotation of village studies in Bangladesh and West Bengal – A review of socio-economic trends over 1942-88, BARD Comilla **1990**

7 **Ahmad, A.** Agricultural stagnation under population pressure - The case of Bangladesh, Dhaka, **1984**

8 **Ahmad, A.J.M.U., Hossain, M.A., Mian, M.H.U., Hossain, M.A.**; Energy crisis in a Bangladesh village, Bogra, **1986**

9 **Ahmad, N.** An economic geography of East Pakistan, 2nd ed., London, **1968**

10 **Ahmad, N.** A new economic geography of Bangladesh, New Delhi etc., **1976**

11 **Ahmad, P.** Income earning as related to the changing status of village women in Bangladesh - A case study, Women for Women Study and Research Group, Dacca, **1980**

12 **Ahmad, Q.K., Hossain, M.**; Rural poverty alleviation in Bangladesh - Experiences and policies, In-depth Studies Series No.10, FAO, **1984**

13 **Ahmad, R.S.**; Financing the rural poor - Obstacles and realities, Dhaka, **1983**

14 **Ahmed, A.** Patterns of land transfer 1972-81 - A survey of two villages in Comilla, Comilla, **1987**

15 **Ahmed, A.B.S.**; Changing pattern of social structure in rural Bangladesh, in: Khan, M.M., Husain, S.A.(eds.), Bangladesh studies: Politics, administration, rural development, and foreign policy, Dhaka, **1985**

16 **Ahmed, J.U.**; Agricultural development strategies: Bangladesh - A comparative analysis of effects on production and distribution, Göttingen, **1984**

17 **Ahmed, M.** Effects of modern production technology on employment, income shares and efficiency in Bangladesh, Diss. Cornell, Ithaca, **1983**

18 **Ahmed, M.** Bangladesh agriculture - Towards self sufficiency, Dhaka, **1988**

19 **Alam, M.M.-U.**; Leadership pattern, problems and prospects of local government in rural Bangladesh, BARD Comilla, **1976**

20 **Alam, N.S.M.**; A new look at the dynamics of social and politcal structure in rural Bangladesh, *Asian Profile*, Vol.14, No.2, pp. 155-164, **1986**

21 **Alam, S.M.N.**; Marginalization, pauperization and agrarian change in two villages of Bangladesh, Diss. Purdue Univ. **1983**

22 **Alam, S.M.N.**; An analysis of cost, productivity and returns of rice production in Bangladesh: A case study of two villages, *Journal of Social Studies*, No.36, pp. 76-96, **1987**

23 **Alamgir, M.** Bangladesh: A case of below poverty level equilibrium trap, BIDS Dacca, (**1980**)

24 **Alamgir, M.** Famine in South Asia - Political economy of mass starvation, Cambridge, Mass. **1980**

25 **Alamgir, M.** An approach towards a theory of famine, in: Robson, J.R.K. (ed.), Famine: Its causes, effects and management, New York etc., **1981**

26 **Alamgir, M., Ahmed, S.;** Poverty and income distribution in Bangladesh, in: Srinivasan, T.N., Bardhan, P.K., Rural poverty in South Asia, New York, **1988**

27 **Alamgir, M.K.;** Development strategy for Bangladesh, Dacca, **1980**

28 **Alamgir, M.K.(ed.);** Land reform in Bangladesh, Dacca, **1981**

29 **Alauddin, M., Mujeri, M.K.;** Employment and productivity growth in Bangladesh agriculture: An inter-district analysis, *Marga*, Vol.8, No.1, pp. 50-72, **1985**

30 **Alauddin, M., Tisdell, C.;** Patterns and determinants of adoption of high yielding varieties: Farm-level evidence from Bangladesh, *The Pakistan Development Review*, Vol.27, No.2, pp. 183-210, **1988**

31 **Alauddin, M., Tisdell, C.;** Poverty, resource distribution and security: The impact of new agricultural technology in rural Bangladesh, *The Journal of Development Studies*, Vol.25, No.4, pp. 370-550, **1989**

32 **Ali, A.M.S.;** Changes in near-saturated agro-ecosystems: a comparison of paddy agriculture in six villages in Bangladesh. (Volumes 1 and II), Diss. Clark Univ. (UMI), **1987**

33 **Ali, A.M.S.;** Intensive paddy agriculture in Shyampur, Bangladesh, in: Turner II, B.L. et al. (eds.), Comparative farming systems, New York, London, **1987**

34 **Ali, R., Rahman, M.M.;** An evolution of Women Development Programme of Mymenshingh District (A Programme Assessment), Bangladesh Agricultural University Mymenshingh, **1978**

35 **Alim, A.** Bangladesh rice, Dhaka, **1982**

36 **Arefeen, H.K.;** Changing agrarian structure in Bangladesh, Shimulia - A study of a periurban village, Dhaka, **1986**

37 **Arens, J., Beurden, J. van;** Jhagrapur - Poor peasants and women in a village in Bangladesh, Amsterdam, **1977**

38 **Arn, A.-L.;** Noakhali Villages - A description of the socio-economic conditions in four villages in Noakhali District, Bangladesh, Copenhagen, **1986**

39 **Asseldonk, J.S.O. van;** Energievoorziening in rural Bangladesh (Energy Supply in rural Bangladesh), *Landbonwkundig Tijdschrift*, Vol.95, No.7/8, pp. 21-28, **1983**

40 **Aziz, K.M.A.;** Kinship in Bangladesh, ICDDR,B Monograph Series No.1, Dacca, **1979**

41 **Bairagi, R., Langsten, R.L.;** Sex preference for children and its implications for fertility in rural Bangladesh, *Studies in Family Planning*, Vol.17, No.6, pp. 302-307, **1986**

42 **Bala, B.A., Karim, M.M., Dutta, D.P.;** Energy-use pattern of an electrified village in Bangladesh, *Energy*, Vol.14, No.2, pp. 61-65, **1989**

43 **Balakrishnan, M.D.;** Rural marketing: myth and reality, *Economic and Political Weekly*, Vol.13, No.34, pp. 1175-1180, **1978**

44 **Bardhan, P.K.;** Interlocking factor markets and agrarian development: A review of issues, *Oxford Economic Papers*, Vol.32, pp. 82-98, **1980**

370

45 Basu, D.R.; Food policy and the analysis of famine, *Indian Journal of Economics*, Vol.64, No.254, pp. 289-302, **1984**

46 Beck, T.; Survival strategies and power among the poorest in a West Bengal village, *IDS Bulletin*, Vol.20, No.2, pp. 23-31, **1989**

47 Berry, L.; Environment: A critical aspect of development and food production in Bangladesh, in: Robson, J.R.K. (ed.), Famine: Its causes, effects and management, New York etc., **1981**

48 Berry, R.A., Cline, W.R.; Agrarian structure and productivity in developing countries, Baltimore, London, **1979**

49 Bhaduri, A., Rahman, H.Z., Arn, A.L.; Persistence and polarization: A study in the dynamics of agrarian contradiction, *Journal of Peasant Studies*, Vol.13, No.3, pp. 82-89, **1986**

50 Bhaduri, A., Rahman, H.Z., Arn, A.-L.; Persistence and polarization in rural Bangladesh: Response to a debate, *The Journal of Peasant Studies*, Vol.16, No.1, pp. 121-123, **1988**

51 Bhagavan, M.R., Giriappa, S.; Class character of rural energy crisis - Case of Karnataka, *Economic and Political Weekly*, Vol.22, No.26, pp. 57-69, **1987**

52 Bhuiya, A., Wojtyniak, B., D'Souza, S., Zimicki, S.; Socio-economic determinants of child nutritional status: boys versus girls, *Food and Nutrition Bulletin*, Vol.8, No.3, pp. 3-7, **1986**

53 Bhuiya, A., Zimicki, S., D'Souza, S.; Socioeconomic differentials in child nutrition and morbidity in a rural area of Bangladesh, *Journal of Tropical Pediatrics*, Vol.32, pp. 17-23, **1986**

54 Bhuiyan, M.S.R.; Influence of tenurial status of land on the adoption of improved production technology in an area of Bangladesh, *Bangladesh Journal of Agricultural Economics*, Vol.10, No.2, pp. 89-99, **1987**

55 Bhuiyan, M.S.R., Mandal, D.S.; Tenurial status of farm, resource endowment, resource use and productive efficiency in Mymensingh District of Bangladesh, *Indian Journal of Agricultural Economics*, Vol.42, No.2, pp. 209-220, **1987**

56 Bhuyan, K.C.; Education, fertility and family planning practice in a rural area of Bangladesh, *Journal of Family Welfare (India)*, Vol.33, No.2, pp. .3-15, **1986**

57 Blanchet, T.; Meanings and rituals of birth in rural Bangladesh, Dhaka, **1984**

58 Bohle, H.-G.; Role and potentiality of traditional market systems in third world urbanization - Some observations from South India, *Internationales Asienforum*, Vol.14, No.4, pp. 345-362, **1983**

59 Bose, S.; Agrarian Bengal – Economy, social structure and politics, 1919-1947, Cambridge etc. **1986**

60 Boserup, E.; Population and technology, Oxford, **1981**

61 Boserup, E.; The impact of scarcity and plenty on development, in: Rotberg R.I. et al. (eds.), Hunger and history, Cambridge, **1985**

62 Bowonder, B., Prakash Rao, N., Dasgupta, B., Prasad, S.S.R.; Energy use in eight rural communities in India, *World Development*, Vol.13, No.12, pp. 1263-1286, **1985**

63 Boyce, J.K.; Agrarian impasse in Bengal: Agricultural growth in Bangladesh and West Bengal 1949-1980 - Institutional constraints to technological change, Oxford u.a., **1987**

64 **Boyce, J.K.**; Population growth and real wages of agricultural labourers in Bangladesh, *The Journal of Development Studies*, Vol.25, No.4, pp. 467-489, **1989**

65 **Briscoe, J.**; Energy use and social structure in a Bangladesh village, *Population and Development Review*, Vol.5, No.4, pp. 615-641, **1979**

66 **Butler, L.**; Integration of wheat research and production in Bangladesh, in: Klatt, A.R. (ed.), Wheat production constraints in tropical environments, A proceedings of the international conference, January 19-23, 1987, Chiang Mai, Thailand; CIMMYT Mexico D.F., **1988**

67 **BRAC (Bangladesh Rural Advancement Committee)**; The net - Power structure in ten villages, Dhaka, **1983**

68 **BRAC (Bangladesh Rural Advancement Committee)**; Who gets what and why: Resource allocation in a Bangladesh village, Dhaka, **1983**

69 **BRAC (Bangladesh Rural Advancement Committee)**; Intervention and change in the lives of rural poor women in Bangladesh - A discussion paper, Dhaka, **1983**

70 **BRAC (Bangladesh Rural Advancement Committee)**; Peasants perceptions: Famine, credit needs, sanitation, Dhaka, **1984**

71 **Bähr, J.**; Bevölkerungsgeographie, Stuttgart, **1983**

72 **Bössmann, E.**; Volkswirtschaftliche Probleme der Transaktionskosten, *Zeitschrift für die gesamte Staatswissenschaft*, Vol. 138, pp. 664-679, **1982**

73 **Cain, M.**; The consequences of reproductive failure: Dependence, mobility and mortality among the elderly of rural South Asia, *Population Studies*, Vol.40, pp. 375-388, **1986**

74 **Cain, M.T.**; The household live cycle and economic mobility in rural Bangladesh, *Population and Development Review*, Vol.4, No.3, pp. 421-438, **1978**

75 **Cain, M.T., Khanam, S.R., Nahar, S.**; Class, Patriarchy, and Womens' Work in Bangladesh, *Population and Development Review*, Vol.5, No.3, pp. 405-438, **1979**

76 **Chambers, R.**; Editorial introduction: Vulnerability, coping and policy, *IDS Bulletin*, Vol.20, No.2, pp. 1-7, **1989**

77 **Chaudhury, R.H.**; Determinants of nutrient adequacy in a rural area of Bangladesh, *Food and Nutrition Bulletin*, Vol.8, No.4, pp. 24-31, **1986**

78 **Chaudhury, R.H.**; Adequacy of child dietary intake relative to that of other family members, *Food and Nutrition Bulletin*, Vol.10, No.2, pp. 26-34, **1988**

79 **Chaudhury, R.H.**; Population pressure and its effects on changes in agrarian structure and productivity in rural Bangladesh, in: Rodgers, G. (ed.), Population growth and poverty in rural South Asia, New Delhi etc. **1989**

80 **Chen, L.C., Chaudhury, R.H.**; Demographic change and food production in Bangladesh, 1960-74, *Population and Development Review*, Vol.1, No.2, pp. 201-227, **1975**

81 **Chen, L.C., Huq, E., D'Souza, S.**; Sex bias in the family allocation of food and health care in rural Bangladesh, *Population and Development Review*, Vol.7, No.1, pp. 55-70, **1981**

82 **Chen, L.C., Rahman, M., Sarder, A.M.**; Epidemiology and causes of death among children in a rural area of Bangladesh, *International Journal of Epidemiology*, Vol.9, No.1, pp. 25-33, **1980**

83 Chen, M.; Poverty, gender, and work in Bangladesh, *Economic and Political Weekly*, Vol.21, No.5, pp. 217-222, **1986**

84 Chowdhury, A.; A Bangladesh village - A study of social stratification, Dacca, **1978**

85 Chowdhury, A.; Agrarian social relations and rural development in Bangladesh, New Delhi etc. **1982**

86 Chowdhury, A.K.M.A.; Maternal nutrition in rural Bangladesh, in: Jain, D., Banerjee, N.(eds.), The tyranny of the household - Investigative essays on women's work (Women in Poverty), New Delhi, **1985**

87 Chowdhury, A.K.M.A.; Child mortality in Bangladesh: Food versus health care, *Food and Nutrition Bulletin*, Vol.10, No.2, pp. 3-8, **1988**

88 Chowdhury, M.; The 1987 flood in Bangladesh: An estimate of damage in twelve villages, *Disasters*, Vol.12, No.4, pp. 294-300, **1989**

89 Chowdhury, N.; Parmers' participation in the paddy markets, their marketed surplus and factors affecting it in Bangladesh: A comment, *The Bangladesh Development Studies*, Vol.16, No.1, pp. 100-107, **1987**

90 Chowdhury, O.H.; Agricultural underemployment, industrial growth, real wages and labour absorbtion in Bangladesh economy: 1952-1978, BIDS Research Report New Series No.39, Dhaka,**1985**

91 Clay, E.; The 1974 and 1984 floods in Bangladesh: From famine to flood crisis management, *Food Policy*, Vol.10, No.3, pp. 202-206, **1985**

92 Clay, E.; Floods in Bangladesh, 1974 and 1984: From famine to food-crisis management, in: Curtis, D. et al. (eds.), Preventing famine – Policies and prospects for Africa, London, New York, **1988**

93 Cooper, A.; Sharecroppers and landlords in Bengal, 1930-1950: The dependency web and its implications, *The Journal of Peasant Studies*, Vol.10, No.Nos. 2/3, pp. 226-255, **1983**

94 Crow, B.; Warnings of famine in Bangladesh, *Economic and Political Weekly*, Vol.19, No.40, pp. 1754-1758, **1984**

95 Crow, B.; US policies in Bangladesh: The making and the breaking of famine?, *Journal of Social Studies*, No.35, pp. 22-65, **1987**

96 Crow, B.; Plain tales from the rice trade: Indications of vertical Integration in foodgrain markets in Bangladesh, *Journal of Peasant Studies*, Vol.16, No.2, pp. 198-229, **1989**

97 Currey, B.; The famine syndrome: Its definition for relief and rehabilitation in Bangladesh, in: Robson, J.R.K. (ed.), Famine: Its causes, effects and management, New York etc., **1981**

98 Cutler, P.; Detecting food emergencies: Lessons from the 1979 Bangladesh Crisis, *Food Policy*, Vol.10, No.3, pp. 207-224, **1985**

99 Elias, S.M.; Constraints to production of pulses in Bangladesh, CGPRT No.11, Bogor, **1988**

100 Ellis, F.; Peasant economics – Farm households and agrarian development, Cambridge etc., **1988**

101 Etienne, G.; Bangladesh: Towards a possible future, in: Etienne, G. (ed.), Rural development in Asia, New Delhi etc. **1985**

102 Etienne, G.; Rural development in Asia - Meeting with peasants (revised edition), New Delhi etc. **1985**

103 **Faaland, J., Parkinson, J.R.**; A development perspective for Bangladesh, *Bangladesh Development Studies*, Vol.4, No.1, pp. 49-66, **1976**

104 **Faaland, J., Parkinson, J.R.**; Bangladesh - The test case of development, Dacca, **1976**

105 **Faizullah, M.**; Development of local government in Bangladesh, Dhaka, **1987**

106 **Fauveau, V., Koenig, M.A., Wojtyniak, B., Chakraborty, J.**; Impact of a family planning and health services programme on adult female mortality, *Health Policy and Planning*, Vol.3, No.4, pp. 271-279, **1988**

107 **Feldman, S., Banu, F., McCarthy, F.E.**; The role of rural Bangladeshi women in livestock production, Cornell International Agriculture Mimeograph No.112, Ithaca, N.Y., **1986**

108 **Feldman, S., McCarthy, F.E.**; Persistence of smallholder, withering away of the small farmer: comments on Bhadury, Rahman and Arn, *Journal of Peasant Studies*, Vol.14, No.4, pp. 543-548, **1987**

109 **Fischer, W.E.**; Eine Bank für die Ärmsten der Armen: Das "Grameen Bank Projekt" in Bangladesh, *Entwicklung + ländlicher Raum*, No.3, pp. 13-16, **1983**

110 **FAO**; Review and analysis of programmes for the rural poor in Bangladesh, Dhaka, **1986**

111 **Geertz, C.**; Agricultural involution - The process of ecological change in Indonesia, Berkley, Los Angeles, **1963**

112 **Gerard, R.**; A feasability survey of production/income generating activities for women in Bangladesh, (Reprint), UNICEF Dacca, **1977**

113 **Government of Bangladesh**; 1979 Statistical year book of Bangladesh, Bangladesh Bureau of Statistics, Dhaka, **1979**

114 **Government of Bangladesh**; Bangladesh population census 1981, Bangladesh Bureau of Statistics, Dhaka, **1984**

115 **Government of Bangladesh**; The survey of ponds 1982, Bureau of Statistics, Dhaka, **1984**

116 **Government of Bangladesh**; The Third Five Year Plan 1985-90, Dhaka, **1985**

117 **Government of Bangladesh**; Upazilla statistics Vol.III, Selected minor crops, Bureau of Statistics, Dhaka, **1986**

118 **Government of Bangladesh**; Report of the Bangladesh livestock survey 1983 - 84, Bureau of Statistics, Dhaka, **1986**

119 **Government of Bangladesh**; Census of agriculture and livestock 1983 - 84, VOL.I Bureau of Statistics, Dhaka, **1986**

120 **Government of Bangladesh**; Final report - Labour force survey 1983-84, Bangladesh Bureau of Statistics, Dhaka, **1986**

121 **Government of Bangladesh**; The Bangladesh census of agriculture and livestock: 1983-84 - Vol.II, Cropping patterns, Bangladesh Bureau of Statistics, Dhaka, **1986**

122 **Government of Bangladesh**; Report on labour force survey 1984-85, Bangladesh Bureau of Statistics, Dhaka, **1988**

123 **Government of Bangladesh**; Report of the Bangladesh household expenditure survey 1985-85, Bangladesh Bureau of Statistics, Dhaka, **1988**

124 **Government of Bangladesh**; Statistical yearbook of Bangladesh - 1987, Bangladesh Bureau of Statistics, Dhaka, **1988**

374

125 Government of Bangladesh; The Bangladesh census of agriculture and live-stock: 1983-84 - Vol.III, Sample enumeration of agricultural characteristics, Bangladesh Bureau of Statistics, Dhaka, **1988**

126 Government of Bangladesh; Statistical pocket book of Bangladesh - 1987, Bangladesh Bureau of Statistics, Dhaka, **1988**

127 Government of Bangladesh; Bangladesh education statistics, Bureau of statistics, Dhaka, **1985**

128 Government of Bangladesh; Statistical yearbook of Bangladesh - 1990, Bangladesh Bureau of Statistics, Dhaka, **1990**

129 Government of Bangladesh; Report on the household expenditure survey, 1988-89, Bangladesh Bureau of Statistics, Dhaka, **1991**

130 Government of Bangladesh; Preliminary report, Population census 1991, Bangladesh Bureau of Statistics, Dhaka, July, **1991**

131 Government of Pakistan; 1960 Pakistan census of Agriculture, Vol.1, Final Report – East Pakistan (Part I), Agricultural Census Organisation **1962**

132 Halim, A., McCarthy, F.E.; Women laborers in rice producing village of Bangladesh, in: IRRI (International Rice Research Institute), Women in rice farming, Aldershot and Vermont, **1985**

133 Hannan, F.H., Islam, N.; Women in agriculture - An annotated bibliography, Comilla, **1986**

134 Haq, M.F.; Rural credit in Ullahpara, Bogra, **1985**

135 Haq, M.N.; A pre-election study on socio-economic conditions of the candidates for Union Parishad election to be held in January, 1977, RDA Bogra, **1976**

136 Haque, F.; Bangladesh: A participatory approach in stimulating fischerwomen's activities, *Ideas and Action Bulletin (FAO)*, No.170, pp. 3-6, **1986**

137 Haque, F.; A loan to a woman ... A direct way to adress poverty, *Ceres*, Vol.21, No.1, pp. 27-31, **1988**

138 Haroun er Rashid; Geography of Bangladesh, Dacca, **1977**

139 Hassan, N., Ahmad, K.; Studies on food and nutrient intake by rural population of Bangladesh: Comparison between intakes of 1962-64,1975-76 and 1981-82, *Ecology of Food and Nutrition*, Vol.15, pp. 143-158, **1984**

140 Hassan, N., Ahmad, K.; Household distribution of energy intake and its relationship to socio-economic and anthropometric variables, *Food and Nutrition Bulletin*, Vol.8, No.4, pp. 3-6, **1986**

141 Hassan, N., Huda, N., Ahmad, K.; Seasonal patterns of food intake in rural Bangladesh: Its impact and nutritional status, *Ecology of Food and Nutrition (USA)*, Vol.17, No.2, pp. 175-186, **1985**

142 Hauser, J.A.; Bevölkerungslehre, Bern, Stuttgart **1982**

143 Hayami, Y., Ruttan, V.W.; Agricultural development – An international perspective, Baltimore and London **1985**

144 Helmrich, H.; Animal husbandry in Bangladesh - Conditions, functions and development potential, Sozialökonomische Schriften zur Ruralen Entwicklung, Bd.64, Aachen **1986**

145 Herbon, D.; Strukturelle und funktionale Aspekte eines lokalen Marktsystems - Das Fallbeispiel eines ländlichen Marktsystems in Bangladesh, *Agrarwirtschaft, Zeitschrift für Betriebswirtschaft und Marktforschung und Agrarpolitik*, Vol.33, No.4, pp. 110-116, **1984**

146 **Herbon, D.**; Politische Strukturen eines Dorfes in Bangladesh - Eine empirische Studie, *Verfassung und Recht in Übersee*, Vol.17, No.4, pp. 475-491, **1984**

147 **Herbon, D.**; Ein dörfliches Gesellschaftssystem in Bangladesh - Mechanismen, Funktionen und Dynamik des sozio-ökonomischen Austausches, Sozialökonomische Schriften zur Ruralen Entwicklung, Band 47, Göttingen, **1984**

148 **Herbon, D.**; Sozio-ökonomische Wirkungen von Entwicklungsmaßnahmen - Fallbeispiele aus einem Dorf in Bangladesh, *Zeitschrift für Ethnologie*, Bd.112, H.1, pp. 71-84, **1987**

149 **Herbon, D.**; The social and institutional structure of the microregion, in: Herbon, D. (ed.), Socio-economic strategies of survival in Bangladesh - A preliminary report on empirical findings, Sozialökonomische Schriften zur Ruralen Entwicklung, Bd.77, Aachen **1988**

150 **Herbon, D.**; Institutional support of rural development in Bangladesh - A review of 30 years of development, *Quarterly Journal of International Agriculture* Vol.27, No.1, pp. 20-32, **1988**

151 **Herbon, D.**; Agricultural cooperatives in Bangladesh - An empirical analysis of credit distribution and recovery as indicator for performance and failure, *Quarterly Journal of International Agriculture*, Vol.27, No.3/4, pp. 351-364, **1988**

152 **Herbon, D.**; "Rural-Poor"-Cooperatives in Bangladesh - An empirical analysis of performance and potential, *Quarterly Journal of International Agriculture*, Vol.27, No.3/4, pp. 365-380, **1988**

153 **Herbon, D.**; Agrarethnologie, in: Lexikon der Ethnologie, Klaus E. Müller (Hrsg.) Frankfurt/M **1990** (under preparation)

154 **Herbon, D.**; Irrigation technology in Bangladesh - An assessment of consequences of different technology levels, *Quarterly Journal of International Agriculture*, Vol.29, No.1, **1989**

155 **Herbon, D.**; Individuelle Lebenschancen und agrargesellschaftliche Dynamiken: Bangladesh - Eine system- und individualstrategisch orientierte Untersuchung zu individuellen Handlungsräumen und zur Folgebedingtheit agrargesellschaftlicher Dynamik, Sozialökonomische Schriften zur Ruralen Entwicklung, Bd. 93, Aachen **1992**

156 **Hermans, C., Udo, H.M.J., Dawood, F.**; Cattle dynamics and their implications in Pabna District, Bangladesh, *Agricultural Systems*, Vol.29, No.4, pp. 371-384, **1989**

157 **Heyer, J.**; Landless agricultural labourers' asset strategies, *IDS Bulletin*, Vol.20, No.2, pp. 33-40, **1989**

158 **Hitti, P.K.**; Islam a way of life, London etc., **1970**

159 **Hoque, K.S.**; Agrarian structure, resource distribution, and production conditions in a Bangladesh village, Diss. Purdue Univ. (UMI), **1987**

160 **Hossain, M.**; Rural development in South Asia: Fragments of analysis, DERAP-Working Papers No.A 134, Bergen, **1979**

161 **Hossain, M.**; Agricultural development in Bangladesh: A historical perspective, *Bangladesh Development Studies*, Vol.12, No.4, pp. 29-55, **1984**

162 **Hossain, M.**; Grameen Bank: A hope for the poor in Bangladesh, DERAP-Working Papers No.A 314, Bergen, **1984**

163 **Hossain, M.**; Credit for the rural poor - The experience of Grameen Bank, Dhaka, **1984**

164 **Hossain, M.**; Irrigation and agricultural performance in Bangladesh: Some further results, *Bangladesh Development Studies*, Vol.14, No.4, pp. 37-56, **1986**

165 **Hossain, M.**; Credit for alleviation of rural poverty: The Grameen Bank in Bangladesh, Research Report 65, IFPRI, Washington, **1988**

166 **Hossain, M.**; Nature and impact of the green revolution in Bangladesh, IFPRI/BIDS Washington, Dhaka, **1988**

167 **Hossain, M.**; Tax burden on agriculture - The Bangladesh case, *The Journal of Rural Development*, Vol.18, No.2, pp. 13-48, **1988**

168 **Hossain, M., Islam, A.T.M.A., Saha, S.K.**; Floods in Bangladesh - Recurrent disaster and people's survival, Dhaka, **1987**

169 **Hossain, Mosharaff**; The assault that failed: A profile of absolute poverty in six villages of Bangladesh, UNRISD Genf, **1987**

170 **Huq, J., Begum, H.A., Salahuddin, K., Quadir, S.R.**; Women in Bangladesh: Some socio-economic issues, Dhaka, **1983**

171 **Huq, M.A.(ed.)**; Exploitation of the rural poor - A working paper on the rural power structure in Bangladesh, Comilla, **1978**

172 **Huque, A.S.**; The politics of local government reform in rural Bangladesh, *Public Administration and Development*, Vol.5, No.3, pp. 205-217, **1985**

173 **Huque, A.S.**; Politics and administration in Bangladesh - Problems of participation, Dhaka, **1988**

174 **Husain, A.T.M.A.**; Share cropping systems in four villages of Bogra district, Bogra, **1985**

175 **Hussain, M.S., Barman, S.C., Elias, S.-M.**; Farmers' technology and economics of groundnut cultivation in selected areas of Bangladesh, *Economic Affairs*, Vol.29, No.3, pp. 192-201, **1984**

176 **Hye, H.A.**; Local level planning in Bangladesh, Dacca, **1982**

177 **Hye, H.A.**; Mechanization in agriculture and women in Bangladesh, *Journal of Social Studies*, No.27, pp. 78-100, **1985**

178 **Hye, H.A. (ed.)**; Village studies in Bangladesh, BARD Comilla, **1985**

179 **Hye, H.A. (ed.)**; Decentralization, local government institutions and resource mobilization, Comilla, **1985**

180 **Islam, M.**; Folk medicine and rural women in Bangladesh, Women for women research and study group, Dacca, **1980**

181 **Islam, M.**; Bibliography on Bangladesh women with annotations, Dhaka, **1984**

182 **Islam, M.**; Women, health and culture, Dhaka, **1985**

183 **Islam, M.N.**; Energy and rural development: Critical assessment of the Bangladesh situation, in: Islam, M.N. et al.(eds.) Rural energy to meet development needs - Asian village, Boulder, Col., **1984**

184 **Islam, M.N.**; Rural energy and rural Development, *Geographical Papers*, No.99, Reading **1988**

185 **Islam, N.**; Development planning in Bangladesh - A study in political economy, Dacca, **1979**

186 **Islam, R.**; What has been happening to rural income distribution in Bangladesh?, *Development and Change*, Vol.10, No.3, pp. 385-401, **1979**

377

187 **Islam, S.**; Rural women in Bangladesh - Socio-economic conditions and educational needs, FREPD General Studies Series, Dacca, **1979**

188 **Islam, S.(ed.)**; Exploring the other half - Field research with rural women in Bangladesh, Dacca, **1982**

189 **Jabbar, M.A.**; Food production in Bangladesh: Policy, strategy and consequences, *Bangladesh Journal of Agricultural Economics*, Vol.8, No.1, pp. 45-52, **1985**

190 **Jahangir, B.K.**; Differentiation, polarization and confrontation in rural Bangladesh, Centre for Social Studies CSS, Dacca, **1979**

191 **Jahangir, B.K.**; Rural society, power structure and class practice, DERAP-Working Papers No.A 228, Bergen, **1981**

192 **Jahangir, B.K.**; Women and property in rural Bangladesh, *Journal of Social Studies*, No.34, pp. 87-95, **1986**

193 **Jahangir, B.K.**; Women and property in rural Bangladesh, *Economic and Political Weekly (India)*, Vol.22, No.36/37, pp. 1561-1562, **1987**

194 **Jaim, W.M.H.**; Change in the land ownership pattern and the process of landlessness in rural Bangladesh, *Economic Affairs, India*, Vol.30, No.4, pp. 232-237, **1985**

195 **Jana, M.M.**; Hierarchy of market centres in lower Silabati Basin, *Geographic Review of India*, Vol.40, No.2, pp. 164-174, **1978**

196 **Jannuzi, F.T., Peach, J.T.**; The agrarian structure of Bangladesh - An impediment to development, Boulder, Col., **1980**

197 **Jansen, E.G.**; Rural Bangladesh - Competition for scarce resources, DERAP Publication No.162, Bergen, Norway, **1983**

198 **Jensen, K.M.**; A study on the economic viability of blacksmiths and carpenters in Noakhali District, BIDS/CDR, Feni, Copenhagen, **1983**

199 **Jensen, K.M.**; Non-agricultural occupations in a peasant society - Weavers and fishermen in Noakhali, Bangladesh, CDR Copenhagen **1987**

200 **Jensen, K.M., Devnath, S.B., Das, S.P.**; By the river Meghna - Fishermen in Ramgati, Bangladesh, BIDS/CDR Copenhagen, **1985**

201 **Jensen, K.M., Paul, P.B., Devnath, S.R., Amin, S.N.**; A study of the group activities within the BSCIC/DANIDA supported cottage industries in Noakhali District, BIDS/CDR, Feni, Copenhagen, **1983**

202 **Jiggins, J.**; Women and seasonality: Coping with crisis and calamity, *IDS Bulletin*, Vol.17, No.3, pp. 9-18, **1986**

203 **Johnson, B.L.C.**; Bangladesh, London, **1975**

204 **Johnson, B.L.C.**; India: Resources and development, London, **1979**

205 **Johnson, B.L.C.**; South Asia (2nd ed.), London, **1981**

206 **Kabeer; N.**; Do women gain from high fertility?, in: Afshar, H. (ed.), Women, work, and ideology in the Third World, London, **1985**

207 **Kabeer, N.**; Organizing landless women in Bangladesh, *Community Development Journal*, Vol.20, No.3, pp. 156-326, **1985**

208 **Kabir, M., Ahamad, M.M., Moslehuddin, M.**; Differential infant and child mortality rates in Bangladesh, *Food and Nutrition Bulletin*, Vol.8, No.3, pp. 63-68, **1986**

209 Kabir, M., Moslehuddin, M., Howlader, A.A.; Husband-wife communication and status of women as a determinant of contraceptive use in rural Bangladesh, *The Bangladesh Development Studies*, Vol.16, No.1, pp. 54-85, **1987**

210 Kahrs, F.; The rural non-farm sector of the microregion, in: Herbon, D. (ed.), Socioeconomic strategies of survival in Bangladesh, Socioeconomic Studies in Rural Development, No.77, Aachen **1988**

211 Kahrs, F.; Existensicherung durch Handwerk, Handel und Dienstleistungen - Eine empirische Studie über den informellen Sektor in einer Mikroregion im ländlichen Bangladesh, Sozialökonomische Schriften zur Ruralen Entwicklung, Bd. 87, Aachen **1991**

212 Karim, A.H.M.Z.; The pattern of rural leadership in an agrarian society: A case study of the changing power structure in Bangladesh, Diss. Syracuse Univ. (UMI), **1987**

213 Kashem, M.A.; Land ownership pattern and tenancy relationships in Bangladesh, *The Journal of Rural Development*, Vol.18, No.1, pp. 49-59, **1988**

214 Katona-Apte, J.; Coping strategies of destitute women in Bangladesh, *Food and Nutrition Bulletin*, Vol.10, No.3, pp. 42-47, **1988**

215 Kennes, W., Parikh, J.K., Stolwijk, H.; Energy from biomass by socio-economic groups - A case study of Bangladesh, *Biomass*, Vol.4, No.3, pp. 209-234, **1984**

216 Khan, A.A.; Rural - urban migration and urbanization in Bangladesh, *Geographical Review*, Vol.72, No.4, pp. 379-394, **1982**

217 Khan, A.R.; Real wages of agricultural workers in Bangladesh, in: Khan, A.R., Lee, E. (eds.), Poverty in rural Asia, ILO Bangkok, **1984**

218 Khan, A.R., Hossain, M.; The strategy of development in Bangladesh, OECD London, Paris **1989**

219 Khan, A.R., Islam, R., Huq M.; Employment, income and mobilization of local resources - A study of two Bangladesh villages, ARTEP (Asian Employment Programme,) Bangkok, **1981**

220 Khan, M.M.; Time allocation pattern in rural Bangladesh: A theoretical and empirical analysis, Stanford univ. (UMI), **1987**

221 Khan, S.; The fifty percent - Women in development and policy in Bangladesh, Dhaka, **1987**

222 Khan, Z.R.; Women's economic role: Insights from a village in Bangladesh, *Journal of Social Studies*, No.30, pp. 13-26, **1985**

223 Khandker, S.R.; Women's role in household productive activities and fertility in Bangladesh, *Journal of Economic Development*, Vol.12, No.1, pp. 87-115, **1987**

224 Khandker, S.R.; Determinants of women's time allocation in rural Bangladesh, *Economic Development and Cultural Change*, Vol.37, No.1, pp.111-126, **1988**

225 Khuda, B.-E.; The nuclearization of joint family households in a rural area of Bangladesh, *Jounal of Comparative Family Studies*, Vol.16, No.3, pp. 387-400, **1985**

226 Koenig, M.A., D'Souza, S.; Sex differences in childhood mortality in rural Bangladesh, *Social Science Medicine*, Vol.22, No.1, pp. 15-22, **1986**

227 Koenig, M.A., Fauveau, V., Chowdhury, A.I., Chakraborty, J., Khan, M.A.; Maternal mortality in Matlab, Bangladesh: 1976-85, *Studies in Family Planning*, Vol.19, No.2, pp. 69-80, **1988**

228 Kreiser, K., Diem, W., Majer, H.G. (Hrsg.); Lexikon der islamischen Welt, Stuttgart etc., **1974**

229 Kuhnen, F.; Die Entwicklung der Bodenordnung in Indien, *Zeitschrift für Ausländische Landwirtschaft*, Vol.4, No.4, pp. 314-340, **1965**

230 Kuhnen, F.; Mehrfachbeschäftigung in der asiatischen Landwirtschaft, in: Jauch, D, Kromka, F. (Hrsg.), Agrarsoziologische Orientierungen, Ulrich Planck zum 65. Geburtstag, Stuttgart **1987**

231 Kunert, C.; Bangladesh ertrinkt in der Armut - Die mörderischen Launen der Natur geißeln regelmäßig das ärmste Land der Welt - Dämme und Deiche könnten Katastrophen verhinden helfen, *Vorwärts* 1.6. **1985**

232 Lasson, A.de, Dolberg, F.; The causal effect of landholding on livestockholding, *Quarterly Journal of International Agriculture*, Vol.24, No.4, pp. 339-354, **1985**

233 Lewin, K.; Feldtheorie in den Sozialwissenschaften, Bern, Stuttgart, **1963**

234 Lipton, M.; Labor and poverty, World Bank Staff Working Paper No.616, Washington D.C. **1983**

235 Lipton, M.; Poverty, undernutrition, and hunger, World Bank Staff Working Paper No.597, Washington D.C. **1983**

236 Lipton, M.; Demography and poverty, World Bank Staff Working Paper No.623, Washington D.C. **1983**

237 Lipton, M.; Land assets and rural poverty, World Bank Staff Working Paper No.744, Washington D.C. **1985**

238 Lipton, M.; Seasonality and ultrapoverty, *IDS Bulletin*, Vol.17, No.3, pp. 4-8, **1986**

239 Lipton, M.; The poor and the poorest – Some interim findings, World Bank Discussion Papers No.25, Washington D.C., **1988**

240 Lipton, M., Longhurst, R.; Modern varieties, international agricultural research, and the poor, World Bank, Consultative Group on International Agricultural Research, Study Paper No.2, Washington D.C., **1985**

241 Longhurst, R.; Household food strategies in response to seasonality and famine, *IDS Bulletin*, Vol.17, No.3, pp. 27-35, **1986**

242 Longhurst, R., Chambers, R., Swift, J.; Seasonality and poverty: Implications for policy and research, *IDS Bulletin*, Vol.17, No.3, pp. 67-70, **1986**

243 Luchesi, B.; Familie und Verwandtschaft in einem Dorf in Bangladesh, Berlin, **1983**

244 Mabud, M.A.; Women's development, income and fertility in Bangladesh, Dhaka, **1985**

245 Maloney, C., Ahmed, A.B.S.; Rural savings and credit in Bangladesh, Dhaka, **1988**

246 Maloney, C., Aziz, K.M.A., Sarkar, C.P.; Beliefs and fertility in Bangladesh, Institute of Bangladesh Studies, Rajshahi University. Rajshahi, **1980**

247 Manig, W.; Ländliche Gesellschaftsstruktur und institutioneller Wandel in Nordpakistan, Diskussionspapiere Nr.3, Institut für Rurale Entwicklung, Göttingen **1990**

248 Martius-von Harder, G.; Die Frau im ländlichen Bangladesh, Saarbrücken, **1978**

249 Martius, H.; Entwicklungskonforme Mechanisierung der Landwirtschaft in Entwicklungsländern: Bangladesh, Saarbrücken, **1977**

250 Marum, M.E.; Rural women and work in Bangladesh, Diss. Berkley **1982**

251 Mashreque, M.S.; Structure of kinship relations in a peasant community of Bangladesh, *Eastern Anthropologist*, Vol.39, No.2, pp. 93-106, **1986**

252 Mellor, J.W.; Agricultural product and input markets in south Asian smallholder agriculture, in: Anschel et al.(eds.), Agricultural cooperatives and markets in developing countries, New York, **1969**

253 Mitra, S.N., Kamal, G.M.; Bangladesh contraceptive prevalence survey - 1983, Dhaka, **1985**

254 Muqtada, M.; Poverty and famines in Bangladesh, *Bangladesh Development Studies*, Vol.9, No.1, pp. 1-34, **1981**

255 Muqtada, M.; Determinants and possibilities of employment expansion in the crop sector, in: Islam, R., Muqtada, M. (eds.), Bangladesh - Selected issues in employment and development, ILO/ARTEP New Delhi, **1986**

256 Muqtada, M., Alam, M.M.; Hired labour and rural labour market in Bangladesh, in: Hirashima, S., Muqtada, M. (eds.), Hired labour and rural labour markets in Asia - Studies based on farm-level data, ILO/ARTEP New Delhi **1986**

257 Murshed, S.M.M.; Production performance of Bangladesh agriculture, 1967-70 to 1976-79: An analysis by component elements of growth, *Bangladesh Journal of Agricultural Economics*, Vol.6, No.1/2, pp. 1-24, **1983**

258 Murshid, K.A.S.; Weather, new technology and instability in foodgrain production in Bangladesh, *Bangladesh Development Studies*, Vol.15, No.1, pp. 31-56, **1987**

259 Müller, H.-P.; Landnutzungssystem in Bangladesh - Tausch und Nutzungsstrategien zur Existenzsicherung, Sozialökonomische Schriften zur Ruralen Entwicklung, Bd. 103, Aachen **1993**

260 Nannen-Gethmann, F.; Energy in the rural economy - A case study of the Philippines and Bangladesh, Saarbrücken etc., **1983**

261 Nebelung, M.; Mobilisierung und Organisation von Kleinbauern und Landarbeitern im ländlichen Bangladesh, Berlin, **1988**

262 Nomani, M.M.; Islamic faith and practice, Academy of Islamic Research and Publications, Lucknow (India) 4th ed., **1977**

263 Nur Begum, N.; Pay or purdah - Women and income earning in rural Bangladesh, Dhaka, **1987**

264 Pandian, M.S.S.; Persistence and polarisation in rural Bangladesh, *Journal of Peasant Studies*, Vol.14, No.4, pp. 532-548, **1987**

265 Pandian, M.S.S.; On the so-called stability of small landowners in Bangladesh, *Journal of Peasant Studies*, Vol.14, No.4, pp. 534-537, **1987**

266 Parikh, J.K., Krömer, G.; Modelling energy and agriculture Interactions – II: Food-fodder-fuel-fertilizer relationships for biomass in Bangladesh, *Energy*, Vol.10, No.7, pp. 805-817, **1985**

267 Pryer, J.; When breadwinners fall ill: Preliminary findings from a case study in Bangladesh, *IDS Bulletin*, Vol.20, No.2, pp. 48-57, **1989**

268 Pulte, P.; Bevölkerungslehre, München, Wien, **1972**

269 Qadir, S.R.; Bastees of Dacca - A study of Squatter settlement, Local Government Institute, Dacca, **1975**

270 Qadir, S.R., Quddus, M.A.; Women's education and home development program. Seventh Report July, 1973 to June, 1977, BARD Comilla, **1979**

271 Qazi, A.K.; Cultivation of leguminous crops in Bangladesh, *Quarterly Journal of International Agriculture*, Vol.25, No.1, pp. 59-67, **1986**

272 Quasem, M.A.; Adoption of HYV paddy in Bangladesh: Its potential acreage and constraints, *Farm Economy*, Vol.3, No.1, pp. 61-79, **1982**

273 Quasem, M.A.; Farmers' participation in the paddy markets, their marketed surplus and factors affecting it in Bangladesh, *The Bangladesh Development Studies*, Vol.15, No.1, pp. 84-104, **1987**

274 Quasem, M.A.; Farmers' participation in the paddy markets, their marketed surplus and factors affecting it in Bangladesh: A reply, *The Bangladesh Development Studies*, Vol.16, No.1, pp. 108-111, **1987**

275 Quddus, M.A., Solaiman, M., Karim, R.; Rural women in households in Bangladesh - With a case study of three villages in Comilla, Comilla, **1985**

276 Räder, C.; Haushaltsökonomie im ländlichen Bangladesh - Suche nach Existenz zwischen Haus, Feld und Markt, Sozialökonomische Schriften zur Ruralen Entwicklung, Bd. 94, Aachen **1993**

277 Rahaman, M.M.; The causes and effects of famine in the rural population: A report from Bangladesh, in: Robson, J.R.K. (ed.), Famine: Its causes, effects and management, New York etc., **1981**

278 Rahman, A.; Rural power structure - A study of the local level leaders in Bangladesh, Dacca, **1981**

279 Rahman, A.; Land concentration and dispossession in two villages in Bangladesh, *Bangladesh Development Studies*, Vol.10, No.2, pp. 51-83, **1982**

280 Rahman, A.; Demands and marketing aspects of Grameen Bank - A closer look, Dhaka, **1986**

281 Rahman, A.; Peasants and classes - A study in differentiation in Bangladesh, Dhaka, **1986**

282 Rahman, A.; Persistence and polarization in rural Bangladesh. Small farmers are being proletarianised - A note on 'persistence and polarization' by Bhaduri et al., *The Journal of Peasant Studies*, Vol.16, No.2, pp. 283-287, **1988**

283 Rahman, Atiur; Rural power structure: A study of the Union Parishad leaders in Bangladesh, *Journal of Social Studies*, Vol.4, pp. 87-119, **1979**

284 Rahman, Atiq, Islam, R.; Labour use in rural Bangladesh – An empirical analysis, *The Bangladesh Development Studies*, Vol.16, No.4, pp. 1-40, **1988**

285 Rahman, K.M.; Development of agricultural marketing in Bangladesh, BARD Comilla, **1973**

286 Rahman, M.L., Islam, M.M.; Rural Bangladesh - A diagnostic study, *Economic Affairs, India*, Vol.30, No.3, pp. 153-169 (192), **1985**

287 Rahman, M.M., Rahman, A.K.M.F., Islam, M.M.; Land redistribution programme in Bangladesh, *Economic Affairs*, Vol.28, No.2, pp. 675-686, **1983**

288 Rahman, P.M.M.; Some aspects of income distribution in rural Bangladesh, *Applied Economics*, Vol.20, No.7, pp. 1007-1015, **1988**

289 Rahman, P.M.M., Ali, M.M.; Distribution of landholding and its inequality in Bangladesh, *Indian Journal of Agricultural Economics*, Vol.39, No.1, pp. 40-52, **1984**

290 **Rahman, R.I.**; Implications of seasonality of rural labour use pattern - Evidences from two villages in Bangladesh, *Bangladesh Development Studies*, Vol.9, No.1, pp. 77-96, **1981**

291 **Rahman, R.I.**; The wage employment market for rural women in Bangladesh, BIDS Dhaka, **1986**

292 **Rahman, R.I.**; Time budget studies and the measurement of time spent on child care by rural women in Bangladesh: A note on methodology, *Bangladesh Development Studies*, Vol.14, No.1, pp. 106-116, **1986**

293 **Rahman, R.I.**; Seasonality of workload of women in rural areas of Bangladesh: Some male-female comparison, *Bangladesh Development Studies*, Vol.14, No.4, pp. 123-130, **1986**

294 **Rangasami, A.**; 'Failure of exchange entitlements' theory of famine - A response (1), *Economic and Political Weekly*, Vol.20, No.41, pp. 1747-1752, **1985**

295 **Ravallion, M.**; Agricultural wages in Bangladesh before and after the 1974 famine, *Bangladesh Development Studies*, Vol.10, No.1, pp. 75-89, **1982**

296 **Ravallion, M.**; Markets and famines, Oxford, **1987**

297 **Ray, J.K.**; To chase a miracle - A study of the Grameen Bank of Bangladesh, Dhaka, **1987**

298 **Ray, R., Ray, R.**; The dynamics of continuity in rural Bengal under the British Imperium: A study of Quasi-State equilibrium in underdeveloped societies in a changing world, *Indian Economic and Social History Review*, Vol.10, No.2, pp. 103-128, **1973**

299 **Rodinson, M.**; Islam und Kapitalismus, Frankfurt/Main, **1971**

300 **Roy, S.K., Haider, R.**; Is nutritional status deteriorating in Bangladesh, *Health Policy and Planning*, Vol.3, No.4, pp. 325-328, **1988**

301 **Sadeque, S.**; The rural financial market and Grameen Bank Project in Bangladesh: An experiment in involving rural poor and women in institutional credit operations, *Savings and Development*, Vol.10, No.2, pp. 181-196, **1986**

302 **Sadeque, S.Z.**; Capital accumulation, the state and the structure of bangladeshi agriculture: A sociological study of the first decade, 1972-1982, Diss. Cornell Univ. (UMI), **1986**

303 **Samad, S.A.**; Real wages in Bangladesh, *Internationales Asienforum*, Vol.12, No.2/3, pp. 189-204, **1981**

304 **Saqui, Q.M.A.H., Akhtar, K.**; Village studies in Bangladesh - An annotated bibliography, Dhaka, **1987**

305 **Sarkar, S.**; Marketing of foodgrains - An analysis of village survey data for West Bengal and Bihar, *Economic and Political Weekly*, Vol.16, No.39, S.A103-A108, **1981**

306 **Sattar, E.**; Women in Bangladesh: A village study, Dacca, **1974**

307 **Sattar, E.**; Universal primary education in Bangladesh, Dhaka, **1982**

308 **Sattar, M.G., Showkat Ara Begum**, Impact of agricultural development programmes on rural women - A study of two women, *The Journal of Rural Development*, Vol.18, No.2, S.49-96, **1988**

309 **Schendel, W.van**; Peasant mobility - The odds of life in rural Bangladesh, Assen, **1981**

310 **Scott, G.L., Carr, M.**; The impact of technology choice on rural women in Bangladesh - Problems and opporunities, World Bank Staff Working Paper No. 731, Washington D.C., **1985**

311 **Scott, J.C.;** The moral economy of peasants - Rebellion and subsistence in South-East Asia, New Haven, **1977**

312 **Sen, A.;** Poverty and famines - An essay on entitlement and deprivation, Oxford, **1982**

313 **Shahid, A., Herdt, R.W.;** Land tenure and rice production in four villages of Dhaka District, Bangladesh, *Bangladesh Development Studies*, Vol.10, No.4, S.113-124, **1982**

314 **Sharma, U.;** Unmarried women and the household economy: A research note, *Journal of Social Studies*, No.30, pp. 1-12, **1985**

315 **Shawkat Ali, A.M.M.;** Role of fertilizer in food production, *Administrative science review*, Vol.12, No.1, pp. 9-17, **1982**

316 **Siddiqui, K.;** The political economy of rural poverty in Bangladesh, Dacca, **1982**

317 **Siddiqui, K.(ed.);** Local government in Bangladesh, Dhaka, **1984**

318 **Sikdar, M.F.S., Banerjee, B.N.;** Trends in area, production and yield of jute in West Bengal and Bangladesh - A comparative study, *Economic Affairs*, Vol.29, No.3, pp. 152-161, **1984**

319 **Sikder, F.S., Elias, S.M.;** Marketing and storage of pulses in Bangladesh, CGPRT Report No.12, CGPRT Centre, Bogor, Indonesia, **1988**

320 **Sobhan, S.;** Legal Status of women in Bangladesh, Bangladesh Institute of Law and International Affairs, Dacca, **1978**

321 **Sohail, M.;** Differentials in cumulative fertility and child survivorship in rural Bangladesh, *Bangladesh Development Studies*, Vol.7, No.3, pp. 53-78, **1979**

322 **Spinatsch, M.;** Boda: Ein Dorf am Rande der Welt, Saarbrücken u.a., **1984**

323 **Stepanek, J.F.;** Bangladesh - Equitable growth? New York etc., **1978**

324 **Streefland, P., Ahmed, H., Nafisa M., Barman D.C., Areffen H.K.;** Different ways to support the rural poor - Effects of two development approaches in Bangladesh, Amsterdam, Dhaka, **1986**

325 **Swift, J.;** Why are rural people vulnerable to famine? *IDS Bulletin*, Vol.20, No.2, pp. 8-15, **1989**

326 **Tahziba Khatun;** Women's education and home development (A Report on the Pilot Project of Bangladesh Academy for Rural Development, 1970-73), Comilla, **1975**

327 **Thorp, J.P.;** Power among farmers of Daripalla - A Bangladesh village study, Dacca, **1978**

328 **Todd, H.;** "Bicycle bankers" target poor clients: Poor women are the main customers of a rural development bank in Bangladesh, *Third World*, No.8, pp. 45-47, **1987**

329 **Uchida, H.;** Analysis of rice production variability in Bangladesh, *Journal of Irrigation Engineering and Rural Planning*, No.10, pp. 21-33, **1986**

330 **Unicef;** Report of a feasability survey of productive/income generating activities for women in Bangladesh, United Nations Childrens Fund, Dacca, **1977**

331 **Unicef;** Simple technologies for rural women in Bangladesh, United Nations Childrens Fund, Dacca, **1977**

332 **Unicef;** Training for women in Bangladesh - An inventory and sample survey of training programmes, United Nations Childrens Fund, Dacca, **1977**

333 **Unicef;** Bangladeshi village women on the move, United Nations Children Fund, Dacca, **1980**

334 Venzky, G.; Das Land am Tropf, *Die Zeit*, No.23, **1985**

335 Venzky, G.; Verheerender als die Jahrhundertkatastrophe - Am Elend in Bangladesh sind nicht nur Naturgewalten schuld, *Stuttgarter Zeitung*, 8.Sep. **1987**

336 Venzky, G.; Die nächste Flut kommt bestimmt - Bangladesh zwischen Überschwemmung und Dürre: Die Chancen für Präventivmaßnahmen stehen schlecht, *Frankfurter Rundschau* 28.Okt **1988**

337 Vylder, S.de; Agriculture in chains - Bangladesh: A case study in contradictions and constraints, New Delhi usw., **1982**

338 Vylder, S.de, Asplund, D.; Contradictions and distortions in a rural economy - The case of Bangladesh, Report from Policy Development and Evaluation Division, SIDA, Dacca, **1977**

339 Wanmali, S.; Networks of distribution of goods and services in rural India: Some spatial considerations, in: ICRISAT (ed.), Agricultural markets in the semi-arid tropics, Patancheru, A.P., India **1985**

340 Weber, M.; Wirtschaft und Gesellschaft (5.Aufl.), Tübingen, **1972**

341 Wennergren, E.B.; Land redistribution as a developmental strategy in Bangladesh, *Land Economics*, Vol.62, No.1, pp. 74-82, **1986**

342 Wennergren, E.B., Antholt, C.H., Whitaker, M.D.; Agricultural development in Bangladesh, Boulder Col., **1984**

343 Westergaard, K.; Boringram - An economic and social analysis of a village in Bangladesh, RDA Bogra, o.J. **(1980)**

344 Westergaard, K.; Pauperization and rural women in Bangladesh - A case study, Comilla, **1983**

345 Westergaard, K.; State and rural society in Bangladesh - A study in relationships, Copenhagen, **1985**

346 Willke, H.; Systemtheorie, Eine Einführung in die Grundprobleme (2., erweiterte Auflage), Stuttgart, New York **1987**

347 Women for Women - Research and study Group; Women and education, Bangladesh 1978, Dacca, **1978**

348 Women for Women - Research and study Group (eds.); The situation of women in Bangladesh, Dacca, **1979**

349 Women for Women; Disadvantaged children in Bangladesh: Some reflections, Dhaka, **1981**

350 Women for Women; Collected articles 1982, Dhaka, **1983**

351 Wood, G.D., Huq, M.A.; The socio-economic implications of introducing HYV in Bangladesh, Proceedings of the International Seminar Held in April, 1975, BARD Comilla, **1975**

352 World Bank/Government of Bangladesh; Bangladesh agricultural credit review Vol.I, Vol II, Dhaka, **1983**

353 World Bank; Bangladesh: Development in a rural economy, 3 Vols., Washington **1974**

354 World Bank; Bangladesh: Economic trends and development administration, Vol.1: Main Report, Report No. 4822, Washington DC., **1984**

355 World Bank; Bangladesh: Employment opportunities for the rural poor - A feasibility report, Washington, **1985**

356 World Bank; Bangladesh: Food and nutrition sector review, Report No.4974, Washington, **1985**

357 **World Bank**; Bangladesh - Recent economic developments and medium term prospects, Washington, **1986**

358 **Zaidi, S.M.H.**; The village culture in transition - A study of East Pakistan rural society, Honolulu, Hawaii, **1970**

359 **Zingel, W.-P.**; Bangladesh, in: Nohlen, D., Nuscheler, F. (Hrsg.), Handbuch der Dritten Welt, Bd.4, Unterentwicklung und Entwicklung in Asien, Halbband I, Afghanistan - Laos, Hamburg, **1978**